My Darling...

99 Love Letters

Shared by:

Kathleen Kincanon Nosek

My Darling,... 99 Love Letters
Copyright: 2020 by Kathleen Kincanon Nosek

ISBN: 978-1-7358278-3-4 (pbk)
978-1-7358278-7-2 (ebook)
978-1-7358278-4-1 (hardback)

www.thewriteviews.com

Kathleen Kincanon Nosek

June 3, 1944

Contents

Dedicated to the Memory
of My Mom and Dad,
and Their Amazing Love Story

Special Thank you:
To My Sister Lynn Kincanon who inspired me to write this book. Lynn is an author of many beautiful poems. She is the writer /poet in our family. I can only hope this book is half as good as many of her writings and it makes her proud.

To my Mom, Mary Eileen Ruhnke Kincanon who left us too soon. I miss her every day. Her story in the pages that follow is, in a small part, my story too. My desire is to tell my parents story in hopes that it touches your heart as it does mine every day.

To my Dad, Louis Bernard Kincanon, who is the author of all but one of the letters in this book. Through these love letters I got to know so much more about my dad as a boyfriend, a soldier, a son, a future husband and father. He surprises me every time I read one of his writings. I hope you feel the love in these Letters and get to know the man he was and the woman he loved with all his heart!

Much love to my brothers
Michael, Larry, and Bill.

To my husband Joe, who always supports me in whatever I do, thank you from the bottom of my heart.

To my son Tim; my daughter-in-law Julie; my two grandchildren, Colin James and Kellie Ann…the loves of my life! Maybe you will write my story someday, I am sure I have given you a lot of material! (Start writing it down)

Preface

The writing of this book came to life five years after the death of my Mom.

Mom's passing was a tremendous loss for all of us. I have four siblings; three brothers and a sister. I am smack dab in the middle of them in birth order, "and the first daughter." Each of us had our own special relationship with Mom.

At the time of Mom's passing we were all grown adults, four of us have adult children of our own and three of us were grandparents. Mom was a great-grandmother of six when she died. Since then there has been one other great-great-granddaughter born and a great-great-grand-son on the way. My sister Lynn lives in Loveland, Colorado and has been there for twenty years, my older brother Michael lives in Naples, Florida and had made his home there since July 2001. The rest of us; an older brother, Larry, younger brother, Bill and me, all stayed local in Illinois, close to Oak Park, Illinois, where we all grew up.

All of us had been out of the family home, raising our families and working hard on our careers when Mom and Dad had to make the tough decision to move out of their home in Oak Park. This was when I first saw the many letters Mom had tucked away in a filing cabinet in their Oak Park home. I noticed the plastic bag and what looked to me like yellow tinged envelopes. I remember being alone with Mom in their bedroom when I saw the letters, and asked her what they were. The quick, brief answer from Mom was "they are my letters." I left it alone not because I was not curious, but because we had so much to do that day. Mom and I could really get waylaid just finding a couple old pictures. Many years went by before they were brought to light again during another move, but that is later in the story. But, once they were "unearthed" after my Mom passed, I discovered they were letters written to Mom from Dad during 1942-1945. Wartime love letters, from my Dad!

My Mom would talk to me about her childhood and growing up without a father, but she never talked to me about her years beyond high school when she met Dad, except to say how they met and a few stories about his mother and the rest of the family. She never, ever went into detail about the trying times they had as a young couple in love and all the obstacles they faced. I have since, pieced much of that together through our Dad's letters.

The reading of the letters from my Father to my Mother, dated from 1942-1945 changed so many things

I am sharing with you, a love story that spans over seventy years.

Chapter 1

The First Reading

Nine months after my Mom died my sister came back home from Colorado to Illinois for a visit. When my sister Lynn comes into town it is a great excuse for the family to gather, not that we ever need an excuse. My husband Joe and I live in Glen Ellyn, Illinois, a western suburb of Chicago. Our home is where the family comes together no matter the season. Our home is the heart of our family and I welcome every bit of it. On this particular day my son Tim, his wife Julie; my two grandkids, Colin and Kellie; my younger brother Bill and his wife Toni were visiting. We were all gathered in our home which always makes me happy. Our home is a single level ranch with an open floor plan. Some of us were sitting around our dining room table and the others were sitting on the couch in the living room watching tv, but, they were still able to be a part of the conversation.

All of us have a real sense of family and the importance of supporting each other. After Mom died that became even more important to us. On this day we were talking about Mom, and the conversation became a life changing conversation, at least for me.

Lynn started to talk about the letters we all knew existed. Once my younger brother Bill heard this his ears perked up! He loves to dive into family history, pictures, visit everyone's grave sites at least once a year, take a drive around to see many of the relative's old homesteads where our childhood was molded. He got off the couch and came to the table to hear more about Lynn's idea.

Lynn had a plan to exhibit the letters in her hometown of Loveland, Colorado. She has a great circle of artist friends where she lives, and they had just completed a project in their town to save a large feed and grain building built in the early 1900's. The plan was to refurbish the building and make it into artist studios and an exhibit hall with comfortable couches where artist could meet to read poetry and show their fine works of art.

A showcase of many local artists was in the planning stage and Lynn's idea was to put our Dad's letters on display. These love letters were written during WWII, when Dad served in the Army. The early letters were from the states when he served in what was called Special Services. Dad was a great right-handed pitcher and the Army had a baseball team which was stationed in North Carolina.

This particular night, with family sitting around the dining room table, the letters came out of that plastic bag and everything changed. The words on those pages tell such a compelling story of two people, their love and struggle during a time of war. We all sat around our dining room table and read little snippets from one letter after the other, being very careful with them, as they are old and fragile. Each letter was in their own envelope carefully tucked away years ago. The return address on many of them struck us all, as we began to realize what we were holding. These letters are our Dad's own words, before any of us were born! They were his intimate thoughts during a time of war and during a blooming romance. Each letter had a date on the top of the first page and in many cases a location. I noticed a change with that much later in the dated letters, when for what I believe was an Army security reason; Dad would only write "Somewhere Overseas" or "Somewhere in Europe"

All of us were laughing and crying, all because of the words coming from our Dad to our Mom. We were enjoying some of the words he used to describe Mom, such as, "Swell Gal," "Darling," and others so enduring. My grandson Colin actually has a recording of us reading and enjoying the words that were jumping off the pages and into our hearts.

The initial attraction for my Mom to my Dad may have started because of her love of baseball, and the fact that Dad was a baseball player who had a great fast ball. But that initial attraction evolved into a lifetime of respect, love and family values. All of which have been generously passed down to their five children and to their children.

When the contents of the letters become clear it is a true miracle that our family did not end at one son, Michael Bernard. There is a story just in his name which of course will become clear throughout this book.

My hope is that you enjoy the reading of the letters and at the same time realize what war can do to the families and the men and woman that serve.

F1.1 Feed and Grain Building Loveland Colorado

F.1.2 My sister Lynn's display at the Feed and Grain.

F.1.3 Notice the letters & My Dad's Army picture.

Chapter 2

The Fall

F.2.1 Our Family Home in Oak Park Illinois 1958-1995

The Beginning

Our home in Oak Park, Illinois where Mom and Dad raised our family holds wonderful memories and some tough ones too. We lived in our home for thirty-eight years. We moved in when I was in kindergarten in 1958.

It was 1995 and the time had come for Mom and Dad to move out of our family home. Cleaning, purging, and getting ready for a move after so many years in a home is a huge undertaking. It was time to downsize from the home they raised their family and shared so many memories for nearly forty years. It was also time for a one level ranch without any stairs and no outside maintenance. Mom and Dad were getting on in age and the big house along with all that goes with it was becoming too hard for them to maintain on their own, not to mention the two-story layout.

Right before the decision to move, Dad had taken a really bad fall down a flight of stairs. The day of this catastrophic fall was the same day he had Cataract surgery. He was told by his doctor to stay on the first floor and avoid stairs, but Dad did not heed the doctor's advice. He went up to their bedroom on the second floor anyway.

Our home was a two-story, four-square style with what could be described as a treacherous staircase up to the second-floor bedrooms, even for the sure footed. We learned to traverse it quickly and easily as children, but as a handicapped, elderly person it was a hazard to say the least.

The second floor had two bedrooms, and two other rooms that were considered more like attic space. These rooms were a little scary when we were kids, but we always hoped one of the rooms would one day be turned into an extra bathroom. That did not come to pass while we lived there because my parents just could not afford to make that change. So, our only bathroom was on the main level.

Dad got up in the middle of the night, nearly blind from his surgery, and you can only imagine the rest of this scenario. He took a terrible fall down those stairs. My mom talked many times of how when Dad hit the bottom he called out over and over again for his "mommy." He had a knot on his head the size of a golf ball. I don't think he had any idea where he was. After his fall that night, it was the beginning of the end for my Dad. He was never quite the same after that. It seemed like it took away a piece of him, and for the next five years it was a slow progression of loss of cognitive reasoning. They called it "multiple systems degeneration," which I think was a way of saying dementia. It was so sad to witness. Mom and I took Dad to many doctors for an evaluation, hoping they would give him a simple answer or a pill, so we could get our Dad back, and Mom could have the man she loved for all these years, but they really had no answers. We just saw the husband and father we knew slowing leaving us.

The move out of our Oak Park home was very difficult for all of us. We spent our entire childhood in this home, but we all knew it was one of those necessary moves that was in the best interests of everyone.

The home was sold, and all decisions were made as to what was going and what was not. It did not take long to find them a place that was absolutely perfect. I hired a Realtor that was referred to me by a friend to help us in the search for a new home for Mom and Dad. We let him know all the things we were looking for which included, no stairs, no outside maintenance, attached garage, one car was ok, two bedrooms and most importantly a location close to family. We narrowed the location down to the western suburbs which would put them in-between all of us. Our Realtor was amazing, he was funny, engaging, and kept all of our concerns forefront in his mind. While looking, our Realtor, Bob, told me I should consider a career in real estate since I was really enjoying this entire process so much. That one statement changed the course of my life. A few months later I was a licensed Realtor and at the time of this writing I own my own real estate company, and I have been helping families find their dream home for twenty-two years. This is what Bob did for our parents, and for us.

He found them the perfect one level ranch townhome in Darien, Illinois. The location was perfect for everyone. It had everything we asked for and more. It was in a great community not to mention it was "on the pond" where Mom and Dad could lounge on their patio and watch the ducks and geese fly into the water. It was light and cheerful because of their eastern exposure. No stairs, attached garage, updated kitchen with stainless appliances, full size laundry right off the kitchen, which was such a change from our home in Oak Park where Mom had to go down into the basement on another pretty tricky staircase. Mom certainly loved having the washer and dryer just steps away from the bedrooms. Best of all, it had two full bathrooms which was always a joke since at times we had nine people in our home with one bathroom for our entire life. My Dad always got such a kick out of that fact.

The entire clan gathered for moving day in Oak Park to witness the end of an era, to say goody-bye to the nooks and crannies that were our safe places for all our lives. It was not an easy day for any of us. One place I can still remember physically going upstairs to say good-bye and thank you to, was my bedroom closet. As a young girl I used to sit on the floor in there and stare out the tiny oblong window where the church next door stood. The church had a mesmerizing stained-glass window that used to capture my imagination as a child. Sometimes, if there was a service being held, I could hear the music from their organ. It also served as a soft place to land when I wanted to hide or just be alone. Taking the time to go up to my room that my sister Lynn and I shared; I walk into the closet as a grown woman, it brought tears to my eyes saying thank you closet, thank you window, thank you church and your gorgeous windows. You saved me many times. I am sure each one of us had their own set of good-byes to say that day.

We met the moving truck in Darien where we were well aware that this was going to be a challenging day. It was time to reorganize and get things in their rightful place. All of this was hard to do when things are so new and different, especially, for a couple that spent nearly forty years in a place that was so familiar to them. All five of us helped them with that task which made it easier for everyone. One of the best things about the move into their new place, it was all on one level!

The previously mentioned filing cabinet with the letters, was now loaded onto the moving truck to join them in their new home in a brand-new walk-in closet in their bedroom.

My Mom and Dad really did like their new place and they were very comfortable there, and that sure made this Life Changing transition easier on all of us. We all know that change can be hard, but after a while you settle in, and life goes on, as it did, for all of us.

Things seemed normal for quite a while. Dad was doing okay, for lack of a better term. Dad's "dementia," was still a worry, but we all supported Mom and helped where and when we could. Thankfully I had a job selling real estate which allowed me to be flexible and more available for them. I was around whenever Mom needed me. Mom and I were really close, and I truly enjoyed her company.

Joe and I also made a move to a south suburb not too far from their new place. It was a great move for us and we loved the area and enjoyed our new home. It had over an acre of land and it was as close to rural country living as we could find.

Mom and Dad came over often and spent time just hanging out with us. We were all enjoying life in our new homes.

Chapter 3

The Filing Cabinet

My sister moved from our home in Oak Park Illinois when she was nineteen years old and was fortunate to live in many different states before landing in Loveland, Colorado in 2000.

Because I was the only girl left at home, I was the daughter who would be asked to help Mom clean out her closets. It seemed that was something that happened way too often in my opinion. I tried to make these cleaning days a little bit lighter by giving my Mom a lot of grief while hanging up her clothes and picking items off the floor. Mom would sit on the edge of the bed watching me and telling me where things should go. I remember telling her, "if you know where things are supposed to go, then why didn't you put them there?" We would both laugh. Cleaning her room gave me the same feeling I had as a child. I was reliving some of the Saturday's when my sister and I were young. Mom would make us clean our rooms before going outside to play. Lynn and I tried to get away with shoving our clothes in the drawers just to get them put away, so we can go out. Saturday's were for fun not for chores! We would get away with that some of the time, but there would be those awful days where Mom would come up and check on us. "Oh, My, Gosh!" Lynn and I would hold our breath praying she would not try to open the drawers. When she did the drawers stopped an inch of the way out. Those drawers were not going anywhere! Well, Mom got it open and took every drawer and all the clothes that were stuffed inside and dumbed them in the middle of our room! It was the worst thing I had ever seen! Where in the world did she get that brilliant idea? She and her coffee clutch ladies must have shared some of their own pearls of wisdom and now my sister and I were paying the price. Thanks a lot whoever you were!

Anyway, you know that old saying; what goes around comes around? Yes, that is what I did. I was reenacting that same crazy stunt on my Mom. On one occasion, as there were many, my Mom was sitting on the edge of her bed, my brother Michael was visiting from Florida and my sister Lynn was in from Colorado. Michael was standing at the doorway inside the bedroom, he came in because he was hearing all this laughter, and yelling, and more laughter. I was tossing things out of Mom's closet right at her as she sat on the edge of her bed facing us and her walk-in closet. I said, "How does it feel?"

My brother, who by the way never had to endure the same clothes dumping trick that my sister and I did, was just standing there shaking his head, he could not believe the scene he was witnessing. He said to Mom, "you let her do that to you?"

What the heck did he know? That was my Mom and I; we loved the specialness we had between us.

The last item on the list for the day was organizing the filing cabinet. I immediately noticed that bag of yellow tinged letters which I had seen just before their move. They were hard to miss because they seemed so out of place between the files, bills, and, bank statements. I remembered Mom telling me that they were "her letters." I paid much more attention to them now versus the day when we were organizing for the move. When I asked about the letters again, she told me they were letters Dad wrote to her during the war. Right away I asked if I could read them and that is when she told me, "You can read them when I am gone!"

I never asked again or even gave them much thought. I saw them often after this, but also respected her wishes not to invade her privacy. I am glad that I did because I know that if she and I would have read them together, Mom would have had to analyze the words line by line, and it would have changed the way I interpreted the words on those pages.

Reading the letters revealed to me a huge correlation in her life and mine. I never realized before reading them and getting to know my Mom and Dad during the early years of their relationship, how much it mirrored my own experience with young love. I bring this fact to light in this book. If I had the chance to talk to Mom, I would love to tell her, I am so grateful for her never ending support at a time when I needed it the most. I know now it was because she understood me more than any other person in my life and more than she was willing to share. Mom's unconditional love and support is what I truly miss each and every day.

I would love to introduce you to my parents one chapter at a time.

Chapter 4

Mom

F4.1 Mom 19 years old 1942

Mom

The year is 1942.

Mom was a tall 5'10" beautiful nineteen-year-old with a gorgeous enviable head of dark raven hair that fell just below her shoulders. Her hair was stunning when she wore it down, but glamorous pulled back or up. The women of this era, the early 1940's, all had "the look." They dressed like every day was Sunday. Pearls were the jewelry of choice. If you look at most high school yearbooks from that era you will notice that many of the girls were wearing pearls over very soft cashmere sweaters.

My Mother was a woman who always loved talking about her life as a young girl, and knowing that, made me think I knew it all. Even if I didn't, she was there to refresh my memory or answer questions as they came up… until the time she wasn't.

My husband and I still drive along familiar roads that we traveled many times with my Mom, and we will say out loud: "You know I used to swim there as a kid," or "Gosh I would hate to live there," or "I used to ride my bike here," or, "this is where my brother and I went to daycare, can you believe it is still here?"

And it is still there off Harlem Avenue in Oak Park, with the high brick wall keeping the children safely inside & prying eyes out!

F4.2 Oak Park & River Forest Day Nursery

F4.3 Oak Park Nursery on Harlem Avenue Since 1912

F4.4

According to a short memoir my grandmother wrote:

> “the cost in the early 1920’s for each child in their care was only ten cents per day.”

My mother had a difficult life as a child. Her father died when she was only five years old. She would often talk about the day he died in their apartment in Oak Park on Harrison Street. Mom could point to the very window where, as a little girl, she would watch for her father to come home from work. Mom would say "I look at pictures of myself as a child and I am never smiling." She wondered if she was always sad because she had a hole in her heart from her father's absence. I think she may have been right about that. I know from what Mom had told me her father was waked in their own home which had to be very hard for a child to witness. He died of lock jaw which is a spasm of the jaw muscle causing it to remain tightly closed, it is typically a symptom of tetanus, but in the recent weeks or months prior he had had Scarlet Fever which may have contributed to his early death. One of the other stories mentioned in my grandmother's writings was the fact that Mom's father had a tooth pulled and it became infected right before he became ill. Penicillin was not discovered until 1928 and not even in mass production until the mid 1940's. In-fact, the first person treated with the drug was in early autumn 1940. While I was researching for this book, I read that during WWI there was a death rate of 18% just from bacterial pneumonia and that fell to less than 1% by WWII because of penicillin.

Mom was an older sister to her brother Bill who was four years younger. She became his caretaker, because their mother, now a single parent had to work to make ends meet. She often spoke of how independent she was. She was ten years old when her mom let her go to the World's Fair in Chicago in 1933-1934 which was a Celebration of Chicago's Centennial.

F4.5 Chicago World's Fair 1933

F4.6 Wrigley Field Chicago Illinois Home of the Chicago Cubs

Mom's mother used to let her take the "L" which is slang in Chicago for the elevated railway which took commuters from west of the city of Chicago into the city and surrounding areas, like Wrigleyville. This is where her favorite baseball team, the Cubs played. Mom and her little brother Bill were the first of the bleacher bums, that was the name they gave the fans that could only afford the seats in the "nosebleed" section, but they did not care. Mom was a Cub fan from the 1930's until the day she died. We always wanted that World Series Win for her but that was not to be. We all give her, and the many Cub Fans that have passed away some of the credit for their World Series Win in 2016 as the "Angels in the Outfield." Boy, did her sons give her the business about her loyalty to that team, but she was never swayed, she was a true Cubs fan, that was all there was to it.

Mom was a second-generation Oak Parker; she went to grammar school at St. Edmunds on Oak Park Avenue where later she would marry our Dad. Mom was a graduate from Oak Park River Forest High School, Class of 1941. She found her passion in high school on stage, playing roles for the drama club and Pastime Players. One of her dreams was to be a Soap Opera star. Guiding Light Perhaps? After all, it was her mother's favorite day time radio show, which became one of the longest running daytime soap operas on TV. The times were hard, and she was a daughter without a father, and she needed to help her family. So, immediately after high school she got a job at Modern Modes which was a dress form company in downtown Chicago located at 216 N. Clinton Avenue.

Here is an original pay stub from Mom's job at Modern Modes

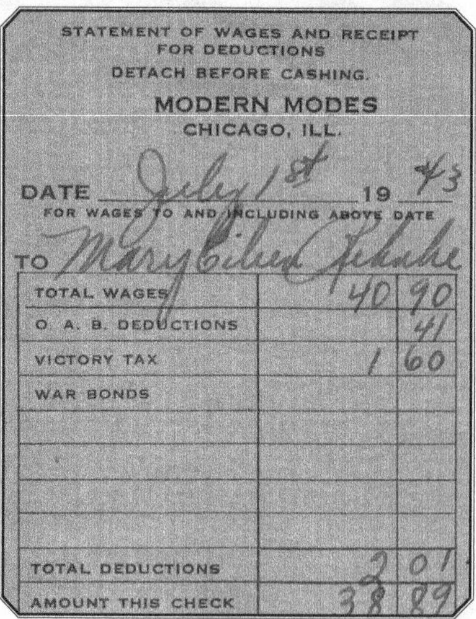

STATEMENT OF WAGES AND RECEIPT
FOR DEDUCTIONS
DETACH BEFORE CASHING.

MODERN MODES
CHICAGO, ILL.

DATE July 1st 19 43
FOR WAGES TO AND INCLUDING ABOVE DATE

TO Mary Eileen [illegible]

TOTAL WAGES	40	90
O. A. B. DEDUCTIONS		41
VICTORY TAX	1	60
WAR BONDS		
TOTAL DEDUCTIONS	2	01
AMOUNT THIS CHECK	38	89

F4.8 Pay Stub Modern Modes July 1, 1943. Total Pay $38.89

F4.7 Dress Forms like those at Modern Modes

Her 1040 income tax form from 1942 stated: Annual Salary $1,093.10

Mom would commute to her job at Modern Modes every day from Oak Park. This is the place where her life would take a turn. Mom was about to meet the love of her life and put her own dreams aside.

Her obsession for The Cubs and baseball in general gave her a reason to set her sights in a different direction, when she was introduced, at a distance to Bernie Kincanon. Mom's best friend Jean also worked at Modern Modes. Jean pointed out a fellow she knew and thought Mom would like to meet. Mom told me once that the only reason Jean felt this way was because she knew her best friend was a crazy sports fan, and this six-foot two inches tall handsome guy with a gorgeous head of hair, and a smile that would light up any room was a baseball player and a pitcher to boot! Mom was more than interested in meeting him, and she and her best friend made it happen, of course they did! Jean and her boyfriend Harry set up a double date which included dinner, and poor Bernie did not know what hit him. My Mom set her sights on Dad long before the formal introduction. She was in hot pursuit. Although Mom told me how she and Dad met, she never shared openly with me how the relationship blossomed; however, through my father's own words in his letters I have learned just that.

Here is one of his first letters to Mom, from Ocala, Florida while pitching for the Milwaukee Brewers and before he went into the Army. As I read the letter to follow, I can feel the insecurities of a new relationship being tested by time and distance. I do not know if this is the very first letter my Dad wrote to Mom, but it is the first one in chronological order of all the ones I have. He is definitely a man in love, but unsure if the woman he left behind will wait for him.

What do you think when reading his letter?

The first letter

F4.9 First envelope addressed to Mom March 11, 1942

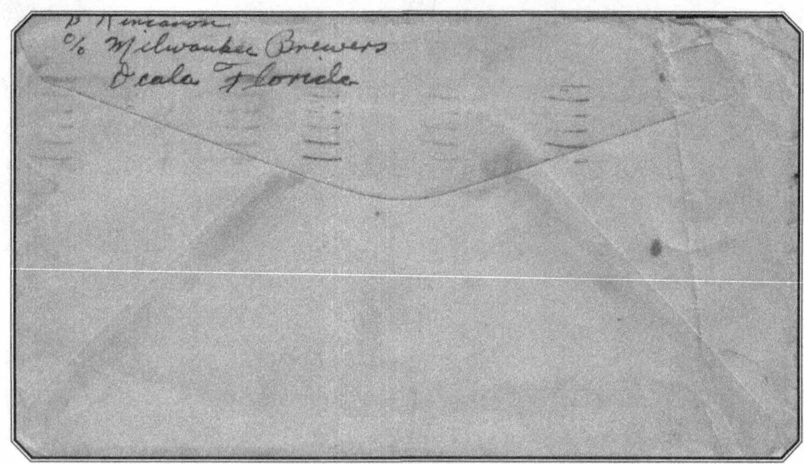

Return address from first letter

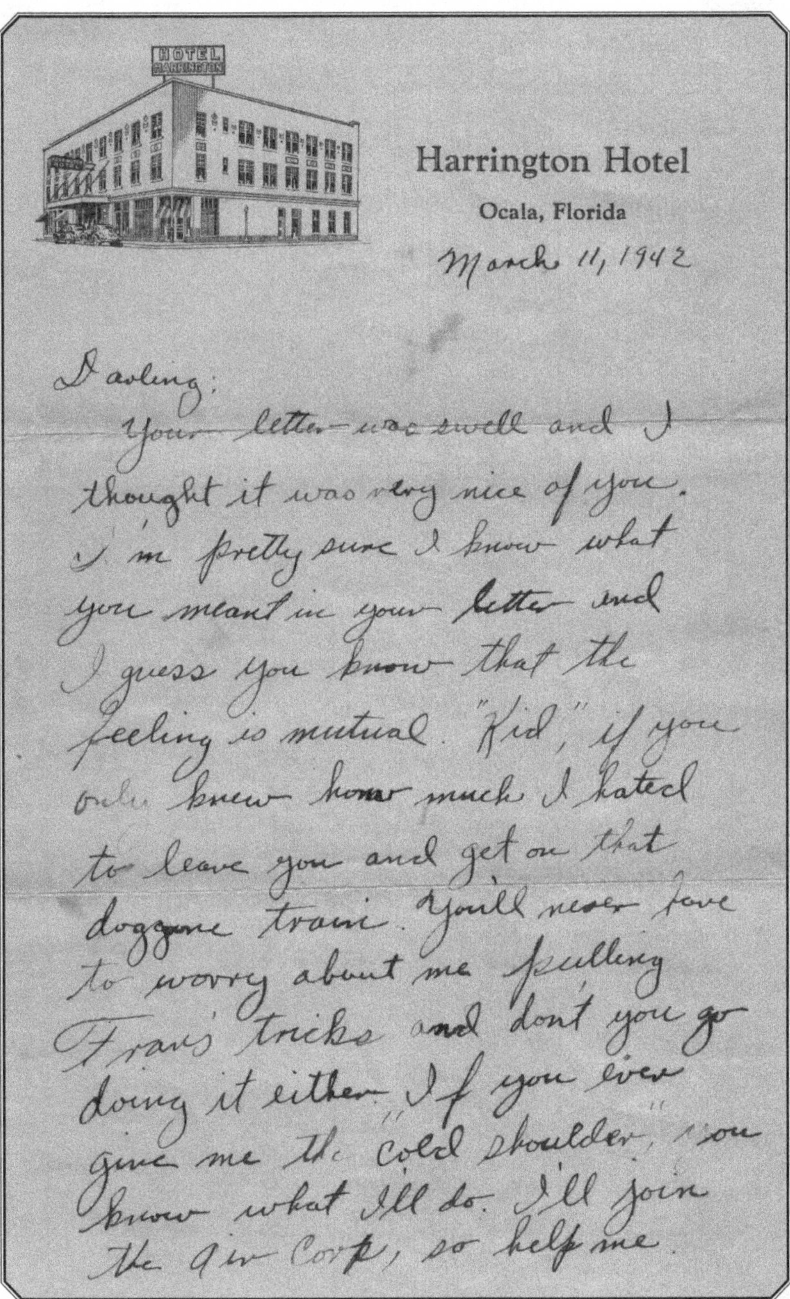

Harrington Hotel
Ocala, Florida
March 11, 1942

Darling:

Your letter was swell and I thought it was very nice of you. I'm pretty sure I know what you meant in your letter and I guess you know that the feeling is mutual. "Kid," if you only knew how much I hated to leave you and get on that doggone train. You'll never have to worry about me pulling Fran's tricks and don't you go doing it either. If you ever give me the "cold shoulder," you know what I'll do. I'll join the Air Corp, so help me.

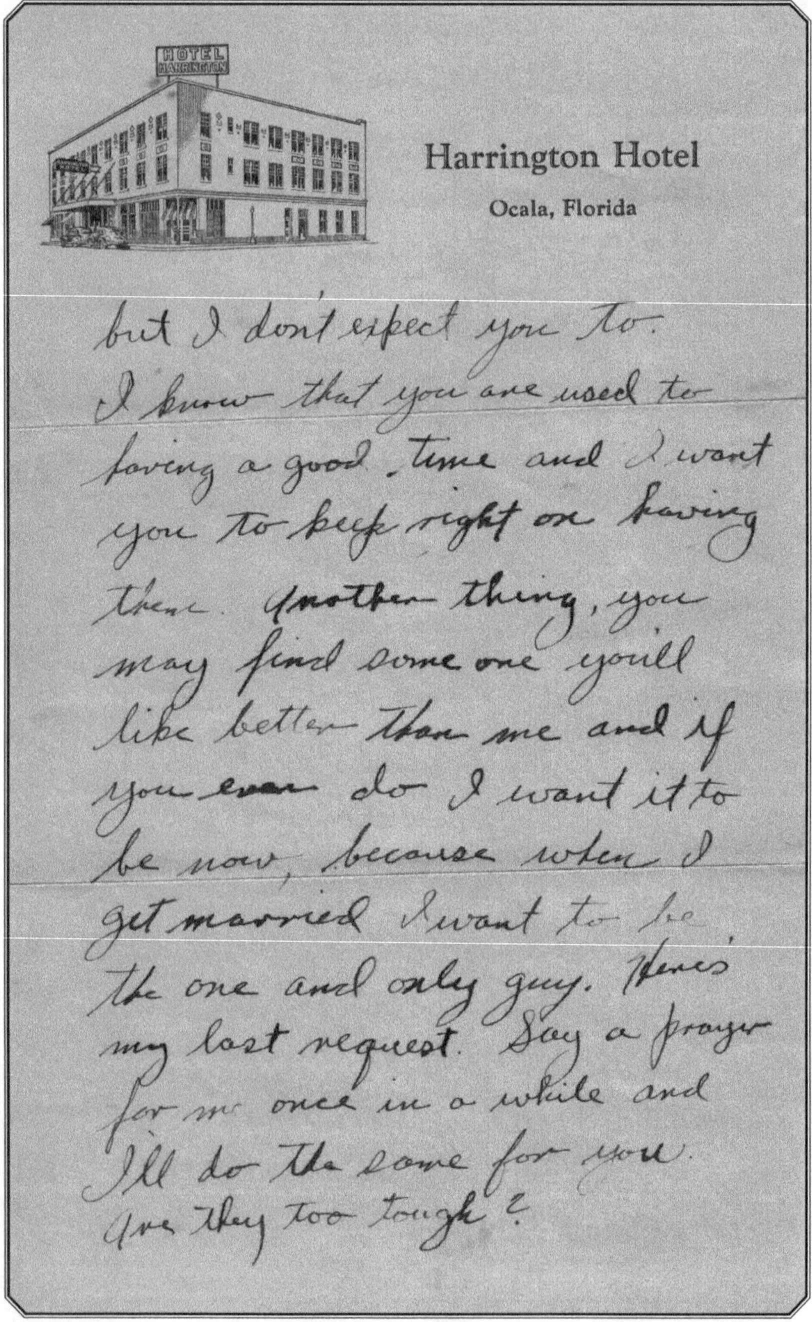

Harrington Hotel

Ocala, Florida

but I don't expect you to.
I know that you are used to
having a good time and I want
you to keep right on having
them. Another thing, you
may find some one you'll
like better than me and if
you ever do I want it to
be now, because when I
get married I want to be
the one and only guy. Here's
my last request. Say a prayer
for me once in a while and
I'll do the same for you.
Are they too tough?

Mary Ilene, what did the fortune teller tell you? Hope it was something good because even if we don't believe in them we can build castles anyway.

Darling, I'm in an awful fix here. My mind is full of pleasant thoughts about you but somehow they just won't come out and form a sentence. Maybe in my next letter, I'll do better and in the meantime please write soon. Take good care of yourself and think of me a little because I've fallen in love with you.

I agree with you, your Mother is swell but how could she be anything else with a daughter like you. Give my regards to all and Goodbye now. Love

Bernie.

Chapter 5

Mom and Me

F5.1 Mom and Me Thanksgiving 2011

All the letters have made me realize so much about my Mom and our own relationship, when I was a young girl and falling hard for my first love. My Mom was always my biggest fan. She supported me no matter what and boy I tested her many times. Not intentionally mind you, but let me just say she never, ever let me down. When I was fifteen years old, a few years younger than she was when she met my Dad, I met a boy named Jim who stole my heart. I had a part time job working Saturday's at Pete's Pizzeria on Oak Park Avenue, just blocks from our home. How I got that job is interesting. My brother Larry was away serving four years in the Navy during the time of the Vietnam War. Back home; he was dating a girl named Camille. Camille's father, Mr. T. (as all the kids called him), owned the Pizzeria.

I think it was the summer of 1968 at my brother's urging, I went into Pete's Pizzeria and introduced myself to Camille. Camille often reminisces about that day, and the one thing she remembers is this young skinny girl, with brown horn-rimmed glasses looking up at her and asking if she was Camille. I remember that too.

My sister Lynn and I used to go up and down some of the small businesses on Oak Park Avenue and ask the owners if we could help them by doing small chores for them. So, this was a perfect opportunity for us to get another little job. We never knew a business owner! We got paid a nickel for emptying garbage at a little dress shop, and sometimes we even got some gum balls as a tip. I helped out at the Flower Shop on the corner of Oak Park Avenue and Lexington Avenue just one block from our home, called Arthington's. The owner was a nice, little man named Fred. I loved the smell of that place. All those fresh flowers. I can still remember the little bell that would jingle every time someone would come or go. He actually taught me how to make corsages and small flower arrangements which he would let me bring home to my Mom. She loved that perk! I remember I used the skills of corsage making in high school when I had to demonstrate something in a speech class.

Needless to say, I ended up working at Pete's Pizzeria and that is where I met some older high school kids that would come in on Saturday's. It was my job to bring their food and clean up after them. I was taught how to make dough for the pizzas using the dough machine and how to make beef sandwiches the way most people liked them…Juicy! I was allowed to eat lunch on the days I worked, and it was such a treat. We were a family of seven, so, it was rare, if ever that we went out to eat. I never in my life had anything like the Italian Beef Sandwich. The Saturdays I worked it would not be unusual for me to eat two or three of those juicy beefs over the course of my shift. Mr. T. used to say I was eating his profits. My pay was five dollars a day and the beef sandwich(s). The high school kids that used to come in there also hung around over the bridge at Avenue Pharmacy. They were called "The Avenue Gang" but the word "gang" had a much different meaning in the early 1970's. I started becoming friends with many of them even though they were at least one or two years older than I was. We were just a fun group of kids hanging at the pharmacy, much to Mr. Hare's chagrin. He was the manager of the pharmacy and a really nice man, but we did test his patience. There was a bank drive through right next to the drug store, so many of us used to loiter there, especially when the bank was closed and there were no cars to worry about. This is when and where I met Jim. He was a tall handsome guy, at least 6'1, had a full head of hair and gorgeous blue eyes. What I noticed about Jim right away was how he was kind to everybody. He was always for the "underdog" and I really liked that about him. He had much of the same qualities I saw in my Dad. Jim was very respectful, and he had this big laugh that was so contagious. He had a twin sister, Laurie. She was so funny and pretty with gorgeous blonde hair that I envied. I grew to love her like a sister, I still do. Jim started out as my good friend, but I knew I was crazy about him. Our friendship turned into boyfriend and girlfriend when I was in my early sophomore year at Oak Park River Forest high school and he was a senior planning for college and his future. By my junior year at Oak Park River Forest and Jim's freshman year in college at Wisconsin State University, we were in love.

I was raised a "good Catholic girl," and certainly not ready for an intimate relationship, but I also knew I loved Jim. We talked about our future even at our young age. Jim never, ever pressured me, he always respected me. He was a true gentleman. We both knew we were in love and committed to each other. In order to be "together" we had to be married. Now how in the world we were going to accomplish that was not yet planned out. However, since I can remember my Dad always told my sister and I that we were getting a ladder (so we could elope). I guess that was his way of telling us they could not afford any big weddings, but I did not understand that at the time. One of my Dad's other pearls of wisdom he would always point us in the direction of Highway 41 to Crown Point, Indiana. I have no idea where he got the information that you could be underage and get married in Crown Point, but he said it many times. Little did he know at the time, he was paving my destiny. The hard part for me was getting to Indiana. It seemed nearly impossible. My Dad was very over-protective to say the least. I could not see how it would be possible to get away for that much time, since I was hardly let out of the house. But, we made the plan and went so far as to get a witness to join us on our adventure. His name was Tom, he was our friend from high school and part of The Avenue Gang. It was February 1970, the King of Hearts Dance was going on at the high school, and Jim was coming in from Wisconsin State University to go with me. Only, we were not going to the dance. Jim, Tom and I were all dressed up headed toward Highway 41 to Crown Point Indiana. My whole life I had been told, almost programed, that that is where you go if you want to get married. My understanding was that you could be under the Illinois legal age for marriage. So, that is where we were headed. How crazy were we? Crazy enough to think a government office with a justice of the peace would be open after 5:00 p.m.! We found the office we were looking for, the one that was going to change our lives. Of course, they were closed! But the trip was not a total waste of time. We at least found out their hours from the sign on the door and would not make that mistake again. My Mom would call me off sick from school most Friday's when Jim would come home from college. The plan was to take that opportunity the following Friday and head back down Highway 41, which we did. We went directly to the Justice of the Peace's office, walked upstairs, and asked a clerk for a marriage license. The man working behind the counter asked us both how old we were. Of course, we told him, Jim was nineteen and I was seventeen. The next words that came out of his mouth were not at all what we were expecting. He said, "kids, where are you from?"

We told him Illinois, and the next thing he said was, "you cannot get married here until you are both eighteen, it is the same in

Illinois." I don't remember, but I think I cried most of the way home. Since my eighteenth Birthday was a year away in March, we left there very disappointed. Jim and I had only one night together that weekend and we gave in, we tried to do the "right thing" and be a married couple, but fate was not on our side, or was it? This one night, this one time, I became pregnant. No one was happy about this news, except Jim and me. We were beyond thrilled!

Now, this book is not all about me, but there is a correlation that came to me after reading my Dad's letters to my Mom. I realized that my Mom was so supportive of my relationship with Jim because of her own experiences with my Dad.

Wow! It became so clear, why, when I would come home from school, she would play little games with me with the letters Jim would write me from college. I would be running home to check the mail for a letter from Jim. He used to write things in code, and always included a large "41" on the envelope. She tried all the time to figure that out. Jim and I knew it was Highway 41, but Mom never knew what any of it meant. She would have three or four of the letters hidden from me and tease me. Mom would throw me one letter at a time. I know the writing on the back of Jim's envelopes drove her crazy. How we would laugh about that even years later. What she must have been feeling and never expressing.

Mom would take me to the pharmacy at night to use the pay phone to call Jim at college, she would call me in sick on Friday's from school because Jim would be home on Thursday night from Wisconsin State. All the subtle ways she was telling me she was on my side and she understood. During the time I was writing this book I had a conversation with Jim, where we talked about my Mom. I mentioned the fact that he is mentioned in my book (a lot). We spoke about how reading my Dad's letters to Mom gave me insight as to why Mom was so supportive of us when we were so young. Jim said very easily, that he knew she was and always felt the support of Mom from the very beginning. He knew how she felt about him and she had no problem telling him when she knew she was dying. He was visibly emotional about that memory and so was I.

One very clear memory I have, I was crying when Jim was leaving for college after a weekend home. He was going all the way to Wisconsin State University in Oshkosh. Mom said,

"Oh, for Pete's sake, you would think he is going off to war!"

What a profound statement coming from her! Did I get it then? Not at all! Do I now? You bet I do.

Chapter 6

Dad

F6.1 Dad 1942

DAD

My Dad was from a poor family, not so unusual in the days of the depression. His mother and father moved their family off the farm from southern Illinois, sure that the world of farming was not for them and their three children. My Dad was the oldest of three. He was the only son of Magdalene, brother to Bernice, and Edith. His father, Louis had passed away at an early age of fifty-three and that left Dad to be the "man" of the family when he was only twenty-three years old. The times, and the fact he was now the man of the house did not allow him to finish high school. He went to work to help support his family. I never asked how he ended up at Modern Modes, but I accepted that as destiny. My father was a kind and very tolerant man. He never said an unkind word about anyone. He was brilliant, self-taught and self-read. He had a thirst for learning about other religions, cultures, and people. He always had a book in his hand and would read whenever he had time to spare. We used to call him "the book worm." The Maze Branch public library on Gunderson in Oak Park, was about a twelve-minute walk from our house, but with Dad's long strides it was more like ten-minutes. This library was his haven. I have come to believe, after reading all of his letters, that his love for reading gave him the escape from his days in the army during WWII.

Having these Love Letters penned by my Dad… this surprised me for reasons I will explain.

It is a very sad realization that your father went to war in 1942 a young, loving, demonstrative man and came home someone very different. I have learned from these letters that he had a very deep love for my mother. He was able to express that love on the written page without hesitation. These letters as you will see, were not written by a man who had a hard time expressing his feelings. I think if that were the case there would be a lot less of them, and they would only be a page or two in length. This is not the reality of dad's letters. His letters were sometime five, six, seven, pages long. That is so unbelievable to me.

The Dad I grew up knowing, well yes, I know he loved all of us, but he did not know how to express that love easily. Giving my Dad a hug was visibly an uncomfortable embrace for him to accept. He had this little giggle that let me know he was not quite sure how to accept it. He did, but I was the one who wanted it more than he did. I always wanted to be "daddy's little girl" but that did not happen until I was well into my thirties. I loved my Dad for the man I knew he was. He was a hardworking guy who provided for his five children as best he could. He was as dependable as a clock. He was the one who thought if you were on time, you were late. He would be out in the car waiting, before any of us had our coats on. I am much like him in that way. I spend a great deal of time waiting in my car!

I think he always wished he could have gone further in school, so he could have provided a better life for his family. I remember when he died, I wished there was a way he could leave his vast knowledge behind, with me. Dad was a true Democrat, progressive beyond the times. He was all about fairness to all people. He was kind, inclusive, and an empathetic man. He could show his emotions, he could cry. I loved that about him, but it also scared me at times.

I remember watching a movie with him when I was a little girl, I was too young to know what it was about and honestly, I do not remember even paying attention to it at all. I know my Mom and my grandmother, (dad's mother) my brother Michael and sister-in-law Marge, were there as well. As a matter of fact, Marge brought this up to me recently when we were talking about Dad. She remembered this entire incident very well. All of a sudden, I heard this sound I had never heard before coming from my father. It scared the daylights out of me! He was crying, no, he was sobbing, at whatever was happening in this movie. He rushed from the room, and I do remember my Mom saying that this movie always makes him sad. It is very interesting because the name of the movie came to me out of the blue! How I remembered it? Well… I give all the credit to my angles! The movie is Our Town an adaptation of a Pulitzer Prize winning play of the same name by Thornton Wilder, starring William Holden. It was made in 1940 and was nominated for an Academy Award for best picture and best actress, Martha Scott. I will make a point of watching it to see what touched my father so deeply that day. Maybe you will too!

One of the things that surprised me about him is that he still loved to take walks. He had mentioned many times how he had to walk long distances in the Army, and he was always so cold, colder than he had ever been in his life. He told me once all the men had terrible boots that never fit them properly. I always wondered why the Army did not take better care of the soldiers that were putting their lives on the line for our country. I think the walks he took after the war gave him the alone time he needed, and the feeling of freedom he once was deprived of for so long. He would say hello to strangers when walking down the street, people did not always return the gesture, but he did not care, that was the farmer in him.

His time as a soldier did, however, make him absolutely hate standing in line no matter what we were doing, that is when his impatience would rear its head. I did not understand it, but I accepted that about him.

Dad had a very overbearing mother and many times it was difficult for him. He never wanted to be disrespectful to his mother because he loved her deeply. My grandmother did not want her son to travel for baseball, she wanted him at home with her. She was afraid of everything. She never let him learn to swim, for fear he would drown. Now, there was another thing my grandmother was afraid of…her name was Mary Eileen!

I know in those days' men joined the Army, Navy, or Marines because it was their patriotic duty. Dad, being who he was, would want to do the right thing. I do know after his horrific experience, the wars that followed in his lifetime, he was totally against. My Father hated the Vietnam War from the very beginning. This brought him much ridicule at work by men that told my father, a WWII POW that he was Un-American!! He was alone in his beliefs downtown at his job working at the Merchandise Mart for the Chicago Transit Authority (CTA). It took many years for the ones that were the hardest on him to later apologize and tell my Dad he was right all along! Dad waited a long time to hear that, but it did nothing for all the years he suffered at that job he hated. I believe he hated it because of the treatment he received and because he wanted to be more and do more for his family. Little did Dad know when he was twenty-four years old, before all of this he was to experience, he would have many more obstacles to overcome.

F6.2 Merchandise Mart in Chicago Dad worked here for forty years

Chapter 7

The Early Days

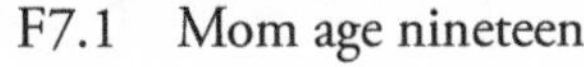

F7.1 Mom age nineteen F7.2 Dad age twenty-four 1942

It was the year 1942, Dad and Mom were in the early stages of their relationship. Mom was nineteen and Dad was twenty-four. Dad was a right-handed pitcher for the Milwaukee Brewers and Mom would go to see him play whenever she could. Most times, sitting alone because she was not at all accepted by Magdalene, my Dad's mother. Mom would often speak about Uncle Charlie, he was married to my great Aunt Catherine, (Caddie for short), my Dad's aunt, and the youngest sister of his mother, Magdalene. Caddie and Charlie did not have children of their own and both were crazy about their nephew, Bernie. They followed his sports career with the dedication of parents. Since Aunt Caddie was my grandmother's younger sister, she knew better than to do anything that would make her mad, but Charlie, he was the one who would buck the "Matriarche" and go sit by Mom in the bleachers. She never forgot his kindness and spoke of it often.

Dad had his dreams and was torn between all of them; baseball, the mother he loved, and now the girl that he knew was someone very special, was added to the equation. He had a decision to make and he knew it.

Dad's love of baseball drove him and that was his passion. That love, and passion was what brought Mary and Bernie together and started their Love Story you are about to read. Not only from my words, but the words right off the pages from my Dad's letters he wrote to my Mom before and during war time. The letters date from 1942-1945. They are heartfelt and tell a truly wonderful story of love, wartime, and the horrors of war when the one you love is "Missing in Action."

Chapter 8

"Wild Man"

It was 1942. War was on the horizon and love was blooming.

Mom and Dad's relationship was growing closer as you can tell when you read his letters. Dad is away now for the baseball season and a few of the early letters are from that period. Mom knew in her heart he was going to be her husband. These were words she never spoke to me, but they are conclusions I have drawn from the contents of the letters I will share with you. Here is his second letter from Ocala Florida while playing ball. Dad was responding to one of Mom's letters, it is one of those times I wish I had her letters too, because Dad is pretty emotional in this letter and it seems to be in response to Mom's letter and their time together. When Dad said in his letter, "I have left your house most every time looking like a Wild Man." It really made me think to myself, WOW, Mom!

Mom was a woman who always knew what she wanted.

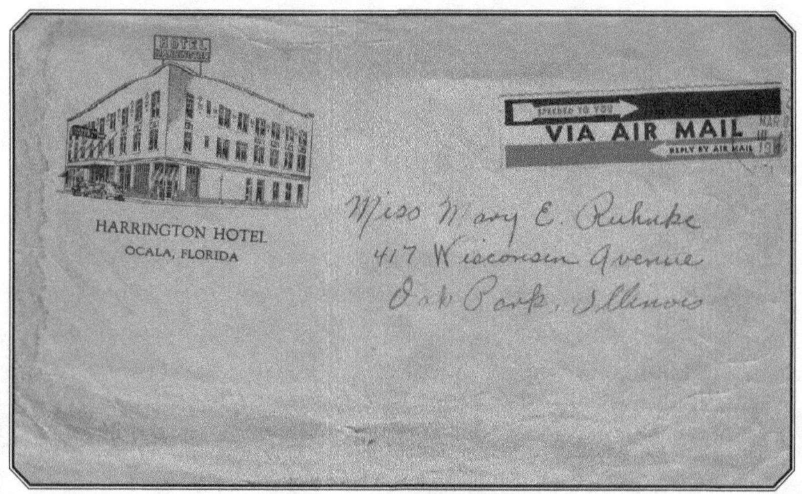

F8.1 March 26, 1942

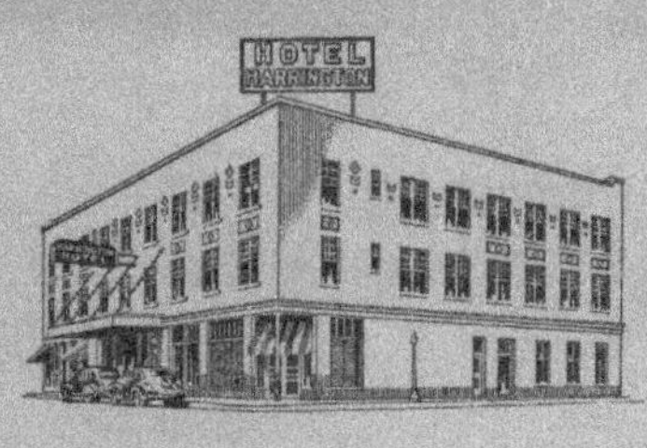

Harrington Hotel
Ocala, Florida

March 26, 1942

Dearest:

Yes, Hon, I asked you to write often and I must say that your really swell to be doing it. The only draw back is that you make me ashamed of myself. Have been pretty slow in writing you this time but don't ever let that bother you. I'm not much at writing to you but if you only knew how much I think about a certain girl, you'd forgive me. I hope.

Darling, I wish I was "your man" for good and could attend that Mission with you this very minute.

your letter really brought the war back to mind. Since I left home I had hardly thought about it. Guess its' the absence of radio's and your morning paper.

Say, you and Mom seem to be getting pretty friendly. You two aren't cooking up a conspiracy against me, are you? Boy, what a lucky guy. Two women in my life and they're the best.

Honey, if you ~~miss~~ me like I miss you then I know exactly how you feel. It's awful, isn't it? What's more, it does get worse every day. No, your letters aren't silly Sometimes I think mine are a little that way too but after

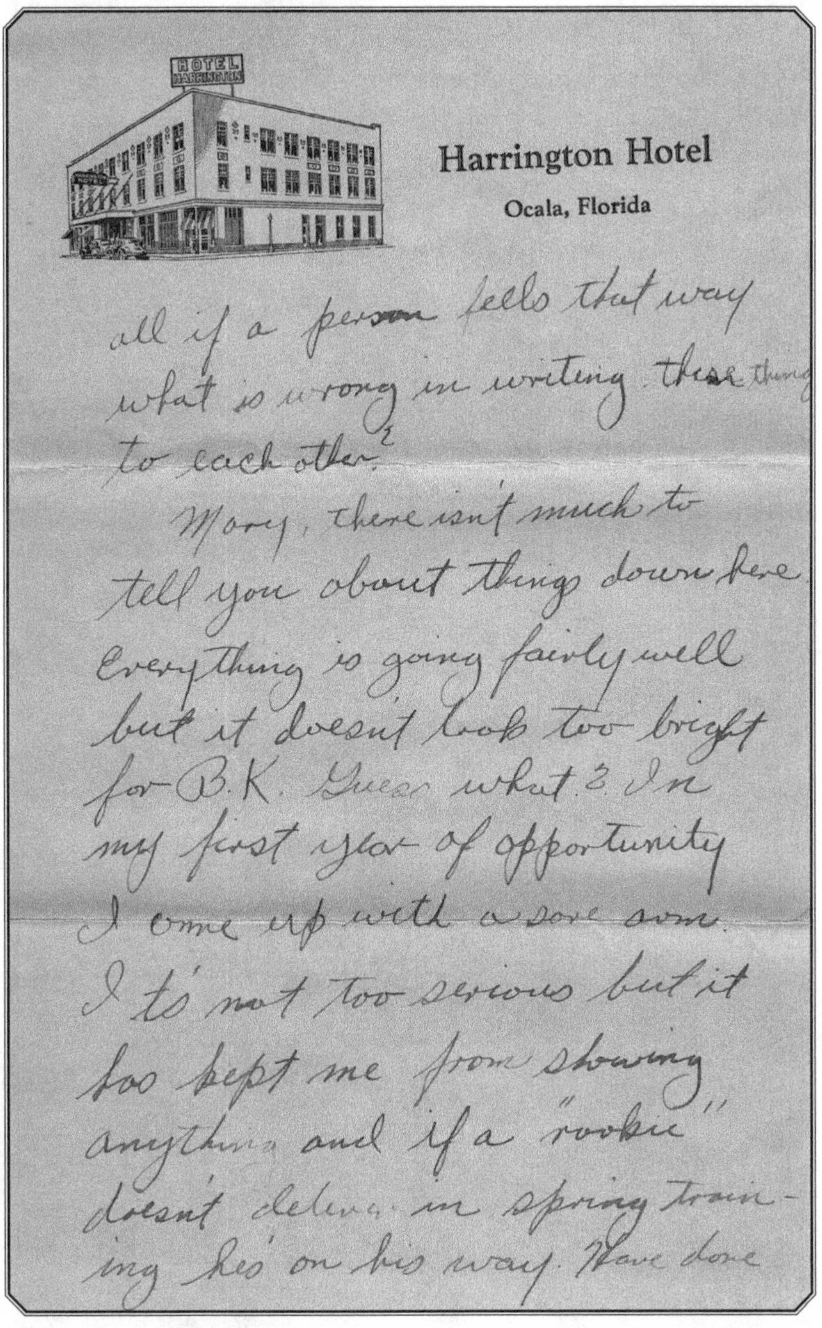

Harrington Hotel

Ocala, Florida

all if a person fells that way
what is wrong in writing these things
to each other?

Mary, there isn't much to
tell you about things down here.
Everything is going fairly well
but it doesn't look too bright
for B.K. Guess what? In
my first year of opportunity
I come up with a sore arm.
It's not too serious but it
has kept me from showing
anything and if a "rookie"
doesn't deliver in spring training he's on his way. Have done

everything to work that soreness out of my shoulder but it's no go. Can't understand it because it's the first time I've ever hurt it and it would happen this year. Do you think I'm an, "Alibi Ike"? Truly though I'm still confident and if the trouble clears up, I'll still give them all a battle. Isn't this good news? The Sox are still taking it out on ~~your~~ or should I say our Cubs? Let's hope for the best. Maybe they'll get going when it really counts.

Referring to your other letter you do rate an X for your excellent will power that night. As I remember,

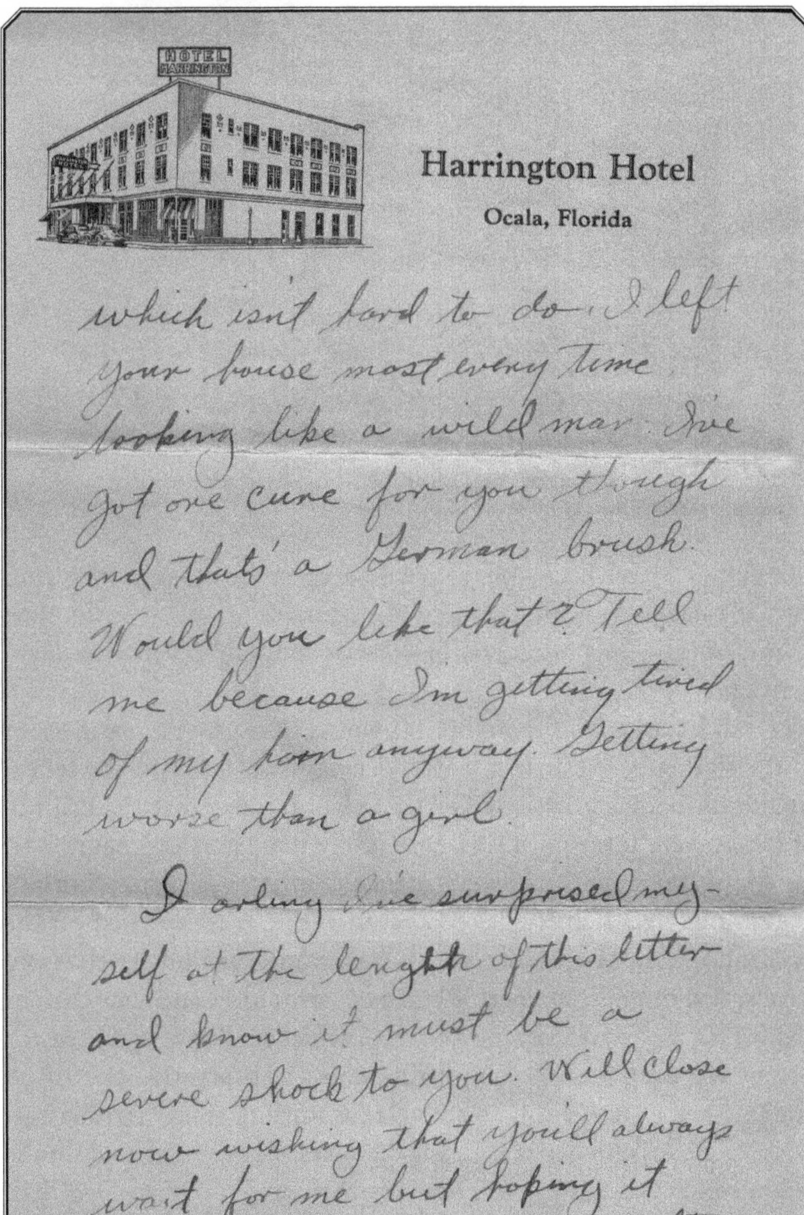

Harrington Hotel
Ocala, Florida

which isn't hard to do. I left your house most every time looking like a wild man. I've got one cure for you though and that's a German brush. Would you like that? Tell me because I'm getting tired of my hair anyway. Getting worse than a girl.

Darling I've surprised myself at the length of this letter and know it must be a severe shock to you. Will close now wishing that you'll always wait for me but hoping it will not be necessary too often.

Love
Bernie XXX

F8.2 Dad handsome as can be in his baseball uniform.

The things I have been able to piece together are coming long after my Dad has passed. He has been gone for twenty years at the time of this writing and my Mom has passed too; and seven years have gone by.

I did not know it then, but if I would have given more thought to the timing of the letters, I would have asked Mom if the letters were from both my Mom and Dad. I had no idea that the bag full of letters were from my Dad alone. Only one letter was penned by my Mom and it ended in mid-sentence. It is dated January 15, 1945. My siblings and I all tried to come up with a reason, based on the date and timing of the letter as to why her one and only letter would have ended in mid-sentence. We had our own ideas and speculations about this, but obviously, no concrete evidence. I have searched the letters and telegrams for correlating dates to explain it, but to no avail. This is during a time where Dad is missing after a terrible battle in Germany. All Mom had was the news she read or heard on the radio, which was not good. There has been no word from Dad for a month. Mom is alone, pregnant with their first child, and she is left worried and wondering where her husband is, and if he is even alive.

Chapter 9

Our Front Porch

I remember I would watch for my Dad on the front steps of our home in Oak Park where we lived on South Euclid Avenue. It was a lovely treelined block. The trees were like a canopy that covered one side of the street to the other. It made you feel safe within its branches. The leaves in all three seasons were our nest. There were a lot of children on our block as there were many Irish Catholics in Oak Park. Our family of five children was small in comparison to some of our friends like the Jirasek's who lived across the street had nine children! All of our neighbors spent a lot of time outside. The front porch was a place my Dad and Mom loved to relax and read.

Dad would move his lawn chair to follow the sun as he read his books or just watched the world go by. It felt natural to be outside on the front steps waiting for his return home every evening. I knew his walk from a mile away. He was tall and had a confident walk, long straight up strides that were double what I could keep up with as a little girl, especially since I am the shortest of all the kids. Dad and Mom were both tall and had four other tall children. I must have gotten my five-foot five height from my grandmother who never even made it to five feet. Although according to statistics, five foot five is not short, it's average. I am a brown eyed, average female.

We were so blessed to be raised in Oak Park, on our exact block. We had many neighborhood friends and we spent hours upon hours playing with them outside. We played games such as kick the can, tag, jump rope, and hide and go seek, and four-square at the church next door. In the winter, the park was only a block away where we would go ice skating, play crack the whip, build forts and have major snowball fights. My younger brother Bill often talks about how the boys used to hitch rides on the back of car bumpers and glide along the icy street. My sister Lynn and I would skate until we were frozen solid and never noticed it until we were walking home with frozen stiff gloves that no longer kept our frostbitten fingers warm. Our feet would betray us on the way home and give way to how really cold they were. I think some days there were actual tears because we knew we stayed a little too long and we were paying for it as we walked that long block home. It seemed so much closer on the way to the park! We would finally get home and take the frozen clothes off, gloves first. They would hit the floor with a thud still in the solid shape of our hands. The radiators in our home were perfect for thawing out those precious commodities.

I can see Dad now in my mind's eye, coming down our block at 5:00 p.m. every night from work. Mom would be in the kitchen and dinner was on the table at 5:15 p.m. like clockwork, it was comforting. We had a full table! Five children and two wonderful parents. In the summertime that table grew to nine as my grandmother, my Mom's mother, and her husband, Marty would come in every summer for three months to beat the heat of Florida and sometimes dodge hurricane season in West Palm Beach, Florida.

Mom and Dad were busy raising five children, but they did so in a very cohesive home. There was the fact that Dad did not like his job, and I am sure that caused some issues. Maybe we were just one of those families where the parents had enough sense to keep their troubles hidden from their children. I know there were weeks when money was tight. Mom would say every now and then that they were lucky if they had five dollars at the end of the week. I think some of the money stretching had to do with the weekly poker games at my grandmother's house over the weekend.

We lived in a middle-class household, in a wonderful neighborhood. We did not have everything, but really wanted for nothing. We had food on the table, although sometimes dinner was breakfast to save money. When mom did serve breakfast for dinner, I had the horrible job of buttering the toast. Trying to keep up with a two-slice toaster, hard butter and seven people? It was a nightmare. But we were all together and that alone was a blessing.

Chapter 10

Ocala Florida Milwaukee Brewers

There were two letters in this one envelope dated April 2, 1942 and April 7, 1942

This letter covers a lot of what both of them were feeling as they were a part and missing each other. Dad tells Mom how he will always be in debt to Jean, mom's best friend for introducing them at Modern Modes. He does not seem so taken with that place and feels mom could do so much better, but he is so grateful that they met there!

Destiny!

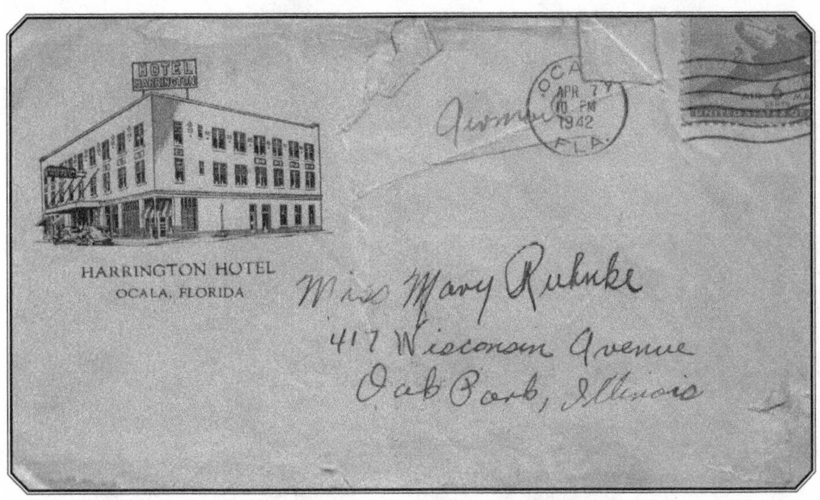

F10.1 April 2, 1942

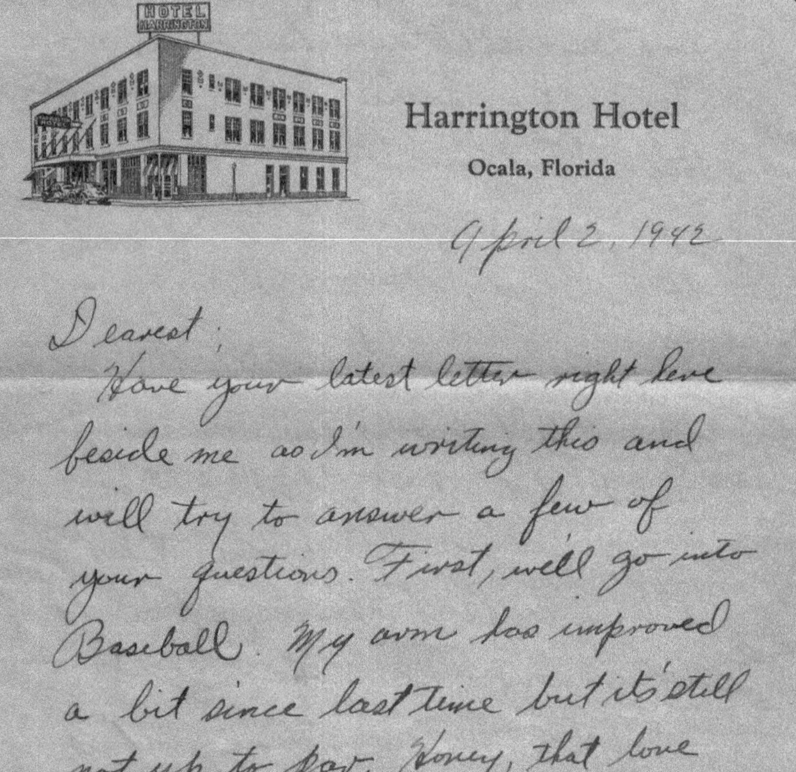

Harrington Hotel
Ocala, Florida

April 2, 1942

Dearest;
Have your latest letter right here beside me as I'm writing this and will try to answer a few of your questions. First, we'll go into Baseball. My arm has improved a bit since last time but it's still not up to par. Honey, that love sickness the Cubs came up with is a little funny but there is some truth in it. You told me yourself how you were acting at work and I've been some-what the same. You know, dreamy and melancholy.

About that clipping: it's very good and it better be true, or else. You know I'm the gangster type, don't you. People down here think so. Maybe it's the reputation Chicago has.

Darling, If I were you I wouldn't worry too much about that job at M. M. It's no place for you anyway. What a bunch. Bet there's not a crazier gang anywhere. It suprises me every time I think about it but I can't figure out how I ever found you in that place. I'll owe Jean my thanks forever now.

Mary, I have a new name for you. It is neglected. Like it? Bet you feel that way sometimes. Know how I'd

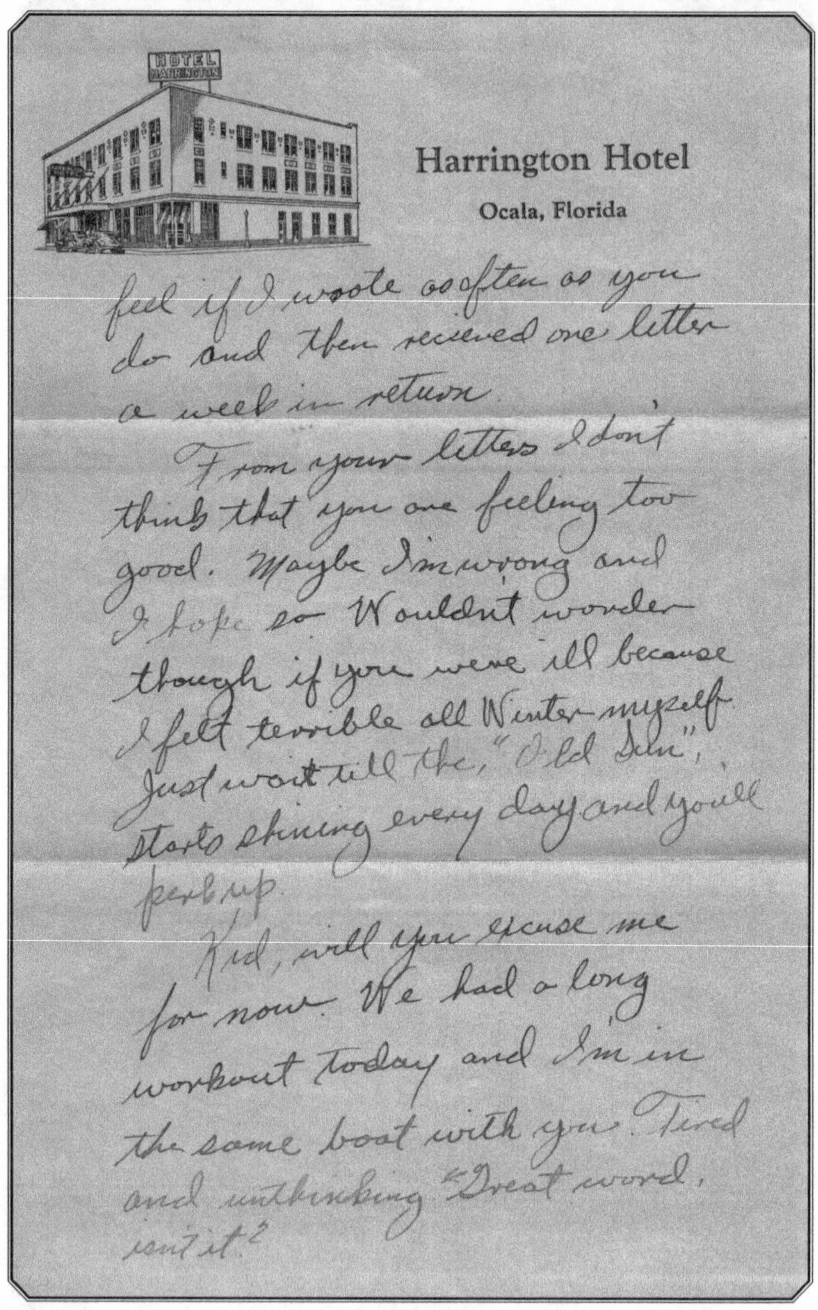

Harrington Hotel

Ocala, Florida

feel if I wrote as often as you do and then recieved one letter a week in return.

From your letters I dont think that you are feeling too good. Maybe I'm wrong and I hope so. Wouldnt wonder though if you were ill because I felt terrible all Winter myself. Just wait till the, "Old Sun", starts shining every day and you'll perk up.

Kid, will you excuse me for now. We had a long workout today and I'm in the same boat with you. Tired and unthinking. "Great word, isnt it?

Write and take care of yourself.

Love
Bernie. XXX XXX

We break camp the 12th of this month but up to now I'm in the dark as to where I'll be. I'm getting very anxious to see you.

My regards to your Mother and Bill.

Chapter 11

You are My First Darling, Also the Last

I was sad when I read the following letter. I felt sorry for what Dad was experiencing. His arm was not responding to whatever treatment they were giving him, and it seems by what his letters say, his baseball season is over. They want him to go somewhere, no idea where. But I think, by the sound of this letter, my Dad just wanted to go home and see his girl.

Dad tells her, **"You are the first Darling in my life, also the last."**

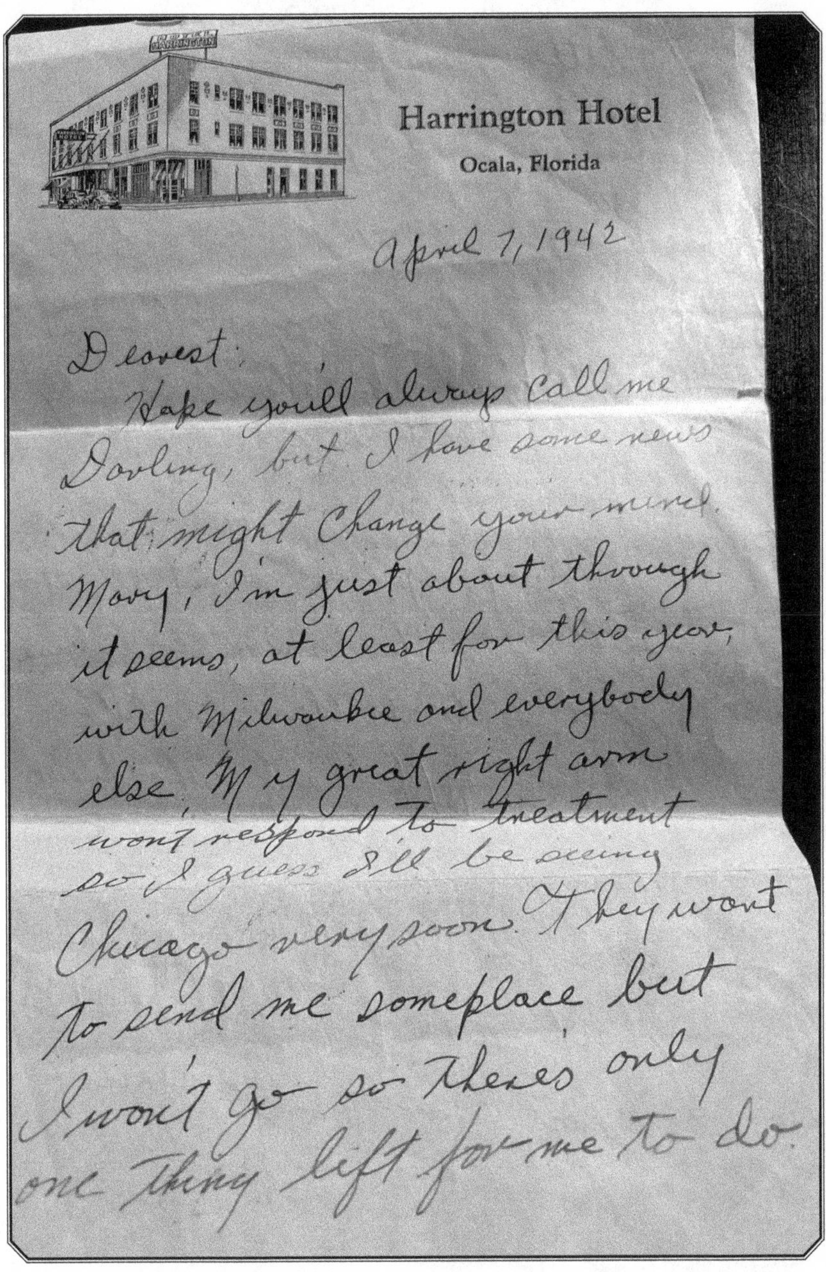

Harrington Hotel

Ocala, Florida

April 7, 1942

Dearest:

Hope you'll always call me Darling, but I have some news that might change your mind. Mary, I'm just about through it seems, at least for this year, with Milwaukee and everybody else. My great right arm won't respond to treatment so I guess I'll be seeing Chicago very soon. They want to send me someplace but I won't go so there's only one thing lift for me to do.

F11.1 April 7, 1942

Wasn't that a gloomy start in
a letter from me to you?
Your last letter was swell,
Eight pages. Do you think
I rate all that? Tell Bert
that he has a very good idea
but don't you take it seriously.
You do very well and I'm
proud of you.

Honey, you are right about
Fate. I'm beginning to believe
that thats all there is to life.
Things happen and who knows
why. We just go along from
day to day trusting that
all goes well and if they
dont, whose fault is it.?
I don't know. Do you?

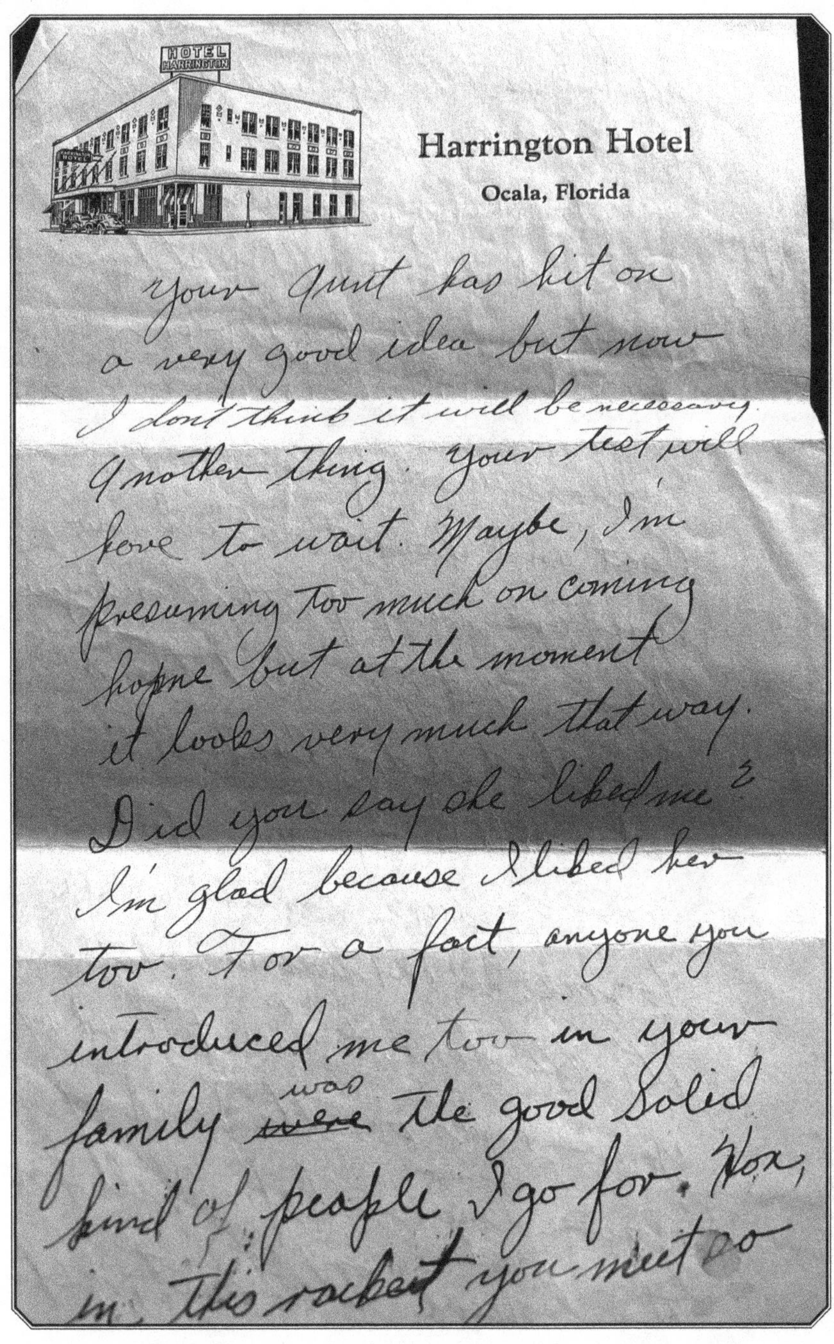

Harrington Hotel
Ocala, Florida

your Aunt has hit on
a very good idea but now
I dont think it will be necessary.
Anothe thing. Your test will
have to wait. Maybe, I'm
presuming too much on coming
home but at the moment
it looks very much that way.
Did you say she liked me?
I'm glad because I liked her
too. For a fact, anyone you
introduced me too in your
family ~~were~~ was the good solid
kind of people I go for. Hon,
in this racket you meet so

many fakes. They can look you
square in the eye and tell the
darnedest lies you ever heard.
Darling, I'm used to
crazy hats so, I'll just love
to take a look at yours.
Bet you made quite a picture,
Easter Sunday in your new
Coat and Bonnet. You know
you are very pretty don't you?.
Know that you don't think
so but I do. Can't explain
it but every time I look at
your picture something happens
to me. Don't know whether
it's the honest direct look of
your eyes or the pout of
your lower lip. Will have
to figure that out, next

Harrington Hotel

Ocala, Florida

time I see you.

Mary, Easter was OK with me and I'm sure that yours was fine also. I'm sorry about not sending you a card but will explain that later.

Darling, I've run out of thoughts so will close for now. Take care of yourself and maybe I'll see you soon.

Love XXX

Bernie XXX

By the way your the first Darling in my life, also the last.

My thanks to Sue.

(Over)

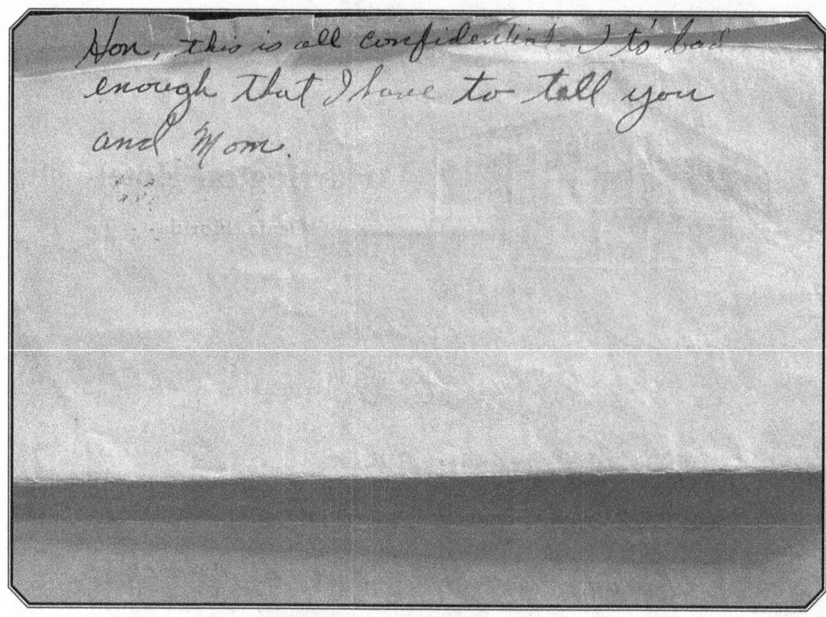
Hon, this is all confidential. It's bad enough that I have to tell you and Mom.

Dad seems to be really smitten in this letter and tells Mom that he never ever wanted to fall in love. He was really missing her, and he mentioned a song on the radio, **"You Made Me Love You"**

There is some of Mom's handwriting on the back of the envelope. It looks like she is planning on taking a train to go see Dad.

The writing says:

"Argue me out of taking the 8:00 train…
that was only to get away quicker

Well, you read the rest.

F11.2 April 16, 1942

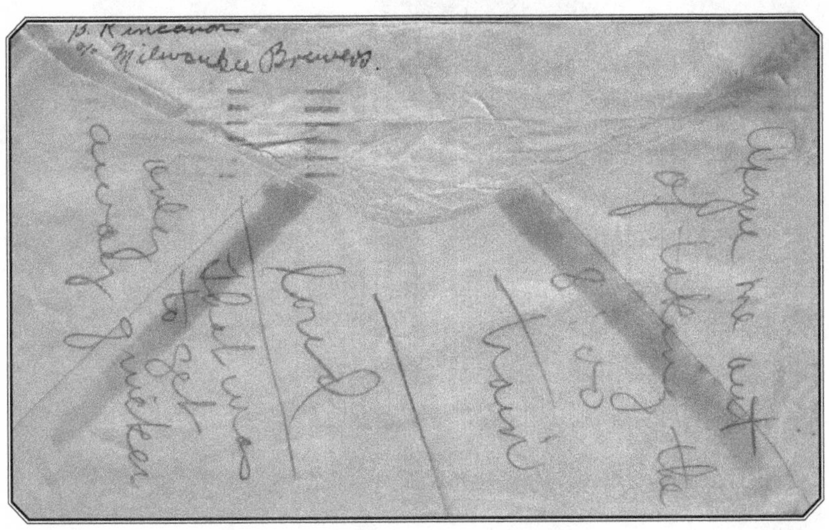

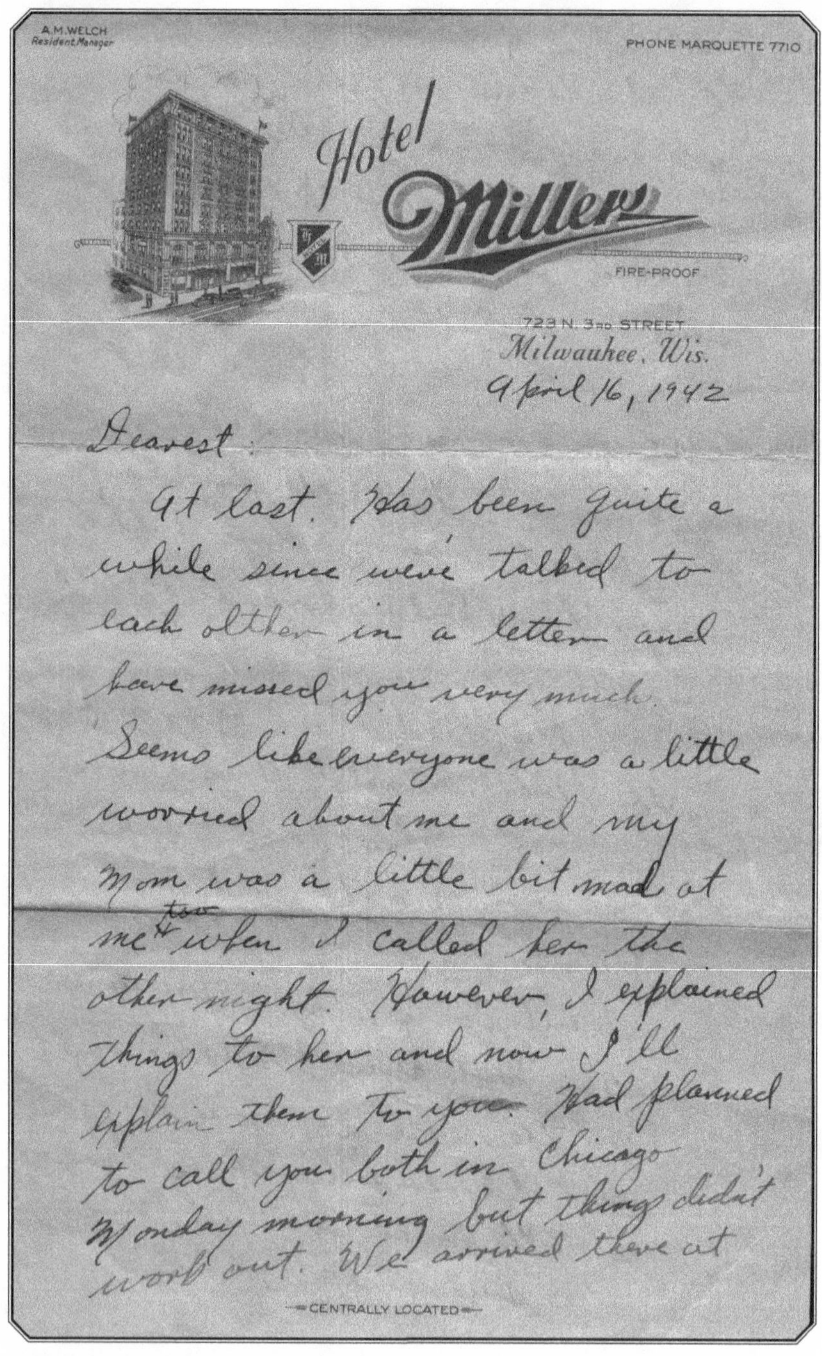

April 16, 1942

Dearest:

At last. Has been quite a while since we've talked to each other in a letter and have missed you very much. Seems like everyone was a little worried about me and my Mom was a little bit mad at me too when I called her the other night. However, I explained things to her and now I'll explain them to you. Had planned to call you both in Chicago Monday morning but things didn't work out. We arrived there at

7:30 AM and as soon as we got off the train we all jumped into a Parmalee Bus and went to the Union Depot. We arrived there at train time and I didn't have a chance to do anything. Knew that everyone would wonder where I was but up untill Sunday I didn't know where I'd be myself. What's more it is still a mystery.

Honey, did I bore you with all those details? Am I in a bad way. Want to see you so darn much that I'm getting desperate. Talking about Songs, this, "You Made Me Love You", hits me right on the nose. Do you know that I never believed in love untill now? Even if there was such a thing I didn't

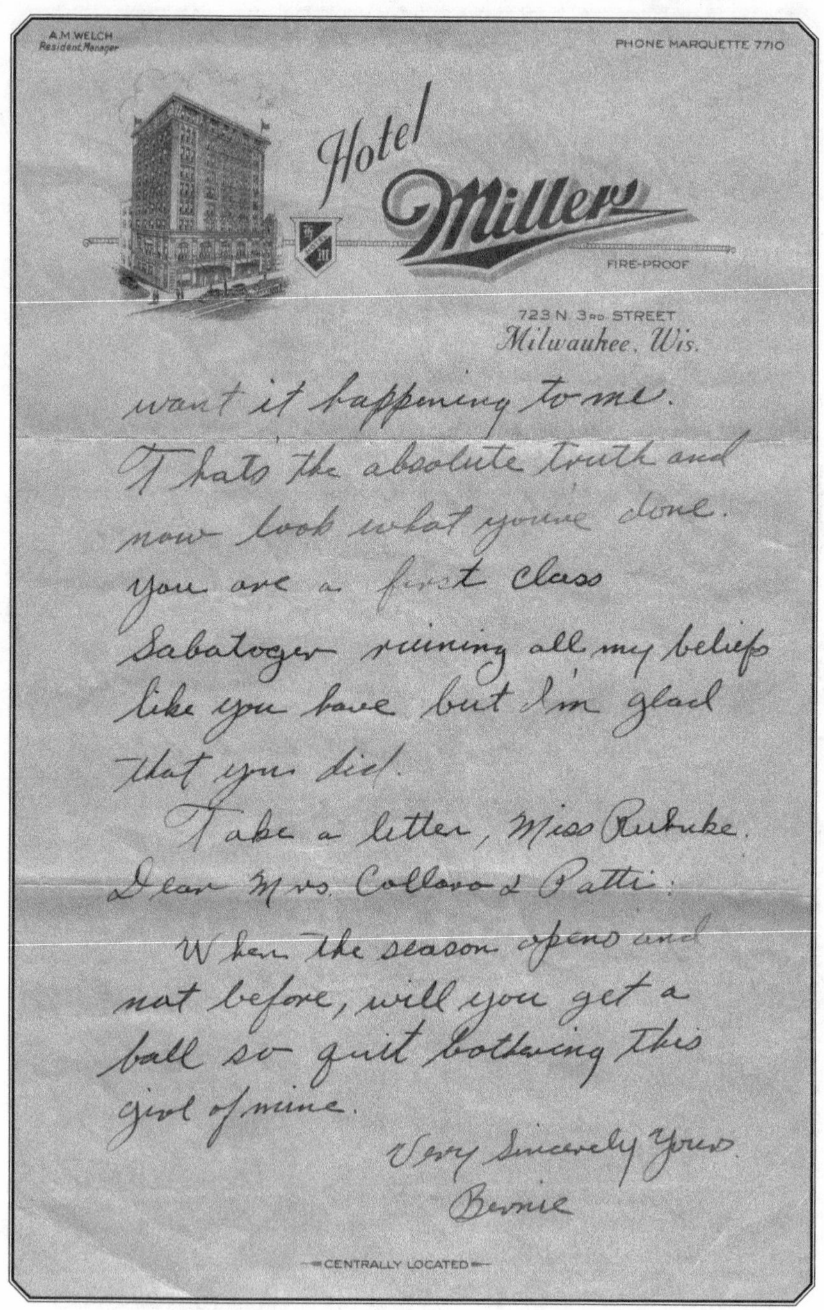

want it happening to me.
Thats the absolute truth and now look what you've done. You are a first class Sabatoger ruining all my beliefs like you have but I'm glad that you did.

Take a letter, Miss Rubuke.
Dear Mrs. Collaro & Patti:

When the season opens and not before, will you get a ball so quit bothering this girl of mine.

Very Sincerely Yours.
Bernie

Suppose you take quite a bit of kidding, Hon, but if they don't get smart, it's O.K.

Darling, the season opens here today and if nothing else I will get to see it anyway. They should let me know something soon so will write you as soon as they do.

Mary, this hasn't been much of a letter but there'll be more and better too. For now I'll close and hope to hear from you soon.

Love
Bernie XXX
XXX

Regards to your Mom & Bill

You made a hit over the weekend.

The letter you just read is the last letter from 1942 and Dad's baseball season. I have no idea when the season ended or if he was with the team the entire time. My guess is he went home to Chicago and his girl because there are no more letters, until, almost one year has passed! I find in a later letter this question is answered.

1942 Letters Transcribed

1942

March 11, 1942
Ocala, Florida

Darling,

Your letter was swell, and I thought it was very nice of you. I'm pretty sure I know what you meant in your letter and I guess you know that the feeling is mutual. "Kid," if you only knew how much I hated to leave you and get on that doggone train. You'll never have to worry about me pulling Fran's tricks and don't you go doing it either. If you ever give me the "cold shoulder" you know what I'll do. I'll join the Air Corp, so help me.

Glad to know that Susie's better but she shouldn't take it so hard. The way I feel now, I can understand it a little, but after all if he doesn't return her love than he's not worth worrying about. Right?

We've just finished our third workout and am I stiff and sore. Outside of that, everything is tops. The weather here is perfect, and we couldn't ask for a better playing field. Oh yes, I forgot one thing. I wish you were here and that's no lie.

Honey, as far as instructions go, I haven't any. It would ease my mind a little if you would sit home every night, but I don't expect you to. I know that you are used to having a good time and I want you to keep right on having them. Another thing, you may find someone you'll like better than me and if ever you do, I want it to be now, because when I get married, I want to be the one and only guy. Here's my last request. Say a prayer for me once in a while and I'll do the same for you. Are they too tough?

Mary Eileen, what did the fortune teller tell you? Hope it was something good because even if we don't believe in them, we can build castles anyway.

Darling, I'm in an awful fix here. My mind is full of pleasant thoughts about you but somehow, they just won't come out and form a sentence. Maybe in my next letter I'll do better and, in the meantime please write soon. Take good care of yourself and think of me a little because I've fallen in love with you.

I agree with you, your mother is swell but how could she be anything else with a daughter like you. Give my regards to all and Goodbye now.

Love,
Bernie

March 26, 1942
Ocala, Florida

Dearest:

Yes, Hon, I asked you to write often and I must say that you're really swell to be doing it. The only drawback is that you make me ashamed of myself. Have been pretty slow in writing you this time but don't ever let that bother you. I'm not much at writing to you but if you only knew how much I think about a certain girl, you'd forgive me. I hope.

Darling, I wish I was "your man," for good and could attend that Mission with you this very minute. Your letter really brought the war back to mind. Since I left home, I had hardly thought about it. Guess it's the absence of radios and your morning paper.

Say, you and mom seem to be getting pretty friendly. You two aren't cooking up a conspiracy against me, are you? Boy, what a lucky guy. Two women in my life and they're the best.

Honey if you miss me like I miss you then I know exactly how you feel. It's awful, isn't it? What's more it does get worse every day. No, your letters aren't silly. Sometimes I think mine are a little that way too but after all if a person feels that way what is wrong in writing these things to each other?

Mary, there isn't much to tell you about things down here. Everything is going fairly well but it doesn't look too bright for B.K. Guess what? In my first year of opportunity I come up with a sore arm. It's not too serious but it has kept me from showing anything and if a "rookie" doesn't deliver in spring training he's on his way, which isn't hard to do. Have done everything to work the soreness out of my shoulder but it's a no go. Can't understand it because it is the first time, I've ever hurt it, and it would be this year. Do you think I'm an "Alibi Ike"? Truly though, I am still confident and if the trouble clears up, I'll still give them all a battle. Isn't this good news?

The Sox are still taking it out on your or should I say our Cubs? Let's hope for the best. Maybe they'll get going when it really counts.

Referring to your other letter you do rate an X (kiss) for your excellent will power that night. As I remember, which isn't hard to do, I left your house most every time looking like a wild man. I've got one cure for you though, and that's a German Brush. Would you like that? Tell me because I'm getting tired of my hair anyway. Getting worse than a girl.

Darling I've surprised myself at the length of this letter and know it must be a severe shock to you. Will close now wishing that you'll always wait for me but hoping it will not be necessary too often.

Love
Bernie XXX

April 2, 1942
Ocala, Florida

Dearest,

Have your latest letter right here beside me as I'm writing this and will try to answer a few of your questions. First, we'll go into Baseball. My arm has improved a bit since last time but it's still not up to par. Honey, that love sickness the Cubs came up with is a little funny but there is some truth in it. You told me yourself how you were acting at work and I've been somewhat the same. You know, dreamy and melancholy.

About that clipping, it's very good and it better be true, or else. You know I'm the gangster type, don't you? People down here think so. Maybe it's the reputation Chicago has.

Darling, If I were you, I wouldn't worry too much about that job at MM (Modern Modes) It's no place for you anyway. What a bunch. Bet there's not a crazier gang anywhere. It surprises me every time I think about it, but I can't figure out how I ever found you in that place. I'll owe Jean my thanks forever now.

Mary, I have a new name for you. It is neglected. Like it? Bet you feel that way sometimes. Know how I'd feel if I wrote as often as you do and then received one letter a week in return.

From your letters I don't think that you are feeling too good. Maybe I'm wrong and I hope so. Wouldn't wonder though if you were ill because I felt terrible all Winter myself. Just wait 'till the "Old Sun" starts shining every day and you'll perk up.

Kid, will you excuse me for now, we had a long workout today and I'm in the same boat with you. Tired and unthinking. Great word isn't it?

Write and take care of yourself. Love Bernie XXX XXX

We break camp the 12th of this month but up to now I'm in the dark as to where I'll be. Am getting very anxious to see you.

My regards to your Mother and Bill.

April 7, 1942
Ocala Florida

Dearest,

Hope you'll always call me Darling, but I have some news that might change your mind.

Mary, I am just about through it seems, at least for this year with Milwaukee and everybody else. My great right arm won't respond to treatment, so I guess I'll be seeing Chicago very soon. They want to send me some place, but I won't go so there's only one thing left for me to do. Wasn't that a gloomy start in a letter from me to you?

Your last letter was swell, eight pages. Do you think I rate all that? Tell Bert that he has a very good idea, but don't you take it seriously. You do very well and I'm proud of you.

Honey, you are right about Fate. I'm beginning to believe that that's all there is to life. Things happen and who knows why. We just go along from day to day trusting that all goes well and if they don't, whose fault is it? I don't know, do you?

Your aunt has hit on a very good idea but now I don't think it will be necessary. Another thing, your tests will have to wait. Maybe I'm presuming too much on coming home, but at the moment it looks very much that way. Did you say she liked me? I'm glad because I liked her too. For a fact, anyone you introduced me to in your family were the good solid kind of people I go for. Hon, in this racket you meet so many fakes. They can look you square in the eye and tell the darndest lies you ever heard.

Darling, I'm used to crazy hats so, I'll just have to take a look at yours. Bet you made quite a picture Easter Sunday in your new coat and Bonnet. You know you are very pretty don't you? Know that you don't think so, but I do. Can't explain it but every time I look at your picture something happens to me. Don't know whether it's the honest direct look of your eyes or the pout of your lower lip. Will have to figure that out next time I see you.

Mary, Easter was O.K. with me and I'm sure that yours was fine also. I am sorry about not sending you a card but will explain that later.

Darling, I've run out of thoughts so will close for now. Take care of yourself and maybe I'll see you soon.

Love,
Bernie XXXXXX

By the way you're the First Darling in my life, also the last.

My thanks to Sue.

Hon, this is all confidential. It's bad enough that I have to tell you and mom.

April 16, 1942
Milwaukee, Wisconsin

Dearest,

At last. Has been quite a while since we've talked to each other in a letter and have missed you very much.

Seems like everyone was a little worried about me and my mom was a little bit mad at me too when I called her the other night. However, I explained things to her and now I'll explain them to you. Had planned to call you both in Chicago Monday morning, but things didn't work out. We arrived at 7:30 a.m. and as soon as we got off the train, we all jumped into a Parmalee Bus and went to the Union Depot. We arrived there at train time and I didn't have a chance to do anything. Knew that everyone would wonder where I was but up until Sunday I didn't know where I'd be myself. What's more it is still a mystery.

Honey, did I love you with all those details? Am I in a bad way. Want to see you so darn much that I'm getting desperate. Talking about songs, this "You Made Me Love You" hits me right on the nose. Do you know that I never believed in love until now? Even if there was such a thing I didn't want it happening to me. That's the absolute truth and now look what you've done. You are a first-class saboteur ruining all my beliefs like you have, but I'm glad that you did.

Take a letter, Miss Ruhnke.

Dear Mrs. Collaro and Patti:

When the season opens and not before, will you get a ball, so quit bothering this girl of mine.

Very Sincerely Yours,
Bernie

Suppose you take quite a bit of kidding, Hon, but if they don't get smart it's okay.

Darling, the season opens here today and if nothing else I will get to see it anyway. They should let me know something soon, so will write you as soon as they do.

Mary, this hasn't been much of a letter, but there'll be more and better too. For now I'll close and hope to hear from you soon.

Love
Bernie XXXXXX

Regards to your mom and Bill.

You made a hit over the weekend.

Chapter 12

He's in the Army Now

Dad's Army letters begin March 21, 1943
You can see by the envelope he is now:
PVT. Louis B. Kincanon Anti Tanks Company 424th
Infantry A.P.O. 443 Fort Jackson, South Carolina

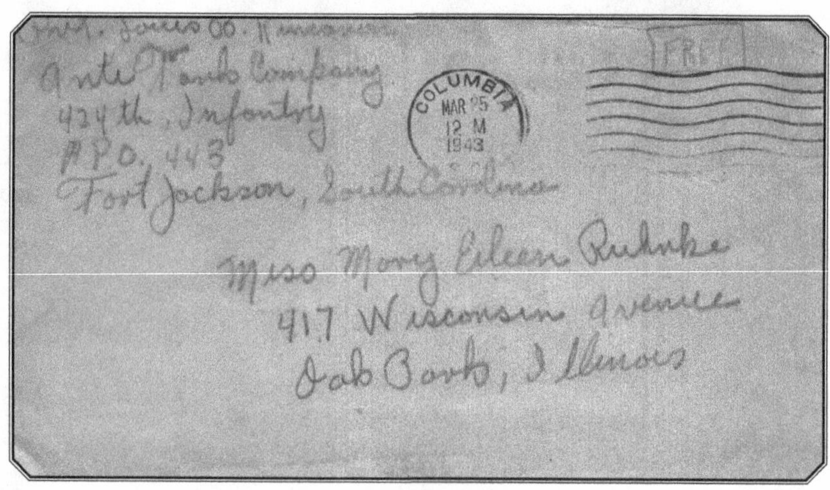

F12.1 March 21, 1943

March 21, 1943

Dear Mary:

Surprised you, didn't I? Seems quite a while since I left Chicago and all you nice people. Just the same things happen fast and before you know it, your on a mysterious journey. We left Camp Grant, Friday afternoon at 4:00 PM and arrived here in Fort Jackson, South Carolina at 6:00 this morning. The trip was very tiring because we had no berths and we just sat there day & night. It's raining pretty hard here today and it being Sunday we have nothing to do. Some of the guys are shooting dice, some sleeping and others like myself writing like the good boys we are.

Hope all of your family and yourself are doing o.K. Pardon me just a minute. Mary the games getting interesting. These guys sure don't have much regard for money. Pretty high stakes.

This is, I know a poor excuse for my first letter to you but I don't want to bore you or anyone, going through all the details of Army Life.

Mary, they told us to tell everyone not to write for a

while because we are not settled as yet in our permanent barracks.

Please give my regards to everyone and my next letter will be more informative. Take care of yourself and I'll write soon. Good-bye for now and Love

Bernie XX

Call my Mom up once in a while, will you <u>Chub</u>?

Excuse the pencil. This is the Army, Miss Ruhnke.

No, I'm not in the Medical Corp. Don't even know what I am in.

Dad was still in South Carolina at Fort Jackson. His letter is full of appreciation and gratitude. It seems as though Mom sent him some items in the mail such as gum and a prayer missal. The picture below is the actual missal Mom sent him. The back of it actually has raised beads almost like brail to say the rosary. He is responding to one of her letters where I assume, she is telling him how she feels and there seems to be some talk about marriage. Dad is trying to assure her in his letter that he loves her but needs more time.

There is a lot more in this letter regarding their relationship, Army Life and a try out for the Army Baseball Team.

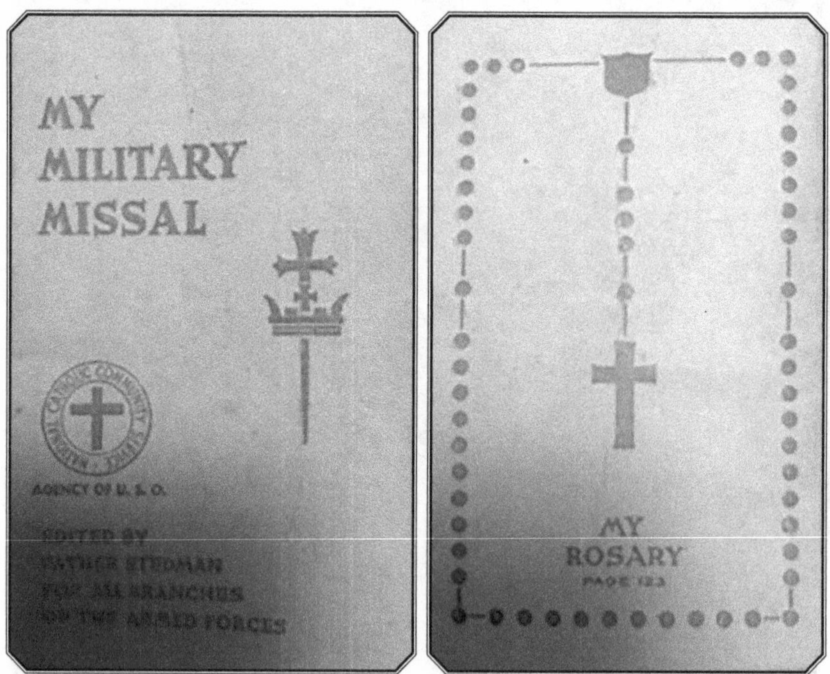

F12.2 March 28, 1943

March 8, 1943

Dear Mary E.

Oh you Brat. Am I mad. I'm tearing my hair out, that is what's left of it. If there isn't a letter from you in the mail tomorrow well, I just won't read it that's all. Seriously, I can't understand why my letters are so slow in reaching you. I'm sure I wrote you from Camp Grant and that's over a week ago, and my last letter from here has had plenty of time to get there. I understand that the poor Mailman has a tough time finding Oak Park so maybe that's the reason.

Since my last letter nothing much has happened unless I mention the thousands of miles I've walked since then, the shots I've taken and the speeches I've listened too. A guy has to be a genius to remember all they teach you in one day let alone a week of instruction. Even so its not so hard and in time all these things will be routine.

Hows your Mom & Bill? They should both be feeling

much better now that they don't have to look at me anymore. Is Bill playing ball yet? Seasons getting pretty close now and am I getting anxious to play. We played a little Soft Ball today but its like playing house or something. No thrill. Mary, bet you $5.00 Bill makes a good Ball player have never seen him play but the way he throws and handles himself tells a story. Don't tell him this or he might

got high hat on the rest
of the family. Inject a
laugh after that sentence
please. Know he has
more sense than to get
that way. It's a very
bad trait. If you don't
understand some of these
words just write me a
letter and tell me so I can
explain them to you.

After all this idle
banter, I suppose you
are expecting a change
to the serious side of
life. Know there is
such a thing because
thats the way I feel
when I say I miss you
all very much and take

you think of me (once in a while.)

The above for all
&
the below for you Brat.
Not hearing from you has left me a little weak in the stomach. You know the way you used to tell me you felt when we were at war. I always felt the same way myself and admit I was silly at times but I thought so much of you that even the slightest thing I heard about you bothered me. Enough of that or else we'll both be crying.

Will close for now
hoping to hear from
you soon and I mean
soon. Best regards &
all my love,
Bernie

Pvt. Louis B. Kincanon
Anti Tank Company
424th Infantry
Fort Jackson, South Carolina

COLUMBIA
APR 16
1 PM
1943
S.C.

Miss Mary E. Ruhnke
417 Wisconsin Avenue
Oak Park, Illinois

F12.3 April 1, 1943

April 1, 1943

Dearest;
Have recieved your numerous letters and have read every one through, even the [illegible] The gum also arrived and as you know, appreciated. You 2, I don't know what to call you. You know you actually overwhelm me, When I read your letters I'm speechless, numb, and dumbfounded. Have always hoped for the complete love of a good decent girl and the way you write my

wish seems to have come
true. Mary, you've heard
me say that if I couldn't
be perfectly happy, married
I would never take the
leap. If you think as
much of me as you say you do
we have nothing to fear.
Don't ever doubt my feelings.
A year or more should be
enough for me to know
for sure. I miss you very
much, still love you,
so you must be the
one & only.

Hon, I'm glad the family
is feeling fine and their
few lines in your letter was swell

Suppose all of you are still working hard. Life is like that it seems. It gets pretty monotonous at times especially when Saturday's & Sunday's are just the same as the rest. Have just about reconciled my-self now to work eat and sleep. No more Mary for a while and that's a pretty tough reconciliation. Gee, you've even got me doing it, Mush.

You ask me to explain army life, what I do and all stuff like that there. So far we've been learning

Close order drill - Column Right - Right Flank and all that stuff. We are learning so many things, our Rifles, Guard Duty Identification of Airplanes Tent Pitching and a few more things that escape me now. Whats more we've only started and from now on we really hit the ball. Speaking about the ball I have gone out for the Regimental team and soon that will be under way. Darlin, hate to tell you all this because it's all about me and I'd rather talk about you

You never would let me, remember? Just a glutton for punishment, aren't you?
Have written to Mom tonight and she also has a detailed account of A.L.
Dearest, I'll close now. Lights out at 9:30 just 15 minutes from now. Know I haven't answered 1 tenth of your questions but time forbids. Besides this is more fun anyway, telling you I love you.
My best regards and love to all. Bye
Bernie (over)

I'll kiss you goodnight by mental telepathy. Hope it works, but I doubt it. Bye

The Missal was really something. Must have taken a lot of patience + time. I liked it very much and the time of reading was about 15 minutes.

Chapter 13

Absence Makes the Heart Grow Fonder

The next sweet letter is dated April 9, 1943 and mailed on April 10, 1943.

My Dad is becoming more and more smitten with Mom with each letter. I can only imagine what my Mom is writing to him. You can use your own imagination here. I can sure tell that some of his mushy comments are in response to something she had said, and it had made him happy and feeling more and more secure with his tall brunette. He is in love and in his mind engaged, although not officially.

I just noticed none of these letters have zip codes. When did they come into play? I was interested enough to look this up. According to GOOGLE by the early 1960's a more organized system was needed, and a non-mandatory five-digit ZIP Codes were introduced on July 1, 1963.

F13.1 April 9, 1943

April 9, 1943

Dearest:

I'm still hearing from you regularly and you are not making me a bit mad. You know we can't get enough letters from such people as you. Tall, dark and beautiful, at least some people say so, I don't think they know what they are talking about, though. Seriously, Mary. I do think your very pretty especially when you are all dressed up and no place to go. It does seem funny but I didn't have to go places and do things to have a good time when we were together.

Maybe it was love, why sure
it must have been. Does
absence make the heart grow
fonder? It must the way
I'm writing to you. Guess it
has always felt this way
but was too dumb to admit
it. About being engaged
I wish it were so but
as things stand it's im-
possible. As far as that goes
I can see very little hope
for the future but I'll
work something out somehow,
Can't stop now because it's
much too late. Mine
is a lost cause. Hon, be-
tween us two we are

definitly engaged.

A guy was just here telling me he writes his girl once ~~or~~ twice every day. Can you imagine me doing that? What can a guy write about? I often wonder how you do it but you do & your letters are always long & interesting. It must be a gift.

Mary, about Bill's Glove, I'm not sure what to tell you because I don't know what you want to pay. I can tell you to get him an infielders glove. They generally have short fingers and then it makes [illegible] to kick up

those hot grounds. Know
what I mean. Wish I were there
and we'd pick it out together.
Hon, business is picking up
again. We have to clean the
barracks now so will have
to close. This letter has its
good and bad points, mostly bad,
but hope you'll excuse me
because it was done in a
hurry. Give my regards to
all and tell them to write

x Love
Bernie.

Chapter 14

Premonition

I am truly mystified by this next letter, it is dated April 15, 1943 and mailed April 19, 1943. Let me give you a little look into the future.

My Father was born April 17, 1918. Michael (my oldest brother) was born April 12, 1945. This letter is dated April 15, 1943. Almost two years to the day *before* Michael was born and two days after my Dad's birthday.

In this letter there is much talk about marriage and the obstacles...obstacle number one, WAR.

As you read the letter you will discover their talks about marriage and how their future had gone way beyond what the pages of previous letters have told us. My Dad was being the logical one of course, Mom, the emotional one, wanting a marriage while the war was heating up. Dad knew if anything were to happen, she would be left alone, and **"MIKE and No Father!"** I had to re-read this passage a number of times. Dad and Mom had their future planned long before the day they married. It was such amazing timing, the letter, the dates, and in their heart's, they knew they were destined to have a son. This letter is full of love, wanting, army life, KP Duty, and baseball. Dad covers a lot in these seven pages; asking my Mom if it's Leap Year, I guess you can deduct what that was all about?

Oh Mother!

F14.1 April 15, 1943

April 15, 43.

Dearest;

So, there you are, mad again. Also getting witty, aren't you? Well, that joke was just as bad as all the rest and what's more I just read it again in that magazine section, "Yank". Hello? After all that I'll ask you how you are, how's the weather and all that stuff? Gee, this Army's getting me so punchy I can't even write a sensible letter anymore.

If you only knew how
busy they are keeping us.
The Army alone is bad
enough but Baseball
on top of that just gives
me time to eat & sleep.
I'm not lying because
I missed practice tonight
to write you & Mom.
Had my first K P yesterday
and it's all they say it is.
Wash dishes, pots and pans
mop the floor, peel potatoes
and Carrotts, dish out the
food and all that happens
three different times.

The night before I was gigged for being late at retreat and spent an hour walking around our barracks with a full field pack. What a life. Then that wasn't enough this had to happen. Received a letter from you & was reading the first page when the wind blew the other two pages out of my hand & under a building. Was I mad. My only happiness, "Gone With The Wind." Guess you've heard enough misery for

awhile, haven't you? If you
haven't I have much more
to tell you. Don't get
me wrong Chub, I'm
still happy except for
not seeing you. Miss you
more each day & as time
goes on it is bound to
get much worse. Say,
you, is this Leap Year?
You Nut, if I could only
see & talk to you. Don't
you remember what we
decided. Mary, I'm in
the mood as much as you
but if your looking for
a life of misery you'll
find it in a war marrage

As far as I'm concerned
what is there to lose?
You, everything. I can
get married & go away to
war after a few weeks
of happiness. If I don't
come back it wont matter
anyway to me. In your
case you'd probably be
left here waiting & soon
maybe, Mike & no
Father. Hon, this is a
crazy way to talk but
it's true and we must
face it. Let's bide our
time and eventually things
will work out OK, I'm

sure. If you ever feel
that you've waited too
long & don't want to
waste anymore of your single
life let me know and
we'll arrange something.
Before you do that, though
consider everything &
not your heart alone.
If I listened to mine you'd
have been a bride months
ago. That's how much
I love you and want you
but there happens to be
a few barriers up now
and one of them is spelled
war.

Well, gal, I'm about ready to shower & shave now and then to bed. Say hello to Ma & Bill and the rest of your family. also Morty & ask him how his bowling is coming along. By the way one of your Mother's dinners would taste plenty good right now. Hope your as good a cook some day. Will close now with all my love. Keep writing.

X Bernie.

Was I right?

This letter is one I could read a thousand times. It still amazes me, the timing of the letter and the contents. I have noticed through all my readings of these letters and dates on the envelopes that there are many dates that have meaning today in our family. *Is that a numerology thing? I don't know,* but, one of Mom and Dad's numbers that always seemed to pop up for them was "4 1 7" or a combination of those numbers.

Notice the address on all the envelopes it was my Mom's home in Oak Park where she lived with her mother. The numbers "417" was also my father's birthday.

Chapter 15

What's in a Name?

In the previous letter, Dad mentions a son, they were planning ahead, they were planning a family. Dad even went so far as to say the baby's name, Mike! In an earlier chapter I mentioned there was a story just in his name. I will reveal some of the family history on names.

My father's family had a very strange tradition. They all had a first name and a middle name, I know, not so odd, right? But, every single one of them were all called by their middle name. I have no idea why, and this became an issue later as you will learn. I will share a little with you now, as it will not spoil the bigger piece of this story by telling you this much. My second older brother, Larry, and I do not have a middle name. My Mom and Dad decided for reasons you will learn later why this came to be. So, this envelope's return address is Louis B Kincanon, and the letters you are reading are all signed Bernie. Bernard is my Dad's middle name, hence the explanation. Funny thing is, he always liked Louis or Lou better. I found this out many years later when I heard my Dad on the phone with a man, he played horseshoes with every week after he retired. I overheard him leave a message saying, "this is Lou calling," I looked at my Mom and asked, *"who is Lou?"* Mom told me that since Dad's retirement any new people he would meet, he told them his name was Lou, which it was of course, but that was news to me!

Chapter 16

"The Longing"

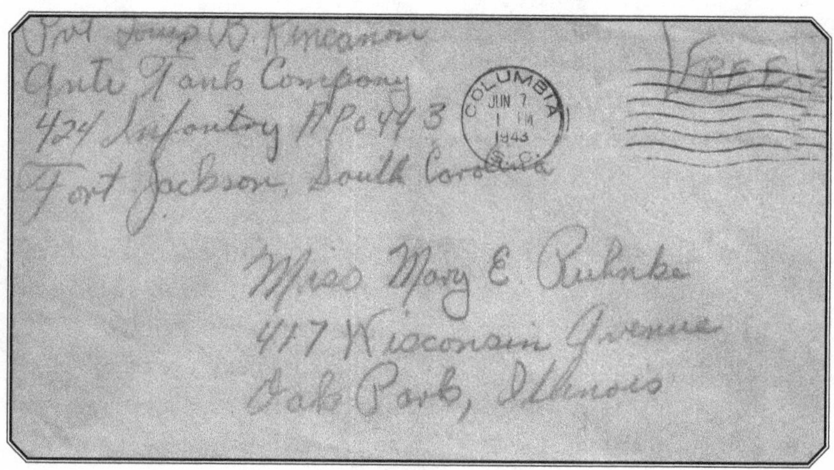

Pvt [illegible]
Anti Tank Company
424 Infantry APO 443
Fort Jackson, South Carolina

COLUMBIA JUN 7 1 PM 1943 S.C.

FREE

Miss Mary E. Ruhnke
417 Wisconsin Avenue
Oak Park, Illinois

F16.1 June 6, 1943

June 6, 1943

Darling:
I know, this letter is
late getting to you & I deserve a bawling out which
probably will come soon. Go
ahead Son, I want you to
& would like to get it in
person. You know it
really was fun to tease
you & make you mad.
Your very cute when
you pout & I couldn't
keep from laughing when

You did. You'll probably kill me for writing this, won't you? Gosh, how I miss you. Knew it would be bad but in all my life I've never longed for anyone like I do you. If I could just put it into words but like yourself, words just won't. Can't explain how I feel. I'm lost without you, Kid. Can't even enjoy myself without you. never—

will be able to, I know,
You see we're in the same
boat. Read your letter with
the Marriage problem in it.
I don't know what to say.
As you know, I'm all for
it but hon, will you
wait till I see you. Have
to talk to you & well de-
cide together. Understand
I'm always thinking of you
& as long as I do it just can't
be.

Here's some Army news. I mean Army Baseball. Have just finished pitching against our hated rivals again, the 100th Division. Beat them 1-0 and allowed four hits. Am I feeling good, Mary. Believe that I'm twice the pitcher this year than I've ever been. Can't understand it but at last I've acquired good control. What a thrill. You, Mom & Baseball, my three loves.

Mary, will you give my
love to your family &
all. Really miss all of
them & tell your Grandmother
I like her very much too.
Bye for now, X

I love you
Bernie.

Dad is talking about his new-found control as a pitcher. He just won a game 7-0 against their rivals, The 100th Division. He was feeling so great about it. I am so happy to learn, even though he was in the Army, he was still able to do the one thing he loved, Play Ball!

I love the way my Dad closes on most of his letter to Mom. He was always telling her to send his love to her mother, brother, or, grandmother. That is the kind of man he was.

Chapter 17

The First Furlough*

*"A leave of absence, especially that is granted to a member of the armed services"

Dad is wondering how he "ever left home without being married" but his fear of the unknown kept him from following his heart. One of the quotes from his letter was, **"Remember me, I'm the guy who loves you."**

Mom and Dad are discussing a visit for Mom to come and see Dad in South Carolina. I do not know if she ever made that trip. Dad's sense of humor is coming out in this letter, so cute! He told her, **"Bring plenty of cotton"** and, **"Well kid I'm still in love with you and always will be."**

It was really difficult not to highlight all the delightful quotes from my Dad's letters written to my Mom. I was torn on which way to present them, but in the end my hope is that you take the time to read them for yourself. The war was touching many in our family, it was taking a toll.

Dad wrote it's been "quite a while" since he wrote last. I just looked at the last letter and it was dated June 13. How awesome is he that 10 days is a long time? How many men do you know that are letter writers?

I am so happy to hear him say in the last few letters that he thought time goes so **"darn fast"**

This letter also confirmed what I suspected in one of the earlier letters. Dad was complaining here about the team pitching him again after only two days of rest on his arm. It was no wonder he was having shoulder problems. Dad had a reputation and they were using it, to his detriment.

F17.1 Dad Furlough 1943

F17.2 Dad and Mom during Dad's first Furlough 1943

F17.3 June 10, 1943

June 10, 1943

Darling:

Hello Beautiful: Do you know what those pictures did to me? They absolutely made a new man of me. Since then I havent stopped looking at them, believe me. There is only one drawback. The longing to see you has increased to where I can hardly stand it. When I sit here & look at you,

I wonder how I ever
left home without being
married. Guess I'm quite
a dope but my love couldnt
quite overcome the fear.
Your letters are still
reaching me regularly &
all seems to be well in
O.P. I'm mighty pleased
that your all fine and you
all had better stay that
way. Sue is having quite
a time for herself. She deserves every minute though
because you never know

when she will get to see
Fran again. I hope that he
doesn't have to leave too soon.
This war is sure beyond
me.

We had quite a ball
game last night. Had to
pitch again with only two
days rest. The Lt. seems
to think I'm the berries
so now I have a reputation.
We played Shaw Field
the team with that good pitcher
& tied 1-1. Both runs were
unearned so we did all right.

Hon, please excuse me
for tonight. It's bedtime
so I'll have to close.
Remember me, I'm the
guy who loves you.
Give my regards to Mom
& Bill.
Love XXX
Bernie

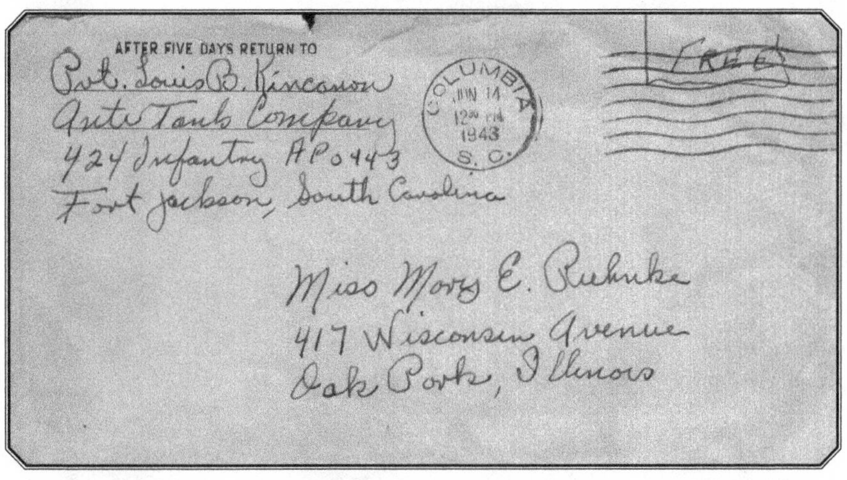

F17.4 June 13, 1943

June 13, 1943

Darling;

Do you mean to tell me that you havent heard from this boy in nine days. How, I must be slipping or else time is going by too fast for me. I'm trying to make it up to you now. I think this is the third this week and a new record has been made.

Mary, you know that your coming here would be

The most welcome thing that
Could happen. You must
forgive me sometimes. I guess
just writing to you makes
me so darn dizzy that I can't
even think. Never even mentioned
your blood donation either &
I wanted to tell you how
proud you make me feel.
Darling, just one thing. Will
you wait untill I notify you
to come? Want you here
now & always but it would
be impossible to be with
you ~~most~~ as much as I'd like too.

We are pretty busy as you
know & getting away evenings
is a tough job. Remember
this. When I do see you
start ducking. Also bring
plenty of cotton. Never had
so much to tell you before
& your ears may become
very weary. Do believe that
for once a man is going
to out talk a woman.

Glad to hear the good
news about Bill. Bet it's
like being out of jail for him.
Know how he feels because
I was in the same boat once &

long time ago. How's Mom & Marty? Tell her I miss her a lot & would like to hear from her. I'll answer it & we won't even let you read it. So there.

Well, kid, I'm still in love with you & always will be as I've said before. Never do get tired of telling you, so you'd better never get tired of hearing it. Have to close now so excuse me please for tonight. Will write again soon.

Love XXXX
Bernie

We won today 10-1. Our other pitcher worked. He's a good boy.

We're still in first place

F17.5 & F17.6 Mom and Dad 1942

F17.7 & F17.8 Mom and Dad 1943

F17.9 June 24, 1943

The following letter was definitely a welcomed one, I'm sure. Dad is telling her they are trying to get everyone on the baseball team to get furloughed at the same time. Mom must have been over the moon with that news. He said that Mom's home in Oak Park was becoming his home. It is obvious reading his words that Dad really truly cared about Mom, but more than that he cared deeply about her family. Dad is still in South Carolina, and by the sound of the letters Mom may have been planning a trip to see him, but with the news of an upcoming furlough, that may not have happened.

June 24, 1943

Darling:

Well, here I am again. It has been quite a while since I wrote you last. As I said before, I can't keep up with the time, it goes so darn fast. Mary, I have some good news. Our furloughs start in about two weeks & I think maybe I'll see you pretty quick. They are trying to get the Ball players' furloughs all at the same time. Don't know exactly when but will soon &

then I'll let you know.
— So all of you people are fine. Please continue to stay that way & don't worry me. It seems that one house in Oak Park is now part of me & I don't want to hear of anything being wrong there.

Hon, your letters are still coming regularly & without them I'm afraid this life would have me down, by now. No kidding. without you to think about

this Army with its monotony
would be too much. At
least, this way I can always
look forward to seeing
you eventually & if not with
your letters to the week,
Darlin, I'm sorry
but this letter has to be
drawn to a close. It's
way past bedtime now
so please excuse me for
tonight. Always remember
I love you & miss you very
much. Will write you

again soon. Love & Best
Regards to Mom & Bill.

I love you, Kid.

Bernice

We lost a double header
Sunday 1–0 and 5–1.
I pitched the 1–0 game
& then the St. decided to
let the other guy hurl.
Last night the Snow Field
team beat me 7–0 but it
doesn't matter anyway. Bye

There is a terribly [illegible] I was
writing them in a big hurry

Chapter 18

Mea Culpa!!!

He's so honest! **"Mary I'm a Bum"** It looks like Dad forgot his girl's birthday! Knowing my Mom, I am sure, with everything Dad was going through so far away from home, Mom forgave him. But it is always nice to get a "MEA CULPA" I loved reading his reason why though, ***"This*** **Army's got me crazy and you have got me in the clouds."** I would take that as a sufficient apology. What is really funny is that the following letter was written the day before her birthday and it was mailed on her birthday, June 29· He writes in the letter how much he had planned for her birthday, to send a card and a present, then totally forgot. He even mentioned that his mother would try to cover for him, but he was taking full responsibility for his own forgetfulness. That was my Dad. He was a man of honor and integrity. You could rely on the fact that if he told you something, it was the truth.

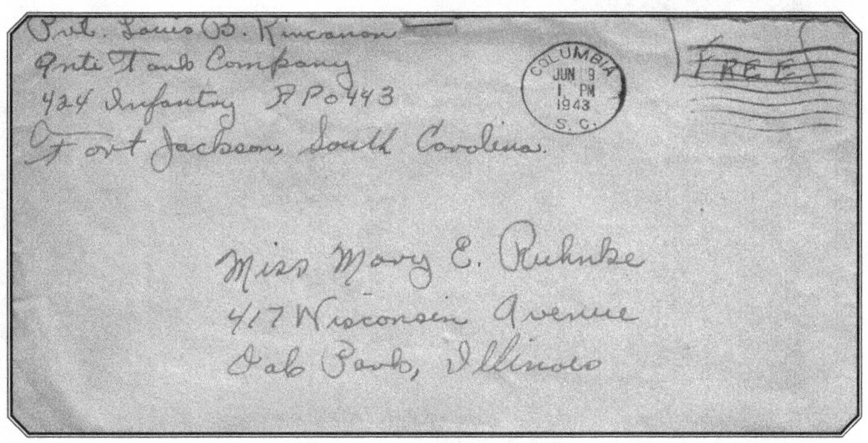

F18.1 June 29, 1943

June 28, 1943

Darling:

Have just finished reading your last two letters & thought I'd better write again, but quickly. Don't blame you. I'm sorry & I hope it will not happen again. Mary, I'm a bum. Here it is your Birthday & not even a card have I sent you. Don't know what the matter is. All this Month I've been thinking & planning for your present & a card but at the very last "good old Bern" forgets all about it. Promise you that I'll make good when I see you though. Mom may give you a present from me. She mentioned it in her last letter. She'll probably make excuses for me saying that I told her to buy something for you, but I didn't. Hon, whatever is wrong, blame it on the Army & also being away from you. This Army's got me crazy & you've got me in the clouds.

ing you would be a problem.
Our Corp tests are coming
up now & will be busy from
dawn till dark. Nothing seems
to work out in this place.
You know I miss you more
each day & talk about loving
someone. Words can't explain
so won't even try.

Hon, as usual there is
work to be done so will
close for tonight. Regards &
love to all & be good.

XXXX I love you, Mary E.
Bernie

Hello to Sue when you write her.

I hope, we finished in third place.
We're knocked out of the top the other night for the first
Time. Lost 7-0.

It sure looks like Dad got his furlough and had a wonderful time home with Mom and their families. I am guessing he may have had three weeks or more by the sound of his next letters, that do not start back up again until July 21, 1943. His first letter is only a one-page letter, which by now you might agree is unusual. From the second letter dated July 25, 1943, you can really feel how hard it was for him to have been home and to leave again.

I do not know how these men and woman do it. It is heart wrenching to read let alone experience it first-hand.

See what you think after reading his letters.

Chapter 19

After the Furlough

F19.1 July 21, 1943

July 21, 1943

Darling:

Here I am safe & sound. The trip was terrible & even Fort Jackson looked good. Haven't much to tell you only that I'm lost again without you. Almost every minute I expect to look up & see you & then boom, back to reality I go.

Hon, will close now but will never stop loving you. Regards to the family & hope you're all fine.

Love xx
Bernie.

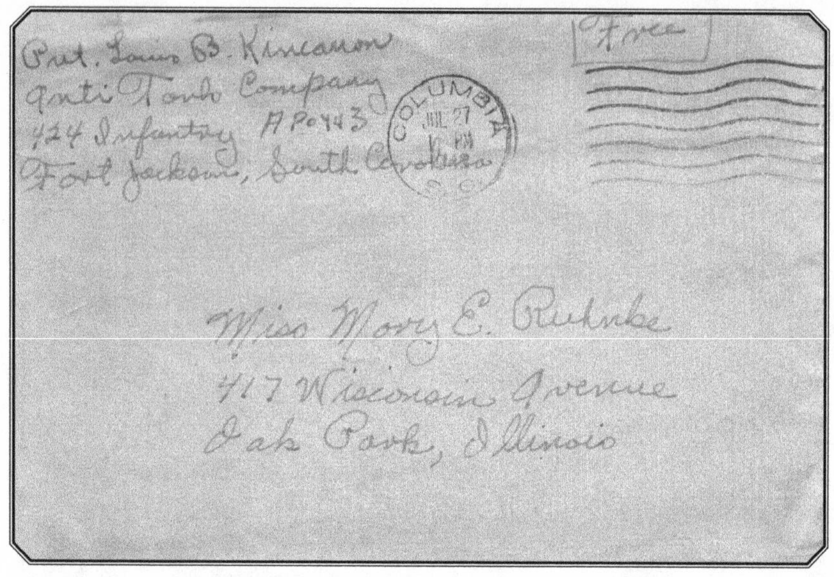

Pvt. Louis B. Kincanon
Anti Tank Company
424 Infantry APO 443
Fort Jackson, South Carolina

Free

COLUMBIA JUL 27 S.C.

Miss Mary E. Ruhnke
417 Wisconsin Avenue
Oak Park, Illinois

July 25, 1943

This letter is heartbreaking, Dad seems so sad and lonely. I cannot even begin to imagine how difficult war time is when families are separated for months at a time. What is it like for the loved ones at home waiting; waiting for a letter or word that they are okay? How we take things for granted. Most of us can relate to a loved one being away on a business trip or vacation. A week, maybe two where we are sleeping alone, doing chores alone, maybe taking out the garbage on our own, or getting up early to let the dog out and make sure they are fed. Taking care of the children, getting them to school, their activities, carpooling. The jobs mostly done or at the very least shared, by the one not at home. I know when that happens in my house, I count the days for Joe to be home, so I don't have to get up at his ungodly hour of 5:30 a.m. But, imagine, your loved one gone for months at a time, not knowing where they are, if they are safe, injured, or even alive? Wouldn't you worry about your children, will they remember their mommy or daddy when they return? Will they return whole in mind and body? When I said we take so much for granted, can you let yourself feel the same? I bet many of you reading this right now have seen videos of father's and mother's coming home and surprising their child at school, or at a sports event? Doesn't that strike emotion in you immediately? It is emotional when you see a video of a dog, left for months at a time while their owner is away serving our country, that reunion enlists tears from me right away. I torture myself by watching that over and over again.

Knowing what I know now after reading my Dad's letters, my heart breaks knowing that my Mom had to go through this by herself. Maybe you know a loved one or a friend that has served or is serving right now. This thought alone makes me take a deep breath and be awed by the sacrifices of these brave souls.

July 25, 1943

Darling;

Am here in the Barracks & have just finished listening to Frank Munn. One of his songs was "Can I Forget You"? It has always been a favorite of mine and now I'll answer the question. Hon, I'll never forget you so long as I live. Those few days at home were the happiest I've spent in four long months. There was one drawback to that happiness, though. We both knew it would come to an end eventually and sure enough it did. Guess I never really appreciated my civilian life with you.

Mary, so far I've done nothing in regard to the operation. Am waiting a bit but it wont be long now.

Sure bet you were glad to see your Grandmother. Hated to miss seeing her but next time well make connections. That California must have something. Sue & her must have fallen hard for the West. Please give her my regards & I hope to see her [illegible] soon.

So you hated to go back to M.M.? Cant say that I blame you because work is hard after all the fun we had. As for myself

every day in trucks, set up
our gun & then lay down in
the shade for two or three
hours. Can't hardly believe
it but that's what we've been
doing. After Basic it seems
like heaven.

Our Baseball team hasn't
been reorganized as yet but they
are planning on doing some
playing.

Mary, I don't know exactly
how our marriage plans will
turn out but in a week or
so I may have the answer.
What it will be depends
on a few thing that I'll
explain later. In the meantime
pray for the best.

Darlin, suppose you are dissapointed in me again. I'll admit this letter should have reached you two days ago but as usual it's late. Don't ever think that I don't want to write you. Guess I'm just plain lazy. Since I am that way this letter will now be drawn to a close. I love you more than ever, think of you always & hope to be a very important part of you soon. Give my love to Mom & Bill. Bye for now.

Love
Bernie

Hon, whenever I put an x on the end of my letters to you, I feel like a sissy. It's more fun in real life anyway.

This is quite a letter, it covers Dad's new duties since completing basic training, baseball, and Mom and Dad's future marriage plans. The talks about their future had begun.

I love the P.S. in this letter. Yes Dad, real life kisses are much better than an "X" on a letter, but the girls still like to see them.

Right Girls?

It is so wonderful to read my Dad's words and be able to feel his sense of humor and his willingness to show his feelings to Mom. Dad was a quiet man and, in my experience not very demonstrative. But one of the sweetest things I am discovering is that Dad did have it in him! Maybe, and this is just my thought, the war had changed him. That was totally possible.

Chapter 20

#3673948

Now that Dad finished basic training, he was assigned his Army number that he no doubt remembered for the rest of his life. He was now,

Private Louis B. Kincanon 424 Infantry
Anti-Tanks Company APO 443 #36739483
Fort Jackson, South Carolina

This Army number got me curious. Curious enough to do a little research. Doing so answered a couple of questions. The first question was one I had been wondering since starting this book; Did Dad volunteer for the Army? I always believed Dad was the kind of guy to do the right thing, to serve his country, at the same time he was such a laid-back, quiet man, that I could not picture him fighting anyone, let alone in a war. Well I was surprised to learn, but probably should not have been, his number, besides being used to identify him, was a planned out coordinated number by the Army which was anything but random. During WWII, the numbers that began in the

"30 000 000 to 39 999 999's" was issued to men born in the United States and voluntarily enlisted. Question number one answered; the thirty-six number was to identify a geographical area. Thirty-six covered Illinois, Wisconsin, and Michigan.

I know my Mom knew Dad's number by heart, I think it makes total sense though. If I have 99 letters written by my Dad, I can bet the number she wrote to him was likely twice that many. When my Dad had to be admitted to the VA hospital in the year 2000, my Mom rattled off his Army number like it was her phone number. I was pretty impressed but not at all surprised!

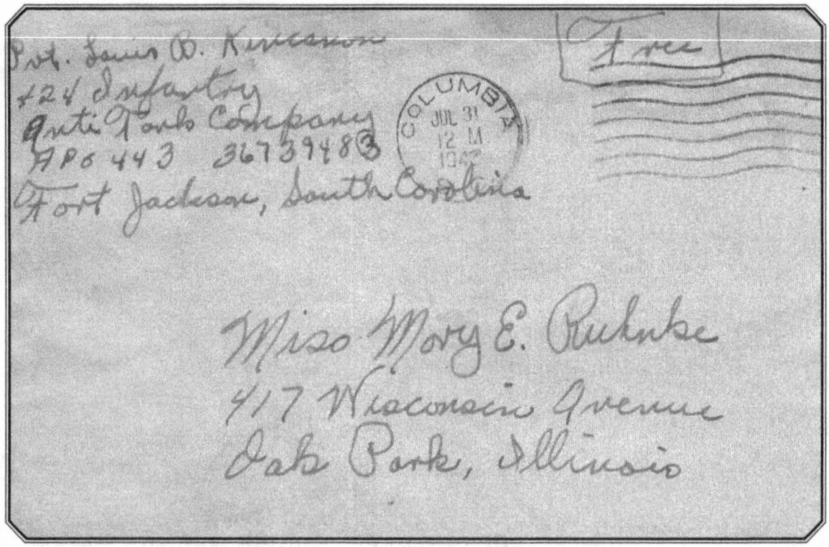

F20.1 July 31, 1943

July 31, 1943

Darling:
Recieved all of your letters & cards & must admit that I can't figure out where you get time to write so often. Mary, nothing pleases me more than a letter from you. You really keep my spirits at high tide & without you I'd be lost. By the way Frank Munn is now singing, "You'll Never Know".

Hon, all of your questions are unanswerable at present but not for long. Mona has written me twice & she is against our marriage

but she's only thinking of
the tough times we'll have
getting along after the war.
More for a fact she really
wants us to be married
but thinks that we should
wait. In a week or so
I'll let you know for
sure. As for the operation
I haven't done a thing, yet.
Maybe I'm a little scared
of these Army Doctors.
Tell Caddy not to worry
because I'll let her know
before it happens. No, we
haven't started playing
ball again & I guess they
have decided to quit for
the year. Don't care too
much. This Army is
tough enough without
added exercise

Darling, did your Mom think that I was going to marry you without asking her? I'll bet she felt neglected. Have wanted to write her but didn't know just how to go about it. Hon, I'm so darn ashamed to even think of getting married under these conditions that asking her is a very hard job. I know how she feels & wouldn't blame her if she'd refuse. Mary, I've always said I'd never take the plunge without security & I'm so far from that now that I feel like a beggar. I do love your Mother & don't ever want to do anything to hurt her. What's more you yourself are my whole life & if I can't make you happy because then I've failed in something that means everything to me. Say, I've really preached a sermon, haven't I? Well, it's all true & am glad that I've gotten these things over to you.

Darlin, am closing now. Remember, I love you & always will. Regards to Mom & Gram & Bill & Sue's family also.

Love
Bernie

Chapter 21

Vera Lynn

My Dad sure did love his music, he mentions another song he was listening to called, **"You'll Never Know."** One thing about Dad, the words to these love songs brought up a lot of emotion for him. I witnessed that myself first-hand when he would be listening to his music at home or in the car.

Dad loved to sing, he had a wonderful, soothing voice. I used to love it when we were kids in the car rides home from my grandmother's house and Dad would break into song. Some of the songs I knew were **"Home, Home, on the Range,"** and of course all the Christmas Carole's. But those war songs brought Dad to a whole different place. One of his favorite war time artists was Vera Lynn. Vera Lynn was an artist that used to sing for the troops. Her music would be piped in for the boys to hear at their base. My mother never made the connection until I asked her many years later, if my younger sister Lynn was named after her? I asked because Mom had told me years earlier that Dad picked out Lynn's name. So, when I asked her, my Mom gave me the funniest look and said with a very serious face and, a bit of a smile, **"I never thought of that;"** *I could tell she hadn't.* I always thought my Mom was jealous of Vera Lynn. Mom never seemed to like her music when Dad played it. When he played it at home, she always made a comment. Maybe it brought her back to a place she would just as soon forget. Vera Lynn passed away during this writing; she died June 18, 2020. She was 103 years old. They named her "The forces Sweetheart. Dame Vera Lynn Rest in Peace. One of your biggest fans is up in heaven with you, say hello to him for me.

F21.1 Vera Lynn then and now. 1917-2020

I have so many questions for my Mom, questions that will never be answered. The number one question I would ask her; ***is the man that went to war, was he the same man that came home?***

I only know my Dad, as my Dad, and that is the way I am sure it is with ninety nine percent of the population. How many children get to read so many letters written by one of their parents long before they were born? Mom would be the only person that could have really answered the question regarding what Dad's personality was like before he went away and was there a change in him when he came home? After all he had been through it would not be surprising.

From reading Dad's letters and being able to feel his emotions through his writings, it makes me believe war did have an effect on him. A man that came home and may have been haunted by his own experiences. There is no judgement, it is just truly heart wrenching to realize this.

My Mom and Dad lived happily married for fifty-six years. All of us kids knew Mom and Dad loved each other, we were very fortunate. However, I never remember them showing much affection around us. They did have a lot in common and enjoyed those things together. Sports was on top of that list especially baseball, but they really liked all sports; in all seasons. ***Much to the girl's chagrin.***

Chapter 22

Magdalene

In the following letter dated August 1, 1943 Dad was telling Mom that his mother did not want them to marry. My Dad's mother, Magdalene, as I mentioned before, ruled the roost! My Mom must have been furious and saddened when she read that. I will give a little history now regarding my Mom and my grandmother's relationship.

One of the stories my Mom told me about my Dad's mother during their dating period was one I will not forget. It explains a lot about my Dad too, and how he chose to get through to his mother.

Dad was away playing ball, I gather now it was the period of time he was in Ocala, Florida playing with the Brewers. That would have meant Dad was away and Mom was home waiting for him. She was surviving the separation with his letters, all the while waiting on his return. At some point, there was a break in the baseball schedule, or the season was over, and Dad was planning his trip home. He of course let Mom know when and what time he would arrive, so she could be there to greet him.

I am thinking it was the April 16, 1942 letter, when she was writing on the back of that envelope about a train schedule. It makes sense because after that letter, the letters stopped until Dad was in the Army.

Of course, Mom wanted to see her man as soon as he pulled in the station. She lived in Oak Park and his family lived on Winnemac Avenue in Chicago. There was definitely a need to take the train, "L" or bus to get where she was going. Well, Mom packed an overnight bag, *yes, she did,* and headed to Winnemac Avenue to be there when Dad arrived home. Here is where it gets crazy, Mom knocked on the door, Magdalene answers, and had this look on her face as if to say, "What are you doing here?" According to my Mom she did not wait for her to ask, she walked in right past Magdalene and said, "Bernie wants me to be here when he gets home." Mom said, she set her overnight bag down and that was that!

Mom was nineteen years old at the time. She told me during this story that she was a "Little Brat" behaving that way to his mother, but she was not going to let my grandmother stop her from seeing her man.

There had been other instances in the past, early on where Magdalene would literally put herself between my Dad and the door of their home. She would throw her hands straight out and tell him "You are not Leaving." Dad was twenty-four years old and there were times when his mother would do this, and he would not go, because he respected her enough not to fight with her. I was told it took my Dad writing his mother a letter about his feelings for Mary Eileen, telling his mother that she was the girl he was going to marry. That must have done the trick, because Dad and his mother never fought about Mom again. It would seem to me that letter writing was Dad's way to get his feelings across, to more than one woman.

I think this is a really good place to say, that my Dad's mother was an amazing grandmother to me, my sister, and, brothers. We spent every Sunday there for dinner and we were spoiled by her, as grandmothers do to their grandchildren. She loved us. We spent many weekends with her and my Aunt Bea going shopping, to the movies, bus rides, food, lots of food. She was a great cook! I loved her and so did my Mom. Mom and "MAW" (Maw was the name for both of our grandmothers) grew to have a great relationship. They respected each other and knew that they both loved Bernie with all their hearts.

My Dad was very close to one of his sisters, Aunt Bea, she was such a lovely person. She never had any children of her own but treated all of us like her own. She was married to Uncle Bill; he was right off the boat from Ireland and he drank like a fish. He was no more than five feet six inches tall and skinny as a rail. I think it was because he would rather drink than eat, not to mention he smoked like most of those boys from Ireland did. He was not a bad looking guy and was really funny and nice when he was sober, but I honestly do not remember much about any real interactions with him. I would watch him mostly from afar, and, wonder what he was talking about. His *brogue** did not help. Half the time I was trying to figure out what he was saying, but as I got older, I knew the liquor was the real problem. My poor Aunt Bea put up with so much from him, until she finally had enough. I think the straw that broke the camel's back was when my aunt found out that the rent was not paid, and that her husband had spent his paycheck at the racetrack instead. That was it for her, Aunt Bea left Uncle Bill and she moved in with my grandmother, which turned out to be so good for everyone. We got to see her a lot more often, and my grandmother was not alone anymore.

Uncle Bill, you will not be surprised to learn, died a pretty ugly death; he was alone, broke, and a drunk. He fell outside, hit a curb in the street, and broke his neck somewhere in the city of Chicago.

Our Aunt Bea lived a few years longer but died suddenly, at age sixty-four, which was so hard on everyone. She went in for a check-up because she was just not feeling right; sadly, it ended up she had something in her x-ray showing a mass on her pituitary gland. The doctors performed and operation, but she did not survive the surgery. We were all so saddened and shocked, she was so young.

Maw was alone again.

Brogue means An Irish Accent when speaking English

Magdalene's House

The drive every Sunday was not a fast one, but we always loved the way my parents would take to get us there. We would take the Eisenhower expressway toward the city and our car would veer off underground to Lower Wacker Drive. Now, you might think being underground would be a little frightening for a child, but those bright green lights that lined the concrete walls were so pretty and not scary at all. When getting in the car to go see Maw, we would always ask if we were going to see the green lights, as we knew there was more than one way to get to our grandmother's house. The other choices were so boring, and it seemed to take much longer. It did not take much to make us happy, plus we knew we were halfway to my grandma's house by the time we reached Lower Wacker Drive and those green lights.

We would arrive on Maw's street in Chicago at 1620 Cullum Street. The streets in Chicago have such a different feel than our neighborhood in the suburbs. The streets seem so narrow, but it soon becomes apparent why, there are cars parked everywhere, on both sides of the street. Wonderful old trees line the streets with row after row of tall apartment buildings all with the same dark brown brick. In the summertime, one could look up and see grey metal window air conditioners bulging out of each floor. It looked to me like they were all in the same window in each apartment. The first entry door was heavy and hard for a small child to open on her own, but Dad was always there to help and guide us inside to the large foyer. I always liked the tile in the foyer, it was small black and white octagon shapes, which was popular during that time and has returned as a tile of choice in many new homes today. There were rows of mailboxes lining the wall with a doorbell and name label of the occupant on each one. My sister and I would run into the foyer up to the line of bells and fight to be the one to ring it first. The deal was that the one who rang the doorbell first would not be the one who got to open the door when our grandmother would magically make the door buzz to release the lock of the second heavy door. The immediate smell of the hallway once that second door opened was familiar and comforting. It was not a distinguishing odor, more like a combination of spices or cleaning products, as the hallways were always clean. I have no idea who resided behind the other doors. As often as we were there, we rarely saw anyone else in the hallways. I always imagined who those people were and what they were cooking in their kitchens. I knew that cooking is what my grandmother was doing in her home, behind her door.

We had a three flight climb up and with each step there was a squeak of the wood that would give way just a bit. Along with the smells, it was a familiar sound that I can still conjure up in my mind. The welcoming party on the third floor knew exactly how far we were by the sounds coming up the stairs, including our laughter. Our young, little legs moved quickly getting us to where we were anxious to be; excitedly, leaving our parents at least a flight behind us, which was great because we liked to get the first hugs and kisses from Maw. I am sure our two older brothers beat us up there, as the boys always were way out in front of the girls, in more ways than one. Once at the top, there was a wide opened door and even wider open arms. Our grandmother was always so happy to see us. We knew it and we felt it. I knew in my heart that she was anticipating our arrival. I imagine her peering out her window watching for us to pull up, park the car, and enter her building, long before we hit the buzzer. We were greeted with happy hello's, hugs and the smells of her cooking. Once inside it was the familiarity of a place of love and safety. We were well cared for and nurtured there. Her dinners were wonderful, she knew each of us and our favorites. Mine was her hot rolls and soft butter for spreading, and there were always plenty for everyone. It was her gift to her family; it was her way of loving us.

Dad also mentions my Mom's mother in his letter. She was such a sweetheart and easy as can be. There was a very stark difference in appearance between the two women. My Mom's mother was a liberal minded woman, especially for the times. I can just see her being very supportive of both of them and their future plans, by the sound of the letters she already thought of Dad as a member of the family and the feeling was mutual. That is just the way she was. But she would want Dad to go about it in the right way and ask her permission for her daughter's hand in marriage.

Chapter 23

"The Irish Bunch"

Long before the breakup of my aunt and uncle, my parents would be at my grandmother's house every weekend. The "Irish Bunch" was the name Mom and Dad would always use to refer to those that gathered at my grandmother's house. Many of the men were relatives and they were straight off the boat from Ireland. And when I say men, some of them were very young, in their twenties, but they were men to me since I was pretty young at the time. They all were big poker players and my Mom and Dad loved playing cards. I swear we missed some meals during the week due to losses from those poker games. Dad did not have a poker face at all! Mom would win, and Dad would lose what she won, so it never seemed they came out ahead. Those card games would go on all night long. I remember Mom telling me there was a church by Midway Airport; it is still there, St. Camillus on Lockwood Ave in Chicago. At that time, they had a 4:00 a.m. mass. I checked their web site and their earliest mass now is 7:00 a.m. They must not have the early birds like they did back in the day. Some of the card players and my parents of course, as they would never miss mass, would attend that service. I am sure there were some prayers about a big win during the service. After mass they would head right back to my grandmothers to finish the game. When they got back to Maw's, the food would come out for their second round of cards and sustenance. I do not know who stayed with us when some of them left for mass, all I know, we were cozy and safe and fast asleep in my grandmother's bed. Some of the guys stayed behind and continued to play and drink their beer. My Dad, he was a total teetotaler, so that was never an issue in our home. But as kids we sure got to see some crazy yelling from the "Irish Bunch" that we were not used to in our home.

This one particular night many years into the weekly card games, a ritual my parents loved and enjoyed for years, was about to change.

The End of the Games

This one night at my grandmothers was different. According to my Mom who told this story many times. There was too much alcohol, along with the Irish temper of some of the boys. The dealer of the cards was my Uncle Bill, he was going around the table turning the first two cards down, then the next card up on everyone's hand announcing each card as he would flip it over. Queen of Spades, ten of hearts, on and on until he got to Danny, as he turned over a two of spades my uncle said, and I quote "and shit for you." Well, Danny came flying across the table at my uncle Bill and a huge fist fight broke out. I don't think either one of them had the wherewithal to aim, let alone hit the other, but it was quite a scene. These two grown men rolling around on the dining room floor was not a pretty sight.

Fortunately, my grandmother put a stop to that kind of behavior immediately, and that was all there was to it. You did not go against Maw!

Mom talked about that night so often because it was the end of the weekend card games, which was a very sad outcome.

I know they loved the game, but they loved the people more! Everyone there was special in their own way. Some of them were god parents to us, some of them were cousins. I remember John and Molly; they were a cute older couple. Molly was short, a little plump with a round face and pretty blue eyes. I don't know what it was about the Irish Brogue, but it pulls you in, partly because you want to listen closely to understand what is being said and the other reason is, to me it was like music. Molly's husband John was a big guy with a half bald head, he always wore a suit, even when playing cards. One of the stories about Molly was when Mom was pregnant with my younger brother, Bill. Mom was thirty-seven years old and must have looked like she was putting on a little weight, but nothing very obvious. Molly went up to my Mom, patted her tummy, and asked her in that wonderful accent, "Do you have a *"gasùr"* * in there"? Mom immediately said and firmly "NO"! The way Mom tells it, she felt like she may had been going through her change of life, being pregnant at thirty-seven was not on her radar at all. Well, Mom confirmed soon after that she was indeed having a baby. Mom always said that it was Molly's fault and appointed them godparents to my younger brother Bill.

Gasùr: Gaelic for small boy, child

Most of the men at the poker table were right off the boat or at least they sounded like it, and some of the younger men were very handsome. I had a couple childhood crushes in those days. Tess and Danny were another wonderful couple. Danny was a really tall burly guy, with a big round red face and a red nose. You could see all these little veins running through his nose and face. It was like a very complicated road map. I think that was from the amount of beer he drank. Tess, his wife, was gorgeous. She looked like a movie star, to me she looked like Sophia Loren and just as pretty. They had a big party every New Year's Eve with all the cast of characters. The entertainment for the evening was of course the card games. Tess was also a great cook and would always have a big turkey in the oven with all the fixings. I do remember that dinner was always served very late at their house. By the time we sat down to eat I was starving. Their home had many great old nooks and crannies and all of us including some of our cousins would play hide and seek for hours.

Danny used to pick me up when I was little and start singing an Irish song to me, ***"I'll Take You Home Again Kathleen"*** with his beautiful Irish voice, but the beauty of his voice did not take away from the fact I was scared to death that he was taking me home. I would cry until he would put me down or I could wrestle myself away and run into the safety of my Mom's arms. I knew Mom was close by when Danny started to sing because he did have a very lovely voice that everyone loved to listen to. He continued that ritual with me until I was too big to pick up. I still liked him though, just not up close where he could take me away!

When we were really young, and told to go to bed, my sister and I used to go around the card table and say goodnight to everyone, and the poker players coming out a little ahead, would always slip us some of their winnings. As we got older, Mom made us say goodnight away from the table. There went our penny candy money! I have to say I did not miss those early morning car rides home in the winter, with no heat in the car. We would finally be asleep, just in time to be awakened by my Mom's voice, "come on kids we're home" The only saving grace was my Mom was smart, she packed our pajamas, so we were already dressed for bed. That I did not miss one little bit, but I know my parents sure did.

Chapter 24

Sad News Back Home

My Dad had just received the following letter with bad news from back home. His favorite Uncle Matt was very ill. Everything I had been told about Matt was, he was a wonderful man and my Dad thought of him like a bother. He says in his letter that he is hoping beyond hope that he will be granted an emergency furlough to come home. Dad does not seem very confident that it will happen because Matt is not immediate family.

The rest of the letter seems like there is a feeling of discontent with the men. Dad mentions they do the same old thing every day and time is standing still. Dad states **"if every moan was a dollar, we'd be rich."** The war is heating up and they may be waiting on orders to go overseas. It is also mentioned that the men want to leave for "over there" it doesn't seem from Dad's words that he is in any hurry to go overseas. He mentions how fortunate he is to be an American and to be born in the USA.

I cannot imagine this. They had no idea what they were about to face and reading these words about leaving the U.S.A. to fight this terrible war. As I was reading the letter, I considered how my Dad had no idea that while he was loving this woman, planning a future and wanting a family; sadly, he was blind to the reality of what was ahead of him and how it would put all those plans at risk. Mom was back home, reading the newspaper, listening to the news of the war on the radio, reading Dad's letters, and she too all the while was hopeful for their future.

The restless men want to get moving, but we now know what they were about to face.

It's a terrifying thought isn't it?

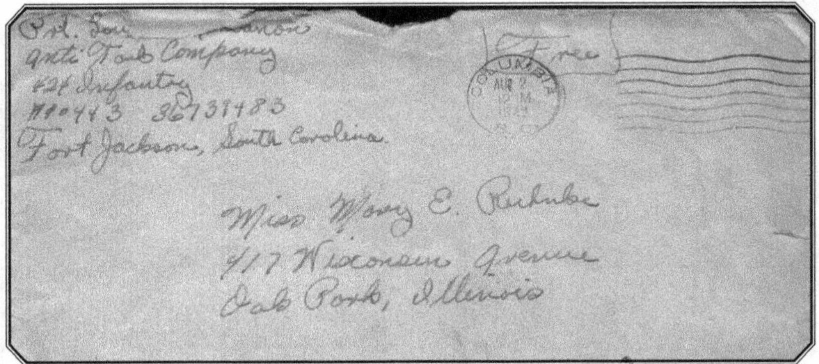

F24.1 August 1, 1943

August 1, 1943

Darling,

Have a few minutes this morning before I go to Mass so will spend them with you. There has been nothing much going on here lately & it seems that we are just getting along as best we can. We go through the same old routine every day & time seems to stand still. However if you'll just keep on writing such swell letters I believe I'll pull through without going completely screwy. Boy, you've never seen such a bunch of disgusted guys in your life. If every moan was a dollar we'd all be rich. A whole lot of them would prefer to go across right now but they'd change their minds in a hurry. We are really fortunate to be able to live in the U.S.A.

Darling, I'm missing you more each day & can't hardly wait for something to happen over there.

Well, Mary it's happened at home hasn't it? Just recieved a telegram from Mom & before I read it, I knew what it was. I'm waiting around now for some word of approval on an emergency furlough. Generally they won't

allow us to go home unless its in the immediate
family. Hoping for the best. Poor Matt. I
Can't explain how this makes me feel. He's been
just like a brother & if he goes its going to
be pretty hard on all of us.

Well hon, I'll close now & may see you soon.
If I'm not allowed to come, I'll call you tonight.
Still love you so much that being away from
you hurts down deep if you know what
I mean. Bye for now & best regards to all

Love
Bernie.

Chapter 25

Mush

Dad was feeling the effects of news back home. He had received nothing but bad news coming from his mother's letters. So, he seemed so grateful for my Mom's letters and her good news, and her sweet "mushiness."

The good news of Mom's cousin Sue getting married had struck a chord. I imagine this was the reason he was telling Mom she will be "The Next Bride." Mom was standing up in her wedding and most likely imagining herself on her own wedding day. How could she not? I can really hear in his letter that he really wished it could be their wedding. He was letting her know that he would understand if she did not wait for him, but he sure hoped that she did.

He wanted her to know he trusted her. I think my Mom was putting the pressure on, and Dad was afraid she would give up on him. But all I am feeling reading the following letters; Dad's insecurities. He knew Mom was back at home alone and lonely. Dad was worried. Mom was always a very active engaged woman, and for her to sit at home and wait was something he was concerned about. Dad had fears writing, *most girls wouldn't.* One of the best lines in this letter for me, **"Darling, you know I left my heart in the train depot last Tuesday, don't you?"**

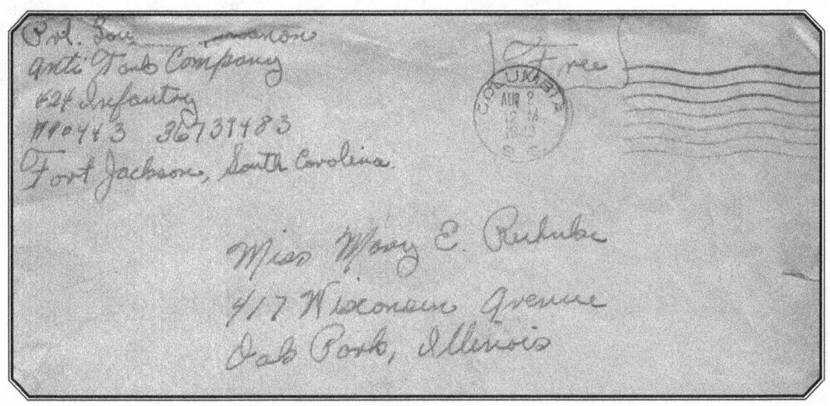

F25.1 August 15, 1943

Sunday. Aug. 15, 1943

Darling:

Just came back from Columbia & wish I hadn't gone. There is nothing there but soldiers & we see enough of them here. We went to a show & saw, "Cabin in the Sky. Was a good show even though it had an all colored cast. Mary, our Baseball Club is being re-organized again & will probably start playing this week. After the season is over which won't be long now, will probably disband for the duration. The Army hasn't changed much. They are going to able to go on. Sure feel sorry for those Rifle Cos. They do nothing but walk & in this heat its murder. So now you see, this isnt such a bad organization. We walk quite a bit but we also ride once in a while.

Darling, you know I left my heart in the train Depot last Tuesday, dont you? You sure looked swell & when your all dressed up like that, I'm lost. You called me bashful & maybe your right. Wanted to give you a much better good-bye but Sunday night was pretty good. It really was one of the happiest nights we've ever had together. Now, I'll close for now thanking you for all the swell letters you've sent & hoping you'll never stop sending them. Give my love to your folks & the best of luck to Fran & Sue. By now it is all over & I sincerely hope they have the best. Can't help but envy them myself because they have done what I hope to do some day.

Love
Bernie

Mary, you've heard this before, but here it is again. As things have turned out

I'm pretty sure your as dissapointed as I am. Know also that asking you to wait for me is asking a lot & some girls wouldn't do it. It's no fun to sit at home day after day waiting & if you do get disgusted I won't blame you. Promise me this, please? If that day comes I'll understand anything you may do only let me know about it beforehand. You are smiling as you read this I suppose but this is how I feel. Understand this, hon, I'm not questioning your honesty be-

Cause I know your on
the square but I don't
want you to feel that I
have a rope tied to you.
I'd like to do just that
but in these days men
don't do that. I'm really
serious about this & hope
you'll recieve it the same
way. Bye now & don't
forget to give some
reply to this sermon.

Again - I love You

Bcon.

F25.2 August 20, 1943

Aug. 20, 1943

Darling:
Your letters have been coming through on schedule, thank heaven. Seems that yours are the only ones to contain any good news. Of course, the "mush," is always welcome. So many things have been happening at home, I'm afraid to open Mom's letters anymore. Every time I do some new tragedy has occurred. I'm sure glad that you at least are feeling O.K. Mary, if something should happen to you, then I would give up. This

life is tough enough without all those troubles at
home. If I could just be
there I could help some I know.
Well, hon, to get on the
brighter side I'm very
glad to hear that you are to
be the next bride. Maybe
that is a good sign, who
knows. The war can't last
forever you know & if it
ended tomorrow you would
be walking up the aisle with
me in no time, or would you?
At last the weather is
cooling off. Last night we
had a problem & nearly
froze. Had to wear our
raincoats to keep warm.
It's a relief though because
that heat was almost too
much. We have been

pretty busy lately &
I'm getting stiffer & sorer
every day. Have to run
the Obstacle Course quite
a bit now & that's quite
a job if you know what I mean
Boy, do I feel my age these
days. Ahem.

Darling, I still miss you
as much as ever & yes, I
do love you. Funny, isn't it?
Don't forget to send me those
pictures, Kid. I'm sure
you looked beautiful.
I'm also very glad that the
wedding came off so well.
Sue & Fran must be very
happy & give them my best.

Hon, I'll close for now

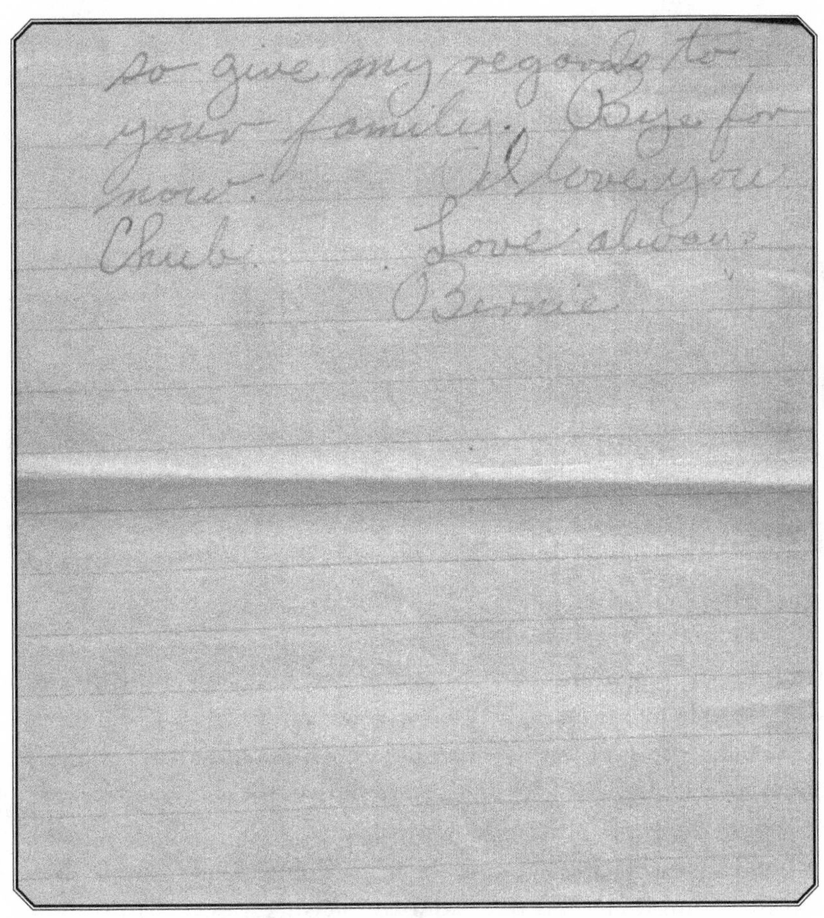

so give my regards to
your family. Bye for
now. I love you
Chub. Love always
Bernie

Chapter 26

Obstacle Course

F26.1 August 25, 1943

Dad was talking about the obstacle course and how hard they are working. He mentions how fit he was, he was down to 170 pounds.

A lot going on in this letter, baseball possibly starting again, Mom wanting to visit him and Dad telling her it is not a great place for her to be. Especially, in an Army Camp.

He's not getting great news from home, Dad's cousin Matt was not doing well, and has had a couple surgeries. It had to be so hard, being so far away and not having a choice to come home to be with the ones you love, especially during difficult times. This was his mother's brother, but he was more than that to Dad. He was feeling so helpless being so far away, but according to the Army, Matt was not his immediate family, so his requests to go home were denied.

August 25, 1943

Darling,

I realize this letter is behind schedule but as usual we are busy. We've been working day & night lately & time to ourselves is something of the past. Mary, my figure is still improving & I'm down to a mere [illegible] lbs. We've been running the obstacle course every morning & it's either going to kill or cure us. By the way they call it, "Tarzan Field," where Jap Killers are made. I've they corny. We play our first game Friday at last. For a while I thought they weren't going to continue.

So you think you've got something, do you? Hon, the feeling is mutual & I hope we always feel the same. I miss you more each day & only wish it were possible for you to come down here. Honestly though I don't believe you'd ever find a place to stay & I don't want you wandering around alone ~~[illegible]~~ in this place. Southern towns aren't too presentable anywhere especially when they are situated near an

Army Camp. If we can just be patient I know some day we'll have all the happiness we can take care of.

Sure hope your family is fine. News from home continues glum but it can't go on forever. Mom told me that Matt has had another operation & so far they don't know how successful it was. Guess its just one of those things that can't be helped.

Darlin, its bed time now so I'll have to close. Tomorrow we arise at 4:45 A.M. & go out to the range. We have some sort of work there for the next ten days so you see we do need our sleep. Bye for now & remember I love you

Bernie

Tell your mom, I'll write her soon.

Sorry about the pencil but some guy borrowed this pen & just returned it.

Chapter 27

"Fight First, then Marry"

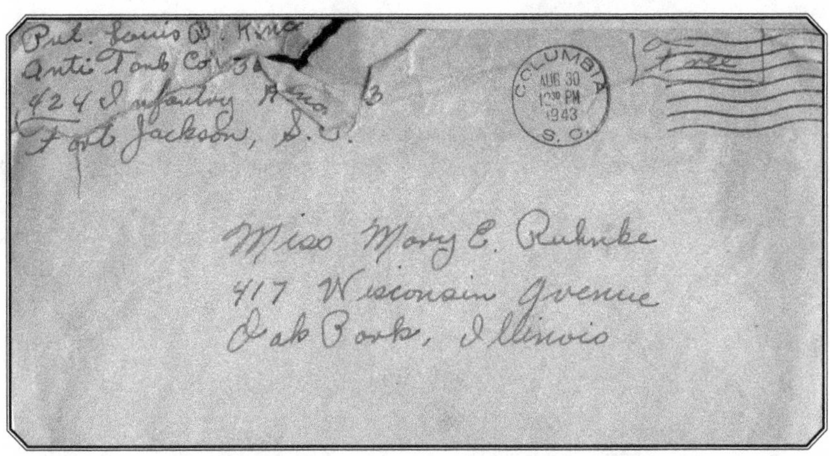

F27.1 August 29, 1943

August 29, 1943

Darling;

Haven't much to say today. Wanted to write you again because I have been neglectful lately, not that I wanted to you understand. If you can figure out that last sentence you're pretty good. Mary, here is another Sunday & nothing to do. I'm quite sure that if I were home with you now things would be much different. We always did have good times together & we always will. Before I forget I want to tell you that your answer to that,

"Sermon", was swell. Hon, if you feel the way you write I'm quite sure I've found the only girl in the world. Its going to be hard on both of us to wait but sincerely I do believe we should. Read an article in the Sunday Visitor this morning entitled, "Fight first then marry". It read very sensible & has convinced me that we would be wiser to wait. Please don't think though that this alone has decided me. I've always been against it but loving you as I do almost changed my mind. If ever you do change toward me don't forget that very serious letter, "Chub".

We played our first

game the other night and
tied 4-4. Relieved in the
fifth & pitched till the finish
of 8 inning when darkness
fell. Gave up two hits
& no runs so wasn't so bad
for an old man, was it?
My arm was creaking
& groaning on every pitch.
Lack of throwing will affect
ones arm like that you know.
Mary, I feel so darn silly
today. Ah, young love. Well
you're young anyway.

Bill seems to be a
jitterbug, doesn't he? Guess
I'll have to wise him up
next time I'm home. Is
he all set for Basketball

this winter? Bet he can't wait. Sure am glad your family takes to athletics. To me it's everything outside of you.

Suppose I'd better close now before you tired reading this. Love you & miss you more each day. Best regards to the family & tell your Mother I won't forget that letter.

Love
Bernie

In that previous letter Dad was telling Mom he read an article in the *Sunday Visitor* about marring during wartime as an enlisted soldier. The article said to **"Fight First, Marry Later."** I cannot image how Mom was feeling receiving these letters from so far away and reading these words. Poor Mom, I felt for her so much. Dad was the one away from home, but my heart goes out to my Mom.

This letter drove me a little crazy as Dad jumped from that article to baseball! Really? That's a man for you, at least the men in my family. *"Sports! Ugh!"* The one thing about the written word, when that is all you have, you keep rereading it and keep torturing yourself. I can just picture Mom doing that, because I know I would.

Dad must have been busy, or he may have had a furlough, I am not really sure. I don't have any letters between August 25, 1943 and September 17, 1943. That is an unusual amount of time between letters for him. Maybe more of his time was taken up with baseball and army life.

Chapter 28

The Runaround

Okay, the question is answered as to the time between the letters. Dad was in the Army Hospital. Dad mentions in the following letter to Mom, **"By now I suppose you know where I am?"** He was in the Army hospital for a hernia, which turns out that was not the reason they ended up operating on him.

Oh, my goodness, these letters to follow are heart breaking. Dad is talking about the war and some of the other men overseas. How very hard war was on everyone, it was keeping families from each other, and in some cases permanently!

Right now, present day, after becoming so familiar with how the war had challenged my Mom and Dad so many years ago, I still cannot image how the men and women who serve our country leave their families behind not knowing if they will ever return home. The ones left behind, must spend every waking hour wondering if they will ever see their loved ones again. As we get further into this love story during war time there is a period of time where my Mom and Dad will go through this very same frightening experience. There will be space, time, and, great distance between letters and no word of where my Dad was, how did they do it? How did his mother do it, let alone my Mom? It almost answers the looming question my siblings and I have always had as to why Dad and Mom never really talked to us about those days. The stories regarding the wartime for them are few and far between. We would get little snippets of something here and there, but never a conversation on what they really went through emotionally or physically for that matter. I am in Awe!

The next few letters that follow find Dad in the Army hospital. Too much time to think, as he writes about the men that were already overseas and how they were taking the brunt of the war on the ground right now. It's 1943 and in his letter, he wrote **"the war news was sounding better, hoping for an early victory!" "Invasion is always costly."**

Two letters had arrived, and he was thrilled. According to his letter to Mom she had told him that she couldn't live without him. He told her being apart so long will make them appreciate being together more than ever. Telling her he knows they were having a hard time of it right now, but they were not alone. That was my Dad. He was the most unselfish, empathetic man and he was not one to think only of himself. He thought of other's feelings, and right then during the middle of war he was thinking of the other men and women that were suffering more than he was, lying there in the hospital bed.

The Army Doctors were not in agreement regarding Dad's treatment. He was admitted, then discharged after two other doctors okayed the operation, but the one that counted said "no."

Right after his release from the hospital, Dad did find out good new about Matt back home. He said, "his getting well makes the world all OK again."

The runaround, where my Dad's health is concerned has happened. He is headed back to the Army hospital. This time it is for an operation, the one he most likely needed when he was released and sent back to base.

From Ward 31 Station Hospital Dad wrote, **"Darling, well here is your perfect specimen again."** Dad's surgery was not what he was expecting. He thought he was going in for a hernia operation and found out he had hemorrhoids. His words in this letter made me smile, only because he sounds a little loopy, like there was some pretty good painkillers involved. His timing could not have been better however, it was baseball season and the World Series was on. If I didn't know better, I would say he had planned it! After all, baseball was one of his priorities in life along with getting home to Mary!

F28.1 September 17, 1943

September 17, 1943

Darling;

By now I suppose you know where I am & why. This sure is a soft life. Came in Wednesday & haven't done a thing. They've given me a blood test & blood count & now I'll just wait for developments.

Since Tuesday my mail hasn't been delivered so one of these days I'll be pretty busy reading your letters.

Somehow, there isn't much to write about today but there is always the weather. It is raining. Well, that takes care of that. War news seems to be much better today. If things keep going like they are we may see an early victory. Finally getting down to the real thing. Do you know wars must be won on the ground. Those poor guys over there now are really taking the brunt of it all. Invasion is always costly but as they say, "that is war".

Hon, just now I recieved two letters from you dated the 13th & 14th. You do say the nicest things. Do you really believe that you couldn't live without me? I'm sure you could, but I hope you'll never have to. It would be equally hard for me you know. Yes, someday we will make up all these lonely days.

Maybe being apart so long
will make us appreciate
being together more than ever.
We are having quite a hard
time of it but we're not
alone. When we finally do
marry, I hope I am able
to make you happier than
you've ever been before.
Whatever happens we must
make a success of our marriage
and we will. Two people
with common sense should
be able to get along together.
Agree?

Well, I'm about to
eat lunch now so will
bid you a fond good bye
for a few days.

Still am very much in
love & miss you always.
Love
Bern.

Best regards to your family
Will write your Mother soon

Pvt. Louis B. Kincanon
Anti Tank Co. 36739483
424 Infantry APO 443
Fort Jackson, S.C.

Free

COLUMBIA
SEP 22
12 M
1943
S.C.

Miss Mary E. Ruhnke
417 Wisconsin Avenue
Oak Park, Illinois

F28.2 September 21, 1943

Sept 21, 1943

Darling:

Guess what has happened now? I have been sent back to duty & I'm getting the old runaround again. They decided I wasn't a serious enough case so they will not operate until I become so bad that it must be done. Hon, this Army has me stumped. Two different Dr's OK'd the operation but the one that counted said no. Mary, every day my debt to & love for you grows greater. Just now your package arrived along with the card & telegram. Don't

know what to say. Know
all this was for a sick guy
& now being back on Duty
I feel funny. When I read
your "Get Well" Card & Telegram
I really laughed because I don't
believe I've ever felt better
in my life. Hon, don't ever
believe that my love for you comes
from all these swell things you
do for me. They all help but
I'd love you if you never
sent me a thing and do wish
you wouldn't be so generous.
Here I am unable to buy
anything for you but some
day I do hope to atone for
everything. Glad that you
visited Matt the other day.
Had a taste of his life, &
its pretty lonesome. He likes
you already & those visits

will make you good friends. I've found out that he can be a very special friend & his getting well makes the World all O.K. again.

Hon, was sorry to hear about your Grandmother. Seems like there has to be trouble always. If it's not one thing it's another. I hope she'll be allright soon & if you will give her my regards.

Darling, don't like to stop writing but as usual, time is limited. Want to thank you again for all you've done. Darn it, words won't and can't express how I feel. Do you

know what I mean? I'm
sure you do so "Wait for
me Mary." It won't be too
long & think of all the swell
years we'll have just looking
back on these lonely days.
Loving you always, I remain
as ever

Your Sweetheart
Bern.

Boy, isn't that a fancy
ending? See what the
hospital did for me? It's
amazing. Do you think I
Could get a "Section 8."
Meaning – Nuts.

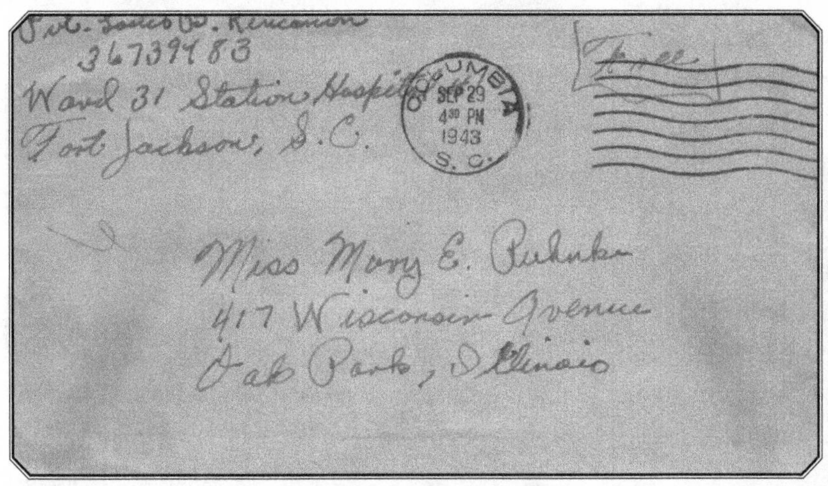

F28.3 September 29, 1943

September 29, 1943

Darling:

Recieved your very swell letter the other day. You'll never know how much a few words from you mean such as, "I love you." Knowing that you really care for me makes these months a little easier to stand. I should say a big little.

Now, it's happened. They've sent me back to the hospital & this time the operation probably will be done. Don't know when or where but I'll let you know when they inform me of the same.

So the Bus threw you
for a loss. Mary, I don't know
what to do about you. I
think you had better marry
me as soon as this war ends.
Remember how I used to
laugh at you on those icy
sidewalks. But you could
have socked me one for that.
Don't let a little thing like
that bother you. I've taken
quite a number of spills
myself without the aid of a
Bus driver.
I'm at a loss for words ex
cept to say that I love you &
miss you very much. This seems
a very short letter in exchange
for your nice long one but
its the best I can do. I'll
write again in a day or so.
By now & Love always
Bern

Give my best regards
& love to your family
& thank your Grandmother for
remembering me.
Suppose Bill is having
quite a time with his "gal".
He sure is way ahead of me.
When I was 16 I didn't
know what a girl was &
didn't care. Give him credit
for being much braver than
me. Bye.

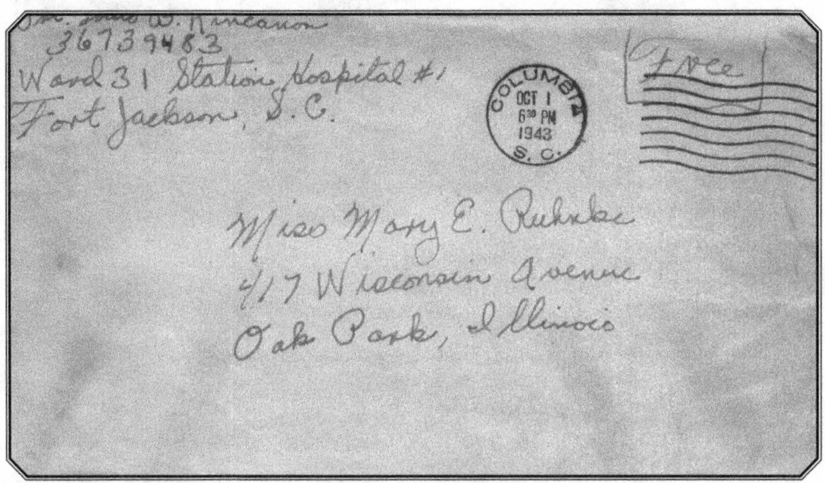

F28.4 October 1, 1943 Ward 31 Station Hospital

October 1, 1943

Darling,

Well, here's your Physical Specimen again. Just think, at one time I was 1A in the Army. Mary, wait till you hear this. I have been through my operation but it wasn't for a Hernia. This time it was Hemmoroids. Do you know what they are. They are pretty painfull & also very embarrassing. They brought me over here Tuesday as you know & yesterday at

9:00 A.M. they gave me
a Spinal & now I'm
Confined to bed for a few
days. The operation itself
was nothing but a
Certain region is a bit
sore at the moment. I
have my compensations,
though. I can write you
more often & I will be able
to hear the World Series.
Pretty slick, aren't I?

Darling will you ex-
cuse this short letter for
now? I'm not at my
best, but the next letter will
be longer, I promise you.
Love you & miss you?
For ever & ever. Bye now

Love always
Bern.

Now don't laugh at me
soon hun

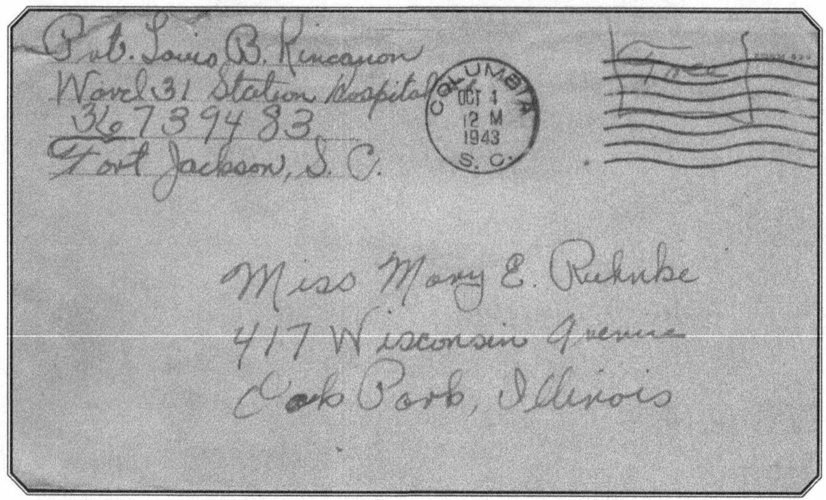

F28.5 October 2, 1943
Letter from the American Red Cross While Dad was recuperating

This letter is from the American Red Cross while Dad was recuberating. Dad had time on his hands and mentioned that he had met some nice men in the hospital. He seemed happy to have them to talk to.

It is World Series time and Dad's team The St. Louis Cardinal's were palying the New York Yankee's. Dad was always a Cardinal Fan even though Mom had tried to get him over to her side with the

Cub's. That made for fun times over the years! Those two teams really were and still are rivals. All three of my brothers ended up as Cardinal Fans too, so poor Mom got so much grief over the years. Well, the Cardinal's did Win and the Cub's kept loosing, but Mom was not a fair-weather fan. She waited her entire life for a World Series Win, but that was not to be!

I am sure that with all the time on his hands he had lots of time to think. This letter mentions more good news regarding the war, but he also is thinking about all the soldiers that are in the thick of it at the time. I can say this because of this quote from his letter, **"I sometimes wonder if people back home appreciate all the things those boys over there are doing. They deserve the best of everything when they come home, and I certainly hope they get it."**

Oct 2, 1943

Darling.
Just had to write you
to keep from going crazy.
That is not the only reason of
course because I really do enjoy
it. Things are very peacefull
& uneventfull here. Believe it
or not but it is now October
the 3rd. Started this letter
with good intentions but one
of the other patients came over
& started a lengthy conversation.
Have made quite a few friends
here & we have a pretty
good time when we are all
feeling good. This operation
is rather painful but in

a week I hope to be my old self again. They claim we'll be here for a month so I'll be writing you pretty often. You may also expect a call sometime soon. I'll let you know before I do though.

Hon, I sure wish that you could be here with me now. Miss you so much but then I shouldn't kick, should I? Mary, I sometimes wonder if the people back home appreciate all the things those boys over there are doing. They deserve the best of everything when they come home & I certainly hope they get it. By the way, the war news looks good, doesn't it?

Are you all enthused
about the World Series next
week? That's something I'm
really waiting for. I'll be able
to hear every game this year.
Want to bet on the outcome? -
Still picking the "Cards" so
you'll have to take the "Yanks".
Well, "Kid", I'm lost
again as usual. I bet your
Mother is still waiting for
her letter. She'll get it real
soon now for I have nothing
else but time. Say, how is
your Grandmother Riehnke?
Haven't heard from you since
last Monday so I don't
know anything. My mail
has been delayed again

but expect all of it tomorrow. Please tell me how all of you are & I hope the news is all good. As you know my side of the house is improving so maybe that's a good sign.

This time for sure is the end. Be a good girl & remember the war can't last forever. All my love always

Bernie

Please excuse this writing. A bed isn't too good a desk.

Chapter 29

The Masterpiece

I have probably re-read this letter a thousand times and each time I did, I found myself wishing, more than anything that I had the letter Mom wrote to Dad to invoke such emotion. When Dad said, **"Hon, that letter, you know which one, was a masterpiece."** He goes on to say he had never read anything that stirred him so much. He expressed such love and gratitude to Mom after reading that letter, **"Your every word was just what I wanted to hear and today my love has grown till it's ready to burst."** My Mom always did know just the right thing to say in any situation.

Dad had two sister's and in all the letters I have read up to now, this is the very first time he mentions them. He told Mom in his letter that he made a call home. Unfortunately, his mom was at the store and he told "the girls" he would call again soon. I can only imagine how really disappointed his mom was to come home to find out she missed a call from her son. I did wonder why he never mentioned his sisters, Bea and Edith. Maybe those "hello's," were reserved for his mom's letters. Who knows, my Dad was such a great brother, he may have been writing them individually.

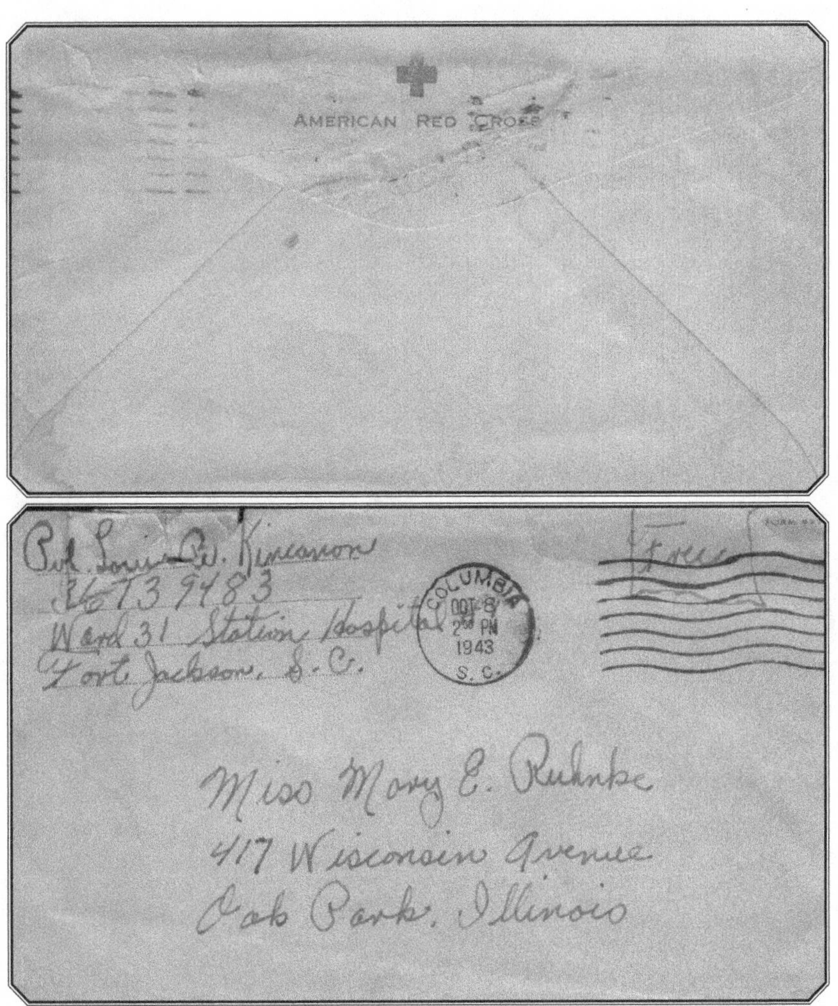

F29.1 October 7, 1943 Still in the Army Hospital

October 7, 1943

Darling:

Have just recived all the mail that has been held back untill now. Hon, that letter, you know which one, was a masterpiece. Never have I read anything that stirred me so much. How did I ever happen to meet such a girl as you? You do have more common sense & understanding than any one I've ever met. You'll never know the feeling of love & gratitude that came over me after ~~I~~ reading that letter. Mary, you know I've never doubted you &

now I never will. My letter to you was very frank & I was hoping that it wouldn't offend you, but I did want you to know how I felt. Just call it a crazy mood that prompted me to write as I did. Girl, have you made me happy. Your every word was just what I wanted to hear & today my love for you has grown till it's ready to burst. By the way in making your choice if I can help it you'll never be sorry. I'll try to be everything you want & expect in a husband. About that "Womens Secrets," business you need not worry. That was just an old saying. There was no reflection on you so

don't worry about it.
Mom, I suppose you & Mom had quite a time laughing over me. Can't say that I blame you because it is kind of funny even to all of us. I'm getting along much better now & in a few weeks I'll be back in harness. Called home today but didn't get to talk to Mom. Unluckily she had just left for the store but I told the girls I'd call her again soon. Friday night I'll try & get through to you so wait for me, don't be disappointed if I fail because sometimes it's

impossible, as you know.
Darling, I'll Close
now but you'll be hearing
often from me. Give my
regards to your family &

All My Love
Bevn.

Will be glad to meet
Lt. Bob also. He must
like you very much,
isn't that strange?

Chapter 30

"Dear Ma"

This is a treat and something different. I was so anxious to read this myself! It is a letter from Dad to my mother's mother, Maw, who Dad fondly called "Ma."

F30.1 October 9, 1943

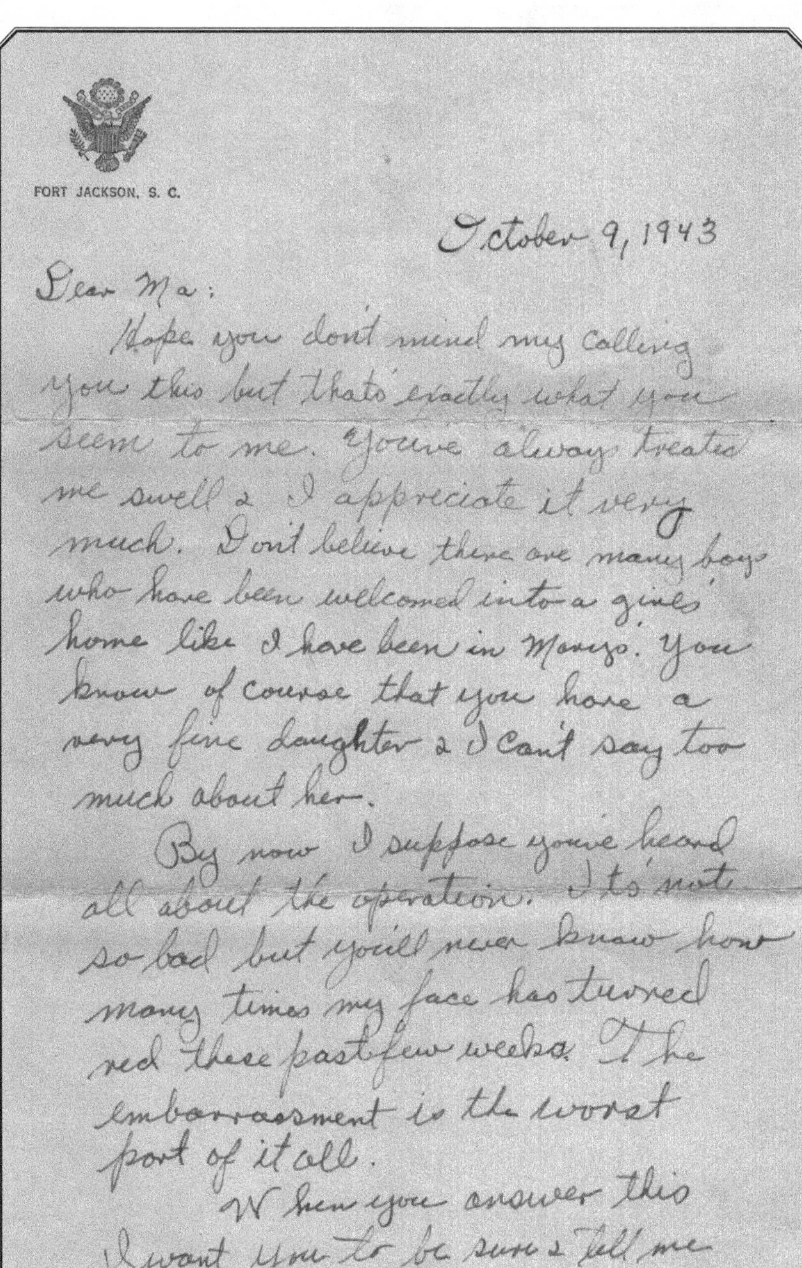

FORT JACKSON, S. C.

October 9, 1943

Dear Ma:

Hope you don't mind my calling you this but that's exactly what you seem to me. You've always treated me swell & I appreciate it very much. Don't believe there are many boys who have been welcomed into a girl's home like I have been in Moreys. You know of course that you have a very fine daughter & I can't say too much about her.

By now I suppose you've heard all about the operation. It's not so bad but you'll never know how many times my face has turned red these past few weeks. The embarrassment is the worst part of it all.

When you answer this I want you to be sure & tell me

what youve been doing & how you are feeling these days. Has your Mother gotten rid of that California love, yet? I have never been to California but so far I've never seen a better place than Chicago or Oak Park. You tell her she'd better stay in the good old Windy City.

I've told you before that I'm not much of a letter writer & this letter proves it. Wish that I could write a long & interesting letter but its not a gift with me. Moxy is about as good at that as anyone I've met. She always manages to tell me all the news at home & then she adds a little "mush." What a gal.

Ma, tell Bill I hope he has a swell season of Basketball & wish that I could see some of his games. Before it was work & now war that has kept me from seeing him play. One of these days I hope to be a free man. Bill is my idea of a good American

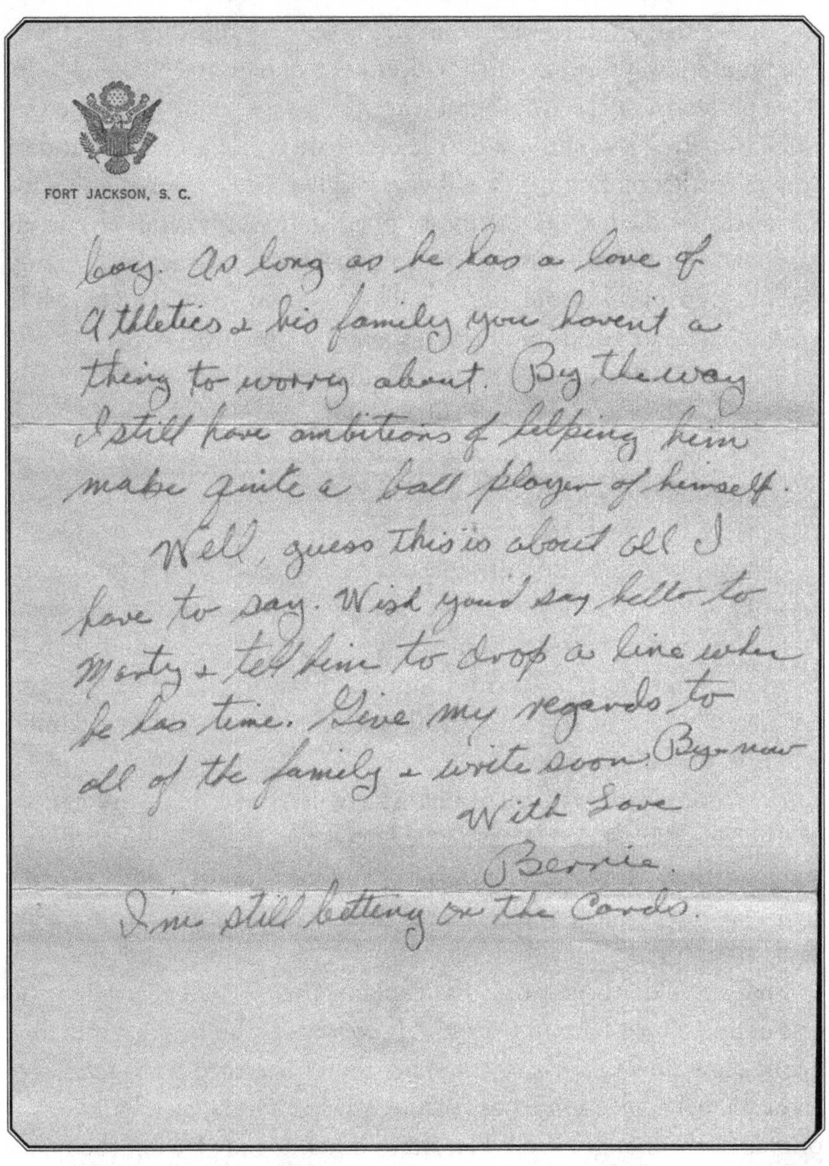
FORT JACKSON, S. C.

boy. As long as he has a love of Athletics & his family you haven't a thing to worry about. By the way I still have ambitions of helping him make quite a ball player of himself.

Well, guess this is about all I have to say. Wish you'd say hello to Marty & tell him to drop a line when he has time. Give my regards to all of the family & write soon. Bye now

With Love

Bernie.

I'm still betting on the Cards.

What a sweet, sweet letter. Yes, that was my grandmother. I loved her so much. She was not even five feet tall and had a heart of gold. Maw had a striking head of silver hair that was never out of place. One of the things that I remember about her is she was "well put together." She would always be very nicely dressed; her hair and makeup were done perfectly, or she would not leave the house. Even when she was in her nineties, I would put a little eye shadow on her eyelids and of course lipstick on her lips. We always laughed when applying the lipstick because she had the thinnest upper lip that it was not always an easy task, but I loved making her up! Maw would always say, "A lady does not go out without her lipstick." We had many laughs while doing that beauty routine. I loved spending time with her.

Maw was widowed at such a young age and as you can already tell by these letters from my Dad, she did a wonderful job of raising her two children Mary Eileen and Bill alone. Maw was way ahead of her time! She was very liberal minded and accepted everything about everybody and their decisions were their own.

Mom and her mother were very close, and their relationship was one I admired. My Dad felt like a member of the family right from the start. Their relationship was very respectful and loving. Every summer, for at least three months, Maw would come up from her home in Florida to stay with all of us. She was always a welcomed addition to our family.

In the letter, Dad mentions Marty, he was a man my grandmother was dating and later married a few years after Mom and Dad were married. Maw would not marry anyone until her kids were settled and married themselves. That was my grandmother, her kids came first. She once told me that "no one was going to tell her how to raise her kids" One story that explains that so well was when she was dating a man named Harold. She was at her home with him and Mom came downstairs and asked her for a quarter to go to the movies and maybe have some popcorn. A quarter would have handled all of that easily enough. Well, Harold told her not to give her the quarter, and that she was spoiling her. Well, that was the end of Harold. She was wonderful! Harold ended up marrying Maw's sister, Aunt Grace, who was ten years younger than my grandmother.

I never thought of Marty as my grandfather, I was never expected to. He was always just Marty. Since Maw married him after Mom got married, Mom was older and never had to think of him as a dad (thank goodness), she never would have anyway. I was never crazy about him, to me he was a dirty old man and always crabby. He was very prejudice about everything and everyone. I never understood what my grandmother saw in him. He was a faithful church goer. Every single Sunday, he played usher and collected the offerings. But in his life outside those church walls, he never seemed to me to be very Christian, considering the negative way he would talk about people and treat others. Maybe, by the time she married him it was for her security more than anything else. I honestly have no other explanation how my sweet loving grandmother ended up with a man like him.

Marty was a very cheap man, he would not part with a dime unless it was to buy his yearly new Cadillac. Every summer when they were due to arrive, we all made bets on the color of their new car. At no time did I ever see Marty take out his wallet. It was not until after Marty died that my grandmother, who by then was in her ninety's, finally had control over the checkbook. Maw went to town! She redecorated her entire home, remodeled the bathroom, and made the kitchen more easily accessible for her. By this time Maw was in a wheelchair, but she still loved to cook so an important modification for her was to bring the kitchen counters down to wheelchair height.

Writing this and putting the time frame together, they had to have had a better relationship then I am giving them credit for, as they were married for close to fifty years. He did take care of her until he died, for that I am grateful.

Chapter 31

Our Matriarch

Before I was born, Maw lived in Oak Park where Mom was raised. I asked my brother Michael if he knew when she moved to Florida and he believed it was in 1950 or there about. He was five years old at the time and remembered Maw and Mom's brother, Uncle Bill both moving south. I always hated that she lived so far away. When I was older and financially able, I went to Florida to see her every year; but when I was young, I had to wait for summer to arrive just to see her. In the months before their visit I would write her letter upon letters. She loved getting them and I know she saved them. I loved making her happy. It is too bad letter writing is a dying art, isn't it? If my family didn't have these letters, ***My Darling*** would not exist now would it?

I remember so much about my grandma's home in West Palm Beach, Florida. I remember the smells, a mixture of grapefruit, and southern mustiness. The grass was rough and hard not at all like the grass at home. My bedroom was full of sunshine, with those old crank windows that were hard to open. When there was a breeze, which wasn't often the blinds would bang against the windows and wake me up at night, but you did not dare close the windows, or you would get so hot and sweaty. I don't remember if they had air conditioning, or if Marty was just too cheap to turn it on. In the morning, my grandmother would always prepare a half of a grapefruit from her tree in her back yard. She would cut each little triangle so it was easy to scoop out, and of course Maw would sprinkle sugar on top to cut the bitterness of that fruit. I was never a big fan of it, but I ate it anyway just to please her; she always went through so much trouble for me, and it was the least I could do. She was always so proud of the fact that the grapefruit came right from her own tree in her back yard. Maw and I used to finish our breakfast and go out to my favorite room in her home, the "Florida Room," it was a lovely, small room with comfortable furniture and a stand-alone TV. She had her favorite shows, like, The Price is Right and Jeopardy. She was pretty good at both! I loved the time I spent with her in that room. We could be out there for hours just talking, laughing, and, cuddling.

In order to let our family know which "Maw" we were talking about, we used to call her "Maw in Florida." I think we could have come up with a better name, like "Little Maw" because there was a definite stature difference between the two of the grandmothers. But I am not too sure if "Chicago Maw" would have liked that nickname for her nemesis, in her mind it might have implied to her that she was "Big Maw." The years before "Little Maw" left for the sunshine state there was a lot of jealousy when it came to the first grandson, Michael.

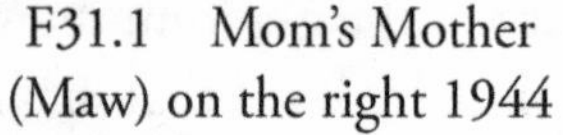

F31.1 Mom's Mother (Maw) on the right 1944

F31.2 Dad (home on furlough 1944)

(left to right) Aunt Edith, Dad, Maw, Aunt Bea

I have already explained how controlling my Dad's mother was with him. She was insistent that every Sunday, Mom, Dad, and Michael went into the city to have dinner. It did not matter what the weather was like or how they were going to get there. In those days, not everyone owned a car. Mom and Dad did not. They would take public transportation from Oak Park on a bus, every Sunday with a baby to keep Maw happy. "Little Maw" was never invited to these Sunday dinners.

Mom told me once that when her mother made the decision to move to Florida, it made life so much easier for her in some ways, and not so much in others. The move south helped to eliminate dividing their time with their first son, Michael, who was by then five years old. I know my Dad, who hated any kind of confrontation, would never say a word about it to his mother, so I am pretty sure he was in his own way relieved too.

Maw's reason for moving south was to follow her son, my Mom's brother Bill. He went there on a vacation and decided he loved the climate. He called my Mom one day and told her he was not coming back. I think that broke her heart. She loved her brother so much. He was the coolest guy. I think my Dad was very sad about him moving too, he was so very fond of him. Dad mentions him in many of his letters. They had so much in common. I know it was a loss for both of them on so many levels. I always thought the way he left was really a lousy thing to do. They had no idea he was even thinking about moving. He actually lived with Mom, Dad and little Michael at the time, so they had to mail him his things. Marty owned and operated a barber shop at the time, so he ended up selling his business to make the move south. My brothers still talk about Marty and how he used to cut their hair so short and was rough with them while doing it. When he moved to Florida, he opened a barber shop on Dixie Highway.

When Marty died at ninety-six, Bill would come over every day before and after work to check on his mother. He did her shopping for her and made sure she had everything she needed. Maw stayed in her home, on her own until a year before she died. The year before her passing, she moved in with Uncle Bill and his wife Lee until she died suddenly from a bleeding ulcer. The really strange thing was, Uncle Bill never traveled anywhere. He was always around. This particular time, when Joe and I were there, he went away for a business trip. It was only for a couple days, but those couple days proved to be the very worst days for him to be away. It was the exact time Maw went into the hospital, and because she passed so suddenly, he did not make it back in time to be there when she died. I know he never really got over that.

To say Maw died suddenly at ninety-nine years of age may sound funny, but she was sharp as a tack. She still cooked, played cards and could tell you everything about her history and what she had for lunch last week. She never missed a thing. Mom was a lot like her, I sure hope I inherited that gene! My husband Joe and I were with my grandmother the day before she died, we were there on our annual visit. The week spent with Maw was wonderful; we went to dinner, we took her shopping for new clothes, and of course we had to get her hair done. It was a great visit as always, and when it was time to leave it was as difficult as it had always been since I was a little girl. But when we left for central Florida to visit some friends of ours, I did not feel the least bit worried when saying good-bye or think for one minute that it would be my last time I would see her. I used to feel that way when I was young because that mean guy Marty she married used to always say, "you better come and say good-bye, you know we may not be here next year!" He was selfish and only wanted that hug for his own pleasure. My sister and I used to walk to school on the day they left to go back home, and we would cry all the way there, thinking we would never see her again. I hated him for that.

Joe and I left on a Friday so happy and fulfilled from our visit! We were looking forward to our visit with Peggy and Larry, long-time friends from Chicago. We all had worked together at Jewel Foods and developed a great friendship that stood the test of distance when they both married and moved south to Florida. That night we arrived we stayed up late laughing and catching up. We finally went to bed around midnight when their home phone rang. There were no cell phones at the time, if there were, very few people owned one. To my shock, the call was for me! It was my Mom calling me, telling me Maw was in the emergency room. I could not wrap my head around what I was hearing. We had just left her that day. I got in touch with my nephew, Tim, who lived in Florida at the time, he was already at the hospital with her. He was telling me while he was laughing that she was in the emergency room asking someone to turn on the World Series for her. Her team, The Braves were in the World Series and she was missing it! That was my grandma, that is my family! I breathed a sigh of relief, while Tim explained what was happening. Maw had a bleeding ulcer and they went in and fixed it. An hour or two later, I called the hospital to check on her. When the nurse answered the phone. I asked how she was doing, and she asked who I was. I told her that I was her granddaughter. She told me "I am so sorry; your grandmother has passed." Evidently, there was more than one bleeding ulcer and she had died peacefully. She just fell asleep. Looking back on this now, I am not at all surprised that a bleeding ulcer was the cause of her death. My grandmother took more aspirin than anyone I know. It was the only medicine she took, and she took it every four hours every day. It was the only thing that helped the pain of her arthritis.

If I know anything at all, I know I am so grateful that we had that week together. That alone was a true miracle because our trips were normally in March for my birthday, but that year we went in October for our Anniversary. I am so grateful.

The time spent with Maw was Priceless!

Joe and I left our friend's home in Leesburg and headed back to West Palm Beach to wait for the rest of my family to arrive from Illinois.

We had just lost our Matriarch!

Chapter 32

"Pleasant Recollections?"

Dad was still in the hospital convalescing. He was able to be up and around but still had a couple more weeks to recover from his surgery. He mentioned in his letter he is also playing pinochle and is one of the few that know how.

I am sure while resting in a hospital you have a lot of time on your hands to think. If it were me, I would be thinking of everyone back home and all the times we had together. This one **"pleasant recollection"** just said so much to me about how most men look at the chores of woman vs men. Dad was thinking about the Sunday dinners with Mom's family. He was literally envisioning her **"plain as day helping with the dinner and then washing the dishes."** These were his pleasant recollections? Oh Brother! He saved himself when he told her they were not the only moments with her that he cherished. When apart from your loved ones it's easy to look back and realize how we take the time spent together for granted.

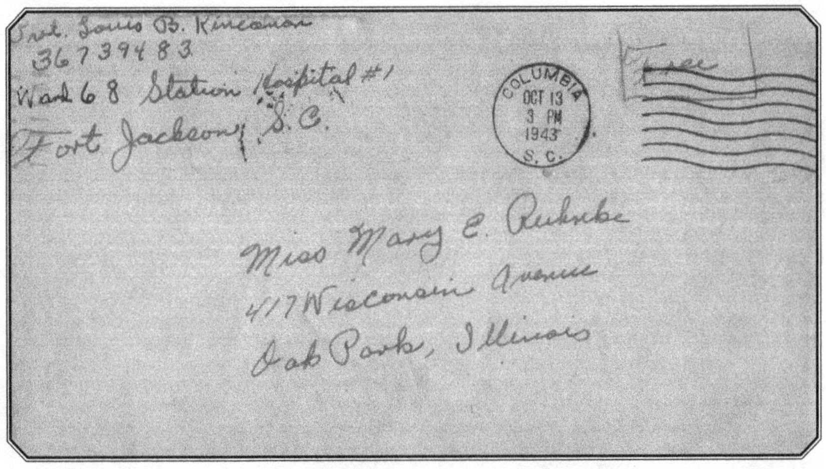

F32.1 October 12, 1943

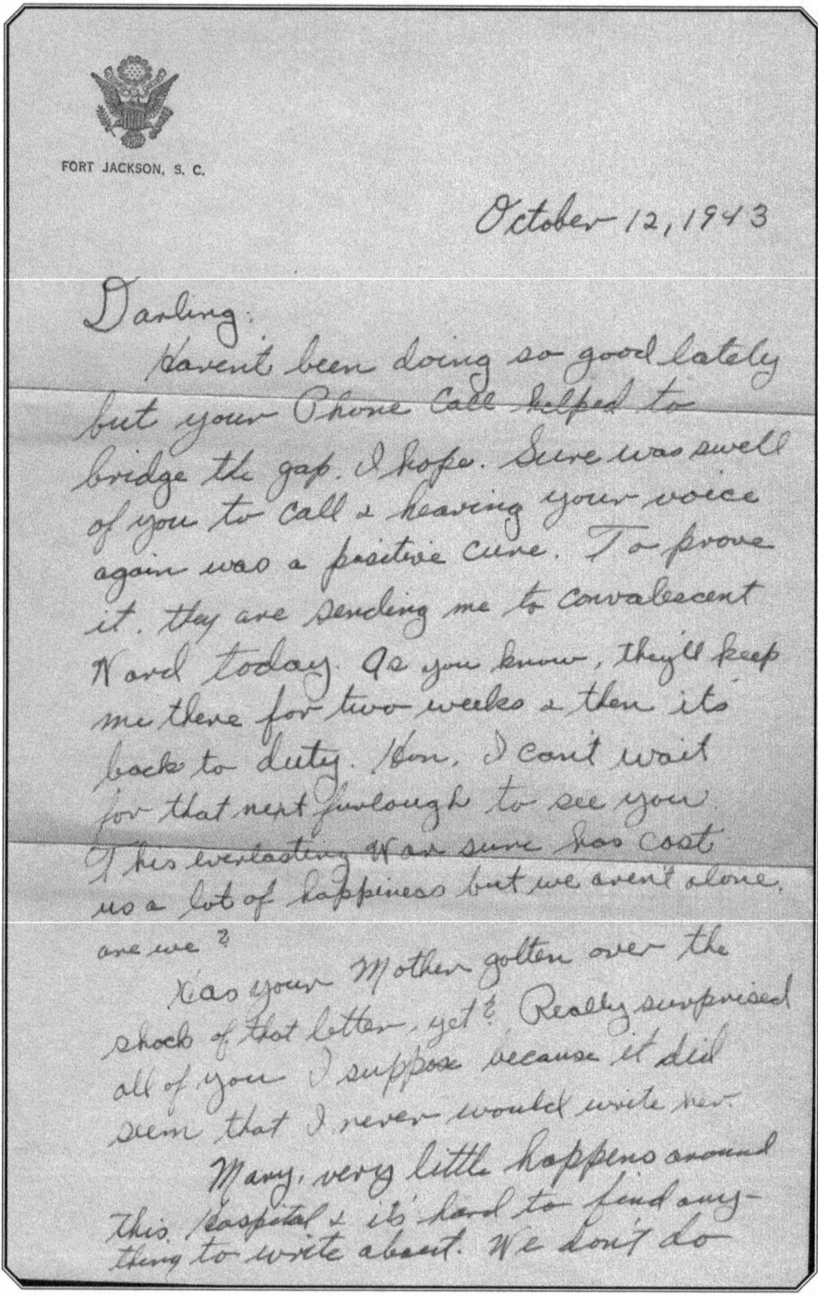
FORT JACKSON, S. C.

October 12, 1943

Darling:

Haven't been doing so good lately but your Phone Call helped to bridge the gap. I hope. Sure was swell of you to call & hearing your voice again was a positive cure. To prove it. they are sending me to Convalescent Ward today. As you know, they'll keep me there for two weeks & then it's back to duty. Hon, I can't wait for that next furlough to see you. This everlasting War sure has cost us a lot of happiness but we aren't alone, are we?

Has your Mother gotten over the shock of that letter, yet? Really surprised all of you I suppose because it did seem that I never would write her.

Mary, very little happens around this hospital & it's hard to find anything to write about. We don't do much here but eat, sleep & play cards once in a while. Now that the World Series is over it will be deader than ever. The Cards aren't quite as good as we thought they were but they did make every game interesting. It's the old story, no hitting in the clutch.

Darling, I hope you'll excuse this poor letter. Just wanted you to know that I'm thinking of you always. Said it over the phone, for once, & I'll say it again, I love you.

Bye now & be good.

Love Always.

Bevo.

Best regards to all, please.

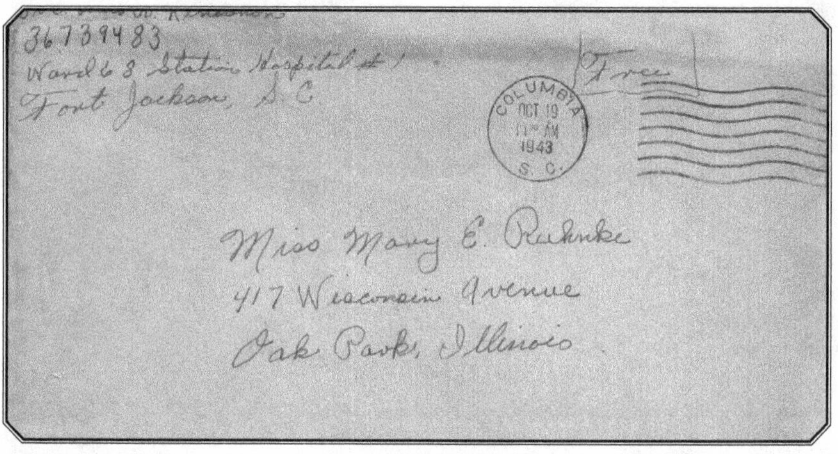

F32.2 October 18, 1943

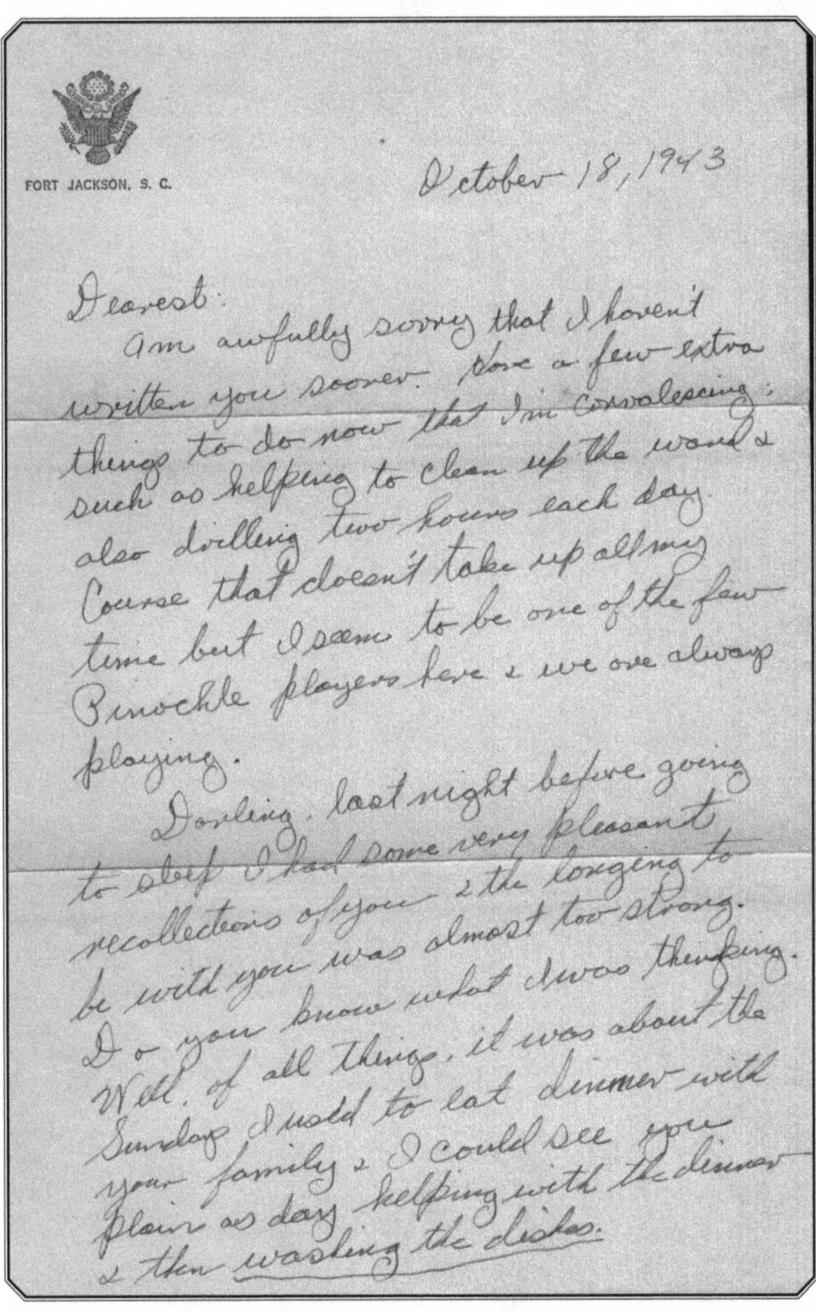

FORT JACKSON, S. C.

October 18, 1943

Dearest:
Am awfully sorry that I haven't written you sooner. Have a few extra things to do now that I'm convalescing; such as helping to clean up the ward & also drilling two hours each day. Course that doesn't take up all my time but I seem to be one of the few Pinochle players here & we are always playing.

Darling, last night before going to sleep I had some very pleasant recollections of you & the longing to be with you was almost too strong. Do you know what I was thinking. Well, of all things, it was about the Sundays I used to eat dinner with your family & I could see you plain as day helping with the dinner & then washing the dishes.

Have you recovered as yet? Mary, those aren't the only moments I've spent with you that I cherish. Every moment was swell but never appreciated like they should have been. Never thought we would have to be apart so long & never did realize how lonesome these months could be. Yes, it must be & is love.

Am glad your Mother liked the letter & tell her I'm awaitin. Speaking of writing letters I believe I owe at least five answers. Recieved a swell letter from the Surface Lines Schedule Dept. and they all said "hello & good health." You know one of those letters where each person writes a few lines. Thought that was pretty nice of them. Don't know if I told you or not but the Queen of Angels Ball Club sent me the same kind so you can see that I have a few letters to get into the mail.

Hon, one page seems to be my limit these days so please have patience. Maybe something of interest will happen soon. In the meantime. I'll keep telling you that I love you & miss you always. Bye now & give my love to your family. Love
Berse.

Dad's letters are getting shorter, but they are full of love. I think his buddies that are also recuperating are into playing cards, and they found the perfect guy. That was always one of his favorite past times. He would play Solitaire if there was no one around to play with him, he did this by himself as long as I can remember. I know how time can fly by when you are doing something you enjoy. I am finding that myself writing this book. It is a labor of love, with each page giving me more of a glimpse into the life of my Mom and Dad, long before I entered the picture.

Dad mentions a couple of people that have sent him get well cards. One place he called the Service Lines Schedule Department, I verified through some papers I found recently that the Service Line Schedule Department, is the department that Dad worked for at the Chicago Transit Authority. The paperwork shows he started working for them at the end of 1942 right before he was in the Army. He also mentioned Queen of Angels Ball Club. I never heard of them, but he must have played ball for their team.

Chapter 33

"It's All About You"

This next letter was a joy to read, I found my Dad in what I would describe as a light-hearted mood. Especially because he was still in the Army hospital. I really enjoyed reading this.

Looks like Dad is out of the hospital rehab in the letter dated October 31. Dad was out of commission for almost two months. I can't help but think that his time in the hospital, may have been his best time in the Army, (except for furloughs home of course) but he just didn't know it yet. I can say that because I know what my Dad had facing him moving forward. Speaking of furloughs, it looked like one was coming up for Dad in the next couple months. He was looking forward to two wonderful weeks back home with his darling.

F33.1 October 26, 1943

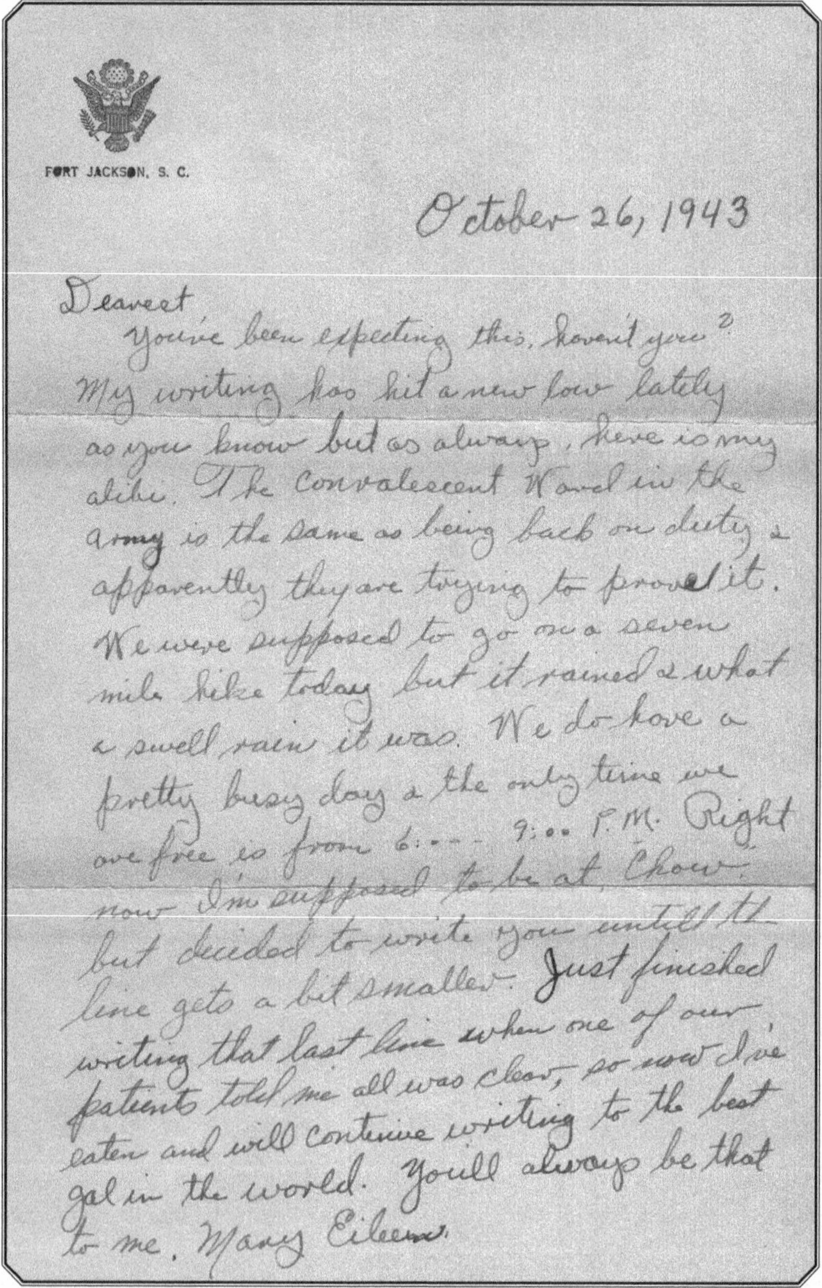

FORT JACKSON, S. C.

October 26, 1943

Dearest,
You've been expecting this, haven't you?
My writing has hit a new low lately
as you know but as always, here is my
alibi. The convalescent Ward in the
army is the same as being back on duty &
apparently they are trying to prove it.
We were supposed to go on a seven
mile hike today but it rained & what
a swell rain it was. We do have a
pretty busy day & the only time we
are free is from 6:-- - 9:00 P.M. Right
now I'm supposed to be at Chow,
but decided to write you until the
line gets a bit smaller. Just finished
writing that last line when one of our
patients told me all was clear, so now I've
eaten and will continue writing to the best
gal in the world. You'll always be that
to me, Mary Eileen.

Well, how was the week end vacation?
Did you girls paint the town "red" or is
it impossible? If it's anything like
Columbia you probably saw a few
shows & then wandered home to listen to
the Radio. I've been to town twice on
passes from the Hospital & what a time I had.
One of the fellows went with me & we saw
a show, ate Hamburghers & played Pool.
Exciting, you bet. Mary, before I go on
I have to tell you about one of the fellows
in our ward. He's from Texas & has the
typical drawl & every time he talks I
laugh. Here's the funniest part about
him though. If he were older & fatter
he'd be a second Wallace Beery. In fact
he should be in pictures himself because
he's crazier than anyone I ever saw. One
thing about the Army is the different
types you meet. Since I've been in
the Hospital I've made a whole bunch
of friends & they are all O.K. Wish they
were in our Company because it seems
that Anti Tank came up with a bunch
of lemons. Guess they are all too young

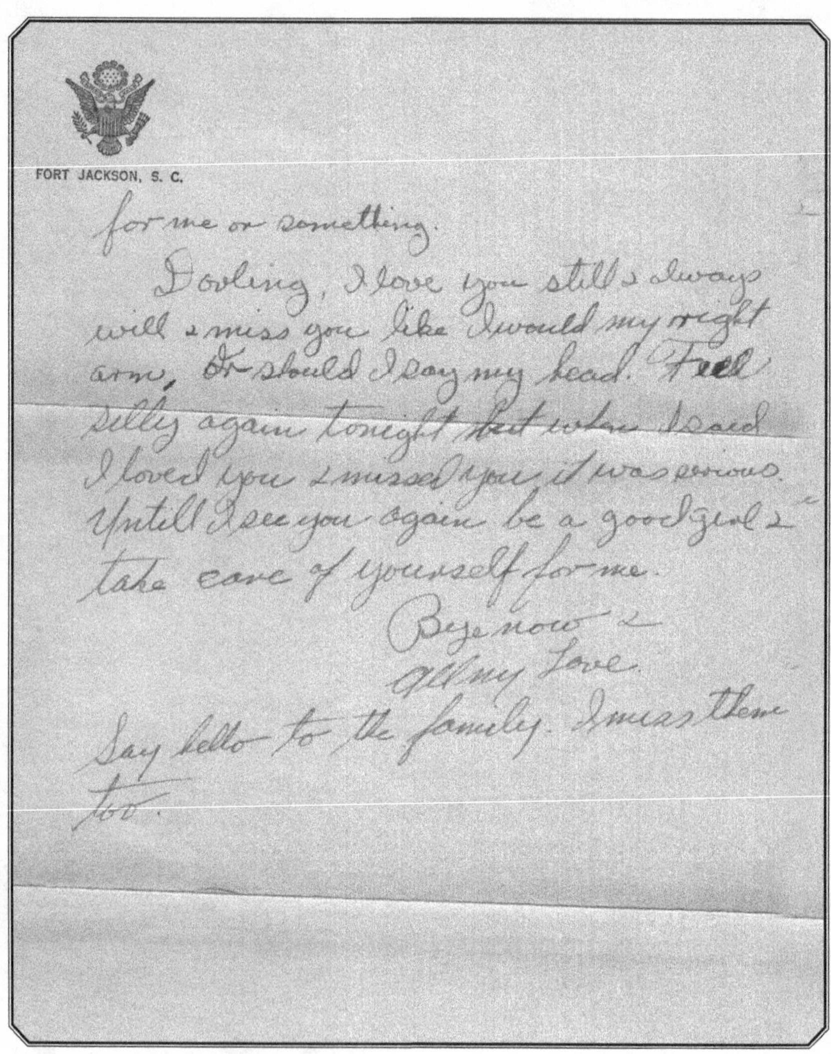

FORT JACKSON, S. C.

for me or something.

Darling, I love you still & always will & miss you like I would my right arm, or should I say my head. Feel silly again tonight but when I said I loved you & missed you it was serious. Untill I see you again be a good girl & take care of yourself for me.

Bye now &
All my Love.

Say hello to the family. I miss them too.

F33.2 October 31, 1943

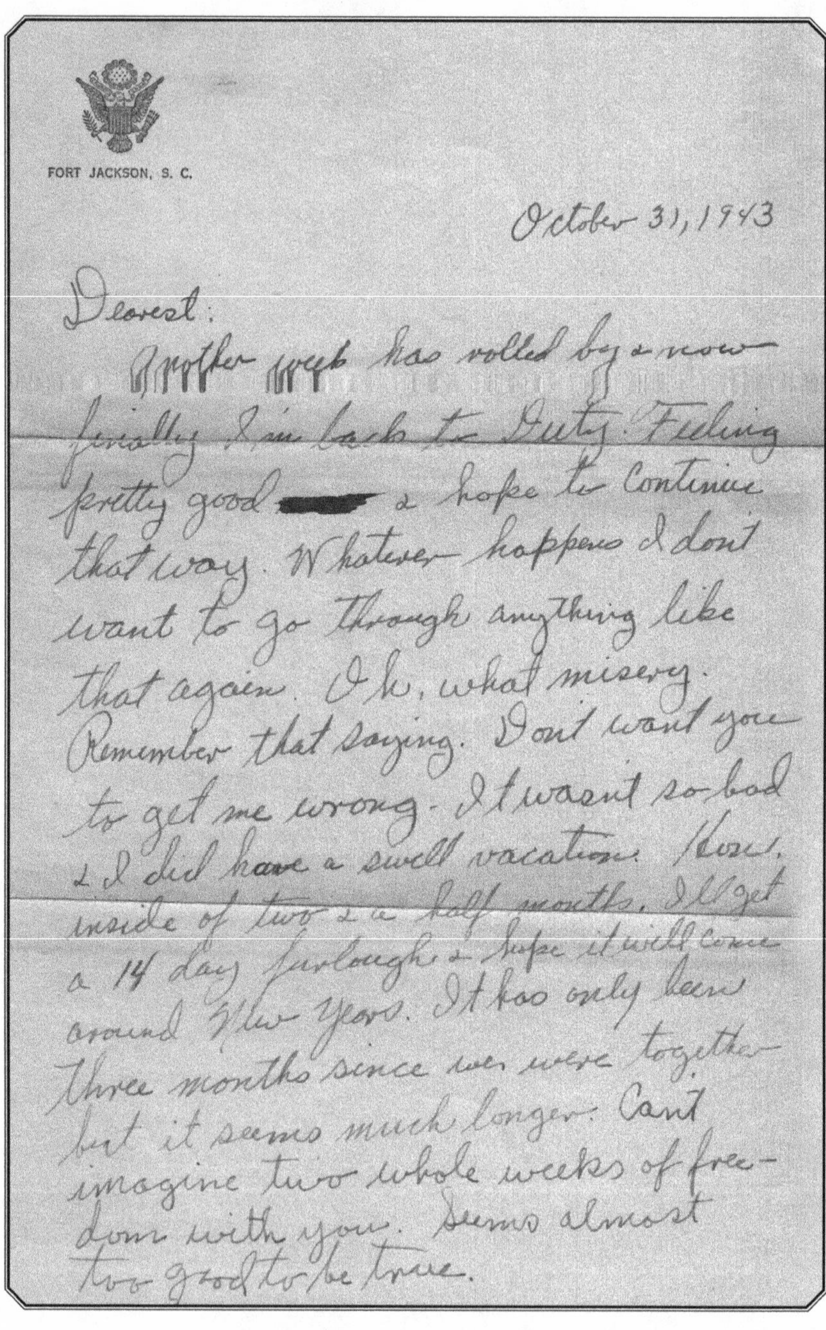
FORT JACKSON, S. C.

October 31, 1943

Dearest:

Another week has rolled by & now finally I'm back to Duty. Feeling pretty good & hope to Continue that way. Whatever happens I dont want to go through anything like that again. Oh, what misery. Remember that saying. Dont want you to get me wrong. It wasnt so bad & I did have a swell vacation. Now, inside of two & a half months, I'll get a 14 day furlough & hope it will come around New Years. It has only been three months since we were together but it seems much longer. Cant imagine two whole weeks of freedom with you. Seems almost too good to be true.

Mary, will you tell your Mother I
recieved her letter & it was swell.
She'll be hearing from me [redacted] & I hope
this time she won't have to wait so long.
Hon, I'm becoming worse & worse at
writing. Have a one way mind these
days & it's all you. All I can think of
is being with you, loving you & never
going away again. If you'll excuse
me for tonight I'll appreciate it.
After tomorrow I may have something
to tell you but until my next letter
I'm stopped. Regards & love to your
family & hope to see all of them soon.
Darling Goodnight & Love Always.
Bevo

What do you think of Notre Dame?
Are these Rebels mad when they win.
Guess they can't stand to see a Catholic
College on top.

Chapter 34

Special Service

Dad's was being transferred to Special Service. He mentioned that the Air Corp. would not take him the way he was, and I am concluding the reason behind that was because of his time spent in the hospital, but he did not go into the entire reason why in his letter. He told Mom he would tell her about it when he got home. His new duties would consist entirely with Athletics. That was right up my Dad's alley. Sports was one of his loves in life. Dad was happy with the appointment and wanted to work hard to merit their confidence in him.

I loved reading how my Dad described my Mom in his letter; he said his taste or preference was the tall stately girls. It seemed to Dad it was the trend of the times and he was lucky enough to have a gal like her. Dad told her she was "perfection." Dad mentions in a following letter how Mom was actually haunting him, because he could think of nothing else but her. He was regretting the fact they were not married as he witnessed other soldiers who had their wives living with them.

He is longing to walk up the isle with her and pledge his love for her. Dad was actually blaming himself that they weren't already "hitched." One of the lines in the letter is totally my Dad. He said, **"I just couldn't see myself giving you nothing and taking all."** My Dad was such a good man.

F34.1 November 4, 1943

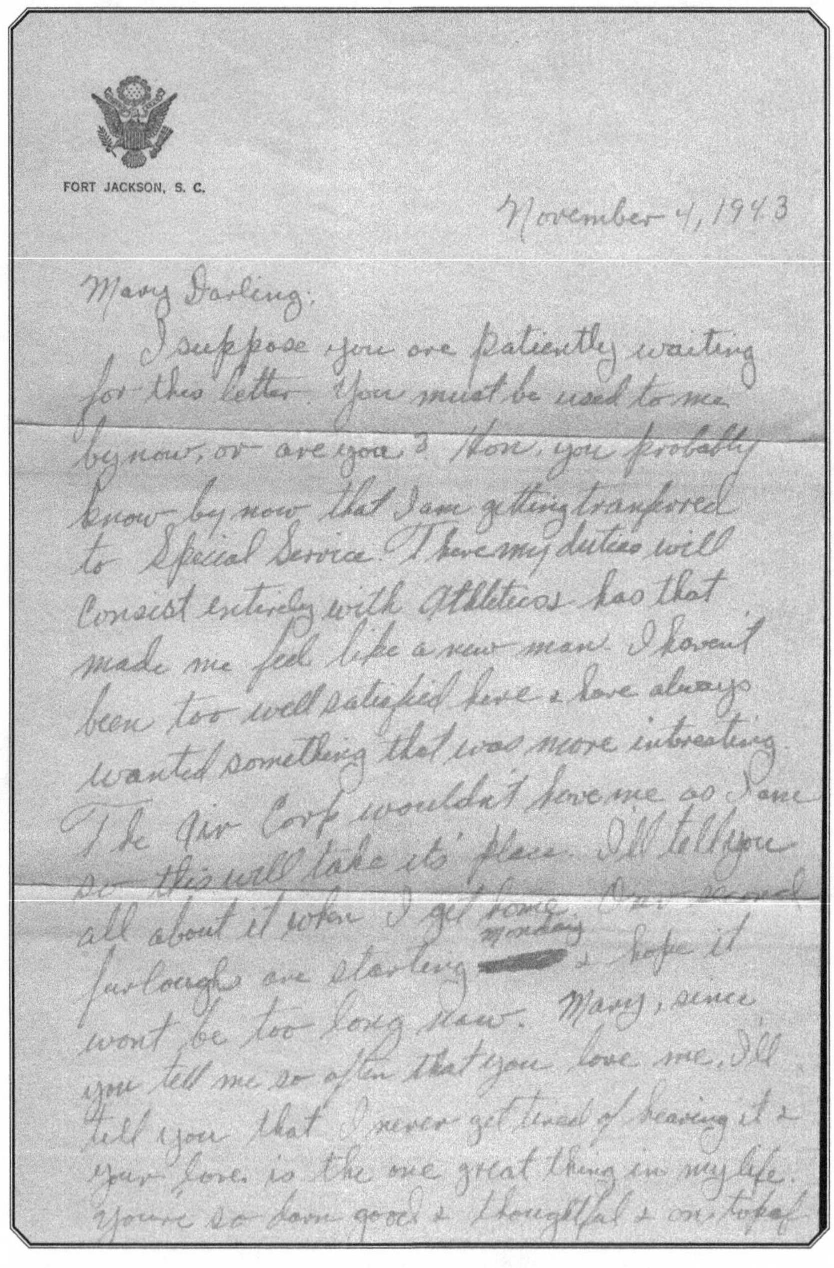

FORT JACKSON, S. C.

November 4, 1943

Mary Darling:

I suppose you are patiently waiting for this letter. You must be used to me by now, or are you? Hon, you probably know by now that I am getting transfered to Special Service. I hear my duties will consist entirely with Athletics has that made me feel like a new man. I haven't been too well satisfied here & have always wanted something that was more interesting. The Air Corp wouldn't have me so I am so this will take it's place. I'll tell you all about it when I get home. Our second furloughs are starting monday & hope it wont be too long now. Mary, since you tell me so often that you love me, I'll tell you that I never get tired of hearing it & your love is the one great thing in my life. You're so darn good & thoughtful & on top of

all that you are a very pretty gal. Every time I
see a tall, dark girl my heart jumps & then comes
the disappointment. You've read where the trend
is leaning towards the tall stately girls now
but I've always preferred them that way. That
Column you send me always mentions about
them so you see you aren't too heavy for
your height. In fact you're perfection.

Mary, we are wearing our O.D.'s
& they are much better than the khaki.
They are much classier & we are the
well dressed soldiers these days.

Hon, after such a long interval this letter
should contain more news but there isn't much
to tell you tonight. Do want you to
give my love to your folks & tell your
Mom I'll do it or bust. Your letters are
still very regular & very interesting so please
don't stop. Goodnight for now & I love
you & miss you always.

Bernie

F34.2 November 8, 1943

FORT JACKSON, S. C.

November 8, 1943.

Darling:

Miss Ruhnke, I recieved your letter & the pictures today & both were swell. Don't think your picture did you justice though. I have one in my wallet that is tops & it is really you. Well, now I'll have my two favorite women folk with me always.

Say, hon, I'm still a Private in this Army. It's true that eventually it will lead to something but I still have to make good. This Basketball & Football business is tough to Referee because I've done very little of it but with experience I should do O.K. It's a swell break & will do my best to merit the appointment.

Do you know that life is very lonesome & uninteresting without you?. I've thought of nothing else but you for so long that I believe you are actually haunting me. Mary, how I envy these Soldiers who have their wives living in

Columbia. If you only knew how much I want to marry you. What I wouldn't do to walk up the aisle & pledge to love you always isn't possible. Do you get that last sentence? It's kind of mixed up but hope you understand. In plain English it means that I want you & need you very much. See —?
It's all my fault I guess that we aren't hitched but hon, I just couldn't see myself giving you nothing & taking all. Does that sound familiar?

So all of you women are going on a diet now? Well, it's a good idea & maybe I should too. They say the less you carry around the longer you live & I want to live with you a long time. By the way I read of a good morning exercise & maybe you'd like to try it. This clipping here will explain all. You know since the Army teaches so much Physical Training, I'll have to keep up with it after the War is over. It really does a lot of good. Don't take this girl's story as a hint. You are & always were 100% with me, long legs.

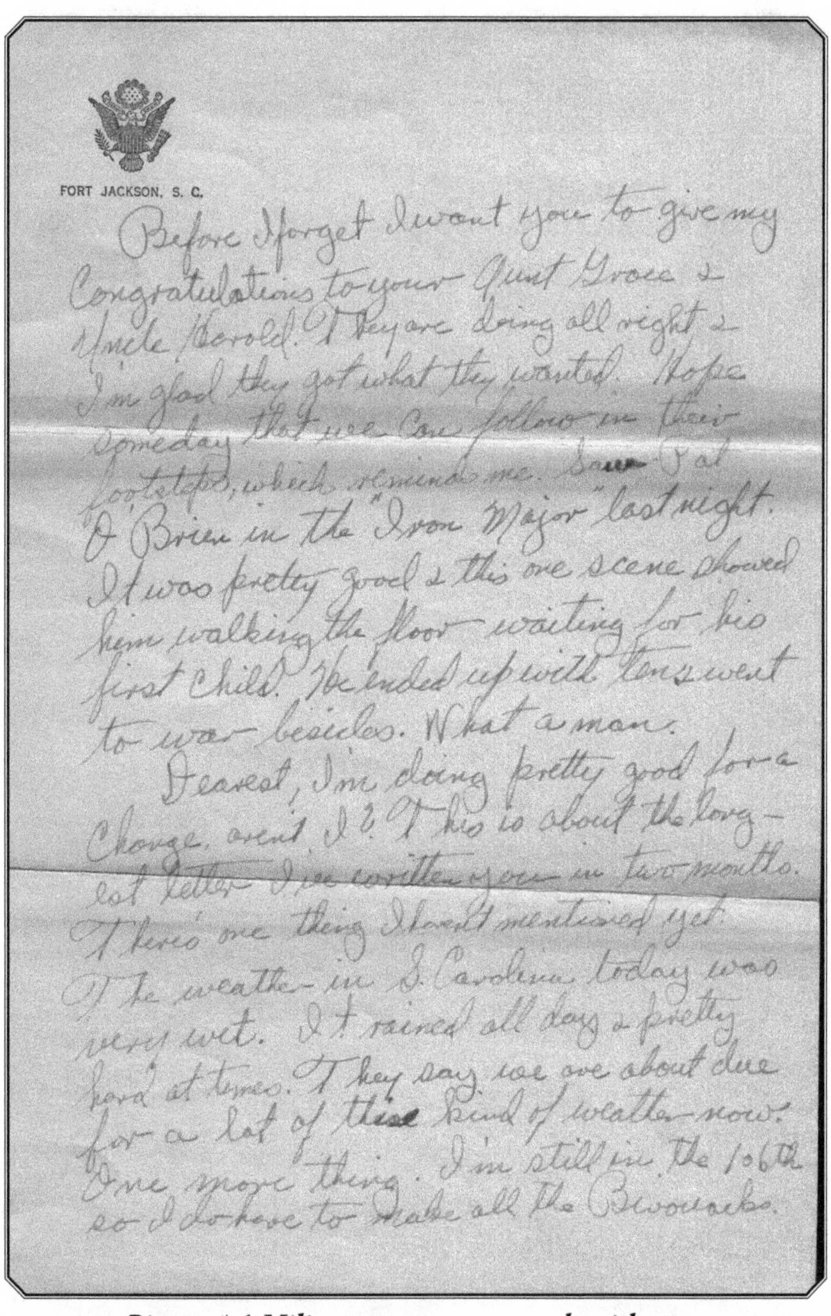
FORT JACKSON, S. C.

Before I forget I want you to give my Congratulations to your Aunt Grace & Uncle Harold. They are doing all right & I'm glad they got what they wanted. Hope someday that we can follow in their footsteps, which reminds me. Saw Pat O'Brien in the "Iron Major" last night. It was pretty good & this one scene showed him walking the floor waiting for his first child. He ended up with ten & went to war besides. What a man.

Dearest, I'm doing pretty good for a change, aren't I? This is about the longest letter I've written you in two months. There's one thing I haven't mentioned yet. The weather in S. Carolina today was very wet. It rained all day & pretty hard at times. They say we are about due for a lot of this kind of weather now. One more thing. I'm still in the 106th so I do have to make all the Bivouacks.

Bivouac* A Military encampment made with tents.

There is one starting Thursday & well be in the field till the 24th of this month. Then we Come in & have our big Thanksgiving dinner. After that my Furlough shouldn't be too far away & Confidentially I Can't wait.

Well, me love, I've rattled enough for Tonight so please excuse me & keep your heart filled with love. I Can Stand every bit of it & hope that you never find cause to change your mind. Guess you know by now what I've been trying to tell you all this time. I love you, you nut.

So long Chub & I'll be seeing you soon, I hope & pray. Bern

Is your Mom still waiting? Give her, your Mom & Bill my love.

Sue wrote me but like a dope I lost her address. Would you all be so kind as to send it to me.

Heard a new song with Gene Autry doing the singing. Its Rosalita & very pretty it is lassie. Bye

You'll find my new address on the envelope

Chapter 35

Thanksgiving 1943

F35.1 November 13, 1943

Dad is sending good news home about his future schedule. He will be home soon on furlough. He will be home on December 6th for ten days. As you read further in the letter you will see more hope for more time together. But the words **"back for Maneuvers"** makes me nervous, I can only imagine how Mom felt.

Dad spent Thanksgiving at the Army base, but he did not seem to mind the meal, but he mentioned that he and the men missed their home holiday gatherings. Dad's letter made it seem that Mom may have been complaining about the lack of letters from him. Mom had sent him some cookies to enjoy and dad said they were **"swell."** He also must have shared them with his buddies because he mentioned "all the fellows think you have great possibilities." They were right, Mom was a great cook!

The next few letters were written right before Dad left for home.

FORT JACKSON, S. C.

Nov. 13, 1943

Darling:

This wont be a very long letter but I want to let you know that I'm still thinking of you. We are out in the field & writing facilities are scarce. Hon, in case you are interested this is about how our schedule will run for the next four month. This Bivouack ends the 24th of Nov. & then Dec. 6, I'll be home for eleven days at least. Our regular training ends Jan. 8, and sometime in February our Manauvers start. So you see we do have most of the hard work over with now. They will, after the Manauvers, give us another ten day furlough so thats not such a bad future is it? We were going to get 15 days this time but they have cut them down a few days. Mary, its hard to believe that I'll be seeing you in person in less than a month.

It will be a little hard leaving you again before Christmas but seeing you anytime is enough for me.

Darlin, I'm sorry this letter is so brief but I'm too excited to write. Pretty soon we can talk to each other again & then you can hear all & so can I.

Tell all the folks hello & give them my love. Bye for now, Beautiful.

Love Always
Bean.

Correct Address from now on.
Pvt. Louis B. Kincanon
36739483
Division Special Service Office
APO 443
Fort Jackson, S.C.

F35.2 November 25, 1943

FORT JACKSON, S. C.

Nov. 26, 1943

Hello Darlin;

Guess by this time you have given up hope of getting this letter. Will admit that I have been very lax & deserve a good talking to. You will get your chance very soon & even that will make me feel swell. Talking to you in any way or on any subject is almost too good to be true. Hon, while out in the field I missed out on some of your letters & have just finished reading all of them. Was sorry to hear that you had a cold & now I'm glad that you are feeling better. So you are doing your daily dozen now. I'll have to watch that some day when I get home. Mary, I'm getting so darn anxious to see you that each day seems a year. It won't be long now though so maybe I

can stand the suspense.
We have just finished eating our
Thanksgiving Dinner & was it swell.
We had Turkey with all the trimmings &
everyone of us had plenty. Wasn't bad at
all but we did miss the home atmosphere
Hon, everything is going fine here &
I'll explain all when I see you. Until
then I'll try & write two or three more
letters just because I love you. You
are absolutely right. I am a terrible
letter correspondent. Be a good girl
& remember always, I love you & miss
you too much. Bye now & say hello
to your family for me.

Love
Bern.

Have to use up a full page some how
Hope all of You had a very nice
Thanksgiving with as good a Dinner
as we. Bye Kid.
Almost forgot to thank you for the
Cookies. They were swell & all of the fellows
think You have great possibilities

Chapter 36

Return to Base

The next letter you will read will be after Dad's furlough and he had returned to his base.

It is a hard read after their time spent together. I know my heart was breaking reading it. I do not think there is anything I can write about this next letter that could explain the sadness in my Dad's words. Two things made me so sad just thinking about how he must have been feeling. Dad wrote; **"these next few months will be the longest and loneliness I'll ever spend"** and **"Death couldn't be much worse than the feeling of emptiness on that lousy train."**

There was so much more instore for both Dad and Mom in the year ahead.

F36.1 December 17, 1943

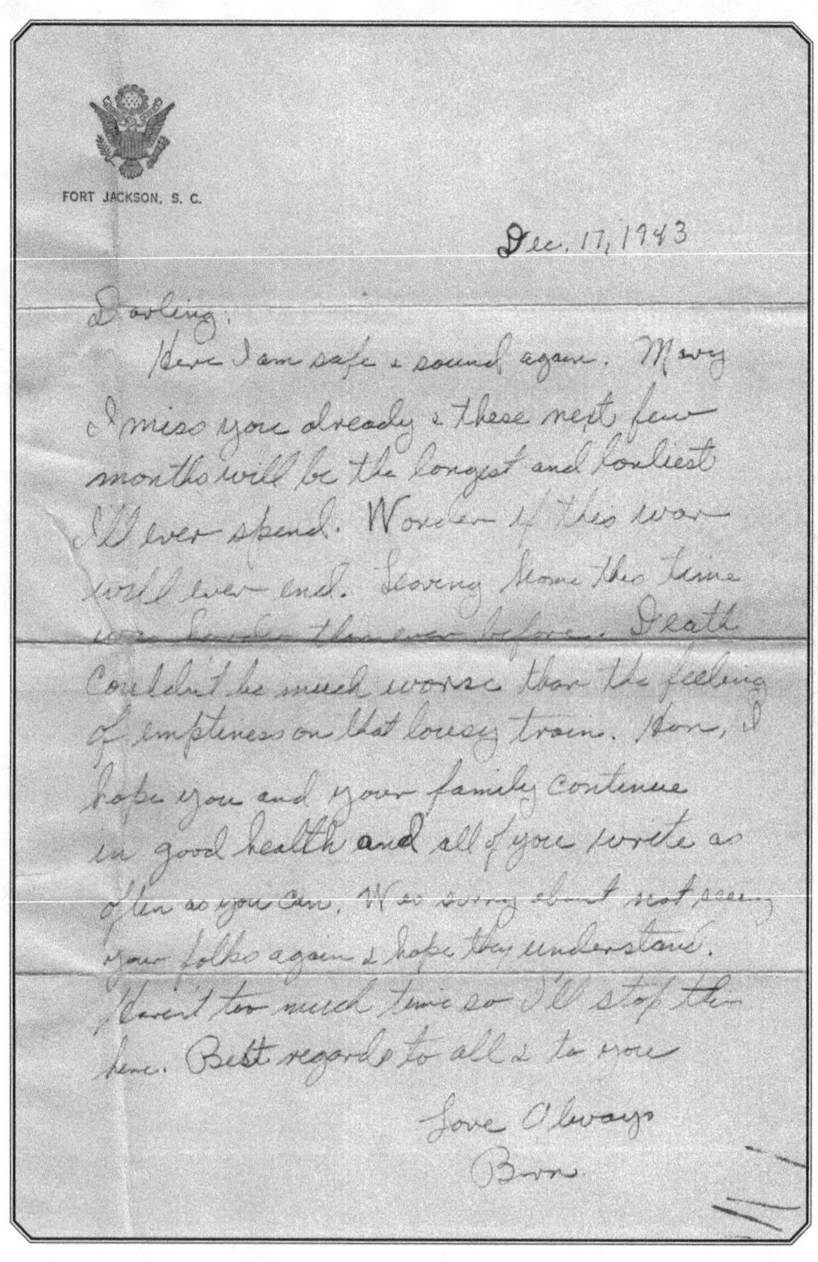

FORT JACKSON, S. C.

Dec. 17, 1943

Darling:

Here I am safe & sound again. Mary I miss you already & these next few months will be the longest and lonliest I'll ever spend. Wonder if this war will ever end. Leaving Home this time was harder than ever before. Death Couldn't be much worse than the feeling of emptiness on that lousy train. Hon, I hope you and your family continue in good health and all of you write as often as you can. Was sorry about not seeing your folks again & hope they understand. Haven't too much time so I'll stop then here. Best regards to all & to you

Love Always

Bon

Chapter 37

Christmas Season 1943

Christmas, just days away in this next letter dated December 23, 1943. Dad said how he hopes that by next Christmas they would be together.

They both had no idea what the future held for them. None of us know what the future holds, but in times like these the future was so uncertain. *I am sure you would have had to keep the faith and plan your life like nothing was going to hold you back from following your dreams.*

Mom and Dad were not together for Christmas in 1943. That fact did not stop Mom from playing Mrs. Clause. I would love to know what gifts she sent Dad, but if I know my Mom it would have been the perfect choices for his current needs. Dad pretty much conveys this in his letter. Mom knew exactly what he needed. But he asked her not to spend all her hard-earned money on him. It seems Dad had taken up pipe smoking, which is funny because I never remember him smoking a pipe. I will have to ask my older brother Michael if he does.

What a Christmas for the men. They were getting right down to "battle conditions" and Dad mentioned how tough it was on them. They had to move in the middle of the night under black-out conditions, along with the cold nights it made for a really hard time.

While reading Dad's letter and realizing he was so far away from home at Christmas, it made me think about our own family

Christmases. I am not sure if Dad ever had a great love for the holidays. I only recall one-time Mom got Dad to get in the car with all of us and drive downtown to the city of Chicago to see the giant Christmas tree and Marshall Field's creatively decorated windows. The traffic was terrible going into the city, which was not unusual, especially this time of the year. Dad let us all know how crazy it was to make this trip just to see a tree. I would rather that he had gotten into the holiday spirit and started singing some Christmas carols with his beautiful voice instead of complaining about traffic.

There was a fun side to Dad we fondly remember. Our family's tradition was to open gifts on Christmas Eve. All the kids were sent upstairs to bed early so Santa would come! Eventually, we would fall asleep, only to be awakened by all this noise and commotion downstairs. Dad would be yelling out the back door, then slam the door, all the while saying, "thank you Santa, Merry Christmas!" That was our que to run downstairs and open our presents that Santa left for us. I remember some of those nights where all of us kids would run out to the back porch to catch a glimpse of Santa's reindeer. My younger brother Bill said so many times, "I see him, I see him." Those are very special memories thanks to my Dad.

AFTER FIVE DAYS RETURN TO
Pvt. Louis B. Kincanon
Div. Special Service Office
36739483 APO 443
Fort Jackson, S.C.

COLUMBIA
DEC 23
3 PM
1943
S.C.

Miss Mary E. Ruhnke
417 Wisconsin Avenue
Oak Park, Illinois

F37.1 December 22, 1943

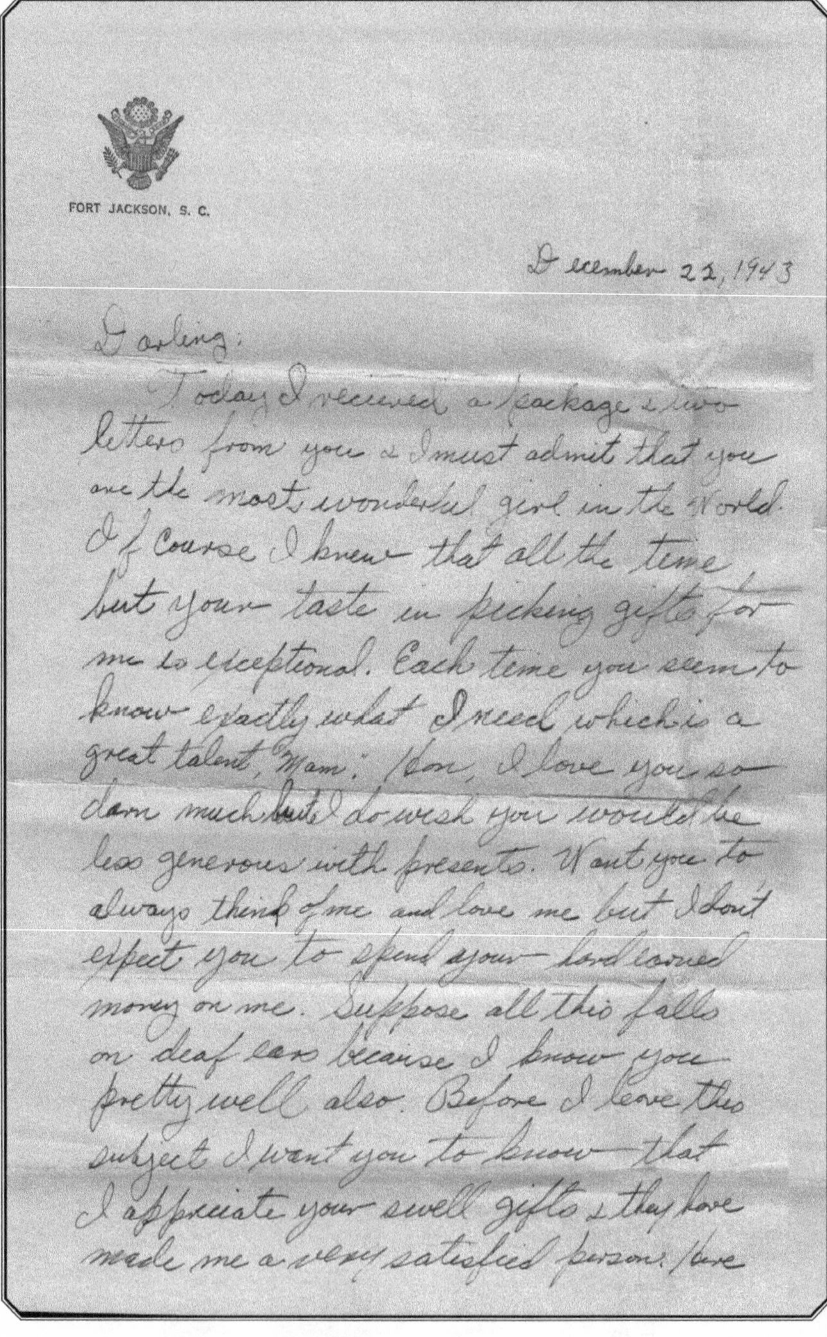

FORT JACKSON, S. C.

December 22, 1943

Darling:

Today I received a package & two letters from you & I must admit that you are the most wonderful girl in the World. Of course I knew that all the time but your taste in picking gifts for me is exceptional. Each time you seem to know exactly what I need which is a great talent, Mam. Hon, I love you so darn much but I do wish you would be less generous with presents. Want you to always think of me and love me but I don't expect you to spend your hard earned money on me. Suppose all this falls on deaf ears because I know you pretty well also. Before I leave this subject I want you to know that I appreciate your swell gifts & they have made me a very satisfied person. Have

I am in love with a great girl & she is in love with me. What else could any man ask for except that she be his wife forever. Some that day will come & I hope & pray it won't be too long now. By the way you may marry an old satisfied pipe smoker. Bought some Bond Street Tobacco today & I really enjoy smoking this new way. Mary, I'll write your Mother soon & thank her for her present. She, like her daughter was far too generous and it makes me feel awful. Here I haven't even sent a Christmas Card her way. Give her my love and thanks.

Well, today at noon we finished our Bivouac & it was a relief. We are getting right down to Battle Conditions now & it is a bit tough. We have to move in the middle of the night under Blackout Conditions & that along with these Cool nights makes for a hard time. We'll be moving again Monday for another nine days so you can see we aren't getting too much time for pleasure.

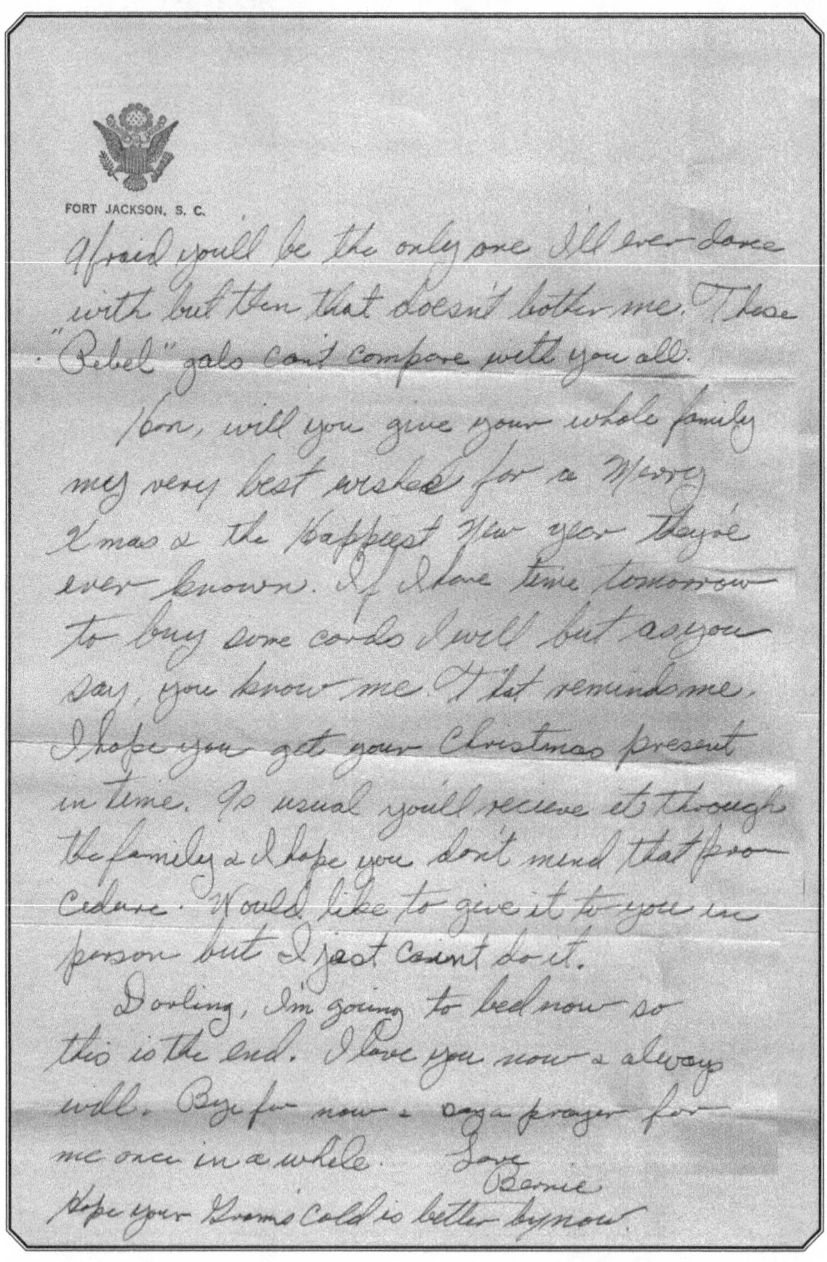

FORT JACKSON, S. C.

Afraid you'll be the only one I'll ever dance with but then, that doesn't bother me. These "Rebel" gals can't compare with you all.

Hon, will you give your whole family my very best wishes for a Merry X-mas & the happiest New year they've ever known. If I have time tomorrow to buy some cards I will but as you say, you know me. That reminds me, I hope you get your Christmas present in time. As usual you'll recieve it through the family & I hope you don't mind that procedure. Would like to give it to you in person but I just can't do it.

Darling, I'm going to bed now so this is the end. I love you now & always will. Bye for now & say a prayer for me once in a while. Love

Bernie

Hope your Gram's cold is better by now.

F37.2 December 25, 1943

FORT JACKSON, S. C.

Dec. 25, 1943
26

Darling Mary,

How do you like that heading? Oh well! Variety is the spice of life they say & why shouldn't I practice it? Don't mind all this "Corny" stuff, hon, I have just returned from a Kay Kyser picture & can't help feeling a bit goofy. The title was "Swing Fever," & it was pretty good. This has been some Christmas Day here in S.C. It has never stopped raining & it made a gloomy setting for such a Wonderful day. Aside from that though we had a swell dinner & everything went O.K. Our Office put on a Dance Christmas Eve & we were all wrapped up in work. Since I've been here in Special Service I have become a "Jack of all trades," but so far Master of none. The Dance was a complete success though which will make our Major happy. He is hard to please so everything we do must be just so.

Mary, let's talk about you for awhile. I'm sure all of you had a nice Christmas & hope to hear about it in your next letter. You'd better not forget to tell me what you had for dinner & how you enjoyed the day as a whole. Hon, next Christmas, I sincerely hope we will be able to be together as married people & enjoy the happiness I know we'll find. Whether you know it or not you've made me very happy already in our very sketchy Courtship. Have you ever read one of Lefty Menzello letters. If you have you'll know where I'm getting all of these fancy words.

Well, "Mush", this is all for the present. Give my love to all & keep up the good work in your writing. You're amazing, finding something different to say every day.

Bye for now, & I love you.

Bern

Hope your Grandmother is feeling better now.

After my Dad's mom passed away, Mom took over the tradition of hosting Christmas dinner. Mom was a wonderful cook. We always had an extra-large juicy turkey that weighed at least twenty-four pounds, stuffed with Mom's famous dressing which is still a family favorite. I still make it to this day and of course, I follow her recipe to the tee. Besides the turkey and stuffing, Mom would make mashed potatoes with her homemade gravy. I have since learned that making good gravy is not an easy task. It was always the last thing she was making while the turkey was out of the oven waiting to be carved and carving a big bird took a lot of skill, one I have yet to master. Sweet potatoes were always on the menu along with a delicious broccoli casserole which was a recipe from my sister-in-law, Marge; it is one dish that all of us love, and I will make it outside of the holiday dinners because it is so darn good.

Mom would always make her cranberry sauce from scratch, this one I still have not tackled. I know my sister Lynn has though. My Aunt Bea's nut bread was a staple that my Mom always made in remembrance of my aunt, and because she loved it herself. Of course, hot rolls and butter were a staple item.

The finale, our Great Aunt Caddie's pumpkin pie with whipped cream on top. Her recipe is another family favorite that has been passed on to all pumpkin pie lovers. This is making me really hungry just thinking about it. I will prepare almost verbatim the same dinner for our family for Christmas, except we will serve a beef tenderloin hot off the grill, instead of a turkey. Joe has that down to a science where it comes out perfectly medium rare.

Mom always set a gorgeous table which showed her true feelings of love for everyone. Being at our family home for the holiday and witnessing the care she took to make the day a wonderful memory for all that were there. I have carried on that tradition as well. The tablecloth with matching napkins folded in a holiday shape, my finest silverware, and crystal glasses all say a very loving welcome to my family. I thank my Mom for showing me how important that was to her, and how I hope I will do the same for my family and for those that go on to raise their own families.

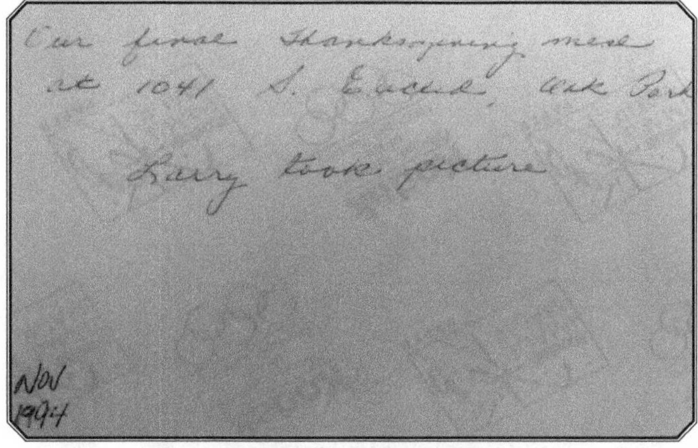

F37.3 November 1994
Our Last Family Thanksgiving at 1041 S Euclid
From the top:
Head of the table Dad
To the right moving forward:
Mom, Kerry, Camille, Michael, Marge, Bill and Jack
Head of the Table in front: Joe
On the Left moving Back:
Rick, Tim, Kristen, Toni, Emily, Kathy and
Aunt Caddie (Larry took the picture)

F37.4 Christmas Dinner 2019 Our Home in Glen Ellyn, Il
I took the picture (Kathy)
From the left front:
Larry, Camille, Tim, Jack, Toni, Bill, Will, Colin, Kellie, and Julie
I have no idea where Joe is…

F37.5
2019 Christmas Table at Our
Home in Glen Ellyn
Mom taught me well.

F37.6
2019 Christmas Table at Our
Home in Glen Ellyn
Mom taught me well.

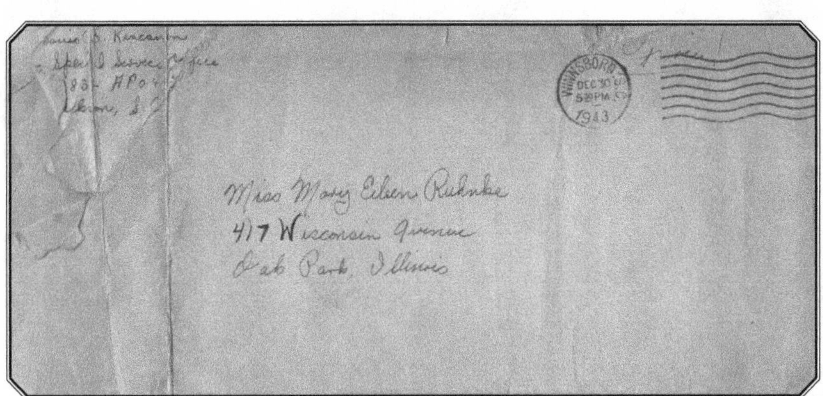

F37.7 December 29, 1943

December 29, 1943

Darling:

Hello again. How you? OK I hope & you'd better stay that way. Say Kid, How do you like the new way of becoming engaged? Bet nobody ever thought of that before. Seriously though, I'm sorry and you'll keep on loving this dope, please?

Well, since I wrote you last a few changes have been made and all for the better. You remember I told you about us facing those two weeks in the field. The Bivouack is on but this lucky guy is sitting in a nice warm Warehouse in Winnsboro S.C. taking life comparatively easy. We are resupplying empty P.X. trucks & outside of a busy time now & then, life is very enjoyable. We are sleeping on beds & for amusement we play Pinochle & listen to a Radio. Do you think I deserve such a break as this?

Your letters are still breaking all records & does that make me mad. If it werent for you I believe I'd be lost. You'll never know just how much each & every one of them mean to me. Yes, hon, you've been my main "Morale Builder" ever since March 17. You did all right those many months before but since then I've needed you much more.

Guess all of you have about recovered from your Christmas day by now. Now all you have to worry about is New Year's Eve. Last year about this time we were having a pretty enjoyable evening & this year? We can always console ourselves though by imagining just what we'll be doing if we were together.

they do I write things like that & it makes me feel worse
instead of better. Chub, you just wait. Some day you're
going to see so much of me you'll wish I were in the
Army again. You'd better not ever wish that, you brat.

Darling, It's 12:30 AM here & about time for
bed. I'll write again soon & let you know all about
this town. Suppose it's about the same as all of these
"Rebel towns." Goodnight & I love you now & forever.
The Radio is playing "Where or When." Hope it's soon.

Love
Bern

By the way, I'll try to be there when you receive
your Wedding Ring.

Give my love & best Regards to all.

1943 Transcribed Letters

1943

March 21, 1943

Dear Mary:

Surprised you, didn't I? Seems quite a while since I left Chicago and all you nice people. Just the same things happen fast and before you know it, you're on a mysterious journey. We left camp Grant Friday afternoon at 4:00 PM and arrived here in Fort Jackson, South Carolina at 6:00 this morning. The trip was very tiring because we had no breaks and we just sat there day and night. It's raining pretty hard here today, and, it being Sunday we have nothing to do. Some of the guys are shooting dice, some sleeping and others like myself writing, like the good boys we are.

Hope all of your family and you are doing ok. Pardon me just a minute, Mary the games are getting interesting. These guys sure don't have much regard for money. Pretty high stakes.

This is, I know a poor excuse for my first letter to you, but I don't want to have you or anyone, going through all the details of Army Life.

Mary, they told us to tell everyone not to write for a while because we are not settled as yet in our permanent barracks.

Please give my regards to everyone and my next letter will me more informative. Take care of yourself and I'll write soon. Good-Bye for now and Love

Bernie XX

Call my Mom up once in a while, will you Chub?
Excuse the pencil. This is the Army Miss Ruhnke.

No, I'm not in the Medical Corp. Don't even know what I'm in.

March 30, 1943

Dear Mary E.

Oh, you Brat. Am I mad. I'm tearing my hair out that is, what is left of it. If there isn't a letter from you in the mail tomorrow well, I just won't read it that's all. Seriously, I can't understand why my letters are so slow in reaching you. I'm sure I wrote you from Camp Grant and that's over a week ago, and my last letter from here has had plenty of time to get there. I understand that the poor mailman has a tough time finding Oak Park so maybe that's the reason.

Since my last letter nothing much has happened unless I mention the thousands of miles I've walked since then. The shots I've taken and the speeches I've listened to. A guy has to be a genius to remember all they teach you in one day let alone a week of instruction. Even so it's not so hard and in time all these things will be routine.

How's your Mom and Bill? They should both be feeling much better now that they don't have to look at me anymore. Is Bill playing ball yet? Season's getting pretty close now and am I getting anxious to play. We played a little Soft Ball today but it's like playing house or something. No thrill. Mary, bet you $5.00 Bill makes a good Ball Player. Have never seen him play but the way he throws and handles himself tells a story. Don't tell him this or he might go high hat on the rest of the family. Inject a laugh after that sentence please. **(from your author: Is this the very first LOL?)**

Know he has more sense than to get that way. It's a very bad trait. If you don't understand some of these words just write me a letter and tell me so I can explain them to you.

After all this idle banter, I suppose you are expecting a change to the serious side of life. Know there is such a thing because that's the way I feel when I say I miss you all very much and hope you think of me (once in a while.)

The above for all and the Below for you Brat.

Not hearing from you has left me a little weak in the stomach. You know the way you used to tell me you felt when we were at war? I always felt the same way myself and admit I was silly at times, but

I thought so much of you that even the slightest thing I heard about you bothered me. Enough of that or else we'll both be crying.

Will close for now hoping to hear from you soon and I mean soon. Best regards and all my love.

Bernie

April 1, 1943

Dearest:

Have received your numerous letters and have read every one through even the missal. The gum also arrived and as you know, appreciated. You? I don't know what to call you. You know you actually overwhelm me.

When I read your letters, I am speechless, numb, and dumbfounded. Have always hoped for the complete love of a good decent girl and my wish seems to have come true. Mary, you've heard me say that if I couldn't be perfectly happy married I would never the leap. If you think as much of me as you say you do, we have nothing to fear. Don't ever doubt my feelings. A year or more should be enough for me to know for sure. I miss you very much, still love you, so you must be the one and only. Hon, I'm glad the family is feeling fine and their few lines in your letter was swell. Suppose all of you are working hard. Life is like that it seems. It gets pretty monotonous at times especially when Saturday's & Sunday's are just the same and the rest. Have just about reconciled myself now to work eat and sleep. No more Mary for a while and that's a pretty tough reconciliation. See, you've even got me doing it, Mush. You ask me to explain close order drill- Column Right-Right-Flank and all that stuff. We are learning so many things, our rifles, guard duty, identification of airplanes, tent pitching and a few more things that escape me now. What's more we've only started and from now on we really hit the ball. Speaking about the ball I have gone out for the Regimental team and soon that will be under way. Darlin', hate to tell you all this because it's all about me and I'd rather talk about you. You never would let me, remember? Just a glutton for punishment, aren't you?

Dearest, I'll close now. Lights out at 9:30 just 15 minutes from now. Know I haven't answered 1 tenth of your questions but time forbids. Besides, this is more fun anyway, telling you I love you.

My best regards and Love to All.

Bye Bernie

I'll kiss you goodnight by mental telepathy. Hope it works, but I doubt it. Bye.

The Missal was really something. Must have taken a lot of patience & time. I liked it very much and the time of reading was about 15 minutes.

April 9, 1943

Dearest:

Am still hearing from you regularly and you are not making me a bit mad. You know we can't get enough letters from such people as you. Tall, dark and beautiful, at least some people say so. I don't think they know what they are talking about though. Seriously, Mary, I do think your very pretty especially when you are all dressed up and no place to go. It does seem funny, but I didn't have to go places and do things to have a good time when we were together. Maybe it was love, why sure it must have been. Does absence make the heart grow fonder? It must the way I'm writing to you. Guess it has always felt this way but was too dumb to admit it. About being engaged I wish it were so but as things stand it's impossible. As far as that goes I can see very little hope for the future, but I'll work something out somehow. Can't stop now because it's much too late. Mine is a lost cause. Hon, between us two we are definitely engaged.

A guy was just here telling me he writes his girl once or twice every day. Can you imagine me doing that? What can a guy write about? I often wonder how you do it but you do & your letters are always long and interesting. It must be a gift.

Mary, about Bills glove. I'm not sure what to tell you because I don't. know what you want to pay. I can tell you to get him an infielder's glove. They generally have short fingers and then it makes it easier to pick up those hot grounders. Know what I mean? Wish I was there, and we'd pick it out together. Hon, business is picking up again. We have to clean the barracks now so will have to close. This letter has it's good and bad points, mostly bad, but hope you'll excuse me because it was done in a hurry. Give my regards to all and tell them to write.

Love
Bernie X

April 15, 1943

Dearest,

So, there you are, mad again. Also getting witty, aren't you? Well, that joke was just as bad as all the rest and what's more I just read it again in that magazine section. "Yank." Hello? After all that I'll ask you how you are, how's the weather and all that stuff? Hon, this Army's getting me so punchy I can't even write a sensible letter anymore.

If you only knew how busy they are keeping us. The Army alone is bad enough but the Baseball on top of that just gives me time to eat and sleep. I'm not lying because I missed practice tonight to write you & Mom.

Had my first KP yesterday and it's all they say it is. Was dishes, pots and pans, mop the floor, peel potatoes and carrots, dish out the food and all that happens three different times.

The night before I was gigged for being late at retreat and spent an hour walking around our barracks with a full field pack. What a life. Then that wasn't enough this had to happen. Received a letter from you & was reading the first page when the wind blew the other two pages out of my hand & under a building. Was I mad. My only happiness, "Gone with the Wind."

Guess you've heard enough misery for a while, haven't you? I have much more to tell you. Don't get me wrong chub, I'm still happy except for not seeing you. Miss you more each day & as time goes on it is bound to get much worse. Say, you, is this Leap Year? You nut, if I could only see and talk to you. Don't you remember what we decided? Mary, I'm in the mood as much as you are, but if you're looking for a life of misery, you'll find it in a war marriage. As far as I'm concerned what is there to lose? You, everything. I can get married & go away to war after a few weeks of happiness. If I don't come back it won't matter anyway to me. In your case you'd probably be left here waiting and soon maybe, MIKE, and no Father. Hon, this is a crazy way to talk but it's true and we must face it. Let's bide our time and eventually things will work out OK? I'm sure. If you ever feel that you've waited too long & don't want to waste any more of your single life let me know and we'll arrange something. Before you do that though consider everything & not your heart alone. If I listened to mine, you'd have been a bride months ago. That's how much I love you and want you but there happens to be a few barriers up now and one of them is spelled war.

Well, gal, I'm about ready to shower and shave now and then to bed. Say hello to Ma and Bill and the rest of your family, also, Marty & ask him how his bowling is coming along. By the way one of your Mother's dinners would taste plenty good right now. Hope you're as good a cook someday. Will close now with all my love. Keep writing.

X Bernie.

April 24, 1943

Darling:

Here it is Saturday night, and I am a long way from where I'd like to be tonight. Do you know what I mean, Toots, or shall I draw you a picture? Time has gone by

Pretty quickly these last few weeks and I'm hoping that it continues to do so. The faster it goes the sooner I can see all of you again and then for all I care it can stand still forever. Hon, I understand perfectly how you feel so you know you're not alone in your misery, if it is that for you.

There isn't much to report in the letter so don't expect too much tonight. After you once hear about the Army you've heard it all. It consists mainly of monotony, hon. Plenty of Physical Exercise and then we start all over again. Don't mind the last two but the first really wears me down. No, I haven't pitched much Mary because my arm is not in the best condition yet, but it won't be long. Baseball will help to change the continual grind so I'm pretty sure I'll make it O.K.

Here is another negative reply. My hair still is very short but is gradually sprouting. Hon, in your next letter will you please tell me all about yourself. Don't talk about me just let me know how you feel, what you do and all kinds of other things.

April 25, 1943

Mary after a pause of about 22 hours, this letter is now being continued. Started this last night and got this far when the lights went out. Today we played another Ball Game and lost 5-4 in ten innings. Didn't pitch until the tenth when with one out he called on me He sure takes it easy with me. I'm glad of that because as you know I'm very delicate and too much exercise wouldn't agree with me at the present. By the way a kid right from our neighborhood was the losing pitcher.

Bet Bill is right in his glory now. Can see in your letter that you and your Mom are about as happy as he is. ˇell him to so his best and he'll get along fine, I know. Hon, can't seem to concentrate no matter how hard I try. There is a radio in the barracks here and the programs are pretty good. Just heard Jack Benny and now **Fitch's Band Wagon with Abe Lyman** is on. Don't get too much time for this sort of entertainment and it sounds good. There are so many things I want to say to you but there seems to be a heavy fog between my thoughts and this paper. Wrote to Mom last night but suppose you'll know about it before this letter reaches you. A couple schemers, aren't you?

Well, Kid, this is the end but there will be more to bore you in the future. Give my regards to all and keep writing you "Bum." You know I'd give a lot to see you just for one day.

After thought, your cards, fudge and taffy candy all arrived and were swell. Thank you Darlin'

Love,
Bernie

Mary, this is a funny thing, but I haven't been able to buy and Easter Card or anything to send you folks. In order to get things like that you have to go to town & I haven't been there once. Evenings & weekends are our only chance and baseball ruins that spare time for me.

Hope you'll understand and forgive me.

Am also receiving the S. News and I'm more grateful then I can say. You think of everything, don't you? No wonder I love you.

May 2, 1943

Dearest:

What's the matter? Haven't you heard? I'm in the Army and when you're in the Army writing even to the girl you love is a problem. Dopey, don't you understand? I'm in love with you and if there was a chance, I'd storm your house with mail, phone calls and everything I could think of but they just won't let me alone. Starting March 17th, I changed from a man into a machine and from now until? I have to do what I'm told and when I'm told. Furthermore what & when occurs one upon the other on into the night and my spare time is limited to minutes. Mary here's a good one. Yesterday we had our First Field Equipment Inspection on the Field. The night before I was up till midnight cleaning and brushing my equipment and clothes and was all set.

The next morning my one pair of clean socks were gone. Consequently, I was gigged*, bawled out and had to work this morning & also miss Mass. Our Lieutenant gave me the devil & told me to quit worrying & thinking about Baseball & I might make a soldier. So now as a result I'm about to give up Baseball & and try to please my esteemed "Looie." (Lieutenant)

Didn't think I deserved the bawling out & everything that went with it, but they won't listen to you, they just talk.

Mary, I wrote Mom & told her about the bawling out & Baseball, but I didn't tell her about being gigged. She worries enough, anyway. It's nothing to worry about because it's a common occurrence and it isn't bothering me at all. In my own mind I've done my best and that's all I can do. Do you see what's so funny about it all? A lousy pair of socks means being a good or bad soldier. What a life. Have I loved you? Know that I have & I'm sorry.

Honey, you know you make me very happy when you say all those nice things. To know that you wouldn't even go to a dance without me makes me feel very proud. I wonder how many fellows in this Army can brag about having a perfect girl like I have.

What a letter this is. Everything I've said has been a mess, except loving you and that you already knew so I've told you nothing. Hon keep up the good work with those swell letters and tell the family hello. I miss all of you very much you know. Bye for now.

Love, Bernie

*Giggled: A demerit given in the military.

May 6, 1943

Dearest:

Hello again yourself, Honey. I'm fine. You know I still love you and always will. Can't help it because life is like that, isn't it? Now that I've replied to your first three lines, I want to say that you make me happier every moment that I know you. Can't understand why you do all these swell things for me, but I do know that without you, life would be pretty tough.

Mary, I was really sorry to hear about Bill. As you say it is a bad break for him & can readily see why he feels so terrible. Wish I was there to help cheer him up, but you can tell him not to let it get him down. It's a funny thing how accidents happen but they do, and we just have to take them as they come. He'll be alright I know.

Hon, in my last letter I told you about quitting Baseball. Well, now that's all changed again. The Captain and Lieutenant of the team personally requested my presence on the team and now everything is OK once more. Have pitched two games so far and won both 5-3 and 4-2. What's more my arm is swell, and do I love you. Am I nuts but can't help it. That thought just popped up so there it is. Hey Kid, I hope your old tummy always does a flip flop when you think of me. Oh, I'm sorry. It's only 19 years old, isn't it?

Did you ever see such a card playing family in your life? The only thing we lack is a license to make it a real gambling house. I'm glad they do play though because Mom enjoys it and she has a little less time to think. Hon, what I was referring to before was as you know the Mother's Day Card. That one thing alone gives me a feeling, you know what I mean. I won't tell you again or you'll get tired reading it. Will you do me a favor. Give your Mother a big Kiss for me on Mother's Day. Thanks. I'll always love her just for having a girl like you besides her own good traits.

Chub, I'm going to close for now but will write you as often as I can. As you know I miss all of you and hope to see you soon. Bye for now.

Love X
Bernie

If I'm Pug, then you'll have to be Chub. Can't wait to see those pictures.

Tell Mom not to worry about Bill too much.

May 13, 1943

Dearest:

Received your two letters today. I was happy to hear that you are still in love. Mary you seem, somehow to worry about me forgetting you, but you shouldn't. The only girls I ever see down here are those in the PX and they don't' bother me a bit. Somehow no matter what girl I look at I always see you smiling through and do they fade in a hurry. So, you see, there is nothing at all for you to worry about. Guess it's only human though because I do myself.

Hon, this letter won't be too long, for it is very late and I'm tired. In one of your letters you asked me about the fellows. To put it plainly, outside of a very few they are the screwiest bunch I've ever seen. Mary, honestly, they don't know which way is up. They are a bunch of kids that have gotten tougher than nails since they got that uniform on. It's really funny to hear them pop off and to watch them strut. Oh well, live and learn they say. By the way three of them just walked in drunker than drunk. You probably think, ah, the wisdom of 25 years. I know it, I'm just a jerk myself.

Well, Chub seeing that things haven't changed much I'm going to close up the shop early this time. Before I do you will want to hear this good news. Sunday, we go on the rifle range for two weeks and I'm afraid letters to you will be few and far between. They tell me that they will keep up busy day and night so there won't be too much extra time. Just remember I still love you and always will. Give my regards to your folks and also your Grandmother. Goodbye for now and be good.

X Love,
Bernie

Kid am I learning the Hill Billy songs. Know you can't wait to hear them.

May 28, 1943

Dearest:

Still lonely. So am I. Yes, Mary a letter from you reaches me every single day and I want to thank you again. I appreciate every single one more than you know. Have been a little busy this week between the Range and the Baseball Field. Haven't had a chance to shoot yet but it won't be long. Had quite a game last night. Played our rivals the 100th Division last night for first place and the game ended in a 0-0 tie. Was pretty hot last night & now I'm sure that my arm is on the way back. It sure feels good to throw hard without a bit of pain.

Imagine Bill is perking up a bit now. Also, his Mother & Sister are probably feeling better right along with him. Funny way to start a sentence, isn't it? It won't be long now or shouldn't be until Bill be as good as ever.

Say, Hon, that Electric Scooter wouldn't be too bad an idea, especially on the 15- and 20-mile hikes. Send it Special Delivery, please. Any more dreams like that, I'll begin to think you're slipping. You know I am. Every day I daydream one mile closer to you, and I'm getting mighty tired of being separated from the one I love. Darlin, there is talk going around about early furloughs. Hope they are true. Can't wait.

Say, do you realize that your letters & the ones I write home have practically the same thing in them. Of course, that excludes all the mush. Mom has a clipping of our game last night so you can read it when you see her.

Kid, I'm getting a bit crowded for time now so will close for the time being. Keep loving me & don't ever change either. By for now.

Love
Bernie

My very best regards to all the Oak Parkers.

June 6, 1943

Darling:

I know this letter is late getting to you and I deserve a bawling out, which will probably come soon. Go ahead hon, I want you to and would like to get it in person. You know it really was fun to tease you and make you mad. You're very cute when you pout, and I couldn't keep from laughing when you did. You'll probably kill me for writing this won't you? Gosh, how I miss you. Know it would be bad but in all my life I've never longed for anyone like I do you. If I could just put it into words but just like yourself, words just won't and can't explain how I feel. I'm lost without you, Kid. Can't even enjoy myself without you and never will be able to, I know. You see we're in the same boat. Read your letter with the marriage problem, in it. I don't know what to say. As you know, I'm all for it hon, will you wait till I see you? Have to talk to you and we'll decide together. Understand I'm always thinking about you and as long as I do it just can't be.

Here's some Army news. I mean army Baseball. Have just finished pitching against our hated rivals again, the 100th Division. Beat them 7-0 and allowed four hits. Am I feeling good, Mary. Believe that I'm twice the pitcher this year than I've ever been. Can't understand it but at least I've acquired good control. What a thrill. You, Mom and Baseball, my three loves.

Mary, will you give my love to your family and all? Really miss all of them and tell your grandmother I like her very much too. Bye for now.

X

I love you, Bernie

June 10, 1943

Darling:

Hello Beautiful; Do you know what those pictures did to me? They absolutely made a new man of me. Since then, I haven't stopped looking at them, believe me. There is only one drawback. The longing to see you has increased to where I can hardly stand it. When I sit here and look at you, I wonder how I ever left home without being married. Guess I'm quite a dope but my love couldn't quite overcome my fear.

Your letters are still reaching me regularly and all seems to be well in Oak Park. I'm mighty pleased that you're all fine and you all had better stay that way.

Sue is having quite a time for herself. She deserves ever minute though because you never know when she will get to see Fran again. I hope that he doesn't have to leave too soon. This war is sure beyond me.

We had quite a ball game last night. Had to pitch again with only two days' rest. The Lt. seems to think I'm the berries so now I have a reputation. We played Show Field the team with the good pitcher and tied one to one. Both runs were unearned, so we did all right. Hon, please excuse me for tonight. It's bedtime so I'll have to close. Remember me. I'm the guy who loves you. Give my regards to Mom and Bill.

Love XXX
Bernie

June 13, 1943

Darling,

Do you mean to tell me that you haven't heard from this boy in nine days? Hon, I must be slipping, or else time is going by too fast for me. I'm trying to make it up to you now. Think this is the third this week and a new record has been made.

Mary, you know that you coming here would be the most welcome thing that could happen. You must forgive me sometimes. I guess just writing to you makes me so darn dizzy that I can't even think.

Never ever mentioned your blood donation wither and I wanted to tell you how proud you make me feel.

Darling, just one thing. Will you wait until I notify you to come? Want you here now and always but it would be impossible to be with you as much as I'd like to.

We are pretty busy as you know and getting away evenings is a tough job. Remember this, when I so see you start ducking. Also, bring plenty of cotton. Never had so much to tell you before and your ears may become very weary. Do believe for once a man is going to out talk a woman.

Glad to hear the good news about Bill. Bet it's like being out of jail for him. Know how he feels because I was in the same boat once a long time ago. How's mom and Marty? Tell her I miss her a lot and would like to hear from her. I'll answer it and we won't even let you read it. So there.

Well, kid, I'm still in love with you and always will be as I've said before. Never do get tired if telling you, so you'd better never get tired of hearing it. Have to close now so excuse me please for tonight. Will write again soon.

Love XXXX
Bernie

We won today 10-1. Our other pitcher worked. He's a good boy. We're still in first place.

June 24, 1943

Darling:

Well, here I am again. It has been quite a while since I wrote to you last. As I said before, I can't keep up with the time, it goes so darn fast. Mary, I have some good news. Our furloughs start in about two weeks and I think maybe I'll see you pretty quick. They are trying to get the Ball players furloughs all at the same time. Don't know exactly when but will be soon and then I'll let you know. So, all of you people are fine. Please continue to stay that way and don't worry me. It seems that one house in Oak Park is now part of me and I don't want anything being wrong there.

Hon, your letters are still coming regularly and without them I'm afraid this life would have me down, by now. No kidding, without you to think about this Army with its monotony would be too much. At least this way I can always look forward to seeing you eventually and if not, your letters will do the trick.

Darlin, I'm sorry but this letter has to be drawn to a close. It's way past bedtime now so please excuse me for tonight. Always remember, I love you and miss you very much. Will write you again soon.

Love and Best Regards to Mom and Bill.

I Love you, Kid.
Bernie

We lost a double header Sunday 1-0 and 5-1. I pitched the 1-0 game and then the LT. decided to let the other guy hurl. Last night the Shaw Field team beat me 7-0 but it doesn't matter anyway. Bye

This is a terrible letter, but it was written in a big hurry.

June 28, 1943

Darling:

Have just finished reading your last two letters and thought I'd better write again but quickly. Don't blame you, I'm sorry and I hope it will not happen again. Mary I'm a bum. Here it is your Birthday and not even a card have I sent you. Don't know what the matter is All this month I've been thinking and planning for your present and a card but at the very last "good old Bern"

Forgets all about it. Promise you that I'll make good when I see you though. Mom may give you a present from me. She mentioned it in her last letter. She'll probably make excuses for me saying that I told her to buy something for you, but I didn't. Hon, whatever is wrong, blame it on the Army and also being away from you. This Army's got me crazy and you've got me in the clouds.

Was good to hear that all of you people are OK. Poor Matt sure has had a bad time of it. Hope from now on he'll be a new man because guys like him deserve the best.

Mary don't know what to say in regard to your coming here. Our furloughs are starting in two weeks, but as yet I don't know anything definite. If these next two weeks weren't going to be so tough, I'd say right now, but seeing you would be a problem.

Our CORP tests are coming up now and we'll be busy from dawn to dark. Nothing seems to work out in this place. You know I miss you more each day and talk about loving someone. Words can't explain so won't even try.

Hon, as usual there is work to be done so will close for tonight. Regards and love to all and be good.

XXXX I love you, Mary Eileen
Bernie

Hello to Sue when you write her.

Oh, yes, we finished in third place. Was knocked out of the box the other night for the final time. Lost 7-0.

July 21, 1943

Darling,

Here I am safe and sound. The trip was terrible and even Fort Jackson looked good. Haven't much to tell you only that I'm lost again without you. Almost every minute I expect to look up and see you and then boom, back to reality I go.

Hon, will close now but will never stop loving you. Regards to the family and I hope you're all fine.

Love XX
Bernie

July 25, 1943

Darling:

Am here in the Barracks and have just finished listening to Frank Munn, *one* of his songs was ***"Can I Forget You?"*** It has always been a favorite of mine and now I'll answer the question. Hon, I'll never forget you as long as I live. Those few days at home were the happiest I've spent in four long months. There was one drawback to that happiness, though. We both knew it would come to an end eventually and sure enough it did. Guess I never really appreciated my civilian life with you.

Mary, so far, I've done nothing in regard to the operation. Am waiting a bit but it won't be long now.

Sure, bet you were glad to see your grandmother. Hated to miss seeing her but next time we'll make connections. That California must have something. Sue and her must have fallen in love with the West. Please give her my regards and I hope to see her soon.

So, you hated to go back to ***Modern Modes?*** Can't say that I blame you because work is hard after all the fun we had. As far for myself things have changed for the better here. We go out every day in the trucks, set up our guns and then lay down in the shade for two or three hours. Can't hardly believe it but that is what we've been doing. After Basic it seems like heaven.

Our Baseball team hasn't been reorganized as yet but they are planning on doing some playing.

Mary, I don't know exactly how our marriage plans will turn out but, in a week or so I may have the answer. What it will be depends on a few things that I'll explain later. In the meantime, pray for the best.

Darlin, suppose you are disappointed in me again. I'll admit this letter should have reached you two days ago, but as usual it's late. Don't ever think that I don't want to write you. Guess I'm just plain lazy. Since I am that way this letter will now draw to a close. I love you more than ever, think of you always and hope to be a very important part of you soon. Give my love to Mom and Bill. Bye for now.

Love
Bernie

Hon, whenever I put an X on the end of my letters to you, I feel like a sissy. It's more fun in real life anyway.

July 31, 1943

Darling:

Received all of your letters and cards and must admit that I can't figure out where you get the time to write so often. Mary, nothing pleases me more than a letter from you. You really keep my spirits at high tide and without you I'd be lost. By the way Frank Munn is now singing ***"You'll Never Know"***

Hon, all of your questions are unanswerable at present but not for long. Mom has written me twice and she is against our marriage but she's only thinking of the tough times we'll have getting along after the war. Mary, for a fact she really wants us to be married but thinks that we should wait. In a week or so I'll let you know for sure. As far as the operation I haven't done a thing yet. Maybe I'm a little scared of these Army Doctors. Tell Caddie not to worry because I'll let her know before it happens. No, we haven't started playing ball again and I guess they have decided to quit for the year. Don't care too much. This Army is tough enough without added exercise.

Darling, did your Mom think that I was going to marry you without asking her? I'll bet she felt neglected. Have wanted to write her but didn't know just how to go about it. Hon, I'm so darn ashamed to even think of getting married under these conditions that asking her is a very hard job. I know how she feels and wouldn't blame her if she refused. Mary, I've always said I'd never take the plunge without security and I'm so far from that now that I feel like a beggar. I do love your Mother and don't ever want to do anything to hurt her. What's more you yourself are my whole life and id I can't make you happy and secure then I've failed in something that means everything to me. Say, I've really preached a sermon, haven't I? Well, it's all true and am glad that I've gotten these things over to you. Darlin, am closing now. Remember, I love you and always will. Regards to Maw and Gram and Bill, and Sue's Family also.

Love
Bernie

August 1, 1943

Darling:

Have a few minutes this morning before I go to Mass so will spend them with you. There has been nothing much going on here lately and it seems that we are just getting along as best we can. We go through the same old routine every day and time seems to stand still. However, if you keep on writing such swell letters, I believe I'll pull through without going completely screwy. Hon, you've never seen such a bunch of disgusted guys in your life. If every moan was a dollar, we'd all be rich. A whole lot of them would prefer to go across right now but they'd change their minds in a hurry. We are really fortunate to be able to live in the U.S.A.

Darlin, I'm missing you more each day and can't hardly wait for something to happen over there.

Well, Mary it's happened at home hasn't it? Just received a telegram from Mom and before I read it, I knew what it was. Am waiting around now for some word of approval on an emergency furlough. Generally, they won't allow us to go home unless it's in the immediate family. Hoping for the best. Poor Matt. I can't explain how this makes me feel. He's been just like a brother and if he goes it's going to be pretty hard on all of us.

Hon, I'll close now and may see you soon. If I'm not allowed to come, I'll call Mom tonight. Still love you so much that being away from you hurts down deep if you know what I mean. Bye for now and best regards to all.

Love
Bernie

August 11, 1943

Darling.

I've been catching up on all your letters since arriving this evening. You did give me the devil, didn't you? Hon, I hated to leave yesterday without you. Seems like things are and have been against us all the time. Sooner or later I have to write you a good long letter and decide once and for all what we are going to do.

The trip almost got me down but I'm still kicking. Am going to bed now so please excuse me for tonight. As ever I love you.

Love Bernie

August 15, 1943

Darling:

Just came back from Columbia and wish I hadn't gone. There is nothing there, but soldiers and we see enough of them here. We went to a show and saw ***"Cabin in the Sky"***

Mary, our Baseball Club is being reorganized again and will probably start playing this week. After the season is over which won't be long now we'll probably disband for the duration. The Army hasn't changed much. They are going to have more "Night Problems" now so we'll be having a few free days. Every time we have one, we are off the next day to rest. Bob sure did have some experience, didn't he? Things like that happen sometimes but as long as he's OK you needn't worry. It reminds me of something we saw the other day. Rifle Company B was out on quite a long hike and they had to make it in a certain length of time. Well, on their last mile almost all of them collapsed on both sides of the road. It was quite a sight to see; a whole bunch of men just lying there unable to go on. Sure, feel sorry for those Rifle Co. guys, they do nothing but walk and in this heat it's murder. So now you see, this isn't such a bad organization. We walk quite a bit, but we also ride once in a while.

Darling, you know I left my heart in the Train Depot last Tuesday, don't you? You sure looked swell and when your all dressed up like that, I'm lost. You called me bashful and maybe you're right. Wanted to give you a much better good-bye but Sunday night was pretty good. It really was one of the happiest nights we've ever had together. Hon, I'll close for now thanking you for all the swell letters you've sent and hoping you'll never stop sending them. Give my love to your folks and the best of luck to Fran and Sue. By now it is all over and O sincerely hope they have the best. Can't help but envy them myself because they have done what I hope to do some day.

Love
Bernie

Mary, you've heard this before but here it is again, as things have turned out, I'm pretty sure you're as disappointed as I am. Know also that asking you to wait for me is asking a lot and some girls wouldn't do it. It's no fun to sit at home day after day waiting and if you do get disgusted, I won't blame you. Promise me this please? If that day comes, I'll understand anything you may do only let me know about it beforehand. You are smiling as you read this, I suppose but this is how I feel. Understand this, Hon, I'm not questioning your honesty because I know you're on the square, but I don't want you to feel that I have a rope tied to you. I'd like to do just that but, in these days, men don't do that. I'm really serious about this and I hope you'll receive it the same way. Bye now and don't forget to give some reply to this sermon.

Again-I love you. Bern

August 20,1943

Darling:

Your letters have been coming through on schedule, thank Heaven. Seem that yours are the only ones that contain any good news. Of course, the "mush" is always welcome. So many things have been happening at home, I'm afraid to open Mom's letters anymore. Every time I do some new tragedy has occurred. I'm sure glad that you at least are feeling OK. Mary, if something should happen to you then I would give up. This life is tough enough without all these troubles at home. If I could just be there, I could help some I know.

Well, hon, to get on the brighter side I'm very glad to hear that you are to be the next Bride. Maybe that is a good sign, who knows. The war can't last forever you know and if it ended tomorrow you would be walking up the aisle with me in no time, or would you?

At last the weather is cooling off. Last night we had a problem and nearly froze. Had to wear our raincoats to keep warm. It's a relief though because the heat was almost too much. We have been pretty busy lately and I'm getting stiffer and sorer every day. Have to run the Obstacle Course quite a bit now and that's quite a job if you know what I mean. Boy, so I feel my age these days. Amen

Darling, I still miss you as much as ever and yes, I do love you. Funny, isn't? Don't forget to send me those pictures, Kid. I'm sure you looked beautiful. I'm also very glad that the wedding came off so well. Sue and Fran must be very happy and give them my best.

Hon, I'll close for now so give my regards to your family. Bye for now.

I Love you Chub.

Love Always
Bernie

August 25, 1943

Darling:

I realize this letter is behind schedule as usual we are busy. We've been working day and night lately and time to ourselves is something of the past. Mary, my figure is still improving and I'm down to 170 lbs. We've been running the obstacle course every morning and it's either going to kill or cure us. By the way they call it "Tarzan Field," where Jap Killers are made. Are they corny. We play our first game Friday at last. For a while I thought they weren't going to continue.

So, you think you've got something do you? Hon, the feeling is mutual, and I hope we always feel the same. I miss you more each day and only wish it were possible for you to come down here. Honestly though I don't believe you'd ever find a place to stay and I don't want you wondering around alone in this place. Southern towns aren't too presentable anywhere especially when they are situated near an Army Camp. If we can just be patient, I know someday we'll have all the happiness we can take care of.

Sure, hope your family is fine. News form home continues glum, but it can't go on forever. Mom told me that Matt has had another operation and so far, they don't know how successful it was. Guess it's just one of those things that can't be helped.

Darlin, it's bedtime now so I'll have to close. Tomorrow we arise at 4:45 A.M. and go out to the range. We have some sort of work there for the next ten days, so you see we do need our sleep. Bye for now and remember I love you.

Bernie

Tell your Mom, I'll write her soon.

Sorry about the pencil but some guy borrowed this pen and just returned it.

August 29, 1943

Darling:

Haven't much to say today. Wanted to write you again because I have been neglectful lately not that I wanted to you understand. If. You can figure out that last sentence you're pretty good. Mary, here is another Sunday and nothing to do. I'm quite sure that if I were home with you now things would be much different. We always did have good times together and we always will. Before I forget I want to tell you that your answer to that, "Sermon" was swell. Hon, if you feel the way you write I'm quite sure I've found the only girl in the world. It's going to be hard on both of us to wait but sincerely I do believe we should. Read an article in the **Sunday Visitor** this morning entitled,

"Fight First then Marry"

It read very sensible and has convinced me that we would be wiser to wait. Please don't think though that this alone has decided for me. I've always been against it but loving you as I do almost change my mind. If ever you do change toward me don't forget that very serious letter, "Chub."

We played our first game the other night and tied

4-4. Relieved in the fifth and pitched till the finish of eight innings when darkness fell. Gave up two hits and no runs so, it wasn't so bad for an old man, was it?

My arm was creaking and groaning on every pitch. Lack of throwing will affect one's arm like that you know. Mary, I feel so darn silly today. Ah, young love. Well you're young anyway.

Bill seems to be a jitterbug, doesn't he? Guess I'll have to wise him up next time I'm home. Is he all set for Basketball this winter? Bet he can't wait. Sure, am glad your family takes to athletics. To me it's everything outside of you.

Suppose I'd better close now before you tire of reading this. I love you and miss you more each day. Best regards to the family and tell your Mother I won't forget that letter.

Love
Bernie

September 17, 1943

Darling:

By now I suppose you know where I am and why. This sure is a soft life. Came in Wednesday and haven't done a thing. They've given me blood tests and blood count and now I'll just wait for developments.

Since Tuesday my mail hasn't been delivered so one of these days, I'll be pretty busy reading your letters.

Somehow, there isn't much to write about today but there is always the weather. It is raining. Well, that takes care of that. War news seems to be much better today. If things keep going like they are we may see an early victory. Finally getting down to the real thing. As you know wars must be won on the ground. Those poor guys over there now are really taking the brunt of it all. Invasion is always costly but as they say, "that is war."

Hon, just now I received two letters form you dated the 13th and 14th. You do say the nicest things. Do you really believe that you couldn't live without me? I'm sure you could, but I hope you'll never have to. It would be equally hard for me you know. Yes, someday we will make up all these lonely days. Maybe being apart so long will make us appreciate being together more than ever. We are having quite a hard time of it, but we're not alone. When we finally do marry, I hope I

Am able to make you happier than you've ever been before. Whatever happens we must make a success of our marriage and we will. Two people with common sense should be able to get along together, Agree? Well, I'm about to eat lunch now so will bid you a fond goodbye for a few days.

Still am very much in love and miss you always.

Love,
Bern.

Best regards to your family. Will write your Mother soon.

September 21, 1943

Darling:

Guess what has happened now? I have been sent back to duty and I'm getting the old runaround again. They decided I wasn't a serious enough case, so they will not operate until I become so bad that it must be done. Hon, this Army has me stumped. Two different Dr's OK'd the operation but the one that counted said no.

Mary, every day my debt to and love for you grows greater. Just now your package arrived along with the card and telegram. Don't know what to say. Know all this was for a sick guy and now being back on Duty I feel funny. When I read your "Get Well" card and Telegram I really laughed because I don't believe I've ever felt better in my life. Hon don't ever believe that my love for you comes from all these swell things you do for me. They all help, but I'd love you if you never sent me a thing and do wish you wouldn't be so generous Here I am, unable to buy anything for you but someday I do hope to atone for everything. Glad that you visited Matt the other day. Had a taste of his life and it's pretty lonesome. He likes you already and those visits will make you good friends. I've found out that he can be a very special friend and his getting well makes the world all OK again.

Hon was sorry to hear about your Grandmother. Seems like there has to be trouble always. If it's not one thing it's another. I hope she'll be all right soon and if you will give her my regards.

Darling, don't like to stop writing but as usual, time is limited. Want to thank you again for all you've done. Darn it, words won't and can't express how I feel. Do you know what I mean? I'm sure you do so "Wait for me Mary." It won't be too long and think of all the swell years we'll have just looking back on these lonely days. Loving you always, I remain as ever

Your Sweetheart
Bern

Boy, isn't that a fancy ending? See what the hospital did for me? It's amazing. Do you think I could get a "Section 8" Meaning----Nuts.

September 29, 1943

Darling:

Received your very swell letter the other day. You'll never know how much a few words from you mean, such as, "I Love You" Knowing that you really care for me makes these months a little easier to stand. I should say a Big Little.

Hon, it's happened. They've sent me back to the hospital and this time the operation probably will be done. Don't know when or where but I'll let you know when they inform me of the same.

So, the bus threw you for a loss. Mary, I don't know what to do about you. I think you had better marry me as soon as the war ends. Remember how I used to laugh at you on those icy sidewalks. Bet you could have socked me one for that. Don't let a little thing like that bother you. I've taken quite a number of spills myself without the aid of a Bus Driver.

I'm at a loss for words except to say that I love you and miss you very much. This seems a very short letter in exchange for your nice long one but it's the best I can do. I'll write again in a day or so. Bye now and

Love always,
Bern

Give my best regards and love to your family and thank your Grandmother for remembering me.

Suppose Bill is having quite a time with his "gal."

He sure is way ahead of me. When I was 16, I didn't know what a girl was and didn't care. Give him credit for being much braver than me.

Bye.

October 1, 1943

Darling

Well, here's your Physical Specimen again. Just think at one time I was 1A in the Army. Mary, wait till you hear this. I have been through my operation, but it wasn't for a Hernia. This time it was for hemorrhoids. Do you know what they are? They are pretty painful and also very embarrassing. They brought me over here Tuesday as you know and yesterday at 9:00 A.M. they gave me a spinal and now I'm confined to bed for a few days. The operation itself was nothing but a certain region is a bit sore at the moment. I have my compensations though. I can write you more often and I will be able to hear the World Series. Pretty slick, aren't I?

Darling will you excuse this short letter for now? I'm not at my best but the next letter will be longer, I promise you. Love you and miss you forever and ever.

Bye now
Love always
Bern

Now don't laugh at me you bum.

October 2, 1943

Darling,

Just had to write you to keep from going crazy. That is not the only reason of course because I really do enjoy it. Things are very peaceful and uneventful here. Believe it or not but it is now October 3rd. Started this letter with good intentions but one of the other patients came over and started a lengthy conversation. Have made quite a few friends here and we a have pretty good time when we are all feeling good. This operation is rather painful but, in a week, I hope to be my old self again. They claim will be here for a month, so I'll be writing you pretty often. You may also expect a call sometime soon. Will let you know before I do though.

Hon, I sure wish that you could be here with me now. Miss you so much but then I shouldn't kick, should I? Mary, I sometimes wonder if the people back home appreciate all the things those boys over there are doing. They deserve the best of everything when they come home, and I certainly hope they get it. By the way, the war news looks good, doesn't it?

Are you all enthused about the World Series next week? That's something I'm really waiting for. I'll be able to hear every game this year. Want to bet on the outcome? Still picking the "Cards" so you'll have to take the "Yanks".

Well, Kid, I'm lost again as usual. I bet your Mother is still waiting for her letter. She'll get it real soon now for I have nothing else but time. Say, how is your Grandmother Ruhnke? Haven't heard from you since last Monday so I don't know anything. My mail has been delayed again but expect all of it tomorrow. Please tell me how all of you are and I hope the news is all good. As you know my side of the house is improving so maybe that's a good sign.

This time for sure is the end. Be a good girl and remember the war can't last forever. All my love always.

Bernie

Please excuse this writing. A bed isn't too good a desk.

October 7, 1943

Darling:

Have just received all the mail that has been held back until now. Hon, that letter, you know which one, was a masterpiece. Never have I read anything that stirred me so much. How did I ever happen to meet such a girl as you? You do have more common sense and understanding than anyone I've ever met. You'll never know the feeling of love and gratitude that came over me after reading that letter. Mary, you know I've never doubted you and now I never will. My letter to you was very frank and I was hoping that it wouldn't offend you, but I did want you to know how I felt. Just call it a crazy mood that prompted me to write as I did. Girl, have you made me happy. Your every word was just what I wanted to hear and today my love for you has grown till it's ready to burst.

By the way in making your choice if I can help it, you'll never be sorry. I'll try to be everything you want and expect in a husband. About that "Women's Secrets" business you need not worry. That was just an old saying. There was no reflection on you so don't worry about it.

Mary, I suppose you and Mom had quite a time laughing over me. Can't say that I blame you because it is kind of funny even to all of us. Am getting along much better now and in a few weeks, I'll be back in the harness. Called home today but didn't get to talk to Mom. Unluckily she had just left for the store, but I told the girls I'd call her again soon. Friday night I'll try and get through to you so wait for me. Don't be disappointed if I fail because sometimes it's impossible, as you know.

Darling, I'll close for now, but you'll be hearing often from me. Give my regards to your family.

All My Love
Bern

Will be glad to meet Lt Bob also. He must like you very much, isn't that strange?

October 9, 1943

Dear Ma:

Hope you don't mind me calling you this but that's exactly what you seem to me. You've always treated me swell and I appreciate it very much. Don't believe there are many boys who have been welcomed into a girl's home like I have been in Mary's. You know of course that you have a very fine daughter and I can't say too much about her.

By now I suppose you've heard all about the operation. It's not so bad but you'll never know how many times my face has turned red these past few weeks. The embarrassment is the worst part of it all.

When you answer this, I want you to be sure and tell me what you've been doing and how you are feeling these days. Has your Mother gotten rid of that California love yet? Have never been to California but so far, I've never seen a better place than Chicago or Oak Park. You tell her she better stay in the good old Windy City.

I've told you before that I'm not much of a letter writer and this letter proves it. Wish that I could write a long and interesting letter but it's not a gift with me. Mary is about as good at that as anyone

I've met. She always manages to tell me all the news at home and then she adds a little "mush" What a gal.

Ma, tell Bill I hope he has a swell season of Basketball and wish that I could see some of his games. Before it was work and now war that has kept me from seeing him play. One of these days I hope to be a free man. Bill is my idea of a good American boy. As long as he has a love of Athletics and his family you haven't a thing to worry about. By the way I still have ambitions of helping him make quite a ball player of himself.

Well, guess this about all I have to say. Wish you'd say hello to Marty and tell him to drop a line when he has time. Give my regards to all of the family and write soon. Bye now.

With Love
Bernie

I'm still betting on the Cards

October 12, 1943

Darling,

Haven't been doing so good lately but your phone call helped to bridge the gap. I hope. Sure was swell of you to call and hearing your voice again was a positive cure. To prove it, they are sending me to convalescent ward today. As you know, they'll keep me there for two weeks and then it's back to duty. Hon, I can't wait for that next furlough to see you. This everlasting war sure has cost us a lot of happiness, but we aren't alone, are we?

Has your Mother gotten over the shock of that letter yet? Really surprised all of you I suppose because it did seem that I never would write her.

Mary, very little happens around this hospital and it's hard to find anything to write about. We don't do

Much here but eat and sleep and play cards once in a while. Not that the World Series is over it will be deader than ever. The Cards aren't quite as food as we thought they were, but they did make every game interesting. It's the old story, no hitting in the clutch.

Darling, I hope you'll excuse this poor letter. Just wanted you to know that I'm thinking of you always. Said it over the phone, for once and I'll say it again, I love you.

Bye now and be good.

Love Always
Bern

Best regards to all please.

October 18, 1943

Dearest:

I am awfully sorry that I haven't written you sooner. Have a few extra things to do now that I'm "convalescing" such as helping to clean up the ward and also drilling two hours each day. Course that doesn't take up all my time but, I seem to be one of the few Pinochle players here and we are always playing.

Darling, last night before going to sleep I had some very pleasant recollections of you and the longing to be with you was almost too strong. DO you know what I was thinking? Well, of all things, it was about the Sundays I used to eat dinner with your family, and I could see you plain as day helping with the dinner and then washing the dishes.

Have you recovered as yet? Mary those aren't the only moments I've spent with you that I cherish. Every moment was swell but never appreciated like they should have been. Never thought we would have to be apart so long and never did realize how lonesome these months could be. Yes, it must be and is love.

AM glad your Mother like the letter and tell her I'm awaitin' Speaking of writing letters I believe I owe you at least five answers. Received a swell letter from the Surface Lines Schedule Department and they all said *"hello and good health"*

You know, one of those letters where each person writes a few lines. Thought that was pretty nice of them. Don't know if I told you or not but the Queen of Angels Ball Club sent me the same kind, so you can see that I have a few letters to get in the mail.

Hon, one page seems to me my limit these days so please have patience. Maybe something of interest will happen soon. In the meantime, I'll keep telling you that I love you and miss you always.

Bye now and give my love to your family.

Love
Bernie

October 26, 1943

Dearest,

You've been expecting this, haven't you? My writing has his a new low lately as you know but as always, here is my alibi. The convalescent ward in the army is the same as being back on duty and apparently, they are trying to prove it. We were supposed to go on a seven-mile hike today, but it rained and what a swell rain it was. WE do have a pretty busy day and the only time we are free is from 6-9 P.M. Right now, I'm supposed to be at chow, but I decided to write you until the line gets a bit smaller.

Just finished writing that last line when one of our patients told me all was clear, so now I've eaten and will continue writing to the best gal in the world. You'll always be that to me, Mary Eileen.

Well, how was the weekend vacation? Did you girls pain the town "red" or is it impossible? If it's anything like Columbia, you probably saw a few shows and wondered home to listen to the radio. I've been to town twice on passes from the hospital and what I time I had. One of the fellows went with me and we saw a show, ate hamburgers and played pool. Exciting, you bet. Mary, before I go on, I have to tell you about one of the fellows in our ward. He's from Texas and has the typical drawl and every time he talks, I laugh. Here's the funniest part about him though. If her were older and fatter he'd be a Second Wallace Beery. In fact, he should be in pictures himself because he's crazier than anyone I ever saw. One thing about the Army is the different types you meet. Since I've been in the hospital, I've made a whole bunch of friends and they are all OK. Wish they were in my Company because it seems that Anti-Tank came up with a bunch of lemons. Guess they are all too young for me or something.

Darling, I love you still and always will and miss you like I would my right arm, or should I say my head?

Feel silly again tonight but when I said I loved you and missed you it was serious. Until I see you again be a good girl and take care of yourself for me.

Bye now and All my Love.

Say hello to the family. I miss them too.

October 31, 1943

Dearest:

Another week has rolled by and now finally I'm back to Duty. Feeling pretty good and hope to continue that way. Whatever happens I don't want to go through anything like that again. Oh, what misery. Remember that saying. Don't want you to get me wrong. It wasn't so bad, and I did have a small vacation. Hon, inside of two and a half months, I'll get a 14-day furlough and I hope it will come around New Years. It has been three months since we were together, but it seems much longer. Can't imagine two whole weeks of freedom with you. Seems almost too good to be true.

Mary, will you tell your Mother I received her letter and it was swell. She'll be hearing from me and I hope this time she won't have to wait so long. Hon, I'm becoming worse and worse at writing. Have a one way mind these days and it's all you. All I can think of is being with you, loving you and never going away again. If you'll excuse me for tonight, I'll appreciate it. After tomorrow I may have something to tell you but until my next letter I'm stopped. Regards and love to your family and hope to see all of them soon. Darling Goodnight and Love Always.

Bern

What do you think of Notre Dame? Are the Rebels mad when they win? Guess they can't stand to see a Catholic College on top.

November 4, 1943

Mary Darling,

I suppose you are patiently waiting for this letter. You must be used to me by now, or are you? Hon, you probably know by now that I am getting transferred to Special Service. There my duties will consist entirely of Athletics and has that made me feel like a new man. I haven't been too well satisfied here and have always wanted something that is more interesting. The Air Corp wouldn't have me as I am, so this will take its place. I'll tell you all about it when I get home. Our second furloughs are starting Monday and I hope it won't be too long now. Mary, since you tell me so often that you love me, I'll tell you I never get tired of hearing it. Your love is the one great thing in my life. You're so darn good and thoughtful and on top of all that you are a very pretty gal. Every time I see a tall dark girl my heart jumps and then comes the disappointment. You've read where the trend is leaning toward the tall stately girls now, but I've always preferred them that way. That column you sent me always mentions about them, so you see you aren't too heavy for your height. In fact, you're perfection.

Mary, we are wearing our O.D.'s and they are much better than the Khakis. They are much classier, and we are the well-dressed soldiers these days.

Hon, after such a long interval this letter should contain more news but there isn't much to tell you tonight. Do want you to give my love to your folks and tell you Mom I'll do it or bust. Your letters are still very regular and very interesting so please don't stop. Goodnight for now and I love you and miss you always.

Bernie

November 8, 1943

Darling:

Miss Ruhnke, I received your letter and the pictures today and both were swell. Don't think your picture did you justice though. I have one in my wallet that is tops and it is really you. Well, now I'll have my two favorite women folk with me always. Say hon, I'm still a Private in this Army. It's true that eventually it will lead to something, but I still have to make good. This Basketball and Football business is tough to referee because I've done very little of it, but with experience I should do OK. It's a swell break and will do my best to merit the appointment.

Do you know that life is very lonesome and uninteresting without you? I've thought of nothing else but you for so long that I believe you are actually haunting me. Mary, how I envy these Soldiers wo have their wives living in Colombia. If you only knew how much I want to marry you. What I wouldn't do to walk up the aisle and pledge to love you always isn't possible. DO you get that last sentence? It's kind of mixed up but hope you understand. In plain English it means that I want you and need you very much. See?

It's all my fault I guess that we aren't hitched, but hon, I just couldn't see myself giving you nothing and taking all. Does that sound familiar?

So, all of you women are going on a diet now? Well, it's a good idea and maybe I should too. They say the less you carry around the longer you live, and I want to live with you a long time. By the way, I read of a good morning exercise and maybe you'd like to try it.

This clipping here will explain all. You know since the Army teaches so much physical training, I'll have to keep up with it after the War is over. It really does a lot of good. Don't take this story as a hint. You are and always were 100% with me long legs.

Before I forget, I want you to give my Congratulations to your Aunt Grace and Uncle Harold. They are doing all right and I'm glad they got what they wanted. Hope someday that we can follow in their footsteps, which reminds me, I saw **Pat O'Brian** in the **Iron Major** last night. It was pretty good, and this one scene showed him walking the floor waiting for his first child. He ended up with ten and went to war besides. What a man.

Dearest, I'm doing pretty good for a change, aren't I? This is about the longest letter I've written you in two months. There's one thing I haven't mentioned yet. The weather in S. Carolina today was very wet. It rained all day and pretty hard at times. They say we are about due for a lot of this kind of weather now. One more thing, I'm still in the 106th so I do have to make all the Bivouacs*. (tents)

There is one starting Thursday and we'll be in the field till the 24th of this month. Then we come in and have our big Thanksgiving Dinner. After that my Furlough shouldn't be too far away and confidentially, I can't wait.

Well, me love, I've rattled enough for tonight so please excuse me and keep you heart filled with love. I can stand every bit of it and I hope that you never find cause to change your mind. Guess you know by now what I've been trying to tell you all this time.

I love you, you nut.

So long Chub and I'll be seeing you soon, I hope and pray.

Bern

Is your Mom still waiting? Give her and your Gram and Bill my love.

Sue wrote me but like a dope I lost her address. Would you all be so kind as to send it to me?

Heard a new song with **Gene Autry** doing the singing. It's **Rosalita** and very pretty it is lassie. You'll find my new address on the envelope. Bye

November 13, 1943

Darling:

This won't be a very long letter, but I want to let you know that I'm still thinking of you. We are out in the field and writing facilities are scarce. Hon, in case you are interested this is about how our schedule will run for the next four months. This Bivouac ends the 24th of November and then December 6th I'll be home for eleven days at least. Our regular training ends January 8th, and sometime in February our Maneuvers start. So, you see we do have most of the hard work over with now. They will, after the Maneuvers, give us another ten-day furlough, so that's not such a bad future is it? We were going to get fifteen days this time, but they have cut the, down a few days. Mary, it's hard to believe that I'll be seeing you in person in less than a month.

It will be a little hard leaving you again before Christmas, but seeing you anytime is enough for me.

Darlin, I'm sorry this letter is so brief, but I'm too excited to write. Pretty soon we can talk to each other again and then you can hear all and so can I. Tell the folks hello and give them my love.

Bye for now, Beautiful.

Love Always,
Bern

November 25, 1943

Hello Darlin:

Guess by this time you have given up hope of getting this letter. Will admit that I have been very lax and deserve a good talking to. You will get your chance very soon and even that will make me feel swell. Talking to you in any way on any subject is almost too good to be true.

Hon, while out in the field I missed out on some of your letters and have just finished reading all of them. Was sorry to hear that you had a cold and now I'm glad that you are feeling better. So, you are doing your daily dozen now, I'll have to watch that some day when I get home. Mary, I'm getting so darn anxious to see you that each day seem a year. It won't be long now though so maybe I can stand the suspense.

We have just finished eating our Thanksgiving Dinner and was it swell. We had turkey with all the trimmings and every one of us had plenty. Wasn't bad at all but we did miss the home atmosphere.

Hon, everything is going fine here, and I'll explain all when I see you. Until then I'll try to write two or three more letters, just because I love you. You are absolutely right; I am a terrible letter correspondent. Be a good girl and remember always, I love you and miss you too much. Bye now and say hello to your family for me.

LOVE
Bern.

Have to use up a full page somehow.

Hope all of you had a very nice Thanksgiving with as good a dinner as we did.

Bye, Kid.

Almost forgot to thank you for the cookies, they were swell all of the fellows think you have great possibilities.

December 17, 1943

Darling:

Here I am safe and sound again. Mary, I miss you already and these next few months will be the longest and loneliest I'll ever spend. Wonder if this war will ever end. Leaving home this time was harder than ever before. Death couldn't be much worse than the feeling of emptiness on that lousy train. Hon, I hope you and your family continue in good health and all of you write as often as you can. Was sorry about not seeing your folks again and hope they understand. Haven't too much time so I'll stop this here.

Best regards to all and to you. Love Always, Bern

December 22, 1943

Darling:

Today I received a package and two letters from you, and I must admit that you are the most wonderful girl in the World. Of course, I knew that all the time, but your taste in picking gifts for me is exceptional. Each time you seem to know exactly what I need, which is a great talent, mam. Hon, I love you so darn much, but I do wish you would be less generous with presents. Want you to always think of me and love me but I don't expect you to spend your hard-earned money on me. Suppose all this falls on deaf ears because I know you pretty well also. Before I leave this subject, I want you to know that I appreciate your sell gifts and they have made me a very satisfied person. Here I am with a great gal and she is in love with me. What else can any man ask for except that she be his wife forever. Hon, that day will come, and I hope and pray it won't be too long now. By the way, you may marry an old satisfied pipe smoker. Bought some Bond Street Tobacco today and I really enjoy smoking this new way. Mary, I'll write your Mother soon and thank her for her present. She, like her daughter was far too generous and it makes me feel awful. Here I haven't even sent a Christmas card her way. Give her my love and thanks.

Well, today at noon we finished our Bivouacs and it was a relief. We are getting right down to Battle Conditions now and it is a bit tough. We have to move in the middle of the night under Blackout conditions and that along with these cold nights makes for a hard time. We'll be leaving again Monday for another nine days, so you can see we aren't getting too much time for pleasure.

Afraid you'll be the only one I'll ever dance with but then that doesn't bother me. These "Rebel" gals can't compare with you all.

Hon, will you give your whole family my very best wishes for a Merry Christmas and the Happiest New Year they've ever known. If I have tune tomorrow to buy some cards I will but as you say, you know me. That reminds me, I hope you get your Christmas present in time. As usual you'll receive it through family, and I hope you don't mind that procedure. Would like to give it to you in person, but I just can't do it.

Darling, I'm going to bed now, so this is the end. I love you now and always will. Bye for now and say a prayer for me once in a while.

Love,
Bernie

Hope your Gram's cold is better by now.

December 29, 1943

Hello again, how are you? OK I hope, and you'd better stay that way. Say Kid, how do you like the new way of being engaged? Bet nobody ever thought of that before. Seriously though, I'm sorry and wish you'd keep on loving this dope, please?

Well, since I wrote you last a few changes have been made and all for the better. You remember I told you about us facing those two weeks in the field? The Bivouacs is on, but this lucky guy is sitting in a nice warm warehouse in Winnsboro South Carolina taking life comparatively easy. We are resupplying empty PX trucks and outside of a busy time now and then, life is very enjoyable. We are sleeping on beds and for amusement we play Pinochle and listen to a radio. Do you think I deserve such a break as this?

Your letters are still breaking all records and does that make me mad. If it weren't for you, I believe I'd be lost. You'll never know just how much each and every one of them mean to me. Yes hon, you've been my main "Morale Builder" ever since March 17th. You did all right those many months before but since then I've needed you much more.

Guess all of you have about recovered from your Christmas day by now. Now all you have to worry about is New Year's Eve. Last year about this time we were having a pretty enjoyable evening and this year?

We can always console ourselves though by imagining just what we'd be doing if we were together.

Why do I write like that? It makes me feel worse instead of better. Chub, you just wait. Someday you're going to see so much of me you'll wish I was in the Army again. You'd better not ever wish that, you brat.

Darling, It's 12:30 A.M. here and about time for bed. I'll write again soon and let you know all about this town. Suppose it's about the same as all of these "Rebel towns," Goodnight and I love you now and forever. The radio is playing "Where or When" Hope it's soon.

Love Bern

By the way, I'll try to be there when you receive your Wedding Ring.

Give my love and best regards to all.

Chapter 38

New Year New Challenges 1944

F38.1 January 1, 1944

Dad missed the year date change from 1943 to 1944. That is not too hard to do when you first write the date at the start of a new year. It takes Dad until his January 12th letter to use 1944 as the year. I am confident about the dates because of the envelope's stamped date. Time must really stand still for these men and women and for the ones at home waiting.

The radio was playing, **"Where or When,"** he told her, and then he wrote, **"hope it is soon… by the way I'll try to be there when you receive your wedding ring?"**

Well this seems to be a more concrete statement that wedding plans are in the works. The only hint to their future plans I can deduct from this letter was the reference to a wedding ring. Dad asked how she liked his way of getting engaged. I have no idea if that conversation took place when Dad was home last or not. It became clearer and clearer how much we don't ask our parents while they are still with us. There is a lesson here for those of you that are reading this right now and are blessed to still have your parents in your life. Ask the questions now, before there is no one left to ask.

Jan 1, 1943

Darling;

A few short lines this evening to a swell girl from a lonely & sad soul. Haven't recieved a letter of any kind for 4 days now but they'll be waiting for me back in Ft. Jackson. As you know your daily letters are my one & only protection from absolute insanity. Our training is now in the very dull & tiresome stages & we keep looking for some outlet. Mary, since being in Special Service I've had a pretty easy life but its not what I had hoped for. We have so much idle time on our hands that the days seem to have no end. While in the A.T. Co they worked us hard & you'd be surprised how fast those months went by. Guess it's the same old story. A fellow is never satisfied in the Army no matter what he is doing. Here I am, safe & sound & still there comes forth from this mortal, loud moans & groans. Maybe it's not the Army life itself but the fact that I can't be with you that accounts for it. Mary, "old kid," if this War doesn't end & allow me to marry you in a very short time, don't blame me for going crazy. I miss you more every day & being under your spell as I am, is, to put it mildly, "hell". Don't tell me. I know I've got

big feet.
How's the family, Hon? Don't know how any of you are but I trust all of you are well & looking forward to a great New Year. By the way, is Bill's team still winning. No matter what sport you're in if it's not a winner the biggest thrill is missing. Tell him I'm wishing him & the team the best of luck. Your Mother & Grandmother will be hearing from me soon. That's the truth, even though you are laughing.
"Honey Chile," due to an important Pinochle game this will now be concluded for tonight. I love you & don't ever forget it. Bye now & best regards to all
Love always
Benn

F38.2 January 2, 1944

Dad figured out he was writing the wrong year on his letters! I love how he expressed himself; **"Dog Gone It."** That was one of my Dad's favorite sayings when I was a kid. It always made me laugh because I couldn't really figure out what it meant. Dog Gone It? A long time later I figured out that it was his very Catholic way of not using the Lords name in vain.

Dog gone it's
Jan. 2, 1943

Darling:

Surprised? Well, here is the reason for this unexpected letter. Forgot to congratulate you on leaving M.M. & taking that swell new job. I've never exactly relished the idea of you working there & now that you're left it suits me fine. Know that they treated you O.K. but outside of a few they weren't the "Elite" of Chicago. Yes, I too have a soft spot in my heart for the place so we won't forget it entirely.

Have you been writing me regularly since last Sunday?

Hope you have because I expect about five of your letters to be waiting for me back in Port.)
Hon, the rumors have us leaving here very soon so don't be too surprised to hear about it in my next letter or two. Maybe they aren't true but who knows? Think I'll be able to tell you where we are going so that's a break, anyway.

Well, that's all for tonight. Be a good girl & pray hard for me. I'll always love you, Mary

Love

Bern.

We've been having a nice week here in this town. It's a lucky break for me because it has been raining quite a bit. Wouldn't be much fun out in the field in this weather. (Quote) "Southern girls are strictly, "Jerks"!" (Unquote)

Chapter 39

The Engagement

January 9, 1944 Mom and Dad are engaged. I am sure they did not actually get engaged on that exact date because engagement was brought up in a previous letter. The following letter where he wrote, that they were now an engaged couple happens to be one of those dates that coinsides with a special date in our family. January 9 is my younger brother Bill's birthday. It just so happens while I am editing this book today, it is January 9, 2020 and it is my baby brother Bill's 60th birthday. The dates throughout Dad's letters have many such dates that have meaning to our family. In a later letter dated January 16, 1944 Dad mentioned their engagement announcement in the paper Mom sent to him and he carried in his wallet. The day when they were married and they could announce it to the world is all he had on his mind.

Dad mentioned at the end of this next letter that after the war he will be back at work and he said, **"for the first time in his life, work will be a pleasure"** the war had taught him that.

I wish I could have reminded him of that when he was so miserable at his job at the CTA for so many years.

F39.1 January 9, 1944

Jan. 9, 1943

Darling:

Hello, for the first time in a week. Now before we go any farther I'll tell you what I'm telling Mom. I have been the busiest guy in the 106th. Our Basketball tournament is in progress & they are running me ragged. It's over Tuesday & what a relief that will be.

Well, my future wife are you happy being engaged to me? You've made a bad bargain but if you aren't complaining, why should I? I do know this much. I'm the happiest & the saddest guy all at the same time.

Happy because we are engaged & sad because we'll have to wait for the end of this war to be married. If you only knew how much I miss you. Well, maybe our love will be that much stronger when we finally do get hitched.

Glad to hear that Bill's team is on top. Know how good a feeling it is to be winning & hope they continue that way. Tell him that the time will come when I can teach him what little I know about hitting. Maybe we'll make a pitcher out of him too. Mary return my love to your family & tell them hello. Bet your Mother is still waiting for her letters.

Why did you call me Mush? Don't you know that its your fault? I can't help it. Hon, the Maneuvers are to be held in Tennessee from the

31st of January till the 27th of March. Our starting point will be from a town called Murphysboro & where will end up nobody knows. Of course this is mostly rumor but it's almost correct anyway. You know, it will seem funny leaving this place but we can't stay here forever.

Darling, will you pardon me for now? I'm a bit tired & want to clean up before going to bed. I'll love you always & keep loving me, will you? So long, hon.

Love
Bernie

So you are keeping up with the rest of the gals. Well, I always claimed you were beautiful & now

you'll probably blame me.
Do want you to buy yourself
all the clothes you need & don't
be saving everything to support
me. It won't take me long to
get going again after the war.
Now, for the first time in my
life work will be a pleasure.
The war has taught me that
anyway.

F39.2 January 12, 1944

Jan 12, 1944.

Hello Hon;

Don't know whether I'll be able to finish this tonight but I'll try. Have just finished K.P. & I will admit to feeling tired. Its a tough job, Kiddo, & here is my Post War & Pre-Marriage Resolution. If you ever ask me to wash or dry a dish be prepared for a fight - quickly. Well, there will be one consolation anyway. You wont be wearing stripes & besides even that would be a pleasure with you near me. Never thought I'd miss you so much but its true & it grows worse daily. Guess what? It is now Jan. 14 at 12:20 in the afternoon. Couldn't

finish this the other night &
since then this is my first free
moment. Worked late last night
again & when I came home
the bed looked too good.

Your Mothers' letter was
swell & now I really have to
sit down & write her.

Mary, as usual, I'm in a
hurry so I'll have to close this
for now. Your letters are
so darn nice & you make me
feel great when you say all
those swell things. I love you
very much & knowing that
you will always be the same helps.
You needn't worry about me so
don't ever. Whatever happens I'll
at least be honest with you &
know that you will be with me.
Bye now & love always.

Bern.

Jan. 16, 1944

Darling:

Your very nice letter came this morning containing the announcement of our engagement. I have it here in my wallet & it is something to be proud of but the day we can tell the World we are married will be the proudest of my life.

Hon, the cookies came this morning & as usual they tasted swell. On top of all your other good characteristics it looks like you are also a good cook. Yes, I have found me a wonderful girl & do I love her.

Mary, we're about set to move out now & Fort. Jackson will soon be a memory.

F39.3 January 16, 1944

Will be a much happier guy when this whole War is a memory & I'm thinking it won't be too long now.

Hon, this letter is just to bridge the gap so I'll cut it short for tonight. Will write you about Thursday & tell you everything. By the way, you'd better stop writing Tuesday or Wednesday because we'll probably be gone this weekend.

Best regards to the family & all my love to you Mush. Bye now

Bern

F39.4 January 19, 1944 Letter to My Grandma

Plans for the future were evidently underway. Dad was thanking Mom's mother for her congratulations and promised to **"make Mary happy!"** In an earlier letter Dad mentioned it was going to be so hard to wait until the end of the war to get married. Do you think Mary Eileen was going to let that happen?

Jan 19, 1944

Dear Ma Ruhnke:

Well, that's almost a reality now & hope it won't be long untill Mary & I can make it final. Your very nice letter was recieved & it was truly welcome. You probably know that a letter means quite a bit to us & we appreciate every one we get. Your wonderful Daughter sure has been swell in writing me every day. Don't know how she does it but each one is interesting & I am always waiting for her next. Maybe love has something to do with it, I don't know. Want to thank you for your Congratulation Wishes. Ma, You needn't worry about me making

Mary happy. If its within my power she'll be one of the happiest because I'd do most anything for her. Don't tell her that because I don't think she suspects me of being so sentimental. She has been so darn good to me that even if I tried I couldn't help but think that she's the best, ever.

Well, we are leaving here Friday for our Maneuver Area in Penn. Will be there for two months & then about the first of April we'll be heading for another Camp. Nobody knows where we'll go so until that day comes one guess is as good as another. Hope its in good Yankee Country though. The South has lost what little appeal it ever had for me.

Mary tells me your Mother is getting ready to leave for California again. It seems like she has found one place better than Chicago. Give her my love & tell her to take care of herself. Maybe, if some of these rumors are true we may see each other out in "the Golden West".

Guess I've reached the end of something to write about for now. Please write again when you can & so will I. Untill then Bye Love

Bernie

Regards to Bill & I'm still pulling for Oak Park. Neptycar he'll be a regular & I hope I'll be able to see most of his games as a citizen (civilian)

P. S. Please note the new address & report same to Mary E.

Chapter 40

On the Move

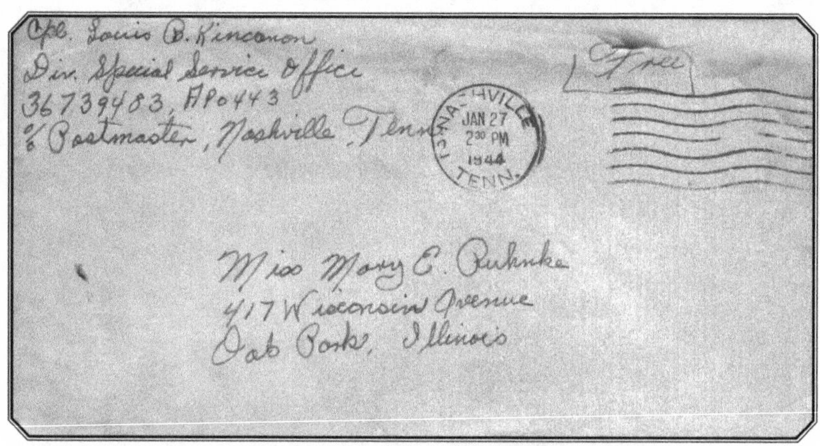

F40.1 January 26, 1944

"Your last six letters caught up with me this morning and what a pleasure they were after five days of loneliness"

Dad was on the move; his troop had left South Carolina and were now stationed in Nashville, Tennessee and he had asked Mom to hold off writing until he knew where he was going to be stationed. Now those letters, six to be exact had reached him and he was one happy man. Tennessee, right outside of Murphysboro, was home to 30,000 soldiers. When Dad went into town, he mentioned that it was overrun with soldiers. The hungry soldiers were not even able to get into any of the restaurants because it was so crowded. He mentioned he only saw a total of 5 civilians while in town. I wonder what the towns people were thinking.

It sure had to be a boost to their economy.

By the sound of this letter Dad was sure feeling his love for his girl back home. It feels to me reading this letter that he was very secure in their love for each other, he writes;

"It sure helps to know that you'll be right there waiting when all this is over" Most fellows haven't the utmost confidence in their gals, as I have in you."

Jan. 26, [illegible]

Hello Darling;

Your last six letters caught up with me this morning & what a pleasure they were after five days of loneliness. Mary, the fellows are beginning to suspect that we love each other. Can you imagine that? They cant understand how I ever fooled you. I cant either but I'm sure glad I did.

Well, we are situated in Tennessee about 5 miles from Murfreesboro. You were right, It really is a burg. We stopped there last night for a cup of Coffee & couldnt even get in a Restaurant. Soldiers have taken the town over & we saw about 5 Civilians. There is another Division here, the 78th, & they will be our Enemy. That makes about 30,000 Soldiers all situated around that one little town. Nashville is 30 miles from here but it may as well be a thousand.

Hon, you do write the nicest letters. It sure helps to know that you'll be right there waiting when all this is over. Most fellows haven't the utmost Confidence in their gals as I have in you. Yes, Mush, some day we will realize all our hopes

& nothing will ever separate us again. As you said getting our happiness the hard way will make us appreciate it much more.

Sorry about the phone call but I couldnt do a thing about it. Your letter telling me about the difficulty didnt reach me untill today. Maybe I'll get a chance to call you one of these days. I have quite a few things to tell you also & the sound of your voice will help a lot.

Mary this isnt much of a letter but there will be more coming. Untill the next, remember I love you very much & miss you always. Be good & give my love to all. Bye now &

Love forever.

Benn.

Remember me to your Grandmother when you write her.

Chapter 41

Good Catholic Girl

F41.1 January 28, 1944

Sometimes, you just have to read the letters. The following letters are full of love, and my words would seem very inadequate.

Jan. 28, 1944

Darling:

It's a bit late to start a letter but I'll try & finish this before retiring. Nothing much has happened the past few days so I haven't much to tell you. The weather continues to be the best & that's a break. We're all holding our breaths though because it can't last. Maybe this winter will be a mild one all over, even Chicago.

Jan 29, 1944

As you can see the tent caught up with me last night & it did feel good. We have been told that after Maneuvers are over we won't be able to sleep in a nice warm bed. Dont hardly believe them [illegible]

2

The floor or ground is hard at first but after a few weeks nothing bothers you. Oh, before I forget, the weather report: A bit cooler but the Sun Continues to shine.

My love, the days are going by pretty fast & I'm wondering just what day in the future will bring us together for good. Furloughs are swell but the after effect is an awful thing. All of these fellows returning from home look like they were doomed to die. The feeling of emptiness stays with you for a month afterwards & then we start looking for another chance to get home. Well, at least we are in the same country, aren't we? The boys over there are not only lonely but they have the threat of death staring them in the face constantly. It must

3

be pretty tough & I don't think
they'll ever forget these years of war.
Mary, you have often told me
that your family & relations think
highly of me. I'm glad they do &
to be truthful I am very grateful.
You have a fine family & swell relations
& to be in their favor means a lot to me.
Now let me tell you what I personally
think of you. Hon, you are all I ever
expected in a girl. You're a good clean
Catholic girl & I have all the respect in
the world for you. Some time when
I'm home we'll have a good talk & I'll
explain how I feel entirely. I know I've
never paid you too many compliments
but if I hadn't loved you & respected you
we wouldn't be engaged. You've been

4

swell to me in every way even
when things weren't looking so
good for us. You bet. I've been
thinking of our first year together
& of all the things you said & did. We
sure have had fun & on the other hand
we've had a few troubles too. Don't
believe anything will stop us from being
happy now because we've come through
everything in good shape. Say, Beautiful,
this is a very rare serious moment with
me, so don't get worried. Maybe it's
the Tennessee Woods.

Excuse me for now & I'll write
you again soon. Love you & miss you
more than ever. Bye now & Love always

Bern.

Hello to Mom & Bill

F41.2 February 3, 1944

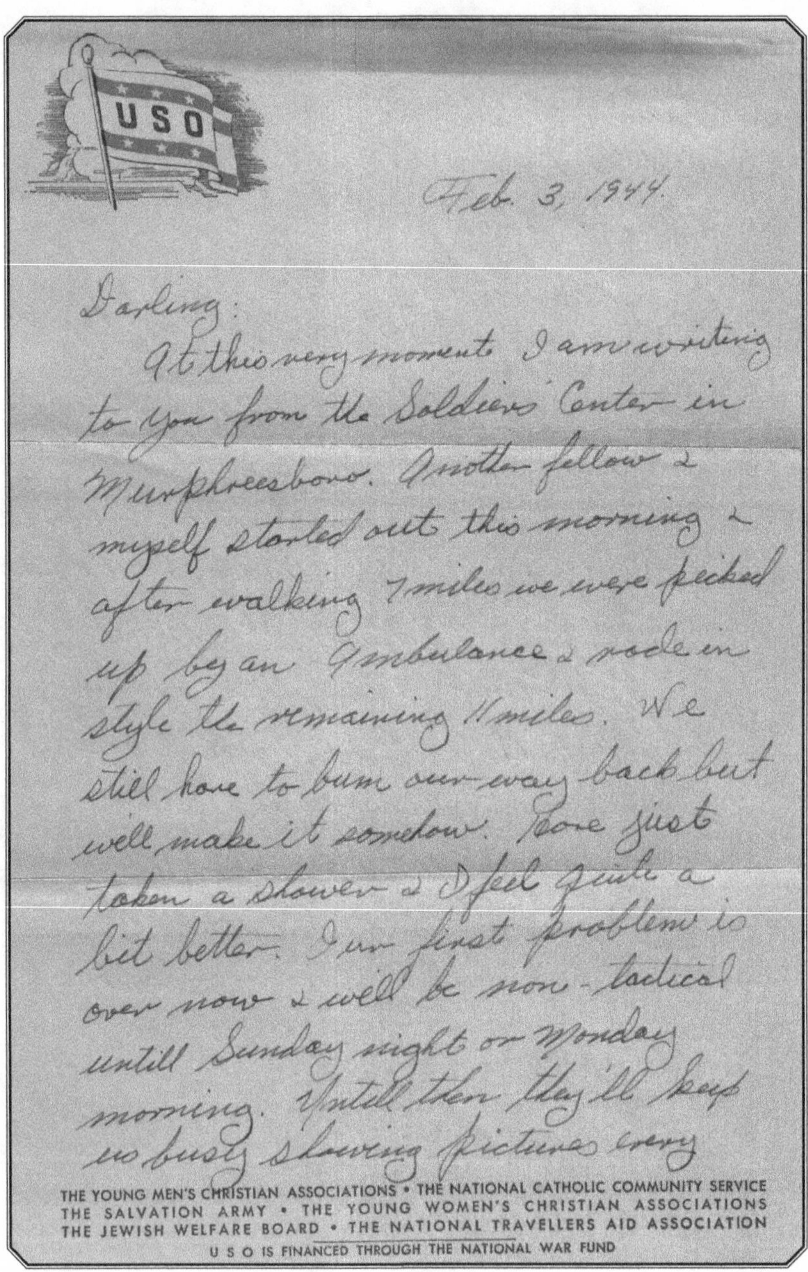

Feb. 3, 1944.

Darling:

At this very moment I am writing to you from the Soldiers' Center in Murphreesboro. Another fellow & myself started out this morning & after walking 7 miles we were picked up by an Ambulance & rode in style the remaining 11 miles. We still have to bum our way back but we'll make it somehow. Have just taken a shower & I feel quite a bit better. Our first problem is over now & we'll be non-tactical untill Sunday night or Monday morning. Untill then they'll keep us busy showing pictures every

THE YOUNG MEN'S CHRISTIAN ASSOCIATIONS • THE NATIONAL CATHOLIC COMMUNITY SERVICE
THE SALVATION ARMY • THE YOUNG WOMEN'S CHRISTIAN ASSOCIATIONS
THE JEWISH WELFARE BOARD • THE NATIONAL TRAVELLERS AID ASSOCIATION
U S O IS FINANCED THROUGH THE NATIONAL WAR FUND

night so you can see that Special Service is always working. It's not so bad though because we do have quite a bit of time to ourselves during the day.

Hon, enough of this Army life. Your letter of the first came this morning & it was swell. Seems like we really do think alike most of the time & that's a good sign. You're swell Mary & I'll always love you.

Darling, I hope you'll excuse me for now. I'm in a hurry to get back but I'll write you again soon. Regards to your folks & I miss them almost as much as I do you. Bye now & love forever

Bernie.

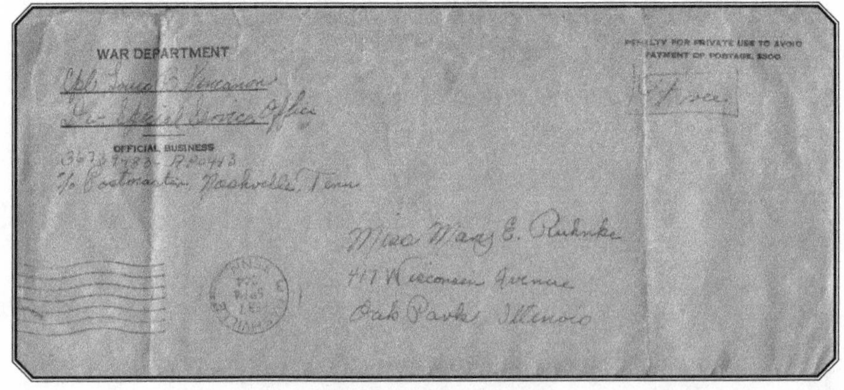

F41.3 February 5, 1944

Feb 5, 1944

Hello Darling:

Before leaving to present a moving picture I'll try to write you a few lines. Nothing new of interest has happened since the last letter. It's still the same old routine of life in the field.

Say, what seems to be the trouble with you? Your last three letters have been telling me that you aren't feeling a bit good. Well, your letter of the 4th just arrived and after reading it through it seems you have recovered. Have a hunch that those visits to the Red Cross aren't agreeing with you. Give you all the credit in the world for doing that but don't let your health

suffer. After all, I do love you
very much & if you're going to
be sick then so am I.
Hon, we can receive packages
out here, but you needn't bother
sending me anything. At the present
time we are eating very well &
besides you've sent me too many
good things already. Some day soon
I hope to repay all the kindness
you have shown me & that's a promise.
Ede does get around doesn't
she? Hope she picks the right guy
out of all those Service men.
Mary, it's time to go now so I'll
leave you for a while. Say hello to
Mom, Bill & Marty for me. In the
meantime I'll go on loving & missing
you as always. Bye Bern.

Please excuse the ripped page. I was in a hurry.

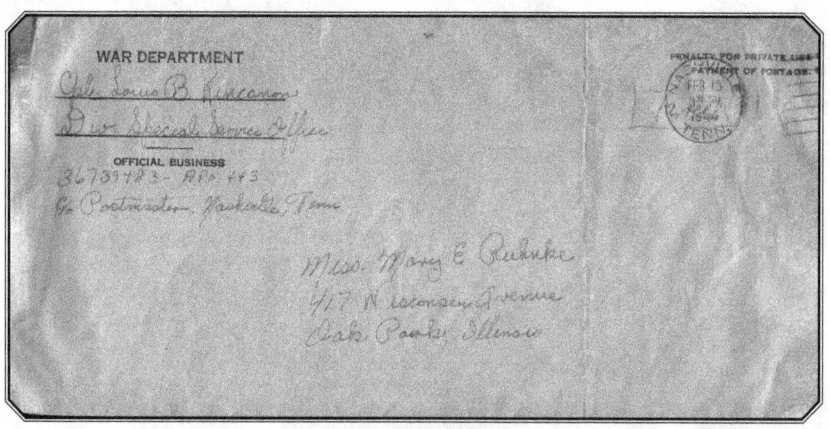

F41.4 February 12, 1944

Feb. 12, 1944

Dearest:

Should have written you before this but it's the same old story. Wednesday night we moved in a pouring rain & Thursday we packed & took off again. Seems like they are really giving this Division the works. The 87th Div. told us that Maneuvers would be comparatively easy but they must have gone at things differently than we are. The days are going by pretty fast though so before we know it we'll be back in some other camp.

Considering your last letter, your Mother had quite a hectic day last week. I hope she didn't hurt herself & that she is feeling OK now.

I recieved another chain letter from the Schedule Dept. & it was swell. They don't forget the boys in Service & every one of us appreciate that fact. One of the boys was wounded in action in Italy & they are all pretty proud of him. Guess he's been in the Army for about two years.

Hon, two months ago we were together but it seems like years. Never will be completely happy untill we are married & together for always. Once I get home it will take quite a necessary trip to ever get me away again. Travel is alright for a while but it doesn't take long to appreciate home & someone like you. That little Poem was absolutely right. Never realized how much I loved you untill I had

to leave & there's an awful empty
feeling with me always.
Mary, that's all for this time. Keep
loving me & pray hard for Victory.
Bye now & regards to Moms Bill.
Love
Ben.
Can't figure out whether I owe your
Mother a letter or not. Please inform
me when you write.

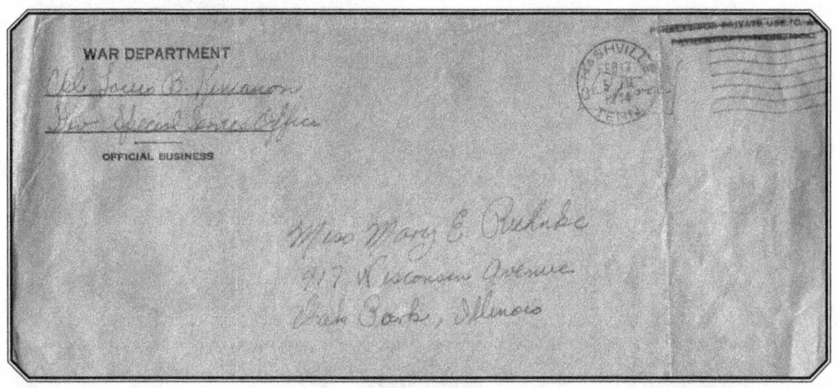

F41.5 February 16, 1944

Feb. 16, 1944.

Hello Hon;

As usual I haven't much to write about but these few lines will help your morale I hope. Many when you hear from me about moving it doesn't mean that we've left Tenn. We just keep jumping around from spot to spot in order to keep up with the rest of the War. When I get home again you'll hear all about Maneuvers & their fine points. While we are out here it's exactly the same as Battle conditions or so they tell us.

So you are having your troubles now? What I am wondering is whether or not you hurt yourself when you fall? What a gal.

Darling, this is a shame I know, closing so suddenly on you but the bed is awaiting. We are due to move again in the morning & sleep tonight is necessary. Will write as soon as possible & promise that the next letter will be much longer. Until then be good, keep loving me & remember I love you & miss you more every day. Bye now Much

Don.

Regards & love to Mom & Bill.

Don't forget, I'm going to collect on all these X's one of these days. You'd better be prepared.

F41.6 February 23, 1944

Feb. 23, 1944
3:00 P.M.

Darling Mary Eileen:

It's a beautiful day in Tennessee for a change. We've had more than our share of rain lately but today it is actually Summer. For some unknown reason we have been at ease all day & all we've done is lay out here & soak up all this swell sunshine.

I hit the "jackpot" in the letter department this morning. Your two letters of the 20th & 21st arrived & two also from home. In other words the two most important people in my life still remember me. Mom also sent some pictures they had taken & did I enjoy them. Everyone looked in the best of health & also very happy. Uncle Matt looks like a different guy now, doesn't he?

Hon, it's surprising how little there is to write to you about these days.

Every day is about the same now but when we hit our new Camp things will pick up again. & when I see you again you'll hear all about these two months. that is if you can stand the boring details. In the meantime I'll keep writing you these short notes to let you know I still think about you day in & day out. Mary, its growing worse every day this lonesome feeling & I'll never be content till we're together for always. Maybe a person is better off never falling in love but I guess not. At least we do have something to look forward to & what we have will be wonderful, I know. This as usual is the end so keep loving me & don't worry for I'll never Change. Bye now & love

Bernie

Mom & Bill will hear from me soon.

Chapter 42

A Beautiful Voice

My Dad loved to sing. He had a wonderful, smooth sounding voice that I loved to listen to in the car rides home from my grandmother's house. Mom also loved to sing, and she was easy to listen to as well. If I had a chance to pick one talent; I would choose to be an amazing singer. In this next letter Dad mentioned that his major heard him singing and asked him to be in a program they were working on. Of course, Dad said "no." He was not the stage performing type. He was never very comfortable being the center of attention, which is a little strange because when he was playing baseball and he was on the mound pitching, he was the center of attention all the time.

Now, Mom and I, we would be the type to be on stage if someone were to ask us. My grandson Colin has that gene too. Colin is a great performer and has an amazing stage presence. He sings, dances, performed in school plays, and dance showcases. He is so much fun to watch. My granddaughter, Kellie is a little shy when it comes to her being the center of attention. She would no more be on stage than fly, but she loves playing sports. She is very talented in soccer, basketball and volleyball. Team sports, that's her thing. I wonder where she got that talent? It is very interesting to write all this down and know in your heart that much of who we are and what we love to do, our likes and dislikes have a direct correlation to our relatives that came before us. We are all connected, we share each other's talents. I love thinking about that, because to me it means that my Mom and Dad live on in all of us. That makes me happy.

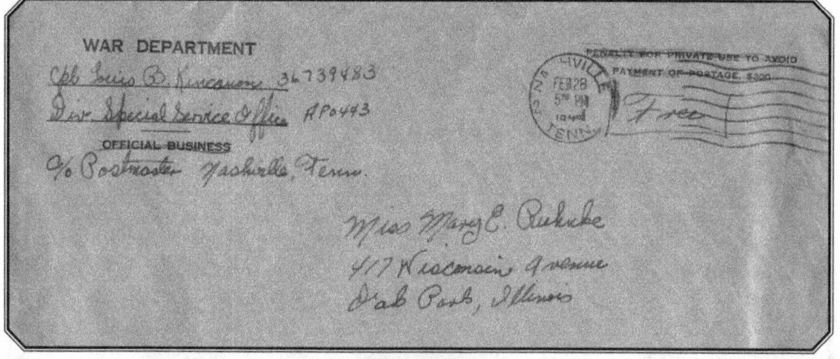

F42.1 February 26, 1944

Feb 26, 1944.

Dearest Darling:

Here's another short note from the "Rainiest State" in the Union. Mary, I have never seen so much rain anywhere & at this very moment we are having a real downpour. It's lucky that we have this large tent or we'd be drowned by now. We just can't seem to keep a dry spot of ground to sleep on & most of the fellows are getting a bit disgusted. One thing about them though. They haven't lost their sense of Humor so they'll get by on that alone. Oh well, there's a great day coming.

Mary, today being so dreary, I miss you more than ever & if I could just see you for a minute the Sun would shine. [illegible] Words fail me to tell you how I really feel but if you love me as I do you then I know you'll understand. In some of your letters you've mentioned about feeling lonesome so we'll have to get together some day & diagnose our case. Anyway when you write me & tell me how much you think of me the "Old Morale" climbs to the sky. Mushy, aren't I. Well, that's the way I feel,

"Mushy" & if you were here, you'd find out.
Hon, didn't I ever thank you for the Valentine
Candy you sent me? Guess not, because
you've asked me about it in some of your latest
letters. I'm sorry you know, & it was swell.
The whole office appreciated it a lot especially our Major. He's a hard candy fiend.
Here's the stopping off point again so
please return Mom & Bill's love & remember
me to all the family. Be good Darling &
I hope to see you in a few months.

Love forever

Bern,

I'm going to brag a little bit, Mary. The
Major heard me singing and now he wants
to use me on our program but I don't wanta.

Sunday. Feb. 27, 44.

Hello again, Hon:

I didn't have a chance to mail this last night. We
went to town last night though & saw "King of the
Cowboys" had a good meal & now we feel better. Funny,
isn't it? Our night off & we go to a show. I still
love you more than ever. See that proves it. Each day it
gets worse. So long for now & keep loving me. BERNIE.

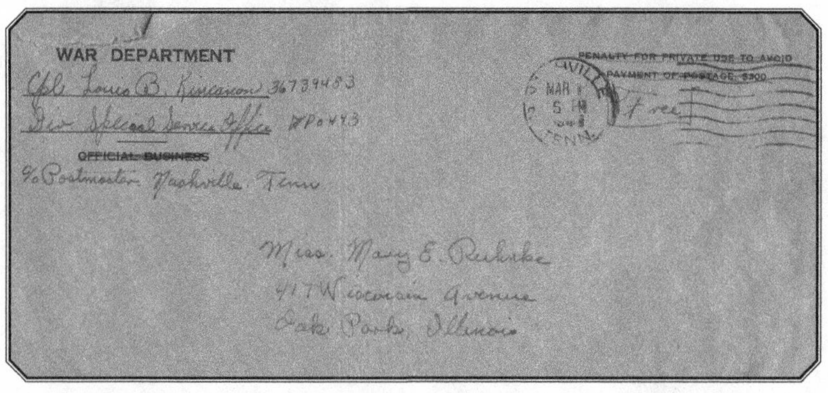

F42.2 February 29, 1944

Feb 29, 1944

Dearest:

Just received your letter telling me of your misfortune. You are very lucky though to recover those things as easily as you have. Can plainly see how you looked & I'll bet you were a very sad soul. That's one of the many reasons I love you Mary. You appreciate every little thing I do for you so much & losing a gift of mine would about break your heart. At least that's what you tell me & I believe you. Now I have a Confession to make. Since leaving Fort Jackson somehow the Cigarette lighter you gave me has disappeared. It may be in my other Barrack's Bag I hope. Don't want to lose it because it means alot to me. Now here's the way we pack our stuff when we go on Maneuvers. We have two Barrack's Bags A & B. In our B bag we put all clothing & equipment that we will not use & it is sent to our new Camp. The A bag is used for all necessary equipment & clothing. So now you know what a Div. does when it packs & takes off. This explanation was for the purpose of showing you that maybe in my haste I put the lighter in the wrong place. Hon, will you be my C Bag?

Don't be mad. That's just a joke we have around here.
You know that you're all the World to me & I couldn't
love anyone more than you. I sincerely hope to prove
these words to you soon & those days eventually will
arrive.

John L. Richards wrote me a letter the other day
& as usual he didn't have much to talk about but John L.
Told me about some "gal" he loves & intends to marry
& that was a surprise. How some guys can fall in
& out & in love again so quickly is beyond me. That's
the third or fourth girl he's fallen for in two years.
In spite of his goofiness I still have a soft spot for
him so after leaving you I'll surprise him & write.

Darling, don't know any more news so will end
this now. Before I do though here is some more flattery but
I mean every word. Want you to know that I carry
all of your pictures around & I'm always looking at my
Beautiful Future Wife. A feeling of pride always hits
me at those times accompanied by that "old bug" loneliness.
Remember the night J Richards came in. Well, that
evening put me on top of the World knowing you were
so attractive & mine. So there too. You're a soft
soaper yourself so now I'm getting even but it's all
true. Bye now, my love. Getting mushier all the time
aren't I?

Love Always
Bern.

Good Detective material.
Bill sure deserves a medal doesn't he?
Say hello to Mom & [illegible].

F42.3 March 8, 1944

March 8, 1944

Darling:

Here is another short note to let you know I'm still thinking of you daily. Nothing has changed here lately except that Maneuvers are drawing to a close. We have about two more weeks of them & then as you probally know we'll take off for Indiana. At least that's the most repeated & reliable news we've had. As for furloughs we don't know anything as yet.

Sorry to hear that Oak Park High lost out in the Tournament. Well just wait till Bill's a regular & then they'll have a champion. Haven't gotten around to writing your Mother but you can tell her to be patient with me. Sure will be glad when I won't have to write anymore letters. Want to be with all of you people forever one of these days & you can be sure that I'll stay right there always.

Mony, remember when I wrote & told you that the weather was improving. Well, I take it all back. Have had rain snow & freezing weather all in the last few days. We certainly will appreciate our new Camp after all this.

Hon, I guess there's no need to keep repeating this but I will. Whether I do or now you can be sure that I love & miss you very much & untill we're together my life will never be Complete.

Now as usual its closing time because I've run out of things to say. Be good now & I hope to see you soon.

Love always.

Bern.

Just recieved your letters of the 6th & 7th & both were interesting. Sorry you lost, Hon but you're bucking a poker-playing family over there. Sure is good to know that you like my family & mix so well with them.

Bye now, Lover.

F42.4 March 13, 1944

March 13, 1944.

Dearest:

I'm a bit late again with this, aren't I? Guess you've hooked up with a very poor letter-writer & I won't deny it. Writing is a hard job for me so you'll just have to suffer the consequences. Anyway, I hope you realize that whether I write you often or not, I think of you always & love you more as time goes by. Being away from you so long is very hard & I sincerely hope that it won't be too long till we get married. Your consistent letters & the packages of cookies and stuff are the main things to me these days so even though you wait so long for letters please don't stop yourself. By the way, last week two very indignant letters reached me & really told me off. Now, when you hear all the dope I'm sure you'll feel a bit different. Just wrote Mom a letter telling her that I'd explain all when the furlough gets here. Women sure are funny people & especially Mothers. Can see her point of view but believe she still thinks I'm a baby without good common sense. Don't tell her that because she's sensitive & I wouldn't hurt her for the world. Don't mean it to sound mean or anything. All I want to bring out is the fact that she's too good a Mother & if I live to be 70 years old she'll still worry about me.

Mary, wish you'd thank your Grandmother for me. She's really swell but being a relation of yours she couldn't be any other way. Yep we'll get along O.K. You like my family & I'm nuts about yours so we can't miss being happy.

My love this is the end of another letter. Can't wait to see you again & from the latest reports it may not be too long. In the meantime keep up the good work & give my love to all.

Love Always
Bern.

Tell Ma I'll write her soon. Bet she gets mighty disgusted waiting for her letter.

Here I am again almost closing without thanking you for your latest box of cookies. Hon, as usual they were delicious.

Chapter 43

The Pressure is On

F43.1 March 20, 1944

In this next letter Dad was writing about Mom's point of view regarding getting married. You can tell by his own words it is something he wants with every fiber of his being, but **"in times like these"** he was so afraid to make that commitment.

March 20, 1944

Dearest Darling:

Late again. Right? Well even so I still love you & its getting very difficult for me to think of anything but you. Sometimes your point of view seems very right to me but I don't know. It's an awfull decision to make in times like these. Hon. believe me I'd give the World to be married to you right now but somehow the thought of it scares me. The responsibility & everything that goes with marriage is hard even in normal times & my better judgement tells me to wait. Guess I'm an awfull dope having such a swell gal as you & [illegible] not taking advantage of these years. I do want you to know that my life is wrapped up in you & always will be. Have quite a bit to tell you about everything when we're together again & hope that's not too far away. Furloughs generally are the rule after Maneuvers so —. The Camp in Indiana is definite now so this Summer should be very enjoyable. Hon. I told Mom not to broadcast about where we're going so I have to ask you also. It [illegible] to do this but its best to keep it quiet. The Army makes rules but the Officers are the first ones to break them. They've sent their wives up there already & I guess everbody in Indiana & Tennessee knows our destination. There's no danger at all in a move such as this so it doesn't make much difference. The only time things are kept under cover is when we take the boat ride.

Hon, Hope you'll excuse the shortness of this letter. I'm saving all the news untill furlough time. Give my love to Mom & Bill & tell her to get well quick. She sure is having a time lately. I'm Glad she understands about me not writing. Good bye hon & Love always.

Bern.

Your Grandmother sent me a swell package & I'm going to write [illegible] & thank her as soon as possible. By the way the Ruhnke family are sure swell people & I love all of you.

Miss O'Ruhnke your package & card sure was appreciated. Thanks very much "Irish".

Chapter 44

Camp Atterbury

F44.1 March 28, 1944

March 28, 1944

Darling:

Haven't much time to write to-
night but I'll do my best. Realize
I should have written you before
but as usual I'm quite a bit late.
Hon we have arrived at Camp
Atterbury & is it swell. Nothing
Connected with the Army ever looked
~~as~~ good as this place did to me.
Last night we stopped over in Fort
Knox, Kentucky & it also was
a good Camp. Seems the farther
North one gets everything improves,
even the girls & I do mean you.
We are now going to Concentrate
on wising up all these "Rebels",
including the Major & Lt.

Mary, I was sorry to hear

about you catching a cold. Hope by now you are feeling better & you'd better stay that way. For some crazy reason, no matter how miserable the weather was on Maneuvers, a cold never caught up with me & that's a break.

Darling, I received the pictures & they weren't so bad. I'll admit my Mary is much prettier in the flesh ~~but~~ don't be [illegible] disillusioned. In regards to seeing you Easter I'll try to call you soon & let you know what the score is. I'll write you again in a day or so ~~a~~ after I found out the way this camp works.

Untill then be good & remember I love you now & always.

Love
Bern.

Regards to Mom & Bill & all the family

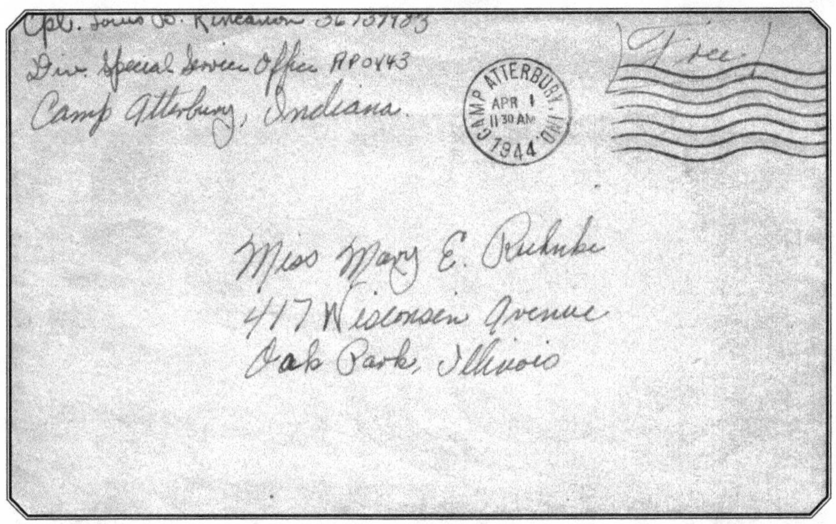

F44.2 March 31, 1944

March 31, 1944

Dearest:

How you doin, hon? Very good I hope & please stay that way. Mary, I dont think there's a chance of me getting home for Easter Sunday. If I was back in the Infantry it would be simple but this office has bad hours & Saturday is just another day of hard work. If its the last thing I do I'll convince Mom about transferring back again. Well, now that you know that I cant make Chicago, you had better come here. Want to see you very much & if you & Ede come down well have a swell time. Have inquired about the Guest House

& when I get the OK from you
I'll reserve one of their rooms.
A Guest is allowed not more
than three days so please tell
me when you'll arrive & leave again.
Hon, this is sure a beautiful Camp
& I know you'll enjoy yourself here.
Guess you know by now
that I'm going to pitch against the
Louisville Colonels next Friday.
Funny isn't it? Had to wait
untill the Army grabbed me to pitch
against an American Association team.
Darling, as I said before, seeing
you again will be great. We'd
hoped to recieve Furloughs after
Maneuvers but we haven't heard a
thing about them. They'll come
eventually but the time is unpredictable
Want to see everyone again & soon.
This letter is awfully mixed up
but guess Baseball not to mention

you has me in a fog.
I'll say so long for now, "Mush"
but you'll hear from me again before
you leave. Give my love to Mom
Bill & the rest of the family. Still
haven't written your Grandmother but
have a good excuse. I've missplaced her
address so will you send it to me.
Good night lover & be good.
Loves Always.
Bessie.
So you caught a cold? That's one
you can't blame on me.

Cpl. Louis B. Kincanon 36739483
Div. Special Service Office APO 443
Camp Atterbury, Indiana

[Free]

Miss Mary E. Ruhnke
417 Wisconsin Avenue
Oak Park, Illinois

F44.3 April 1, 1944

April 1, 1944

Darling.

Just recieved some news today that will change our plans. I expect to be home in about two or three weeks so maybe it would be best for you & Ede to come down some time later on. I know both of you wanted to come & see our swell camp but it would do all of us more good if you'd postpone the trip till about June. Another week or so won't make much difference. It does in a way, but it will make seeing you just that much more enjoyable.

Well, this isn't much of a letter, is it Hon? Anyway I'm a very happy guy & can't wait

to be with you again. I'll
write you regulorly so keep
loving me & remember
you are my only and best girl.
Love always
Bern.

Chapter 45

Wedding Plans

In the previous letter and the few that follow, we find my Dad in the hospital again. This time it is for his pitching arm. Plans were being made for my Mom and Dad's sister Edith to come and visit him but, he was going to be able to go home in the next couple weeks so that visit was put off for another time.

Wedding plans were being discussed which sure surprised me. From the previous letters I know they are now an engaged couple, but he also had been pretty adamant about the timing. His feeling that war time was the worst time to think about getting married but then he mentioned there was nothing he wanted more. I noticed the previous letter was written April 1, 1944 and Dad was in the hospital, planning a furlough, and their wedding for June 3. I wondered, how in the world will they pull it off? Or should I say how did my Mom pull it off? Leave it to a strong woman to know what she wanted and how to get it done. Most weddings today take at least a year to plan.

If the plan was to marry when Dad was on his furlough, the plans had to be made in quite a rush. This could be the number one reason why my Mom was always so upset with herself regarding the guest list. Mom's best friend Jean, who introduced them at Modern Modes, was of course a bridesmaid in their wedding party. Mom was so saddened by the fact she failed to invite Jean's mother, a woman she had known for years and was very close to. It bothered her, her entire life. Things like this happen in the best of circumstances. Planning, timing, and logistics all had to be considered. What a whirlwind! Where did her stunning wedding dress come from? Jean, of course. Mom borrowed it from her. Oh, if we could all be blessed in this life with a friend like Jean. She was a gem who sadly was diagnosed with cancer at the very young age of thirty-eight. When Jean died, Mom and Dad took her death very hard.

I met Jean when I was a baby, I know this only through pictures of me with her and her big dogs, but my memory of her and her family begin around maybe five or six years old. I have some very fond memories of her. I remember she was very pretty and very kind. She and her family lived in the northern suburbs of Chicago. They had a home on a large lot, well over three acres. Jean and Harry had four children and a house full of Great Danes. I used to love going to their home for the summer BBQ's. They had a pool, archery and those gentle giant dogs. This is where I fell in love with the breed and swore that someday I would have my own Great Dane. They were as close to a horse as I was going to get, so having a Dane was on my radar my entire life. This dream was fulfilled. My husband Joe and I have had four Great Danes in our family. They are truly the best dogs. They are expensive to feed and maintain, but I wouldn't have it any other way. At the time of this writing it has been eleven days since we had to make the heartbreaking decision to let our third Dane, KC go. He had been struggling to walk and, in the end, it was the kindest decision we could make for him. He was a gem. KC loved everything and everybody. My grand-daughter Kellie was so attached to him. To say goodbye was one of the hardest things we had to do. He is missed in every corner of our home and our hearts. Because KC was such an amazing part of our family, I think it seems only fitting at this time to include him in this book.

F45.1 KC (named after **K**ellie and **C**olin) Christmas 2019

F45.2 KC F45.3 Joe KC and Kathy F45.4 Majestic KC

F45.5 KC with his buddies Colin and Kellie

F45.6 KC outside enjoying the sunshine!

I want to thank Jean for giving me the gift of loving these majestic dogs, even before I could walk. I was so blessed to have that experience and to share it with my family, especially my grandchildren, who now have a great love and respect for animals of all shapes and sizes.

When Jean passed away, she left behind four children and a wonderful husband. My mom was very fortunate to have had her as a dear friend and she knew it. She always wished that she had more time with her. We wished the same for her and for us.

The following letters are ones where Dad was awaiting his furlough. After this next letter dated May 17, 1944 there was a break in his writings because he went home, he went home to marry his one and only Darling.

F45.7 May 13, 1944

May 13, 1944

Darling,

Here I am again. Back to the Home for the feeble & aged. What an Army Career I've had – How disgusted I am no one knows. Never thought it was possible to have so many things happen in one year. See how I feel, hon?

Now here's some good news I received today. The Captain Called me in today & examined me again. As I believed it's not a hernia but a badly strained muscle so thats a relief anyway. Don't need an operation but plenty of rest. Don't know how long they'll keep me here but I'll be home for our wedding. Mary, know you were very disappointed the other night when I called you. Don't blame you a bit because it did look like a good two months delay in our plans. You sounded very sad over the phone & could just see you so plain. You know marrying me is the beginning of a very bad risk. If I keep on this way you'll be a Hospital Widow.

Hon, I'm going to call Mom this afternoon & tell her the latest dope. She'll probably call you & then this letter won't contain any news for you. Would call you also but making you pay for the call is too much, so this letter is the next best.

Keep writing often & keep loving me & soon we'll be together for always I hope.

By now & Love
Bere.

Give my regards & love to all the family.

By the way, I'm going to quit Baseball for the Summer. Wait till the Major hears that.

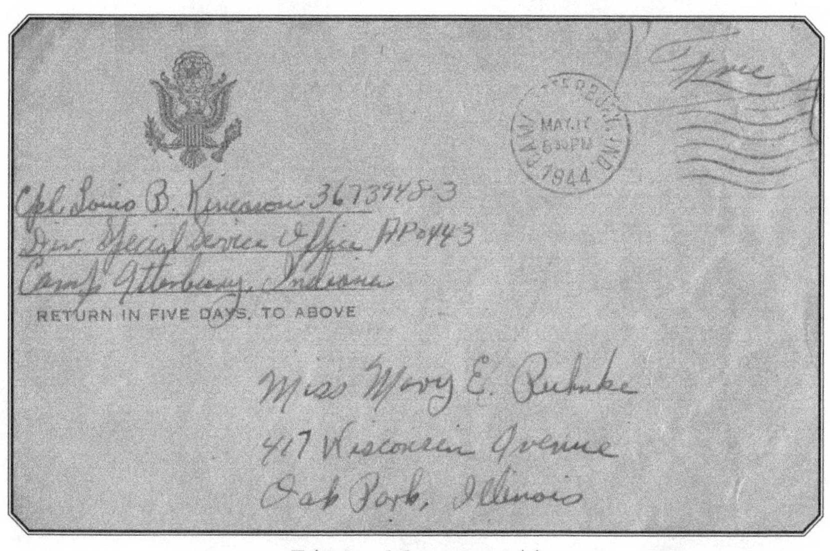

F45.8 May 17, 1944

May 17, 1944

Hello Darling;
Well, here I am again & have made some plans for getting out of here. They haven't done a darn thing for me so can see no good in staying here. By Monday I hope to be free & then maybe the Furlough can be had by June 1st. These Army Doctors are great people. If they can't operate or give you a pill they are lost. He told me to rest but the swelling is still there & any future movement will bring back the pain. He asked me how it was today & I told him

OK so now he thinks he's good.
Have to humor him along & keep up
his Morale.

Mary, how are you doing?
Are you still as anxious as ever
to get hitched? Hope you are
because we've certainly waited
long enough for our complete
happiness. Hon, don't do anything
drastic at your office for awhile.
There are some rumors flying
around again about us moving
& if we ~~~~ are there would be
no sense in you coming here for
a short time & then having to move
to another location. By the time
I get home maybe the whole story
will be out & then I can tell you
all the dope, dope.

Sorry that Bob K. is leaving

the U.S. You don't want to feel too badly though. I'm sure he can take care of himself & being Irish he has plenty of luck on his side. Someday, I'm pretty sure we'll meet & we can't help but like each other. After all we both love you don't we? For the life of me though, I can't figure out why.

Hon, this is an abrupt ending but I'll write you again soon. Give my love to Mom & Bill, Gran & everyone.

Bye now & Love Always
Bern

Chapter 46

"I DO"

June 3, 1944

The plans were made, the day was finally here, and their married life began.

Cpl. Bernard Louis Kincanon weds Mary Eileen Ruhnke

Below is the Army Report Change of Status.
Mary Eileen Ruhnke is now:
Mrs. Mary E. Kincanon

WAR DEPARTMENT

REPORT OF CHANGE OF STATUS AND ADDRESS

[See reverse side for instructions]

APPLICATION No.
X- 2511961

Date [illegible] (Month) [illegible] (Day), 1944

I. Soldier's name Kincanon, Louis (Last) (First) B. (Middle) Army serial No. 36 730 483 Grade Tec 5 (Private, corporal, sergeant, etc.)

Soldier's Army mailing address Div Hq Co., APO #443 Camp Atterbury, Ind.

II. (a) I report that the following *change of status* occurred on June (Month) 3 (Day), 1944, as to—

Name Kincanon, (Last) Louis (First) B. (Middle)

Address [illegible] Ave., (Number and street or rural route) Chicago, (City, town, or post office) Ill (State)

in connection with the family allowances pertaining to the above-named soldier.

[Place check mark (✓) in the proper square indicating which change has taken place]

☐ Birth of child. ☒ Marriage. ☐ Divorce.

☐ Death. ☐ Remarriage. ☐ Dependent reaching 18.

☐ Class B dependent (parent, grandparent, stepparent, brother, sister, half brother, half sister, stepsister, adopted brother, grandchild, etc.) ceased to be dependent upon soldier for substantial portion of support.

☐ Class B dependent (parent, grandparent, stepparent, brother, sister, half brother, half sister, stepsister, adopted brother, grandchild, etc.) became dependent upon soldier for substantial portion of support.

☐ Enter fully any other change of status not covered above Soldier married 3 June 1944 at Church of Saint Edmund, Oak Park, Ill.

(b) Relationship of such person to soldier Wife (Wife, son, mother, brother, etc.)

(c) Explain fully details about change of status

[See instructions as to documentary proof required]

III. In addition to the change reported above the address of the person to whom check is payable has been changed as follows: (If none, write "None.")

Name Kincanon, (Last) Mary (First) E. (Middle) Old address (Number and street or rural route) (City, town, or post office) (State)

New address 417 Wisconsin Ave., (Number and street or rural route) Oak Park, (City, town, or post office) Ill (State)

IV. Other additional information

V. Signature (First name) (Middle name) (Last name) Address (Number and street or rural route) (City, town, or post office) (State)

Relationship to soldier (If report is made by other than soldier, enter relationship to soldier (wife, mother, son, brother, none, etc.)

W.D., A.G.O. Form No. 641
July 14, 1942

16—29737-1

F46.1 Army Report Change of Status

F46.2 St. Edmond's Church in Oak Park June 3, 1944

F46.3 May I Present Mr. and Mrs. Louis Bernard Kincanon
this is the one and only time I ever saw my Dad wearing a wedding ring.

F46.4 Mom and Dad outside St. Edmund's Church. The man in the background is Uncle Matt, who Dad mentions many times in his letters to my Mom.

F46.5 Wedding Day, leaving the church.
The other woman behind mom is her best friend Jean.
Jean is the friend who introduced them.

F46.6 Happy Mary on her big day.
The woman behind her is my Dad's younger sister, Edith.

F46.7 My grandmother, Maw. (Mom's mom).

F46.8 From left to right: My Dad's sister Bernice (Bea)
My grandmother Magdalene, My grandmother Helen.

F46.9 My Mom's brother, Bill and Mom's Mother, Helen

F46.10 Great Friends and Family Celebrating

Certificate of Marriage

IHS

Church of Saint Edmund
Oak Park, Illinois

This is to Certify

That Louis B. Kincanon
and Mary Eileen Oluhnke
were lawfully

Married

on the 3rd day of June 1944
according to the
Rite of the Roman Catholic Church
and in conformity with the laws of the
State of Illinois

Rev. John T. Benz officiating

in the presence of Witnesses: Matthew O'Neill, Edith Kincanon

as appears from the Marriage Register of this Church

Dated June 3, 1944

Seal

John T. Benz asst. Pastor

HILL BROTHERS, HOUSTON, TEXAS

F46.11 Marriage License June 3, 1944

There was a lot more to this time off for Mom and Dad besides their wedding day. This was a time to finally be together as husband and wife. They both knew Dad would have to go back to the Army and report for duty all too soon. I am not sure the exact day he had to report back but I know when the letters began again and that was in August. That gave them a little over a month for their honeymoon. I believe they moved into my grandmother's home in Oak Park on Wisconsin Avenue. I say that because the letters to come were still mailed to that address. This could be a window into some understanding where the push and pull from my Dad's mother came into play. Her son was now living with the "other mother."

I can only imagine what these weeks were like for them. Fitting in so many different visits with all the people they both cared so much about, and at the same time trying to find time for themselves to be alone in a home where they did not have complete privacy as newlyweds. I am pretty sure my grandmother would have made sure she gave them the space they needed.

That is who she was.

When Joe and I were newly-weds 32 years ago at the time of this writing, we had our honeymoon cruise out of Florida for a week, the second leg of our trip was a visit with Maw at her home in West Palm Beach, Florida. Here is a picture of her home on Macy Street.

F46.12 Maw's home in West Palm Beach Florida

I remember when it was time to go to bed my grandmother said to me, ***"you kids can be as noisy as you want, I take my hearing aids out at night, so I won't hear a thing!"*** She was so funny, and yet so in-tuned to everyone's needs and situation. Joe and I still will laugh about that; it was just a little embarrassing coming from my grandmother. But I was glad she couldn't hear because they did have the squeakiest bed even if you were just rolling over. I would not want her to think anything else was going on!

Well, Maw certainly must have given the two of them enough privacy, because while Dad was home on his furlough for their wedding and honeymoon, Mom became pregnant with their first child. Unbeknownst to them; Dad's premonition about a child was coming true. But before they were able to have the future they planned for themselves, there was still a war going on and Dad knew all too well he had to return to serve.

It seems the next letters written in August after Dad has returned from his leave, this is when Mom realizes she may be pregnant.

Chapter 47

Baby on the Way?

F47.1 August 15, 1944
First letter after their wedding and furlough

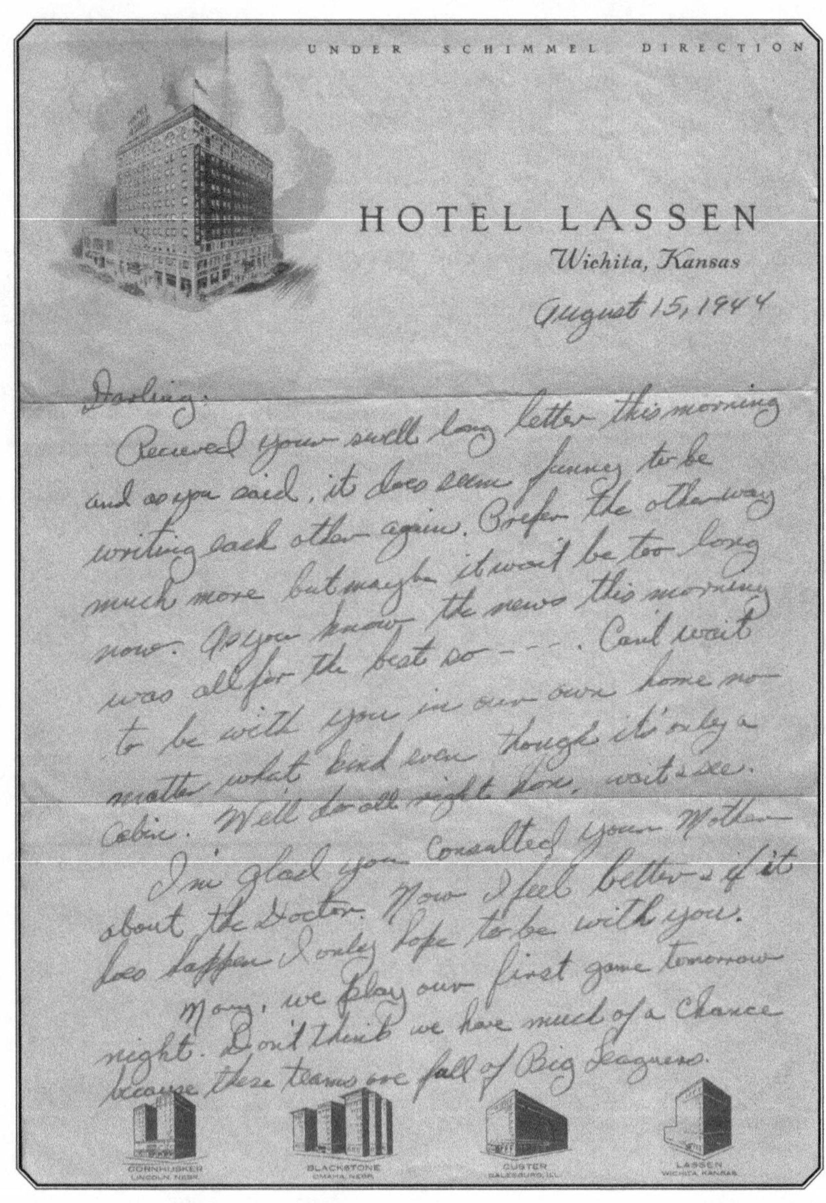

UNDER SCHIMMEL DIRECTION

HOTEL LASSEN
Wichita, Kansas

August 15, 1944

Darling:
Received your swell long letter this morning and as you said, it does seem funny to be writing each other again. Prefer the other way much more but maybe it won't be too long now. As you know the news this morning was all for the best so - - - . Can't wait to be with you in our own home no matter what kind even though it's only a cabin. Well do all right hon, wait & see.

I'm glad you consulted your Mother about the Doctor. Now I feel better & if it does happen I only hope to be with you.

Mary, we play our first game tomorrow night. Don't think we have much of a chance because these teams are full of Big Leaguers.

CORNHUSKER LINCOLN, NEBR. BLACKSTONE OMAHA, NEBR. CUSTER GALESBURG, ILL. LASSEN WICHITA, KANSAS

Can't tell you how long will be here but I'll keep you posted.

Hon, you are quite a working girl, aren't you? Will I be glad when this dope can get back home and make a home for you like I should.

Don't know much else to tell you but you'll be hearing from me again. Tell your Mom & Grom & Bill & everybody hello & hope to see all of you soon.

Love Always

Bern.

When you recieve this letter Honey, please call Mom & tell her theres a letter to her on the way.

Byes now.

F47.2. Mom must have worked in Indiana at Camp Atterbury Civilian Personnel Branch. This was her resignation letter.

W. D., C. P. Div., Form No. 50
(Appd. Apr. 27, 1942)

WAR DEPARTMENT

REPORT OF FIELD PERSONNEL ACTION

Camp Atterbury, Indiana
(Station)

August 4, 1944
(Date)

To: MRS. MARY E. KINCANON

1. Name Kincanon, Mary E.

2. Nature of Action Resignation

3. Effective Date August 7, 1944

	FROM—	TO—
4. Position	Ward Attendant	
5. Grade and/or Salary Allowances	Ungr. 3-1, $.66/hr.	
6. Bureau and/or Other Unit	A S F	
7. Headquarters and duty Station	Fifth Service Command, Wakeman General Hospital, Camp Atterbury, Indiana.	
8. Departmental or Field	FIELD	FIELD

9. C. S. C. REPORT SERIES: P

10. CIVIL SERVICE AUTHORITY: CS Rule XII

11. Appropriation: 555-1180 P 413-01 A 0805 MAHD,A

12. Date of Birth: June 29, 1923

13. Subj. to Ret. Act: Yes x No

14. If Separation, Last Paid Through: 8/7/44

15. Bureau Authority for Action or Position

REMARKS: Last day of actual duty: August 7, 1944

Reason: leaving the vicinity

COPIES TO: (Check)

1. ☐ District Manager—Temporary series only.
2. ☐ C. S. C. copy attached—Permanent series only.
3. ☑ Employee.
4. ☐ Civ. Pers. Field Office—Change in name of graded employee only.
5. ☐ .... (Other)

For the Commanding Officer:

16. [signature] (Signature)

E.J.CROFT, Capt.CMP, C.Civ.Pers.Br.
(Title)

J.Q.M.D. 350M—4-8-43 c-8

Mom's paycheck showing that she made sixty-six cents an hour!

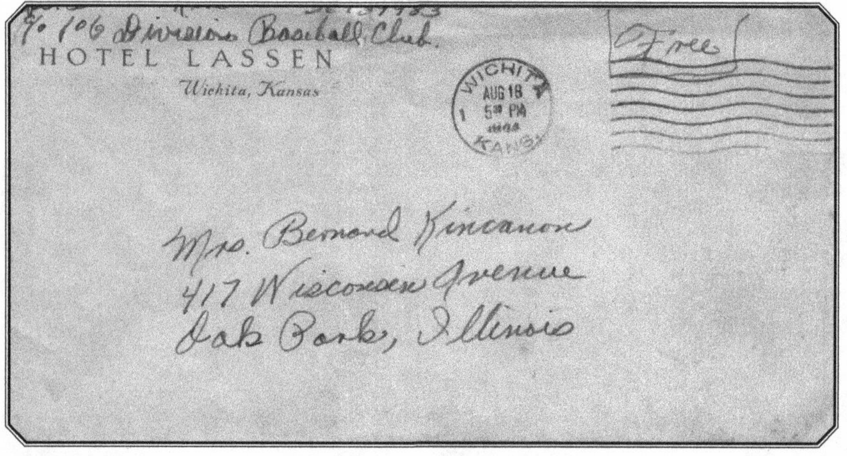

F47.3 August 18, 1944

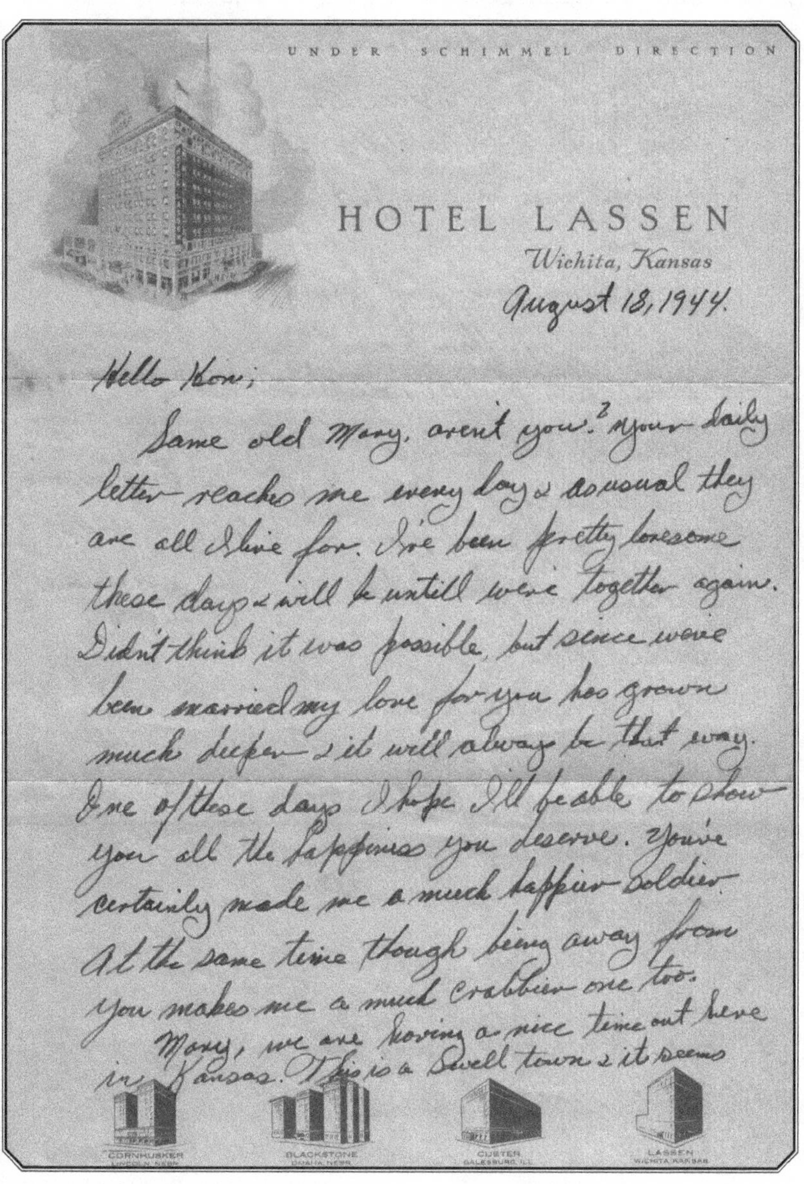

UNDER SCHIMMEL DIRECTION

HOTEL LASSEN
Wichita, Kansas

August 18, 1944.

Hello Hon;

Same old Mary, arent you? Your daily letter reaches me every day & as usual they are all I live for. I've been pretty lonesome these days & will be untill were together again. Didn't think it was possible, but since weve been married my love for you has grown much deeper & it will always be that way. One of these days I hope I'll be able to show you all the happiness you deserve. You've certainly made me a much happier soldier. At the same time though being away from you makes me a much crabbier one too.

Mary, we are having a nice time out here in Kansas. This is a swell town & it seems just like a vacation to all of us. The only thing that spoils it is Captain Daniels & I mean thing. Sure have a lot to tell you about that individual and any respect I ever had for him is gone.

We won our first game the other night but the other team wasn't so hot. Mungo pitched, struck out 17 and gave two hits. Score 5-0. He is still a Big League pitcher but he said he won't be able to pitch again for two weeks. There are plenty of good pitchers out here and we're facing Herman Besse Sunday, formerly with the Athletics. They may pitch me Sunday sure wins all & if they do I'll do my best.

Mary, my love, will you give my regards to all your folks & tell them I hope to see them soon. Bye for now &

Love Always.

Bern.

Address letters same as before only change to Hotel Lassen

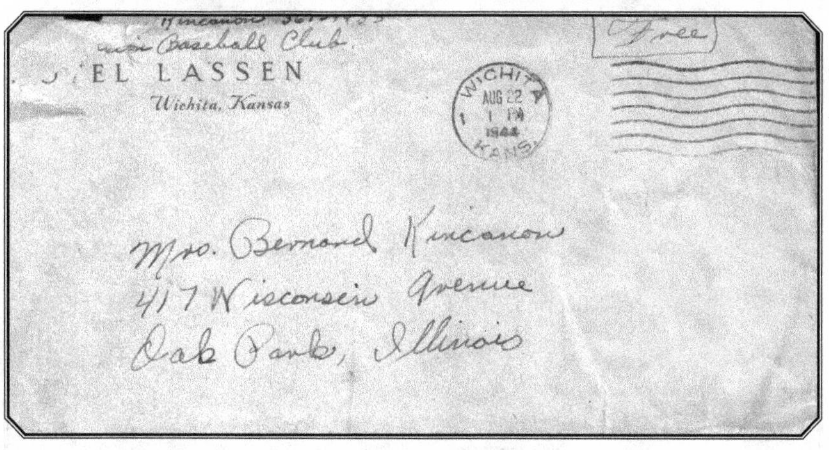

F47.4 August 22, 1944

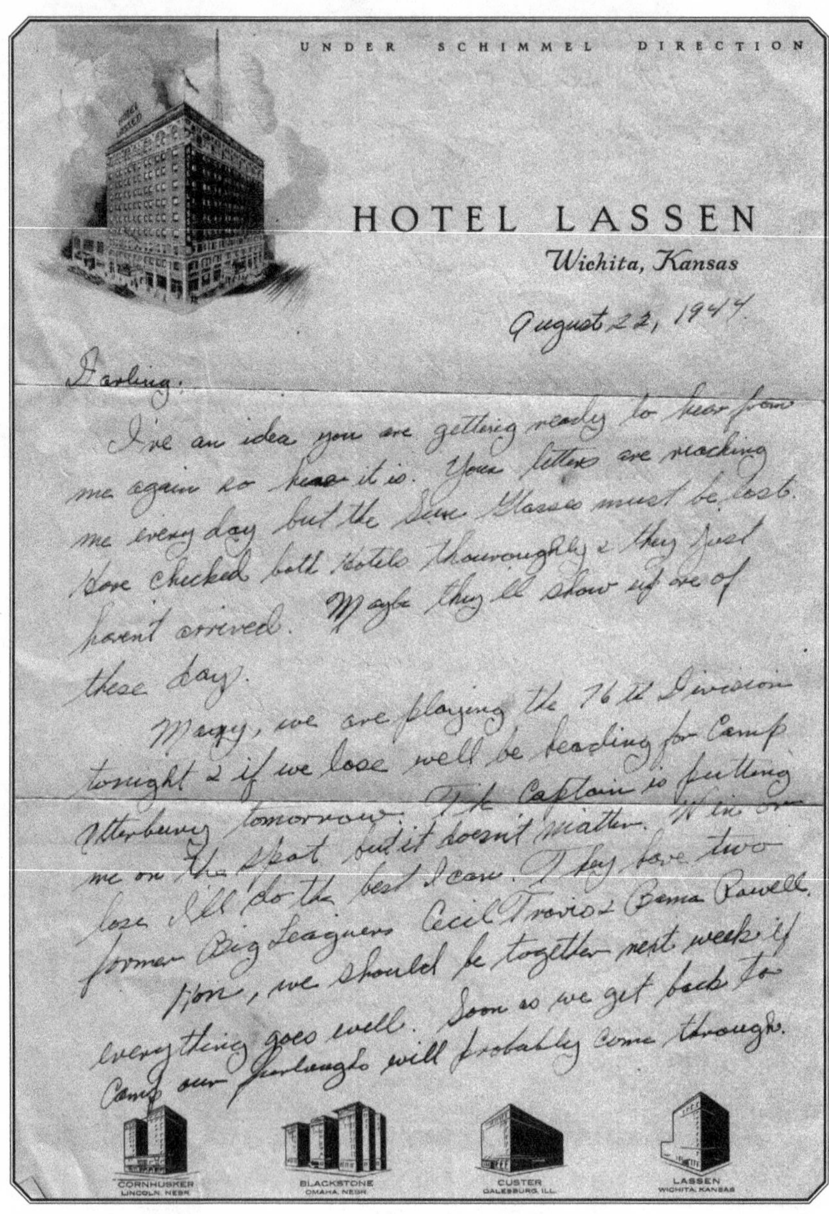

UNDER SCHIMMEL DIRECTION

HOTEL LASSEN
Wichita, Kansas

August 22, 1944.

Darling:

I've an idea you are getting ready to hear from me again so here it is. Your letters are reaching me every day but the Sun Glasses must be lost. Have checked both Hotels thoroughly & they just haven't arrived. Maybe they'll show up one of these days.

Margy, we are playing the 16th Division tonight & if we lose we'll be heading for Camp Atterbury tomorrow. The Captain is putting me on the spot but it doesn't matter. Win or lose I'll do the best I can. They have two former Big Leaguers Cecil Travis & Bama Rowell.

Hon, we should be together next week if everything goes well. Soon as we get back to Camp our furloughs will probably come through.

CORNHUSKER LINCOLN, NEBR. · BLACKSTONE OMAHA, NEBR. · CUSTER GALESBURG, ILL. · LASSEN WICHITA, KANSAS

Can't wait to see everyone again, especially you.
If Hitler only knew what he is doing to me I'm
sure he'd surrender tomorrow. Never before
have I been so lonely as now & it's only been
two weeks since we left each other. Wonder
how some people stand the separation of years
as well as they do.

Aren't these letters of mine interesting?
Just seems to be an empty space in my old
head these days and writing a long interesting
letter is impossible.

Darling, I'll be closing this now & hope you are feeling well. Take things easy "Ma", & I'll be seeing you. Give my love & regards to the family.

Love Always.

Bernie.

Thanks for the two dollars, Brat.
Maybe you'd better stop writing here, Mary.
The team spirit isn't too high & most of
the fellows want to go home on furlough.
Bye my love

Chapter 48

Singin' the Blues

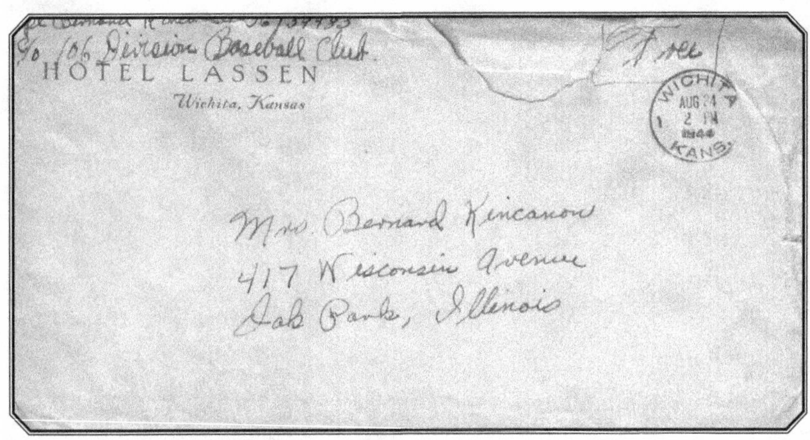

F48.1 August 24, 1944

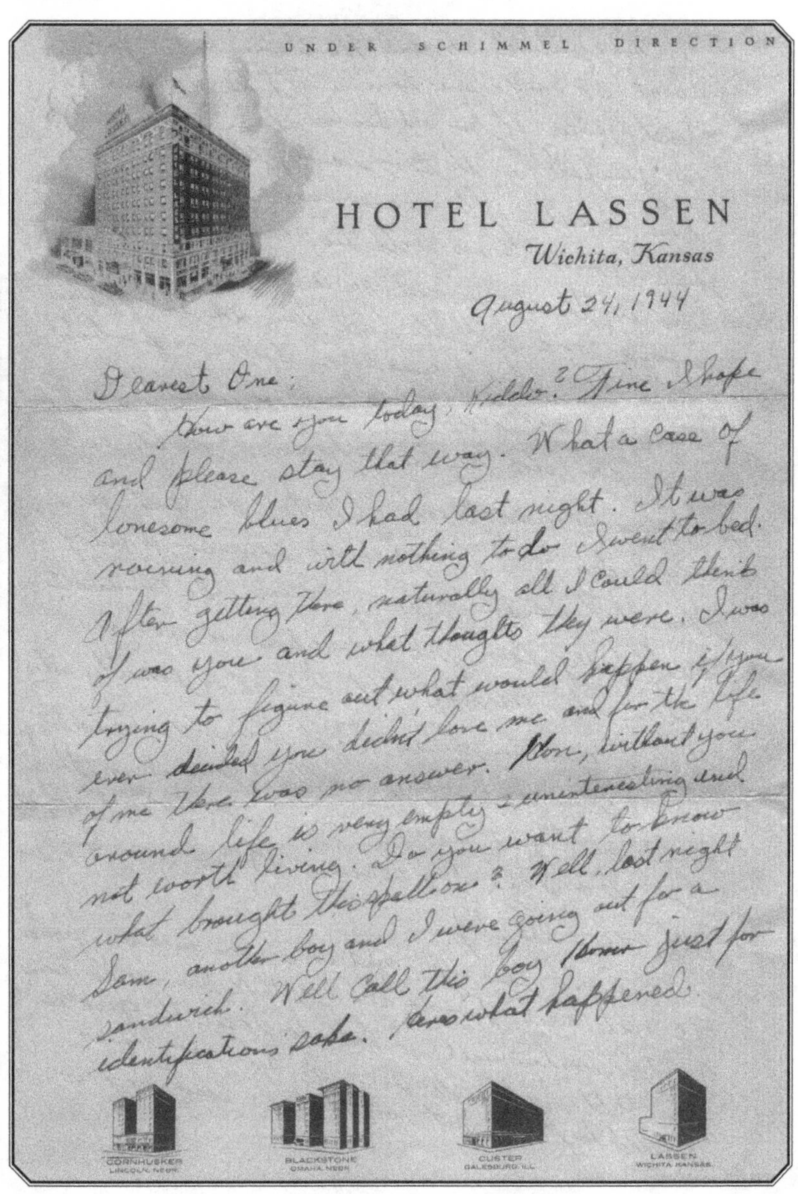

UNDER SCHIMMEL DIRECTION

HOTEL LASSEN
Wichita, Kansas

August 24, 1944

Dearest One:
How are you today, Kiddo? Fine I hope
and please stay that way. What a case of
lonesome blues I had last night. It was
raining and with nothing to do I went to bed.
After getting there, naturally all I could think
of was you and what thoughts they were. I was
trying to figure out what would happen if you
ever decided you didn't love me and for the life
of me there was no answer. Hon, without you
around life is very empty & uninteresting and
not worth living. Do you want to know
what brought this spell on? Well, last night
Sam, another boy and I were going out for a
sandwich. We'll call this boy Homer just for
identifications sake. Here's what happened.

CORNHUSKER
LINCOLN, NEBR.
BLACKSTONE
OMAHA, NEBR.
CUSTER
GALESBURG, ILL.
LASSEN
WICHITA, KANSAS.

a car pulled around the corner and a lady about 38 or 40 was driving. This boy Homer just yelled at her and darned if she didn't stop. He jumped in the car & away they went. Ten minutes after we arrived back to our rooms here Homer comes with his story. Her husband was in the Army and she had been running around some but the last time she had had a date was five weeks ago. Well, you probably know what happened and my first thoughts were for this husband of hers. Possibly he is running around himself but if he isn't he's an unlucky guy. Mary, I've seen so much of this that people begin to seem like animals to me. They have no principles or morals when they act like that. That is exactly why I love you so much. I'd trust you with my life and I always will. Remember this. You can trust me the same way & I know you do. Do I get too serious at times, Mary? If so tell me & I'll stop.

Well, this old right arm won another game. We beat Cecil Travis and his 76th Division team 9-7 Tuesday night. I had to leave the game in the 8th with the score 8-3 in our favor. Wanted to finish but my shoulder said no sir.

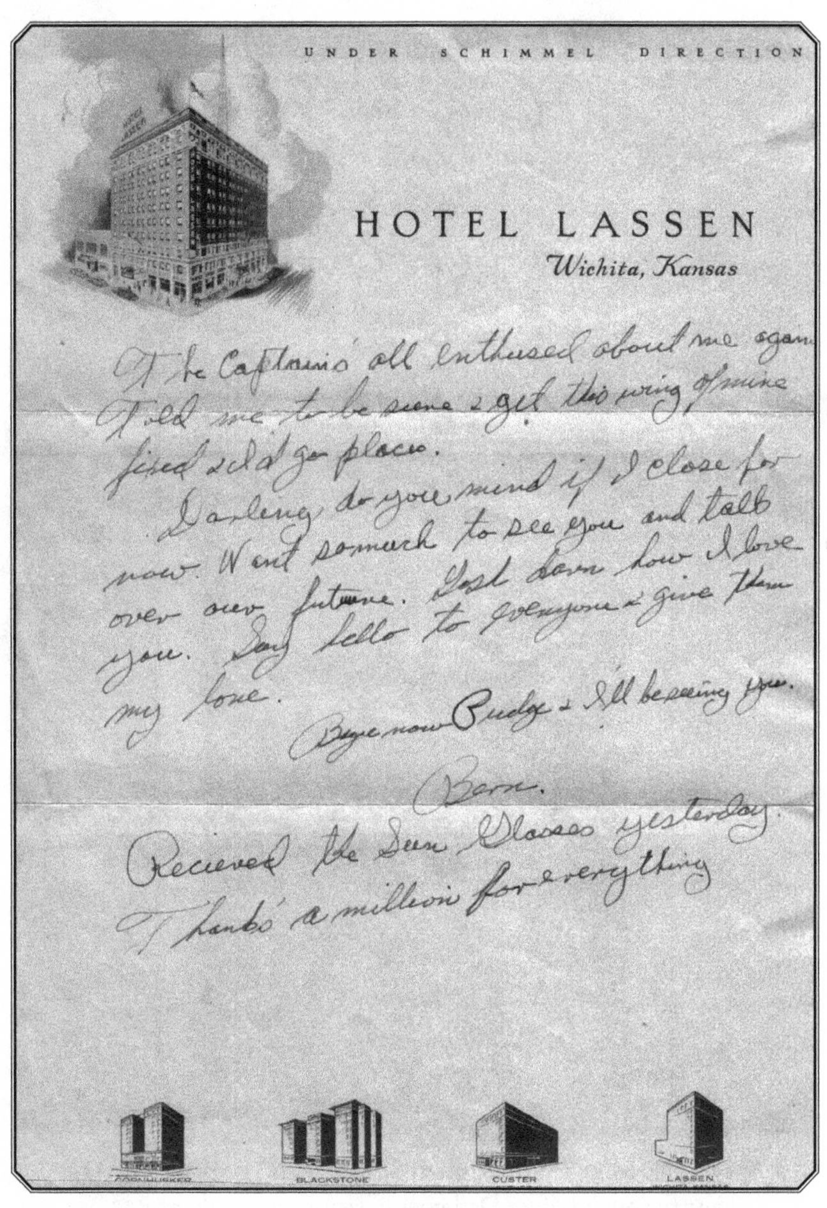

UNDER SCHIMMEL DIRECTION

HOTEL LASSEN

Wichita, Kansas

The Captain's all enthused about me again
Told me to be sure & get this wing of mine
fixed & I'd go places.

Darling do you mind if I close for
now. Want so much to see you and talk
over our future. Gosh darn how I love
you. Say hello to everyone & give them
my love.

Bye now Pudge & I'll be seeing you.

Bern.

Recieved the Sun Glasses yesterday.
Thanks a million for everything

BLACKSTONE CUSTER LASSEN

Chapter 49

Somewhere Overseas

F49.1 Dad, taken three months after their marriage and the last furlough before Dad goes overseas. September 1944

F49.2. October 1944, Dad was deployed overseas, and Mom was three months pregnant.

F49.3 October 1944, Dad was deployed overseas, and Mom was three months pregnant

Cpl. Louis B. Kincanon 36739483
3rd Bn. H.&Co. 423rd Inf. APO 443
c/o Postmaster N.Y. N.Y.

506
26
1944
A.P.O.

Mrs. Louis Kincanon
417 Wisconsin Avenue
Oak Park, Illinois

E. M. Lewis
2nd Lt Inf

F49.4 October 26, 1944 First letter after Dad left from his last furlough

Somewhere in the Eastern part of the U. S.

Darling:

Hope you haven't been worrying too much because you haven't heard from me before now. It's a tough job trying to keep in touch the first few days but from now on the letters will reach you more frequently. This is quite a place, Mary and wish I could tell you more about it. Anyway the food is good and I'm feeling swell.

What I am most interested in is how you are feeling. Have been wondering also how you weathered the trip to good old Oak Park. Please take care of yourself now and don't you worry, I will too. It's only natural that we're going to miss each other but always

remember others are doing it so why
Can't we?
Hon, there isn't much to tell you
tonight so this will have to end for now.
Give my love to your Mom, Gram, Bill and
the rest of the family. To you alone these
few words. You in your love for me
have changed this lonely life to a very
bright one. Were not together now but
I know you're waiting and that makes
the * difference. I'll love you, Mary, always.
A man in love turns poetic once in a while
so why can't I? Bye — Bern
Hey. Mrs Kincanon, don't forget to
put your new name on the Mail Box.

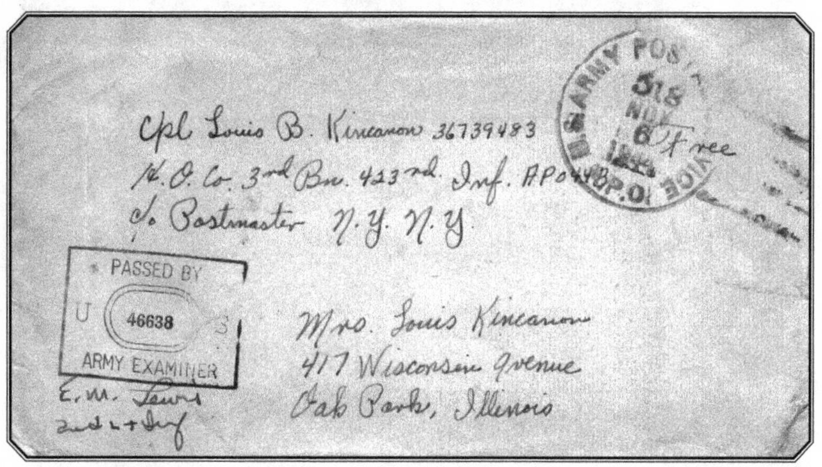

F49.5 November 2, 1944

Somewhere Overseas Nov 2, 1944

Dearest Darling:

Hello again and how are you feeling tonight, Hon? Fine I hope and please stay that way. Know you'll be having your good and bad times from now on but I'll be with you in Spirit at least. Gosh, Mary a guy can be in love but he never knows how much untill he gets so darn far away its impossible to even talk to the Girl over the phone. Well, they can't keep us apart forever and I'm sure we'll appreciate our home that much more after this is all over.

Mary, this is my second letter to you in three days and there isn't much to tell you. My, my life goes on and as usual its all very routine. Outside of Eating Sleeping and Training we are doing nothing. You can see that my conversation does have its limitations.

Sincerely hope my letters aren't too dull and uninteresting but have to express my thoughts to you somehow.

Mom, you take care of Mary and Bill and yourself and sure am waiting for that letter. Gram, that goes for you too. If you get in the writin mood I'd be happy to hear from you.

Mush, here is the conclusion to this. Recieved your letter of the twentieth and want to explain that last letter of mine, from the States. We were in a hurry and they gave us twenty minutes to write. Seeing that I had written you last I decided to write home and include you in it. Was about all I could do, dont ya know.

Bye for now, Honey Chile and I sho do love you.

Bern.

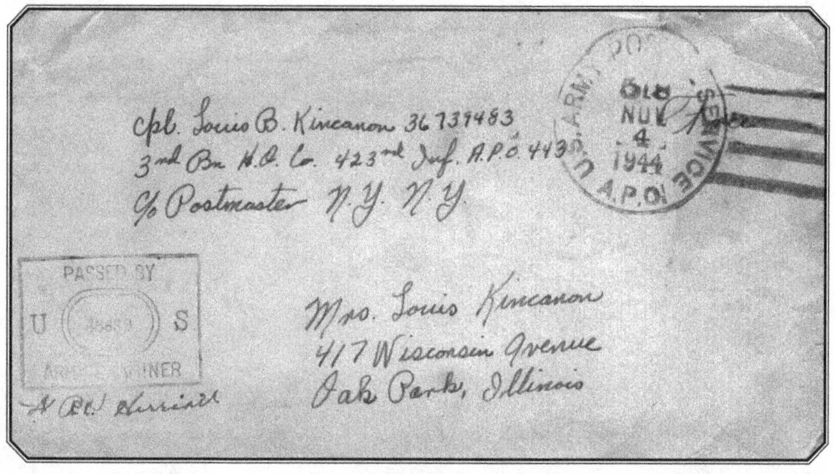

F49.6 November 3, 1944
"On the High Seas"

On The High Seas

My Loving Wife:

Mary, this is one of those real short notes you asked for every so often. There is nothing new to report but maybe later on I'll be able to tell you more about things in general. In the meantime keep writing about everyone at home and I'll be satisfied.

Don't forget I'll love you always and will be looking forward to the time when we can be together forever.

Love

Bern.

Best regards and love to the family.

Somewhere Overseas.

Darling:
Once again I shall indulge in my favorite pastime, writing to you. After a day of Army life it's always a real pleasure to relax and concentrate on you. That sounds like you're in my thoughts only at night but you know better than that. Guess it's a fact that you are on my mind too much at times but I can't help that.

Recieved two more letters from you today. They were swell and was happy to know that all of you are feeling well. One of them made me sympathize

F49.7 2nd letter November 4, 1944

with you though. Can imagine how you felt that Sunday morning you arrived in Chicago. Trouble does seem to come in bunches, doesn't it Hon?

Mary, I've been writing you pretty often and can't remember whether I told you this or not. Your information about our Baby made me so darn proud I couldn't think straight for an hour or more. Boy, won't I have something to come home to. Our Baby and you. What more could any man ask for?

Hon, I had the good fortune of going to town last night. Had a good meal and from there went to the show. Wish I could tell you more about the town but maybe later on my letters will be more informative.

Now, Muah here's the dope on mailing packages. You are allowed to mail them at any time providing they weigh under eight ozs. However, in case I should write home for something special you are required to show my request at the Post Office. That way the package doesn't have to be less than those eight ozs. Now don't forget, Christmas packages can be sent without any Red Tape. This is just information for you in case its ever necessary. Don't want you spending your money on me. Have everything I need and want you to concentrate on keeping yourself happy and as Beautiful as you are. Mary, will you pass this information on to Mom? Don't think I've told her anything about the situation. Tell her also what I said about gifts. I'm sure both of you need the money much more than I need any expensive presents. Knowing you both as I do there's no doubt something will be heading this way. Here are a few thing that will help the morale a bit. Woolen socks, handkerchiefs, Soap, Tooth Paste, Brushless Shaving Cream Candy Cookies and Gum. Thats all I need, honest.

Notice the stamp dated November 29, 1944, mail is moving slowly.

This is probably the longest letter you've ever recieved from me but there's a reason. Started this two day ago and never did get to finish it untill now. See how things are. Takes me five days to gather my thoughts enough to write four pages.

Will close for the present but will write again in a day or two. Give my love and regards to all the family and hope to hear from my new Mom soon.

All my love to you Mary now and always.

Bern.

Chapter 50

‘There is Always a Good Reason”

F50.1 November 5, 1944

In the following letter dated November 5, 1944 Dad writes, **"Hon, in the future if there is a long delay don't be worried because there's always a good reason."**

These words are repeated in other letters and in the one and only letter I have that my Mom wrote to my Dad but never finished. These few words, I am concluding, are words my Mom must have repeated to herself a thousand times. In a little over a month from this very letter, her resolve will be tested.

Knowing what I know about what the future holds for both of them, it is one of the hardest letters to read.

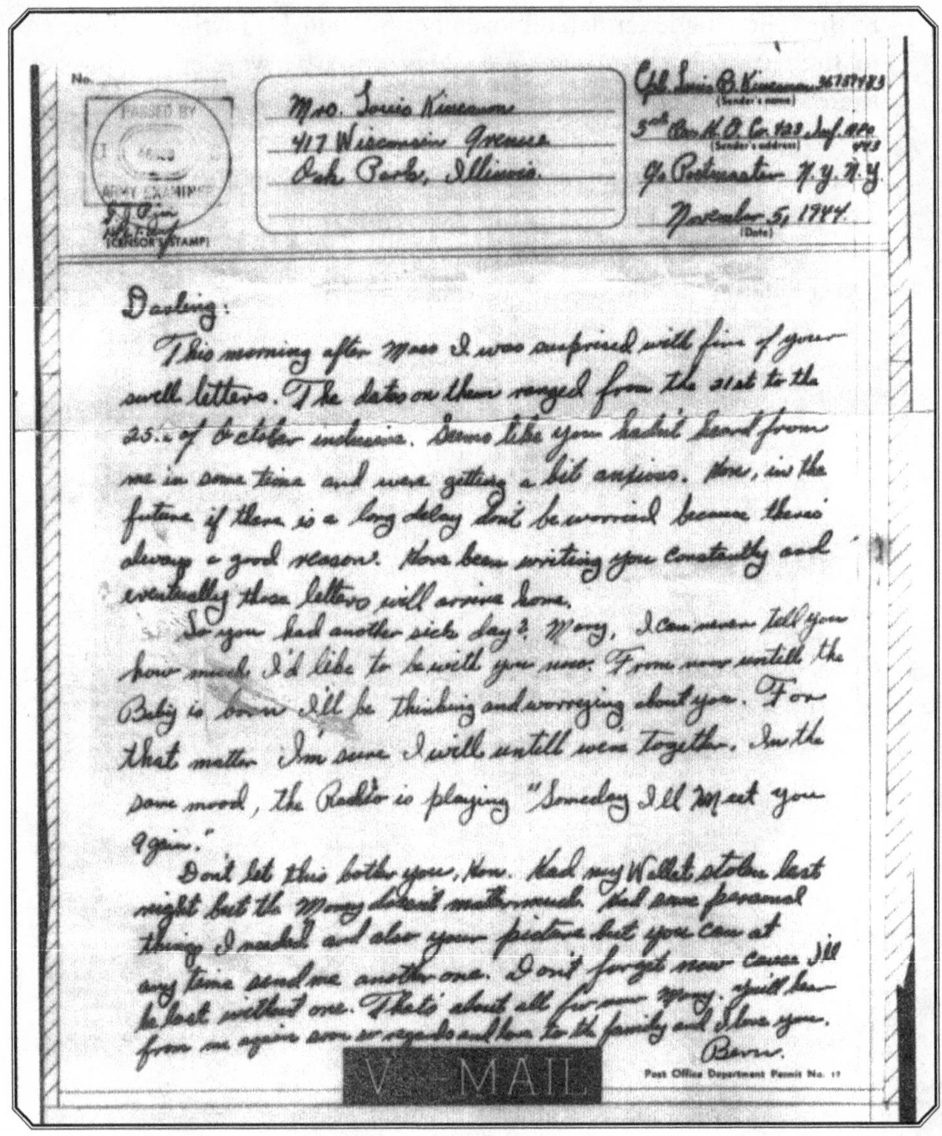

No.

PASSED BY
ARMY EXAMINER
(CENSOR'S STAMP)

Mrs. Louis Kincanon
417 Wisconsin Avenue
Oak Park, Illinois.

Cpl. Louis B. Kincanon 36787483
(Sender's name)
5th Bn. H.Q. Co. 423 Inf. APO 443
(Sender's address)
c/o Postmaster N.Y. N.Y.
November 5, 1944.
(Date)

Darling:

This morning after Mass I was surprised with five of your swell letters. The dates on them ranged from the 21st to the 25th of October inclusive. Seems like you hadn't heard from me in some time and were getting a bit anxious. Hon, in the future if there is a long delay don't be worried because there's always a good reason. Have been writing you constantly and eventually those letters will arrive home.

So you had another sick day? Mary, I can never tell you how much I'd like to be with you now. From now untill the Baby is born I'll be thinking and worrying about you. For that matter I'm sure I will untill we're together. In the same mood, the Radio is playing "Someday I'll Meet you again."

Don't let this bother you, Hon. Had my Wallet stolen last night but the Money doesn't matter much. Had some personal things I needed and also your picture but you can at any time send me another one. Don't forget now cause I'll be lost without one. That's about all for now Mary. Until you hear from me again soon, regards and love to the family and I love you.

Bern.

V-MAIL

Post Office Department Permit No. 1

V-Mail*

*V-Mail Short for "Victory Mail" was a particular postal system put into place during WWII and used between June 1942 through November 1945. The letters were photographed in microfilm. This system drastically reduced the amount of space needed to transport mail, freeing up room for other valuable supplies.

Received 11-14-44.

F50.2 November 6, 1944

Overseas November 6, 1944.

Dearest Darling:

What do you think of your Old Man these days? Doing all right in the writing Department, arent I? Its just one of those things Mary. Every night the urge to write comes upon me and I just cant resist. Dont want to either because its the only way I can satisfy my yearning for you now.

So they're making a Politician of you too. If I know you President Roosevelt cant lose. Wouldnt be surprised to see him sweep the entire 47th Ward. Now, be careful if you do cheat because

I don't want to be telling these guys my Wifes in Jail. Maybe I'd better insert a laugh after that last sentence. The Officer that Censors this may take me serious. We are from Chicago you know and for some reason people have a wrong impression of us Natives.

Darling, here is some further news concerning my Wallet. Didn't mention this but another boy two beds away had his stolen ~~the morning~~ the same night. Well, this morning a Sergeant found both of them in the Latrine, of all places. Everything was there except the Money and that satisfies me. You can still send that picture though and please don't send any Money. Don't need it and if I should I have plenty of friends.

That is about all for tonight Mary. Give my love and regards to Mom, Gram Bill and Marty. Don't forget the rest of the Family. Goodnight Hon and my love to you now and forever.

Bern.

Hon, will you tell me the difference in time between my V Mail letter of last night and this one?

F50.3 November 9, 1944

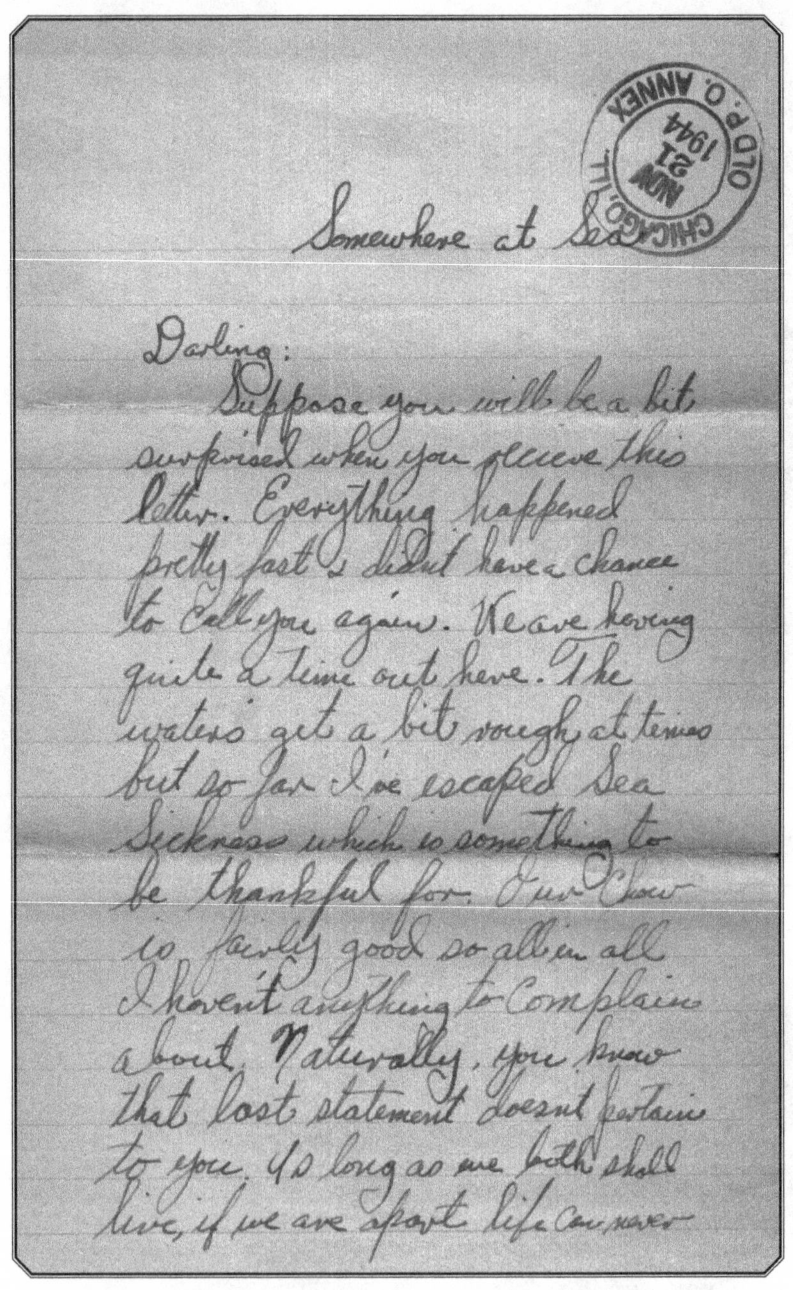

CHICAGO, ILL. OLD P.O. ANNEX NOV 21 1944

Somewhere at Sea

Darling:
Suppose you will be a bit
surprised when you receive this
letter. Everything happened
pretty fast & didn't have a chance
to call you again. We are having
quite a time out here. The
waters get a bit rough at times
but so far I've escaped Sea
Sickness which is something to
be thankful for. Our Chow
is fairly good so all in all
I haven't anything to Complain
about. Naturally, you know
that last statement doesn't pertain
to you. As long as we both shall
live, if we are apart life can never

hold too much enjoyment. You have shown me more happiness than I ever thought possible these past three years and untill were together again maybe these memories will keep us going. I'm sure they will for me and know you'll be all right too. When you do get blue and lonely you know who you can turn to and he'll never fail you. In times like these Religion is our biggest hope and blessing. I'm preaching again but guess you are used to that by now.

Mary, say hello to your Mom and Bill and the rest of the family. Also tell them to write once in a

while. Remember, Hon I love
you now and always.

Bern.

Want to tell you how sorry I
was to hear about your Grand-
Mother. She was a wonderfull
Woman and I'll always remember
her and regret that I never had
the Chance to know her better.

In this letter Dad mentioned how he had recently learned of Mom's grandmother's passing. I can only imagine how sad this news was for Dad being so far away.

Chapter 51

Bernard Michael or Michael Bernard

This following letter is dated November 11, 1944. It was written five months before their new bundle of joy was due on the scene. Chances were, Dad knew he would not be there for their first born. But that did not stop them from planning and discussing baby names. The last few lines in this letter brings tears to my eyes each time I read it. I am at such an advantage knowing the outcome of these written discussions about their future and knowing what lies ahead for both of them.

F51.1 November 11, 1944

Overseas Nov. 11, 1944

Dearest Darling:

Recieved three letters from you yesterday and they were dated Oct 31, Nov 1 and 2nd. The last letter I had recieved from you was dated ~~Nov~~ Oct 25th. so evidently some of your letters have been delayed somewhere. I'm really sorry that you haven't heard from me as yet but I'm positive you will soon. Know how you feel because I was lost untill your letters started to arrive.

So you're working again.[2] What a Gal. I'm glad though that you are able to work and also very proud of you. You don't know how much it helps to know that you are feeling well. Mary, here's a friendly tip. Don't want you to think that I expect you to work. In fact I'd rather you wouldn't. Know that you are planning and saving for our future but Hon, your health means more to me than all the money we could ever save. In other words take care of yourself for me, please? Have I made myself clear that I love you more than life itself and always will?

I'm sorry Mary but I have to cut this letter short. We'll be falling out soon for another days work but I'll write again to-morrow. Give my love to your swell family and I'll be thinking and praying for all of you. Bye Now and Love Always

Bern.

Our Overseas' pay has started and have taken on $18.75 Bond for you. It may help somewhat for the Baby. A good Irish friend of mine, Monahan by name suggested we name him Micheal Bernard or vice versa. If its a Girl he likes Maureen. No doubt about his Nationality is there?

F51.2 November 15, 1944

Overseas Nov 15, 1944.

Darling:

Another night is here so it's time to write the best Wife a guy ever had. I mean that sincerely Mary and it will allways be that way with me. Now, at this very moment, My Boy, Dick Haymes is singing and here are the Titles of his last two Songs. There's a Long Long Trail Awinding and I'll be Seeing You. It may be a Long Long Trail but you can be sure that well be together again. Nothing is going to harm me so you take Care of yourself and look forward to that Great Day.

Nothing out of the ordinary

to tell you tonight. Each Day is about the same and they just keep piling up. By the way, I recieved two more letters from you and I see that you still hadn't heard from me. The dates were the 7th and 8th of November and was positive you would have heard by then. Sure hope by now the Mail Man is getting On The Ball.

Mary, will you excuse me for tonight? Its a bit late and this Old Man is tired as usual. My love and regards to Mom, Grace Bill and Marty and tell them to write when they can. Gosh, how I miss all of you.

Before I close please write and tell me what the Doctor said.

Guess you have by now, but
wanted you to know
that your Health and Well
Being mean everything to me.
Maybe because I love you so
darn much.
Night Hon and Love

Ben.

Chapter 52

England 1944

Being this far along into my Dad's letters, one of the realizations I have had while writing this book and believe me, there have been many, it dawned on me that Dad did a lot of traveling during his time in the army. I am reflecting on his early days in Special Service when his return addresses on his letters were from so many different places, South Carolina; Nashville, Tennessee; Indiana; Kansas; and he had letters sent from many different places in Europe such as England, Scotland, and Germany. He had so many things to write about, especially in his letters from overseas. The reason it struck me; is, I never ever heard him talk about any of these places. He mentioned Scotland as being **"one of the most beautiful places he has ever seen."** I did not know he had ever been there, and I am sure none of my siblings do either.

Did the war do that to my Dad? Did the mere thought of what he endured keep him from letting his mind go anywhere outside of Oak Park, Illinois once he returned home? I will never know.

F52.1 November 18, 1944

Somewhere in England November 18, 1944

Dearest Darling:

At last we are being allowed to tell where we are. It's quite a relief because now my letters may be a bit more interesting. We'll try to give you some idea of England, small though it may be. The first thing we noticed was the Greeness of the Country. The reason for that it seems is the everlasting Dampness. Each morning the ground is as wet as if it had rained all night long. The Weather to be sure isn't agreeable and nine out of every ten caught a cold. We'll get used to it eventually though.

Now here is some more dope
about England and its people.
They have had quite a tough
time of it over here and naturally
we aren't getting the true picture
of the Towns at their best. Most
Everything is rationed including
Food, Clothing, Candy, Ice Cream
and many other things that makes
Life more enjoyable. The people
themselves still have their Cheerfull-
ness and Courage and are very
determined to win this War as
soon as possible. Here is the
last bit of information for tonight. The chief Transportation
here is a very modest Bicycle.
This is the truth. I have
actually seen Women, fifty

to sixty years of age riding a "Bike," to Town. Seems strange doesn't it but it does prove that when things are necessary they can be done. Before I forget I want to tell you that we passed through Scotland and Mary its the most beautiful Country I've ever seen. Haven't seen many but they'd have to be beyond belief to gather my vote.

England is nice to talk about but you're my favorite subject and you always will be. You'll never know how much your letters mean to me and how anxiously I await them. Gosh, I hope you've heard

from me by now. Know just
how you must feel and I
don't want you worrying. In
your last letter you said you
weren't and I'm proud of you.
Just keep feeling that way
because it is the correct
attitude and the only way to be.

Hon, I'm sorry but that's
about all for this time. Take
Care of yourself and keep
loving me. I'm so in love
with you it hurts.

Goodnight and Love

Bern.

Will write your Mom soon.
Give my love to all the family.

Chapter 53

Thanksgiving 1944

F53.1 November 23, 1944

Somewhere in England
November 23, 1944

Dearest

Happy Thanksgiving to you and the entire family. Should have sent this Greeting to you ten days ago but as usual Holidays in the Army creep up on you. Wrote Mom last night and entirely forgot to extend the Seasons' Greetings to my own family.

Two more of your letters came through this week. They were dated October 22 th and November 12. You can see that the Mail is irregular but as long as they get here I'm satisfied. Told Mom this so I'll tell you too. As yet I don't know whether you've heard from me. It has me worried because if you haven't I know exactly how you feel. Have been writing to both of you since the middle of last Month and was certain you'd hear from me by the first of November.

Mary, we had a Company party last week consisting of dancing and refreshments. The Girls invited were the Waaf, Air Corp, and the A.T.C Army. Before the party, the Officer in Charge told us to be as entertaining as possible and to show the Girls a good time. After two hours of sitting around and eating I decided maybe I'd better talk to one of them anyway. A very unfortunate young lady was sitting near by so we struck up a Conversation. She was English and had been in the Service over two years. We talked for about a half hour Comparing our respective Countries and customs and then a boy from our Company Came over to join us so I took off. Then last night a friend and I went to a Show in Town. The Picture was, "Between Two Worlds", and it was good. All in all, you can see that we are having our share of entertainment and relaxation.

Hon, as the days go by I miss you more and more and if its possible my love grows stronger and stronger. Your letters to me are the most important things in my life now. You have a way of making me the happiest guy going and you allways will.

Darlin, that's it for tonight but remember if its possible you'll hear from me as regular as Clock-work. Bye now and Love Always

Bern.

Give your family my love and regards. Don't forget the Boy either. Am I proud? And how.

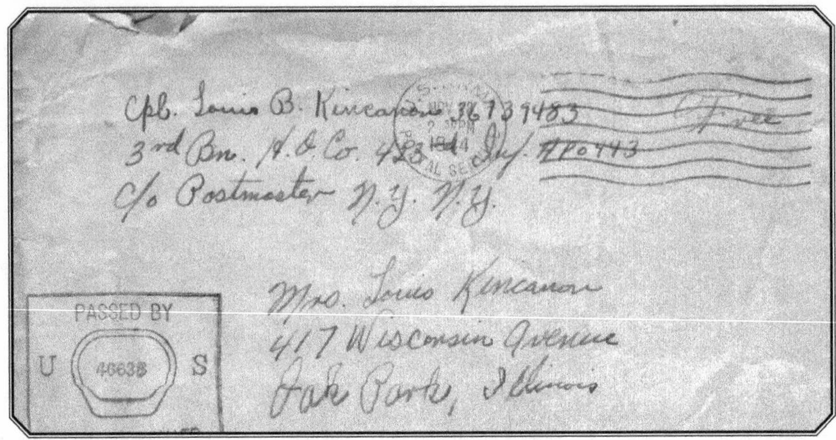

F53.2 November 25, 1944

It has to be so hard for these Soldiers being away from their families anytime, but the holidays have to be especially hard on everyone. I can hear in these holiday letters that Dad is feeling lonely and at the very same time I am sure he had to be sad to be missing this very special time with his new wife as they are preparing to have their first child. My heart goes out to everyone as I read his words.

Somewhere in England
November 25, 1944.

Dearest Darling:

"Hello again, sweetest girl in the World." How's my Wife and our Family today? What a lucky guy this Soldier is. Just to know that you are there waiting for me makes me fear in a way, Coming home to you. Don't know if I'll be able to stand all the happiness that will be inside of me. You can be certain that I'll make every lonely moment up to you when were together again. It's a terrible disappointment to be away from you just when you'll need me most. Hope you'll always remember that you are in my thoughts Constantly and my love for you will never Cease. Please Take Care of yourself and I'll be praying for you and our Baby.

Mrs. Mary, your letters to me aren't censored so you can be just as "Mushy" as you want to. I won't mind a bit.

Haven't heard from you these past few days but will probably get 5 or 6 of them all at once. Recieved four letters from Mom and the Girls and they told me that you Folks had heard from me at last. You can be expecting quite a few letters now because I've been writing pretty often.

Well, Hon, keep writing as often as you can and so will I. Give my love to Mom, Gran and Bill. ~~and~~ Have to write them soon.

Bye now Mary and Love Always

Bernie.

Hope all of you enjoyed your Thanksgiving Dinner and I'm sure you did.

Chapter 54

Another Reminder

The following letter from Dad had another reminder to Mom about the time between correspondence. Again, he tells her that **"there is always a good reason."** He was telling her not to worry when she does not hear from him. These words will turn out to be the only words that keep hope alive for Mom in the coming months. The war is heating up, and Dad will be facing a very difficult time to say the least.

F54.1 November 27, 1944

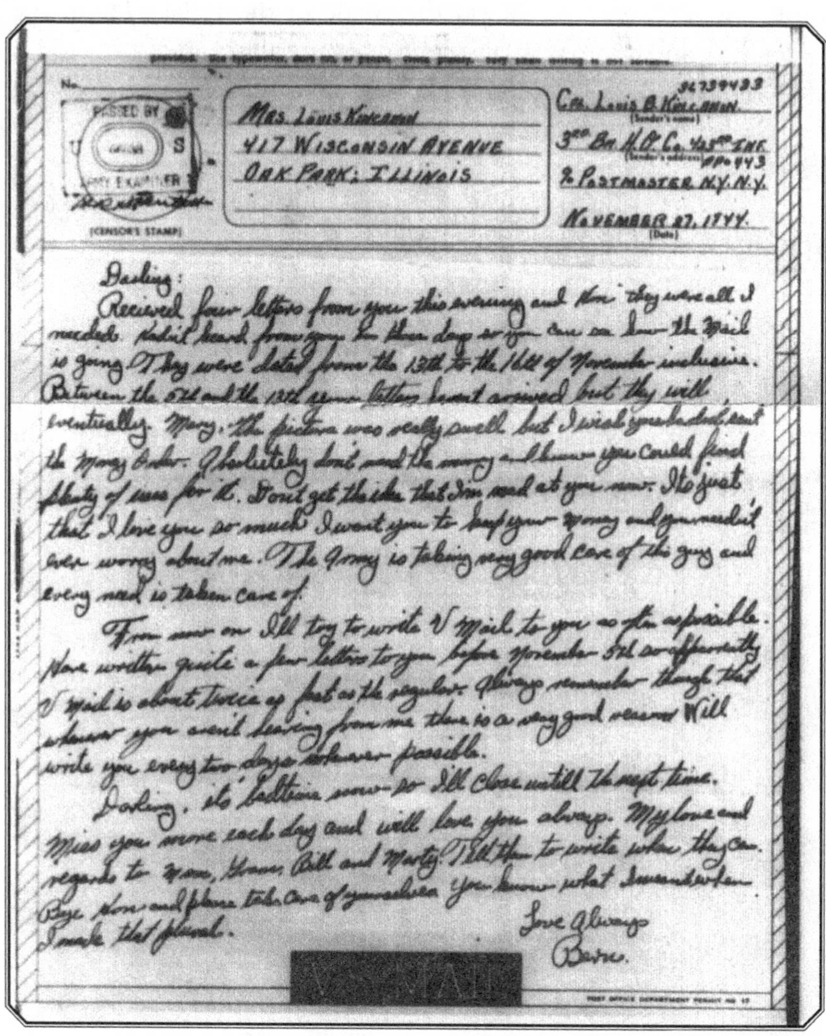

No.

PASSED BY U.S. ARMY EXAMINER
(CENSOR'S STAMP)

MRS. LOUIS KINCANNON
417 WISCONSIN AVENUE
OAK PARK, ILLINOIS

36739433
CPL. LOUIS B. KINCANNON
(Sender's name)
3RD BN. H.Q. CO. 425TH INF.
(Sender's address) APO 443
% POSTMASTER N.Y. N.Y.
NOVEMBER 27, 1944.
(Date)

Darling:

Received four letters from you this evening and [illegible] they were all I needed. Hadn't heard from you in three days so you can see how the mail is going. They were dated from the 13th to the 16th of November inclusive. Between the 5th and the 13th your letters haven't arrived but they will eventually. Mary, the picture was really swell but I wish you hadn't sent the Money Order. Absolutely don't need the money and know you could find plenty of uses for it. Don't get the idea that I'm mad at you now. It's just that I love you so much I want you to keep your money and you needn't ever worry about me. The Army is taking very good care of this guy and every need is taken care of.

From now on I'll try to write V Mail to you as often as possible. Have written quite a few letters to you before November 5th so apparently V mail is about twice as fast as the regular. Always remember though that whenever you aren't hearing from me there is a very good reason. Will write you every two days whenever possible.

Darling, it's bedtime now so I'll close until the next time. Miss you more each day and will love you always. My love and regards to Mom, Gram, Bill and Marty. Tell them to write when they can. Bye Hon and please take care of yourselves. You know what I mean when I make that plural.

Love Always
Bern.

V-MAIL

POST OFFICE DEPARTMENT PERMIT NO. 12

This next letter dated December 13, 1944 will be the last letter you will see from Dad for a very long time.

Three days after the December 13th letter was written and in all probability before my Mom even received this letter, a huge battle broke out in Germany. It was the Battle of the Bulge. The battle began December 16, 1944 and continued through January 25, 1945.

The battle was the last major German offensive campaign on the Western front during WWII. The Battle of the Bulge is the third most lethal American Battle by estimated number of Americans killed (19,276 Killed). If you have been reading my Dad's letters, you are aware of the numerous times he had told Mom that if she is not hearing from him, **"it is for a very good reason."**

In this next letter dated December 13, 1944 Dad tells her, **"Every Mass and Communion are for you and the Baby, that's the best I can do for you now and it makes me feel positively sure you will be alright".**

The big question, will he be alright?

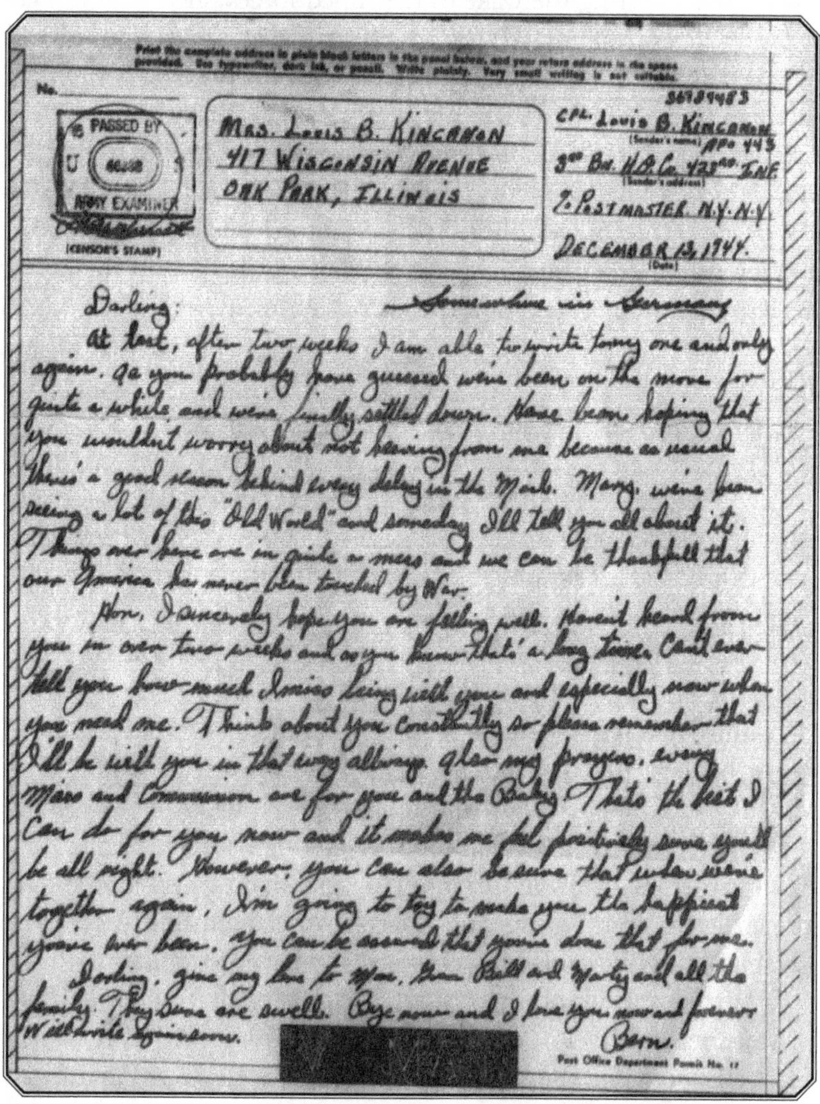

Print the complete address in plain block letters in the panel below, and your return address in the space provided. Use typewriter, dark ink, or pencil. Write plainly. Very small writing is not suitable.

No. ____

PASSED BY
ARMY EXAMINER
(CENSOR'S STAMP)

MRS. LOUIS B. KINCANON
417 WISCONSIN AVENUE
OAK PARK, ILLINOIS

36784483
CPL. LOUIS B. KINCANON
(Sender's name) APO 443
3RD BN. H.Q. CO. 423RD INF.
(Sender's address)
% POSTMASTER N.Y. N.Y.
DECEMBER 13, 1944.
(Date)

Darling: Somewhere in Germany

At last, after two weeks I am able to write to my one and only again. As you probably have guessed we've been on the move for quite a while and we're finally settled down. Have been hoping that you wouldn't worry about not hearing from me because as usual there's a good reason behind every delay in the mails. Marg, we've been seeing a lot of this "Old World" and someday I'll tell you all about it. Things over here are in quite a mess and we can be thankful that our America has never been touched by War.

Hon, I sincerely hope you are feeling well. Haven't heard from you in over two weeks and as you know that's a long time. Can't ever tell you how much I miss being with you and especially now when you need me. Think about you constantly so please remember that I'll be with you in that way always. Also my prayers, every Mass and Communion are for you and the Baby. That's the best I can do for you now and it makes me feel positively sure you'll be all right. However, you can also be sure that when we're together again, I'm going to try to make you the happiest you've ever been. You can be assured that you've done that for me.

Darling, give my love to Mom, Gram, Bill and Marty and all the family. They sure are swell. Bye now and I love you now and forever. Will write again soon.

Bern.

Post Office Department Permit No. 1

F54.2 A little History of The Battle of the Bulge, Courtesy of The U.S. Army Center of Military History

The Battle of the Bulge

In late 1944, during the wake of the Allied forces' successful D-Day invasion of Normandy, France, it seemed as if the Second World War was all but over. On December 16, with the onset of winter, the German army launched a counteroffensive that was intended to cut through the Allied forces in a manner that would turn the tide of the war in Hitler's favor. The battle that ensued is known historically as the Battle of the Bulge. The courage and fortitude of the American Soldier was tested against great adversity. Nevertheless, the quality of his response ultimately meant the victory of freedom over tyranny.

Victory of **FREEDOM** over tyranny

Early on the misty winter morning of December 16, 1944, more than 200,000 German troops and nearly 1,000 tanks launched Adolf Hitler's last bid to reverse the ebb in his fortunes that had begun when Allied troops landed in France on **D-Day**. Seeking to drive to the coast of the English Channel and split the Allied armies as they had done in May 1940, the Germans struck in the Ardennes Forest, a 75-mile stretch of the front characterized by dense woods and few roads, held by four inexperienced and battle-worn American divisions stationed there for rest and seasoning.

After a day of hard fighting, the Germans broke through the American front, surrounding most of an infantry division, seizing key crossroads, and advancing their spearheads toward the Meuse River, creating the projection that gave the battle its name.

Stories spread of the massacre of Soldiers and civilians at Malmedy and Stavelot, of paratroopers dropping behind the lines, and of English-speaking German soldiers, disguised as Americans, capturing critical bridges, cutting communications lines, and spreading rumors. For those who had lived through 1940, the picture was all too familiar. Belgian townspeople put away their Allied flags and brought out their swastikas. Police in Paris enforced an all-night curfew. British veterans waited nervously to see how the Americans would react to a full-scale German offensive, and British generals quietly acted to safeguard the Meuse River's crossings. Even American civilians, who had thought final victory was near were sobered by the Nazi onslaught.

But this was not 1940. The supreme Allied commander, Gen. Dwight D. Eisenhower rushed reinforcements to hold the shoulders of the German penetration. Within days, Lt. Gen. George S. Patton Jr. had turned his Third U.S. Army to the north and was counterattacking against the German flank. But the story of the Battle of the Bulge is above all the story of American Soldiers. Often isolated and unaware of the overall picture, they did their part to slow the Nazi advance, whether by delaying armored spearheads with obstinate defenses of vital crossroads, moving or burning critical gasoline stocks to keep them from the fuel-hungry German tanks, or coming up with questions on arcane Americana to stump possible Nazi infiltrators.

At the critical road junctions of St. Vith and Bastogne, American tankers and paratroopers fought off repeated attacks, and when the acting commander of the 101st Airborne Division in Bastogne was summoned by his German adversary to surrender, he simply responded, "Nuts!"

Within days, Patton's Third Army had relieved Bastogne, and to the north, the 2nd U.S. Armored Division stopped enemy tanks short of the Meuse River on Christmas. Through January, American troops, often wading through deep snow drifts, attacked the sides of the shrinking bulge until they had restored the front and set the stage for the final drive to victory.

Never again would Hitler be able to launch an offensive in the west on such a scale. An admiring British Prime Minister Sir Winston Churchill stated, "This is undoubtedly the greatest American battle of the war and will, I believe, be regarded as an ever-famous American victory." Indeed, in terms of participation and losses, the Battle of the Bulge is arguably the greatest battle in American military history.

Chapter 55

Left in the Dark

Mom's resolve was about to be tested; she was a newlywed, and she was five months pregnant. Mom was totally in the dark about where her husband and soon to be new father was or if he was still alive.

Things had changed for Dad but there was no way of knowing that. There was the news on the radio or in the newspaper, but what good was that when you have no word from your husband, and the news from all the other sources was all bad? Mom was left in the dark.

I knew my Mom, but I cannot in any way fathom what she must have been going through. Mom's upbringing and the things she endured as a child may have prepared her and given her the strength to face what was ahead of her and her baby.

Mom had to grow up fast, as a young child she lost her father, she was the big sister in charge of her little brother, this all made her a very strong woman. Mom had told me many times that growing up without a father made her look at the world differently than most of her friends. Mom knew what she wanted and went after it. We have had some very strong women role models in our family, but she was definitely the one that influenced me the most. Although, my two grandmothers were no "wall flowers." They were both strong in their own way.

We are now at the last letter Dad had written on December 13, 1944; three days before the Battle of the Bulge.

It is winter in Oak Park, and almost Christmas time. The news coming in regarding the war is not good, Mom has no idea where Dad is, his latest letter said he was, ***"Somewhere in Germany."***

Mom is now six months pregnant most likely over her morning sickness and proudly showing off her baby bump to anyone who notices. Her pregnancy was getting a little harder, the hormones, changes to her body and emotions were at an all-time high. Not to mention, The War. Where is Bernie? Why have the letters stopped? I can imagine Mom saying over and over to herself those words she read so many times from Dad, **"If you don't hear from me there is always a good reason."** I am sure that Mom could not help but convince herself that the mail was held up, or he was too busy to write. I do not think Mom could have risked letting her mind go where it will naturally go, because now she had another life growing inside her that needed all of her attention, nurturing, and nutrition. Was she eating properly with all those worries on her mind? December passes and no word, except what she was reading and listening to on the radio. Was she sleeping? She needed her rest for the baby.

Was she crying alone in her room at night? I know I would have been. I am sure she heard of all the casualties but did not let herself think about it. There was no one to ask, no way of knowing.

The other family members that Mom had grown so close to were all feeling the same way, I am sure of it. I just know that they were all worried for Dad and for Mom, and now the new life that was only four months away from entering the world and an unknown future.

The morning sickness may have been over, but now there was that other feeling in her gut that would not go away. It was that constant nagging feeling, and always wondering if there was a letter coming today? The news, it was still drumming in her ears, but she would not let herself go there. Time was moving so slow and still no word. Mom's growing belly was telling her that time was moving along and right into her eighth month. Growing bigger, feeling the baby, a stark reminder, the due date is fast approaching. I am sure it was getting harder to do the normal things at home. Stairs took longer, ankles were swelling, making her very uncomfortable. I am sure Maw was by my Mom's side offering well-intentioned advice. I remember Mom telling me about her right ankle and not knowing what was wrong with it. It was so swollen, much larger than the left. You were so grateful your mother was there with her hot pad while she massaged your leg to help you feel better, but nothing was helping. Thank goodness Mom went to the doctor. She was diagnosed with Phlebitis. It was a very, very serious case. It is an inflammation of a vein; a blood clot which caused extreme inflammation. I remember Mom telling me that the home remedies they had been trying was the worst thing they could have done. The blood clot could have traveled to her lungs resulting in an embolism. Mom was relegated to bed rest for the next few weeks of her pregnancy which took her right up to her due date.

Dad was unaware of any of this. And I am sure lying in bed for the duration of her pregnancy was the last place Mom wanted to be. This was supposed have been one of the happiest times in a woman's life, but I don't think Mom was able to enjoy it. She had too much time to think about her life, her baby's life, and her husband's. There was some letter writing going on during this time by Mom, I am sure. Where those letters went, we will never know. Mom was so brave!

This is what I would want to say to my Mom right now if I could.

Dear Mom, you are an amazingly strong woman, that is the face you presented to the world, your mother, Dad's mother, your brother. You carried the weight for everyone, I know you did. The feeling I get all over my entire body when I think about all you went through; I literally shake from the inside out. I can only imagine how I would have reacted under those same circumstances. I put these words down now to pay tribute to you, one of the strongest women I have ever known.

1944

January 1, 1944

Darling,

A few short lines this evening to a swell girl from a lonely and sad soul. Haven't received a letter of any kind for four days now but they'll be waiting for me back in Fort Jackson. As you know your daily letters are my one and only protection from absolute insanity. Our training is now in the very dull and tiresome stages and we keep looking for some outlet. Mary, since being in Special Service I've had a pretty easy life, but it's not what I had hoped for. We have so much idle time on our hands that the days seem to have no end. While in the Anti-Tank Company they worked us hard and you'd be surprised how fast those months went by. Guess it's the same old story, a fellow is never satisfied in the Army no matter what he is doing. Here I am, safe and sound and still there comes forth from this mortal, loud moans and groans. Maybe it's not the Army life itself, but the fact I can't be with you that accounts for it. Mary, "old kid," if this War doesn't end and allow me to marry you in a very short time, don't blame me for going crazy. I miss you more every day and being under your spell as I am, is, to put it mildly, "HELL."

Don't tell me. I know I've got big feet.

How's the family, Hon? Don't know how any of you are but I trust all of you are well and looking forward to a great New Year. By the way, is Bill's team still winning? No matter what sport you're in, if it's not a winner the biggest thrill is missing. Tell him I'm wishing him and the team the best of luck. Your Mother and Grandmother will be hearing from me soon. That's the truth, even though you are laughing.

"Honey Chile" due to an important Pinochle game this will now be concluded for tonight. I love you and don't ever forget it. Bye now and best regards to all.

Love Always,
Bern

January 2, 1944

Darling:

Surprised? Well, here is the reason for this unexpected letter. Forgot to congratulate you on leaving Modern Modes and taking that swell new job. I've never exactly relished the idea of you working there and now that you've left it suits me fine. Know that they treated you OK but outside of a few they weren't the "Elite" of Chicago. Yes, I too have a soft spot in my heart for the place, so we won't forget it entirely.

Have you been writing me regularly since last Sunday? Hope you have because I expect about five of your letters to be waiting for me back in Fort Jackson.

Hon, the rumors have us leaving here very soon so don't be too surprised to hear about it in my next letter or two. Maybe they aren't true but who knows?

Think I'll be able to tell you where we are going so that's a break, anyway.

Well, that's all for tonight. Be a good girl and pray hard for me. I'll always love you, Mary.

Love
Bern

We've been having a nice week here in this town. It's a lucky break for me because it has been raining quite a bit. Wouldn't be much fun out in the field in this weather.
(QUOTE) "Southern girls are strictly, Jerks" (UNQUOTE)

January 9, 1944

Darling:

Hello, for the first time in a week. Now before we go any further, I'll tell you what I'm telling Mom. I have been the busiest guy in the 106th. Our Basketball tournament is in progress and they are running me ragged. It's over Tuesday and what a relief that will be.

Well, my future wife, are you happy being engaged to me? You've made a bad bargain but. If you aren't complaining, why should I? I do know this much, I'm the happiest and the saddest guy all at the same time.

Happy because we are engaged and sad because we'll have to wait for the end of this war to be married. If you only knew how much I miss you. Well, maybe our love will be that much stronger when we finally do get hitched.

Glad to hear that Bill's team is on top. Know how good a feeling it is to be winning and hope they continue that way. Tell him that the time will come when I can teach him what little I know about hitting. Maybe we'll make a pitcher out of him too. Mary, return my love to your family and tell them hello. Bet your Mother is still waiting for her letters.

Why did you call me Mush? Don't you know that is your fault? I can't help it. Hon, the Maneuvers are to be held in Tennessee from the 31st of January till the 27th of March. Our starting point will be from a town called Murphysboro and where we'll end up nobody knows.

Of course, this is mostly rumor, but it's almost correct anyway. You know, it will seem funny leaving this place, but we can't stay here forever.

Darling, will you pardon me for now? I'm a bit tired and want to clean up before going to bed. I'll love you always and keep loving me, will you?

So long, hon.
Love Bernie

So, you are keeping up with the rest of the gals. Well, I always claimed you were beautiful and now you'll probably blind me. Do want you to buy yourself all the clothes you need and don't be saving everything to support me. It won't take me long to get going again after the war. Hon, for the first time in my life work will be a pleasure. The war has taught me that anyway.

January 26, 1944

Hello Darling,

Your last six letters caught up with me this morning and what a pleasure they were after five days of loneliness. Mary, the fellows are beginning to suspect that we love each other. Can you imagine that? They can't understand how I ever fooled you. I can't either but I'm sure glad I did.

Well, we are situated in Tennessee about 5 miles from Murphysboro. You were right, it really is a burg. We stopped there last night for a cup of coffee and couldn't even get in a restaurant. Soldiers have taken the town over and we saw about five civilians. There is another Division here, the 78th and they will be our enemy. That makes about 30,000 Soldiers all situated around that one little town. Nashville is 30 miles from here, but it may as well be a thousand.

Hon, you do write the nicest letters. It sure helps to know that you'll be right there waiting when all this is over. Most fellows haven't the utmost confidence in their gals as I have in you. Yes, Mush, some day we will realize all our hopes, and nothing will ever separate us again. As you said getting our happiness the hard way will make us appreciate it much more.

Sorry about the phone call but I couldn't do a thing about it. Your letter telling me about the difficulty didn't reach me until today. Maybe I'll get a chance to call you one of these days. I have quite a few things to tell you also and the sound of your voice will help a lot.

Mary, this isn't much of a letter but there will be more coming. Until the next, remember I love you very much and miss you always. Be good and give my love to all. Bye now and Love Forever,

Bern

Remember me to your Grandmother when you write her.

January 28, and 29th 1944

Darling:

It's a bit late to start a letter but I'll try and finish this before retiring. Nothing much has happened the past few days, so I haven't much to tell you. The weather continues to be the best and that's a break. We're all holding our breath though because it can't last. Maybe this winter will be a mild one all over, even Chicago.

As you can see the tent caught up with me last night and it did feel good. We have been told that after Maneuvers are over, we won't be able to sleep in a nice warm bed. Don't hardly believe them but perhaps you'd better start practicing hon. The floor or ground is hard at first but after a few weeks nothing bothers you. Oh, before I forget, the weather report; a bit cooler, but the sun continues to shine.

My love, the days are going by pretty fast and I'm wondering just what day in the future will bring us together for good. Furloughs are swell but the after effect is an awful thing. All these fellows returning from home look like they were doomed to die. The feeling of emptiness stays with you for a month afterwards and then we start looking for another chance to get home. Well, at least we are in the same country, aren't we? The boys over there are not only lonely but they have the threat of death staring them in the face constantly. It must be pretty tough, and I don't think they'll ever forget these years of war.

Mary, you have often told me that your family and relatives think highly of me. I'm glad they do and to be truthful I am very grateful. You have a fine family and swell relations and to be in their favor means a lot to me. Now let me tell you what I personally think of you. Hon, you are all I ever expected in a girl. You're a good clean Catholic girl and I have all the respect in the world for you. Some time when I'm home we'll have a good talk and I'll explain how I feel entirely. I know I've never paid you too many compliments but if I hadn't loved you and respected you, we wouldn't be engaged. You've been swell to me in every way even when things weren't looking so good for us. You brat, I've been thinking. Of our first year together and of all the things you said and did. We sure have had fun and on the other hand we've had a few troubles too. Don't believe anything will stop us from being happy now because we've come through everything in good shape. Say, Beautiful, this is a very rare serious moment with me, so don't get worried. Maybe it's the Tennessee Woods.

Excuse me for now and I'll write you again soon. Love you and miss you more than ever.

Bye now and Love Always. Bern.

January 29, 1944

Dear Ma Ruhnke:

Well, that's almost a reality now and hope it won't be long until Mary and I can make it final. Your very nice letter was received, and it was truly welcome. You probably know that a letter means quite a bit to us and we appreciate everyone we get. Your wonderful daughter sure has been swell in writing me every day. Don't know how she does it but each one is interesting, and I am always waiting for her next. Maybe love has something to do with it, I don't know. Want to thank you for your Congratulation Wishes. Ma, you needn't worry about me making Mary happy. If it's within my power, she'll be one of the happiest because I'd do most anything for her. Don't tell her that because I don't think she suspects me of being so sentimental. She has been so darn good to me that even if I tried, I couldn't help but think that she's the best ever.

Well, we are leaving here Friday for our Maneuver Area in Tennessee. We'll be there for two months and then about the first of April will be heading for another camp. Nobody knows where we'll go so until that day comes one guess is as good as another. Hope it's in good Yankee Country though. The South has lost what little appeal it ever had for me.

Mary tells me your Mother is getting ready to leave for California again. It seems like she has found one place better thank Chicago. Give her my love and tell her to take care of herself. Maybe, if some of these rumors are true, we may see each other out in "the Golden West."

Guess I've reached the end of something to write about for now. Please write again when you can and so will I. Until then Bye.

Love
Bernie

Regards to Bill and I'm still pulling for Oak Park. Next year he'll be a regular and I hope I'll be able to see most of his games as a civilian.

p.s. Please note the new address and report same to Mary E.

February 3, 1944

Darling:

At this very moment I am writing to you from the Soldier's Center in Murphysboro. Another fellow and I, started out this morning and after walking 7 miles we were picked up by an Ambulance and rode in style the remaining 11 miles. We still have to bum our way back, but we'll make it somehow. Have just taken a shower and I feel quite a bit better. Our first problem is over now, and we'll be non-tactical until Sunday night or Monday morning. Until then they'll keep us busy showing pictures every night, so you can see that Special Service is always working. It's not so bad though because we do have quite a bit of time to ourselves during the day.

Hon, enough of this Army life. Your letter from the 1st came this morning and it was swell. Seems like we really do think alike most of the time and that's a good sign. You're swell Mary and I'll always love you.

Darling, I hope you'll excuse me for now. I'm in a hurry to get back but I'll write you again soon. Regards to your folks and I miss them almost as much as I do you.

Bye now and Love forever
Bern

February 5, 1944

Hello Darling:

Before leaving to present a morning picture I'll try to write you a few lines. Nothing new of interest has happened since the last letter. It's still the same old routine of life in the field.

Say, what seems to be the trouble with you> Your last three letters have been telling me that you aren't feeling a bit good. Well, your letter of the 4th just arrived and after reading it through it seems you have recovered. Have a hunch that those visits to the Red Cross aren't agreeing with you. Give you all the credit in the world for doing that but, don't let your health suffer. After all, I do love you very much and if you're going to be sick then so am I.

Hon, we can receive packages out here, but you needn't bother sending me anything. At the present time we are eating very well and besides you've sent me too many good things already. Someday soon I hope to repay all the kindness you have shown me and that's a promise.

Ede does get around, doesn't she? Hope she picks the right guy out of all those Service men.

Mary, it's time to go now so I'll leave you for a while. Say hello to Mom, Bill and Marty for me. In the meantime, I'll go on loving and missing you as always.

Bye
Bern

February 12, 1944

Dearest:

Should have written you before this but it's the same old story. Wednesday night we moved in the pouring rain and Thursday we packed and took off again. Seems like they are really giving this Division the works. The 87th Division told us that Maneuvers would be comparatively easy, but they must have gone at things differently than we are. The days are going by pretty fast though so before we know it we'll be back in some other camp.

Considering your last letter, your Mother had quite a hectic day last week. I hope she didn't hurt herself and that she is feeling OK now.

I received another chain letter from the Schedule Dept., and it was swell. They don't forget the boys in the Service and every one of us appreciate that fact.

One of the boys was wounded in action in Italy and they are all pretty proud of him. Guess he's been in the Army for about two years.

Hon, two months ago we were together, but it seems like years. Never will be completely happy until we are married and together for always. Once I get home it will take quite a necessary trip to ever get me away again. Travel is alright for a while, but it doesn't take long to appreciate home and someone like you. That little Poem was absolutely right. Never realized how much I loved you until I had to leave and there's an awful empty feeling with me always.

Mary, that's all for this time. Keep loving me and pray hard for Victory. Bye now and regards to Mom and Bill.

Love,
Bern

Can't figure out whether I owe your Mother a letter or not. Please inform me when you write.

February 16, 1944

Hello Hon,

As usual I haven't much to write about, but these few lines will help keep your morale, I hope. Mary when you hear from me about moving it doesn't mean that we've left Tennessee. We just keep jumping around from spot to spot in order to keep up with the rest of the War. When I get home again, you'll hear all about Maneuvers and their fine points. While we are out here it's exactly the same as Battle conditions or, so they tell us.

So, you are having your troubles now? What I am wondering is whether or not you hurt yourself when you fell? What a gal.

Darling, this is a shame I know, closing so suddenly on you but the bed is awaitin'. We are due to move again in the morning and sleep tonight is necessary. Will write again soon as possible and promise that the next letter will be much longer. Until then be good, keep loving me and remember I love you and miss you more every day.

Bye now Mush
Bern

Regards and love to Mom and Bill

February 23, 1944

Darling Mary Eileen:

It's a beautiful day in Tennessee for a change. We've had more than our share of rain lately but today it is actually Summer. For some unknown reason we have been at ease all day and all we've done is lay out here and soak up all this swell sunshine.

I hit the "Jackpot" in the letter department this morning. Your two letters department this morning. Your two letters of the 20th and the 21st arrived and two most important people in my life still remember me. Mom also sent some pictures they had taken, and did I enjoy them. Everyone looked in the best of health and also very happy. Uncle Matt looks like a different guy now doesn't he?

Hon, it's surprising how little there is to write to you about these days. Every day is about the same now but when we hit our new Camp things will pick up again. If and when I see you again, you'll hear all about these two month that is if you can stand the boring details. In the meantime, I'll keep writing you these short notes to let you know I still think about you day in and day out. Mary, it's growing worse every day this lonesome feeling and I'll never be content till we're together for always. Maybe a person is better off never falling in love, but I guess not. At least we do have something to look forward to and what we have will be wonderful, I know. This as usual is the end so keep loving me and don't worry for I'll never change. Bye now and love.

Bernie
Mom and Bill will hear from me soon.

February 26, 1944

Dearest Darling:

Here's another short note from the rainiest state in the Union. Mary, I have never seen so much rain anywhere and at this very moment we are having a real downpour. It's lucky that we have this large tent, or we'd be drowned by now. We just can't seem to keep a dry spot of ground to sleep on and most of the fellows are getting a bit disgusted. One thing about them though, they haven't lost their sense of humor, so they'll get by on that alone. Oh well, there's a great day coming.

Mary, today being so dreary, I miss you more than ever and id I could just see you for a minute the Sun would shine. Words fail me to tell you how I really feel, but if you love me as I do you then I know you'll understand. In some of your letters you've mentioned about feeling lonesome, so we'll have to get together some day and diagnose our case. Anyway, when you write me and tell me how much you think of me, the "old Morale" climbs to the sky. Mushy, aren't I? Well that's the way I feel, "Mushy" and if you were here, you'd find out. Hon, didn't I ever thank you for the Valentine candy you sent me? Guess not, because you've asked me about it in some of your latest letters.

I'm sorry you know, and it was swell. The whole office appreciated it a lot especially our Major. He's a hard candy fiend. Here's the stopping point again, so please return Mom and Bill's love and remember me to all the family. Be good Darling and I hope to see you in a few months.

Love Forever
Bern

I'm going to brag a little bit, Mary. The Major heard me singing and now he wants to use me in our program, but I don't want to.

Sunday February 27, 1944

Hello Again, Hon,

Didn't have a chance to mail this last night. We went to town last night though and saw **"King of the Cowboys"** had a good meal and now we feel better. Funny isn't it? Our night off and we go to a show. I still love you more than ever. See that proves it. Each day it

Gets worse. So long for now and keep loving me.

Bernie

February 29, 1944 (Leap Year)

Dearest:

Just received your letter telling me of your misfortune. You are very lucky though to recover those things as easily as you have. Can plainly see how you looked, and I'll bet you were a very sad soul. That's one of my many reasons I love you Mary. You appreciate every little thing I do for you so much and losing a gift of mine would about break your heart. At least that's what you tell me, and I believe you. Now I have a confession to make. Since leaving Fort Jackson somehow the cigarette lighter you gave me has disappeared. It may be in my other Barracks Bag. I hope. Don't want to lose it because it means a lot to me. Now, here's the way we pack our stuff when we go on Maneuvers. We have two Barracks Bags; A & B. In our B Bag we put all clothing and equipment that we will not use, and it is sent to our new camp. The A Bag is used for all necessary equipment and clothing, so now you know what a division does when it packs and takes off. This explanation was for the purpose of showing you that maybe in my haste I put the lighter in the wrong place. Hon, will you me my C Bag?

Don't be mad. That's just a joke we have around here. You know that you're all the world to me and I couldn't love anyone more that you. I sincerely hope to prove these words to you soon and those days eventually will arrive.

John L. Richards wrote me a letter the other day and as usual he didn't have much to talk about, but John L. told me about some "gal" he loves and intends to marry and that was a surprise. How some guys can fall in and out of love and in love again so quickly is beyond me. That's the third or fourth girl he's fallen for in two years. In spite of his goofiness I still have a soft spot for him so after leaving you, I'll surprise him and write.

Darling, don't know any more news so will end this now. Before I do though here is some more flattery, but I mean every word. Want you to know that I carry all of your pictures around and I'm always looking at my Beautiful Future Wife. A feeling of pride always hits me at those times accompanied by that "old Bug" loneliness. Remember the night J Richards came in. Well, that evening put me on top of the world knowing you were so attractive and mine. So there too, you're a soft soaper yourself so now I'm getting even but it's all true. Bye now, my love. Getting mushier all the time, aren't I?

Love Always
Bern

March 8, 1944

Darling,

Here is another short note to let you know I'm still thinking of you daily. Nothing has changed here lately except that Maneuvers are drawing to a close. We have about two more weeks of them and then as you probably know we'll take off for Indiana. At least that's the most recent reliable news we've had. As for furlough we don't know anything yet.

Sorry to hear that Oak Park High lost out in the tournament. We'll just wait till Bill's a regular and then they'll have a champion. Haven't gotten around to writing your Mother but you can tell her to be patient with me. Sure will be glad when I won't have to write any more letters. Want to be with all of you people forever one of these days and you can be sure that I'll stay right there always.

Mary, remember when I wrote and told you that the weather was improving. Well, I take it all back. We've had rain, snow and freezing weather all in the last few days. We certainly will appreciate our new Camp after all this.

Hon, I guess there's no need to keep repeating this but I will. Whether I do or now you can be sure that I love and miss you very much and until we're together, my life will never be complete.

Now, as usual it's closing time because I've run out of things to say. Be good now and I hope to see you soon.

Love Always
Bern

Just received your letters of the 6th and 7th and both were very interesting. Sorry you lost Hon, but you're bucking a poker playing family over there. Sure is good to know that you like my family and mix so well with them.

Bye for now, Lover.

March 13, 1944

I'm a bit late again with this, aren't I? Guess you've hooked up with a very poor letter writer and I won't deny it. Writing is a hard job for me, so you'll just have to suffer the consequences. Anyway, I hope you realize that whether I write you often or not, I think of you always and love you more as time goes by. Being away from you so long is very hard and I sincerely hope that it won't be too long till we get married. Your consistent letters and the packages of cookies and stuff are the main things to me these days, so even though you wait so long for letters please don't stop yourself. By the way, last week two very indignant letters reached me and told me off Hon, when you hear all the dope I'm sure you'll feel a bit different. Just wrote Mom a letter telling her that I'd explain all when the furlough gets here. Women sure are funny people and especially Mothers. Can see her point of view but believe she still thinks I'm a baby without good common sense. Don't tell her that because she's sensitive and I wouldn't hurt her for the world. Don't mean it to sound mean or anything. All I want to bring out is the fact that she's too good a Mother and if I live to be 70 years old, she'll still worry about me.

Mary, wish you'd thank your Grandmother for me. She's really swell but being a relation of yours she couldn't be any other way. Yep, we'll get along O.K. You like my family and I'm nuts about yours so we can't miss being happy. My love, this is the end of another letter. Can't wait to see you again and from the latest reports it may not be too long. In the meantime, keep up the good work and give me love to all.

Love always
Bern

Tell Ma I'll write her soon. Bet she gets mighty disgusted waiting for her letter.

Here I am again almost closing without thanking you for your latest box of cookies. Hon, as usual they were delicious.

March 20, 1944

Dearest Darling,

Late again. Right? Well even so I still love you and it's getting very difficult for me to think of anything but you. Sometimes your point of view seems very right to me, but I don't know. It's an awful decision to make in times like these. Hon, believe me, I'd give the World to be married to you right now but somehow the thought of it scares me. The responsibility and everything that goes with marriage is hard even in normal times and my better judgment tells me to wait. Guess I'm an awful dope having such a swell gal as you and not taking advantage of these years. Do want you to know that my life is wrapped up in you and always will be. Have quite a bit to tell you about everything when we are together again, and I hope that's not too far away. Furloughs generally are the rule after Maneuvers so........The Camp in Indiana is definite now, so this summer should be very enjoyable. Hon, I told Mom not to broadcast about where we are going so I have to ask you also. It's not compulsory to do this but it's best to keep it quiet. The Army makes rules, but the Officers are the first ones to break them. They've sent their wives up there already and I guess everybody in Indiana and Tennessee knows our destination.

There's no danger at all in a move such as this so it doesn't make much difference. The only time things are kept undercover is when we take the boat ride.

Hon, I hope you'll excuse the shortness of this letter. I'm saving all the news until furlough time. Give my love to Mom and Bill and tell her to get well quick. She sure is having a time lately. Glad she understands about me not writing.

Goodbye Hon and love always,
Bern

Your grandmother sent me a swell package and I'm going to write and thank her as soon as possible. By the way, the Ruhnke family are sure swell people and I love all of you. Miss O'Ruhnke your package and card sure was appreciated, thanks very much "Irish".

March 28, 1944

Darling:

Haven't much time to write tonight but I'll do my best. Realize I should have written you before, but as usual I'm quite a bit late. Hon, we have arrived at Camp Atterbury and is it swell. Nothing connected with the Army ever looked as good as this place did to me. Last night we stopped over in Fort Knox, Kentucky and it also was a good camp. Seems the farther North one gets everything improves, even the girls and I do mean you. We are now going to concentrate on wising up all these "Rebels", including the Major and Lt. Mary I was sorry to hear about you catching a cold. Hope by now you are feeling better and you'd better stay that way. For some crazy reason no matter how miserable the weather was on maneuvers, a cold never caught up with me and that's a break.

Darling, I received the pictures and they weren't so bad. I'll admit my Mary is much prettier in the flesh so don't be disillusioned. In regard to seeing you Easter, I'll try to call you soon and let you know what the score is. I'll write you again in a day or so after I find out the way this Camp works. Until then be good and remember that I love you now and always.

Love,
Bern

Regards to Mom and Bill and all the family.

March 31, 1944

Dearest:

How you doin,' Hon? Very good I hope and please stay that way. Mary, I don't think there's a chance of me getting home for Easter Sunday. If I was back in the Infantry it would be simple, but this office has bad hours and Saturday is just another day of hard work. If it's the last thing I do, I'll convince Mom about transferring back again. Well, now that you know I can't make Chicago, you had better come here. Want to see you very much and if you and Ede come down, we'll have a swell time. Have inquired about the Guest House and when I get the OK from you, I'll reserve one of their rooms. A guest is allowed not more than 3 days so please tell when you'll arrive and leave again. Hon, this is sure a beautiful Camp and I know you'll enjoy yourself here.

Guess you know by now that I'm going to pitch against the Louisville Colonels next Friday. Funny isn't it? Had to wait until the Army grabbed me to pitch against an American Association Team.

Darling, as I said before seeing you again will be great. We had hoped to receive furloughs after maneuvers, but we haven't heard a thing about them. They will come eventually but the time is unpredictable. Want to see everyone again and soon.

This letter is awfully mixed up, but I guess baseball not to mention you has me in a fog. I'll say so long for now, "Mush" but you'll hear from again before you leave. Give my love to Mom and Bill and the rest of the Family. Still haven't written your Grandmother but have a good excuse. I've misplaced her address so will you send it to me?

Good night lover and be good.

Love always
Bernie

So, you caught a cold? That's one you can't blame on me.

April 1, 1944

Darling.

Just received some news today that will change our plans. I expect to be home in about 2 or 3 weeks, so maybe it would be best for you and Ede to come down sometime later on. I know both of you wanted to come and see our swell Camp, but it would do all of us more good if you postpone the trip till about June. Another week or so won't make much difference. It does in a way, but it'll make seeing you just that more enjoyable.

Well, this isn't much of a letter Hon? Anyway, I'm a very happy guy and can't wait to be with you again. I'll write you regularly so keep loving me and remember you are my one and only best girl. Love always

Bern

May 13, 1944

Darling.

Here I am again. Back to the Home for the feeble and aged. What an army Career I've had and how disgusted I am, no one knows. Never thought it was possible to have so many things happen in one year. See how I feel, Hon?

Now here's some good news I received today. The Captain called me in today and examined me again as I believed it's not a hernia but a badly strained muscle, so that's a relief anyway. Don't need an operation but plenty of rest. Don't know how long they'll keep me here, but I'll be home for our wedding. Mary, know you were very disappointed the other night when I called you. Don't blame you a bit because it did look like a good two-month delay in our plans. You sounded very sad over the phone and could see you so plain. You know marrying me is the beginning of a very bad risk. If I keep on this way, you'll be a Hospital Widow.

Hon, I'm going to call Mom this afternoon and tell her the latest dope. She'll probably call you and then this letter won't contain any news for you. Would call you also but making you pay for the call is too much, so this letter is the next best.

Keep writing often and keep loving me and soon we'll be together for always, I hope.

Bye now and love,
Bern

Give my regards and love to all the family.
By the way I'm going to quit baseball for summer. Wait till the Major hears that.

May 17, 1944

Hello Darling:

Well, here I am again and have make some plans for getting out of here. They haven't done a darn thing for me so can see no good in staying here. By Monday I hope to be free and then maybe the furlough could be had by June 1st. These Army Doctors are great people. If they can't operate or give you a pill they are lost. He told me to rest but the swelling is still there, and any future movement will bring back the pain. He asked me how it was today, and I told him OK so now he thinks he's good. Have to humor him along and keep up his morale.

Mary, how are you doing? Are you still as anxious as ever to get hitched? Hope you are because we've certainly waited long enough for our complete happiness. Hon don't do anything drastic at your office for a while. There are some rumors flying around again about us moving and if we are, there would be no sense in you coming here for a short time and then having to move to another location. By the time I get home maybe the whole story will be out and then I can tell you all the dope, dope. Sorry that Bob K is leaving the U.S. You don't want to feel too badly though, I'm sure he can take care of himself and being Irish, he has plenty of luck on his side. Someday, I'm pretty sure we'll meet, and we can't help but like each other. After all we both love you, don't we? For the life of me though, I can't figure out why.

Hon, this is an abrupt ending, but I'll write you again soon. Give my love to Mom, Bill and Gram and everyone.

Bye now and love always,
Bern

August 15, 1944 Wichita, Kansas

Darling,

Received your swell long letter this morning and as you said, it does seem funny to be writing each other again. Prefer the other way much more but maybe it won't be too long now. As you know the news this morning was all for the best so.... Can't wait to be with you in our own home no matter what kind, even though it's only a cabin. We'll do all right hon, wait and see.

I'm glad you consulted your Mother about the Doctor. Now I feel better, and if it does happen, I only hope to be with you.

Mary, we play our first game tomorrow night. Don't think we have much of a chance because these teams are full of Big Leagues.

Can't tell you how long we'll be here, but I'll keep you posted.

Hon, you are quite a working girl, aren't you? Will I be glad when this dope can get back home and make a home for you like I should.

Don't know much else to tell you, but you'll be hearing from me again. Tell your Mom, Gram, Bill and everybody hello, and hope to see all of you soon.

Love Always, Bern.

When you receive this letter Mary, please call Mom and tell her there's a letter to her on the way.

Bye, now.

August 18, 1944 Wichita, Kansas

Hello Hon;

Same old Mary, aren't you? Your daily letter reaches me every day and as usual they are all I live for. I've been pretty lonesome these days and will be until we're together again. Didn't think it was possible, but since we've been married my love for you has grown much deeper and it will always be that way. One of these days I hope I'll be able to show you all the happiness you deserve. You've certainly made me a much happier soldier. At the same time though being away from you makes me a much crabbier one too.

Mary, we are having a nice time out here in Kansas. This is a swell town and it seems just like a vacation to all of us. The only thing that spoils it is Captain Daniels and I mean "thing." I sure have a lot to tell you about that individual and any respect I ever had for him is gone.

We won our first game the other night, but the other team wasn't so hot. Mungo pitched, struck out 17 and gave two hits. Score 5-0. He is still a Big-League Pitcher, but he said he won't be able to pitch again for two weeks. There are plenty of good pitchers out here and we're facing Herman Besse Sunday, formally with the Athletics. They may pitch me Sunday sore arm and all, and if they do, I'll do my best.

Mary, my love, will you give my regards to all your folks and tell them I hope to see them soon. Bye for now and,

Love, Always.
Bern

Address letters same as before only change to Hotel Lassen.

August 22, 1944 Wichita, Kansas

Darling;

I have an idea you are getting ready to hear from me again, so here it is. Your letters are reaching me every day, but the Sunglasses must be lost. Have checked both hotels thoroughly and they just haven't arrived. Maybe they'll show up one of these days.

Mary, we are playing the 76th Division tonight and if we lose we'll be heading for Camp Atterbury tomorrow. The Captain is putting me on the spot, but it doesn't matter, Win or lose I'll do the best I can. They have two former Big Leagues; Cecil Travio, and Boma Powell.

Hon, we should be together next week if everything goes well. Soon as we get back to Camp our furloughs will probably come through.

Can't wait to see everyone again, especially you. If Hitler only knew what he is doing to me, I'm sure he'd surrender tomorrow. Never before have I been so lonely as now and it's only been two weeks since we left each other. Wonder how some people stand the separation of years as well as they do.

Aren't these letters of mine interesting? Just seems to be an empty space in my old head these days and writing a long interesting letter is impossible.

Darling, I'll be closing this now and hope you are feeling well. Take things easy "Ma" and I'll be seeing you. Give my love and regards to the family.

Love Always.
Bernie

Thanks for the two dollars Brat. Maybe you'd better stop writing here, Mary. The team spirit isn't too high and most of the fellows want to go home on furlough.

Bye My Love

August 24, 1944 Wichita, Kansas

Dearest One;

How are you today, Kiddo? Fine I hope and please stay that way. What a case of lonesome blues I had last night. It was raining and with nothing to do, so I went to bed. After getting there, naturally all, I could think of was you and what thoughts they were. I was trying to figure out what would happen if you ever decided you didn't love me and for the life of me, there was no answer. Hon, without you around, life is very empty and uninteresting, and not worth living. Do you want to know what brought this spell on? Well, last night Sam and another boy and I were going out for a sandwich. We'll call this boy "Homer" just for identification sake. Here's what happened. A car pulled around the corner and a lady around 38 or 40 was driving. This boy "Homer" just yelled at her and damned if she didn't stop. He jumped in the car and away they went. Ten minutes after we arrived back to our rooms here "Homer" comes with a long story. Her husband was in the Army and she had been running around some, but the last time she had a date was five weeks ago. Well, you probably know what happened and my first thoughts were for this Husband of hers. Possibly he is running around himself, but if he isn't, he's an unlucky guy. Mary, I've seen so much of this, that people begin to seem like animals to me. They have no principles or morals when they act like that. That is exactly why I love you so much. I'd trust you with my life and I always will. Remember this, you can trust me the same way and I know you do. Do I get too serious at times, Mary? If so tell me and I'll stop.

Well, this old right arm won another game. We beat Cecil Travis and his &6th Division team 9-7 Tuesday night. I had to leave the game in the 8th with the score 8-3 in our favor. Wanted to finish but my shoulder said no sir. The Captain's all enthused about me again. Told me to be sure and get this wing of mine fixed and I'd go places.

Darling, do you mind if I close for now? Want so much to see you and talk over our future. Gosh Darn how I love you. Say hello to everyone and give them my love.

Bye Now Pudge and I'll be seeing you.

Bern

Received the Sunglasses yesterday. Thanks a million for everything.

October 26, 1944
Somewhere in the Eastern part of the U.S.

Darling;

Hope you haven't been worrying too much because you haven't heard from me before now. It's a tough job trying to keep in touch the first few days but from now on the letters will reach you more frequently. This is quite a place Mary, and I wish I could tell you more about it. Anyway, the food is good and I'm feeling swell.

What I am most interested in is how you are feeling. Have been wondering also how you weathered the trip to good old Oak Park. Please take care of yourself now and don't you worry, I will too. It's only natural that we're going to miss each other but always remember, others are doing it so why can't we?

Hon, there isn't much to tell you tonight, so this will have to end for now. Give my love to your Mom, Gram, Bill and the rest of the Family. To you alone these few words. You and your love for me have changed this dreary life to a very bright one. We're not together now but I know you're waiting and that makes the difference. I'll love you Mary, always. A man in love turns poetic once in a while so why can't I?

Bye- Bern

Hey, Mrs. Kincanon, don't forget to put your new name on the Mailbox.

November 2, 1944
Somewhere Overseas

Dearest Darling;

Hello again and how are you feeling tonight Hon? Fine I hope and please stay that way. Know you'll be having your good and bad times from now on, but I'll be with you in Spirit at least. Gosh, Mary, a guy can be in love but never know how much until he gets so darn far away. It's impossible to even talk to the Girl over the phone. Well, they can't keep us apart forever and I'm sure we'll appreciate our home that much more after this is all over.

Mary, this is my second letter to you in three days and there isn't much to tell you. Army life goes on and as usual it's all very routine. Outside of eating, sleeping and training we are doing nothing. You can see that my conversation does have its limitations.

Sincerely hope my letters aren't too dull and uninteresting but have to express my thoughts somehow.

Mom, you take care of Mary and Bill and yourself. Sure, am waiting for that letter Gram, that goes for you too. If you get in the writing mood, I'd be happy to hear from you.

Mush, here is the conclusion to this. Received your letter of the 20th and want to explain that last letter of mine from the States. We were in a hurry and they gave us twenty minutes to write. Seeing that

I had written you last, I decided to write home and include you in it; Was about all I could do, don't you know?

Bye for now, Honey Chile and I sure do love you.
Bern.

November 4, 1944 (envelope)
Somewhere Overseas

Darling,

Once again, I shall indulge in my favorite pastime, writing to you. After a day of Army life, it's always a real pleasure to relax and concentrate on you. That sounds like you're in my thoughts only at night, but you know better than that. Guess it's a fact that you are on my mind too much at times, but I can't help that.

Received two more letters from you today. They were swell and was happy to know that all of you are feeling well. One of them made me sympathize with you though. Can imagine how you felt that Sunday morning you arrived in Chicago. Trouble does seem to come in bunches, doesn't it Hon?

Mary, I've been writing you pretty often and can't remember whether I told you this or not. Your information about our Baby makes me so darn proud. I couldn't think straight for an hour or more. Boy, won't I have something to come home to. Our Baby and you. What more could any man ask for?

Hon, I had the good fortune of going to town last night. Had a good meal and from there went to the show. Wish I could tell you more about the town, but maybe later on my letters will be more informative.

Now, Mush, here is the dope on mailing packages. You are allowed to mail them at any time providing they weigh under eight oz. However, in case I should write home for something special you are required to show my request at the Post Office. That way the package doesn't have to be less than eight oz. Now, don't forget Christmas packages can be sent without any red tape. This is just informative for you in case it's ever necessary. Don't want you spending your money on me. I have everything I need and want you to concentrate on keeping yourself happy and as Beautiful as you are. Mary, will you pass this information on to mom? Don't think I've told her anything about the situation. Tell her also what I told her about the gifts. I'm sure both of you need the money much more than I need any expensive presents. Knowing you both as I do there's no doubt something will be heading this way. Here are a few things that will help the morale a bit. Woolen socks, handkerchiefs, soap, toothpaste, brushless shaving cream, candy, cookies and gum. That's all I need, Honest.

This is probably the longest letter you've ever received from me, but there's a reason. Started this two-days ago and never did get it finished until now. See how things are? Takes me five days to gather my thoughts enough to write a few pages.

Will close for the present but will write again in a day or two. Give my love and regards to all the family, and I hope to hear from my new mom soon. All my love to you Mary now and always.

Bern

November 5, 1944
V-Mail

Darling,

This morning after mass I was surprised with five of your swell letters. The dates on them ranged from the 21st to the 25th of October inclusive. Seems like you hadn't heard from me in some time and were getting a bit anxious. Hon, in the future if there is a long delay don't be worried because there's always a good reason. Have been writing you constantly and eventually those letters will arrive home.

So, you had another sick day? Mary, I can never tell you how much I'd like to be with you now. From now until the Baby is born I'll be thinking and worrying about you. For that matter I'm sure I will until we're together. In the same mood, the radio is playing "Some Day I'll Meet You Again"

Don't let this bother you, Hon. Had my wallet stolen last night but the money doesn't matter much. Had some personal things I needed and also your pictures, but you can at any time send me another one. Don't forget now because I'll be lost without one. That's about all for now Mary. You'll hear from me again soon so regards and love to the family and I love you.

Bern

November 6,1944
Overseas

Dearest Darling,

What do you think of your "Old Man" these days? Doing all right in the writing department, aren't I? It's just one of those things Mary. Every night the urge to write comes upon me and I just can't resist. Don't want to either because it's the only way I can satisfy my yearning for you now.

So, they're making a Politician of you too? If I know you President Roosevelt can't lose. Wouldn't be surprised to see him sweep the entire 47th Ward. Hon, be careful if you do cheat because I don't want to be telling these guys my Wife is in jail. Maybe I'd better insert a laugh after that last sentence. The Officer that

Censors this may take me seriously. We are from Chicago you know and for some reason people have a wrong impression of us natives.

Darling, here is some further news concerning my wallet. Didn't mention this but another boy two beds away had his stolen the same night. Well, this morning a Sergeant found both of them in the Latrine, of all places. Everything was there except the money and that satisfies me. You can still send that picture though and please don't send any money. Don't need it and if I should I have plenty of friends.

That is about all for tonight Mary. Give my love and regards to mom, Gram, Bill and Marty. Don't forget the rest of the family. Goodnight Hon and my Love to you now and forever.

Bernie

Hon, will you tell me the difference in time between my V-Mail letter of last night and this one?

November 11, 1944
Overseas

Dearest Darling

Received three letters from you yesterday and they were dated October 31-November 1st and 2nd. The last letter I had received from you was dated October 25th, so evidently some of your letters have been delayed somewhere. I am really sorry that you haven't heard from me as yet, but I'm positive you will soon. Know how you feel because I was lost until your letters started to arrive.

So, you're working again? What a gal. I'm glad though that you are able to work and also very proud of you. You don't know how much it helps to know that you are feeling well. Mary, here's a friendly tip; don't want you to think that I expect you to work. In fact, I'd rather you wouldn't. Know that you are planning and saving for our future, but Hon, your health means more to me than all the money we could ever save. In other words, take care of yourself for me please? Have I made myself clear that I love you more than life itself and always will?

I'm sorry Mary but I have to cut this letter short. We'll be falling out soon for another day's work, but I'll write again tomorrow. Give my love to your swell family and I'll be thinking and praying for all of you. Bye hon and Love Always.

Bern

Our overseas pay has started and have taken an $18.75 Bond for you. It may help somewhat for the Baby. A good Irish friend of mine, Monahan by name, suggested we name him MICHAEL BERNARD or vice versa. If it's a Girl, he likes Maureen. No doubt about his Nationality is there?

November 15,1944
Overseas

Darling,

Another night is here so it's time to write the best wife a guy ever had. I mean that sincerely Mary, and it will always be that way with me. Hon, at this very moment, My Boy, Dick Haynes is singing and here are the titles of his last two songs. "There's a Long Long Trail Awinding," and "I'll Be Seeing You." It may be a Long Long Trail, but you can be sure that we'll be together again. Nothing is going to harm me, so you take care of yourself, and look forward to that Great Day.

Nothing out of the ordinary to tell you tonight. Each day is about the same, and they just keep piling up. By the way, I received two more letters from you, and I see that you still haven't heard from me. The dates were the 7th and 8th of November and was positive you would have heard by then. Sure, hope by now the Mail Man is getting on the ball.

Mary, will you excuse me for tonight? It's a bit late and this Old Man is tired as usual. My love and regards to Mom, Gram, Bill, and Marty, and tell them to write when they can. Gosh how I miss all of you.

Before I close please write and tell me what the Doctor said. Guess you have by now but wanted you to know that your health and wellbeing means everything to me. Maybe because I love you so darn much.

Night Hon and love,
Bern

November 18,1944
Somewhere in England

Dearest Darling:

At least we are being allowed to tell where we are. It's quite a relief because now my letters may be a bit more interesting. Will try to give you some idea of England, small though it may be. The first thing we noticed was the Greenness of the Country. The reason for that it seems is the everlasting dampness. Each morning the ground is as wet as if had rained all night long. The Weather to be sure isn't agreeable and nine out of every ten caught a cold. We'll get used to it eventually though. Now here is some more dope about England and its people. They have had quite a tough time of it over here, and naturally we aren't getting a true picture of the towns at their best. Most everything is rationalized including Food, Clothing, Candy, Ice Cream, and many other things that makes life more enjoyable. The people themselves still have their cheerfulness and courage and are very determined to win this War as soon as possible. Here is the last bit of information for tonight. The chief transportation here is a very modest bicycle. This is the truth. I have actually seen Women fifty to sixty years of age riding a bike to town. Seems strange doesn't it but it does prove when things are necessary, they can be done. Before I forget I want to tell you that we passed through Scotland. Mary it's the most beautiful country I've ever seen. Haven't seen many, but they'd have to be beyond belief to gather my vote.

England is nice to talk about, but you are my favorite subject and you always will be. You'll never know how much your letters mean to me and how anxiously I await them.

Gosh, I hope you heard from me by now. Know just how you must feel, and I don't want you worrying. In your last letter you weren't and I'm proud of you. Just keep feeling that way because it is the correct attitude and the only way to be.

Hon, I am sorry but that's about all for this time. Take care of yourself and keep loving me. I'm so in love with you it hurts.

Good Night and Love
Bern.

Will write your Mom soon. Give my love to all the family.

November 21,1944
Somewhere at Sea

Darling:

Suppose you will be a bit surprised when you receive this letter. Everything happened pretty fast and didn't have a chance to call you again. We are having quite a time out here. The waters get a bit rough at times but so far, I've escaped Sea Sickness. Our Chow is fairly good so all and all I haven't anything to complain about. Naturally, you know that last statement doesn't pertain to you. As long as we both shall live, if we apart life can never hold too much enjoyment. You have shown me more happiness than I have ever felt possible these past few years and until we're together again maybe these memories will keep us going. I'm sure they will for me and know you'll be alright too. When you do get blue and lonely you know who you can turn to and he'll never fail you. In times like these Religion is our biggest hope and blessing. I'm preaching again but I guess you are used to that by now.

Mary, say hello to your Mom and Bill and the rest of the family. Also tell them to write once in a while. Remember, Hon, I love you now and always.

Want to tell you how sorry I was to hear about your Grandmother she was a wonderful woman and I'll always remember her and regret that I never had the chance to know her better.

November 23,1944
Somewhere in England

Dearest:

Happy Thanksgiving to you and the entire family. Should have sent this greeting to you ten days ago, but as usual Holidays in the army creep up on you. Wrote Mom last night and entirely forgot to extend Season's Greetings to my own family.

Two more of your letters came through this week. They were dated October 29th and November 12. You can see that the mail is irregular but as long as they get here I'm satisfied. Told mom this so I'll tell you too. As yet, I don't know whether you've heard from me. It has me worried because if you haven't, I know exactly how you feel. Have been writing to both of you since the middle of last month and was certain you'd hear from me by the first of November.

Mary, we had a company party last week consisting of dancing and refreshments. The girls invited were the Waaf, Air Corp. And the T.C. Army. Before the party the officer in charge told us to be as entertaining as possible and to show the girls a good time. After two hours of sitting around and eating, I decided maybe I better talk to one of them anyway. A very unfortunate young lady was sitting nearby so we struck up a conversation. She was English and had been in the service over two years. We talked for about a half hour comparing our respective countries and customs and then a boy from our company came over to join us, so I took off. Then last night a friend and I went to a show in town the picture was "Between Two Worlds," and it was good. All in all, you can see that we are having our share of entertainment and relaxation.

Hon, as the days go by, I miss you more and more and it's possible my love goes stronger and stronger. Your letters to me are the most important thing to me in my life. You have a way of making me the happiest guy going and you always will.

Darling that's it for tonight but if it's possible you'll hear from me as regular as clockwork.

Bye Now and Love Always,
Bern

Give your family my love and regards. Don't forget the boy either. Am I proud? And How.

November 25, 1944
Somewhere in England

Dearest Darling:

Hello again, "Sweetest Girl in the world" How's my wife and our Family today? What a lucky guy this Soldier is. Just to know you are there waiting for me makes me fear in a way, coming home to you. Don't' know if I'll be able to stand all the happiness that will be inside of me. You can be certain that I'll make every lonely moment up to you when we are together again. It's a terribly disappointment to be away from you just when you'll need me most. Hope you'll always remember that you are in my thoughts constantly and my love for you will never cease. Please take care of yourself and I'll be praying for you and our Baby.

No, Mary, your letters to me aren't censored so you can be just as "Mushy" as you want to. I won't mind a bit. Haven't heard from you these past few days but will probably get five or six of them all at once. Received four letters from Mom and the Girls. And they told me you folks had heard from me at last. You can be expecting quite a few letters now because I have been writing pretty often. Well, Hon, keep writing as often as you can and so will I. Give My Love to Mom, Gram, and Bill. Have to write them soon.

Bye now Mary and Love Always,
Bernie

Hope all of you enjoyed your Thanksgiving Dinner, and I'm sure you did.

November 27,1944 (Mom's mother's birthday)
V-Mail

Darling:

Received four letters from you this evening and Hon they were all I needed. Hadn't heard from you in three days so you can see how the mail is going. They were dated from the 13th to the 16th of November inclusive. Between the 5th and the 13th your letters haven't arrived, but they will eventually. Mary the picture was really swell, but I wished you didn't send the money order. Absolutely don't need the money and know you could find plenty of uses for it. Don't get the idea that I'm mad at you now. It's just that I love you so much I want you to keep your money and you needn't ever worry about me. The army is taking very good care of this guy and every need is taken care of.

From now on I'll try to write V-Mail to you as often as possible. Have written quite a few letters to you before November 3rd, so apparently V-Mail is about twice as fast as the regular. Always remember though that whenever you aren't hearing from me there is a very good reason. Will write you every two days whenever possible.

Darling, it's bedtime now so I'll close until the next time. Miss you more each day and will love you always. My love and regards to Mom, Gram, Bill and Marty. Tell them to write when they can. Bye Hon and please take care of yourselves you know what I meant when I made that pleural.

Love always, Bern

December 13, 1944
(Last Letter Before Capture)
V-Mail
Somewhere In Germany

Darling:

At last, after two weeks I am able to write to my one and only again. We've been on the move for quite a while and we've finally settled down. Have been hoping that you wouldn't worry about not hearing from me because as usual there's a good reason behind every delay in the mail. Mary, we've been seeing a lot of this "Old World" and someday I'll tell you all about it. Things over here are in a quite a mess and we can be thankful that our American has not been trouble by War.

Hon, I sincerely hope you are feeling well. Haven't heard from you in over two weeks and as you know that's a long time. Can't ever tell you how much I miss being with you and especially now when you need me. Think about you constantly so please remember that. I'll be with you in that way always. Also, my prayers, every mass, and communion are for you and the baby. That's the best I can do for you now and it makes me feel positively sure you'll be alright. However, you can also be sure that when we are together again, I'm going to try to make you the happiest you've ever been. You can be assured that you've done that for me. Darling give my love to Mom, Gram, Bill and Marty. They sure are swell. Bye now and I love you now and forever. Will write again soon.

Bern

Chapter 56

Mom's Letter: My Darling

I have the one and only letter written by my Mom to my Dad, it is dated January 15, 1945. The letter ends in mid-sentence, mid page, and, obviously it was never sent. I have no idea what would have caused Mom to stop her writing and never finish this letter. I am very grateful to have this one letter penned by Mom.

Please, you have to read this letter, it brings so much to life, especially the title of this book, ***My Darling.*** The very first paragraph says everything, **"Well honey, no mail again today."** Then repeating his own words to her in her letter to him, **"if there is a delay in the mail there is always a good reason."** This is the reason that this letter is so priceless. History tells us, there will not be a letter from Dad anytime soon.

January 15 - 1945
Monday - 9:30 PM

My darling:

Well, honey, no mail again today. I keep remembering that you've said over and over again that if there's a delay in the mail, there's always a good reason.

Tonight the Secretary of War released the casualty figures since December 16th and darling I could have cried when I saw them. When I think of all you boys over there going through so much! Our prayers are with you always.

Well, Bunnie, I work one more week and then I'm finished. Lillian came back to work today so they won't need me after this week. Gosh, I'm so glad I was able to work this long.

This afternoon I deposited

F56.1 January 15, 1945

7

my poker winnings in the bank. I wrote you last night that I won $14.80 - That was really some game.

Honey, did I tell you that my cousin Jack from Haywood, who was wounded in France, is back in the States? He got back a couple days ago and he's in a hospital in New York, waiting to be transfered to one nearer home. He is the one who was a 2nd Lt. in the Infantry.

Mom can't wait until I'm home all day and can have supper all ready for her at night. At least I'll get a lot of practice, honey, and when we have our own place, I'll be an expert. Darling, that's one thing I can hardly wait for. We'll be so very happy when we

3

are together again. I love you so much, Bernie and I will always. I was thinking last night how lonesome it was here when you were in Kansas, but what was that compared to this ~~tonlate~~ lonliness that we are feeling now. But I guess whenever

UGH! I want more of this letter! Don't you? It's the first time we are hearing from Mom, and not trying to figure out what her letters were saying by what Dad was writing. The letters had stopped coming. But time had kept moving forward, as it does whether you want it to or not. Dad's last letter was December 13, 1944. When Mom wrote this letter, she was six months pregnant.

The following is a poem my sister Lynn wrote about how she interprets Mom's feelings surrounding her unfinished letter to Dad written January 15, 1945

Awakening From a Dream of You

"My darling...I have not heard from you for so long The War Minister says thousands are dead" in an unfinished letter from my mother to my father... January 1945.

Startled, I awaken, and arise confused.
Is that you? Are you near—oh my dear
are you never more
to appear at our door?
This droning dreary news of war
bathed in bullets, bombs and blood
frightens me to my core!
My selfish longing for news of you— brave heart
a call, letter, or telegraph
to tell me that you live still!
Oh let me sleep, for when I dream
your lips I kiss, and I with child
am wrapped inside your loving arms.
I cannot talk of sorrow, or speak of loss!
Crying into the night, beseeching reason— taunts me!
Silence shrouds this room, emptied of thee.
Oh My Darling, Come Home to Me.
Lynn Kincanon

F56.2

Chapter 57

Good News/Bad News

Michael Bernard Kincanon born April 12, 1945.
Sixteen days later a letter from the War Department arrived dated April 28, 1945.

Missing in Action Since Dec 21, 1944

These are quotes from the War Department letter that stand out to me and what I can be confident of, is that my Mom and the rest of the family were torn apart by what is in this letter. The complete letter follows in the next couple pages.

> **"Your distress since he was reported a casualty and your desire to obtain further information regarding him is most understandable."**
>
> **"All communications with the regiment was lost."**
>
> **"Available evidence indicates that the regiment was surrounded by German units."**
>
> **"It is regretted that the War Department has no further details as of April 18, 1945."**
>
> **"My sympathy continues with you."**

UTM/cmm

WAR DEPARTMENT
THE ADJUTANT GENERAL'S OFFICE
WASHINGTON 25, D. C.

IN REPLY REFER TO:
AGPC 201 Kincanon, Louis B.
(19 Feb 45) 36 739 483

28 April 1945

Mrs. Louis Kincanon
417 Wisconsin Avenue
Oak Park, Illinois

Dear Mrs. Kincanon:

There has been forwarded to this office from overseas, your letter of inquiry concerning your husband, Corporal Louis B. Kincanon who has been missing in action in Germany since 21 December 1944.

Your distress since he was reported a casualty, and your desire to obtain further information regarding him is most understandable. A report now available in the War Department shows that on 11 December 1944 the regiment in which your husband was ammunition handler moved up to a defensive position on the battle line in the vicinity of Radscheid, Germany. On 16 December 1944 the German attack began and on 18 December 1944 all communications with the regiment was lost. Available evidence indicates that the regiment was surrounded by German units.

I wish to assure you that upon receipt of any additional information regarding your husband it will be communicated to you immediately. It is regretted that the War Department has no further details as of 18 April 1945.

My sympathy continues with you.

Sincerely yours,

J. A. ULIO
Major General
The Adjutant General

1 Inclosure

F57.1 From the War Department

War Department Bulletin

WAR DEPARTMENT
BULLETIN OF INFORMATION
CONCERNING
ENTITLEMENTS OF MISSING PERSONS AND THEIR DEPENDENTS

With the sympathy of the War Department for dependents of members of the armed forces, absent through hazards of war, is coupled its desire to so administer the pertinent laws as to be helpful to those dependents in matters affecting their welfare. It is the purpose of this bulletin to outline entitlements and benefits of interest to relatives and dependents. In sending the bulletin to the individual who has been officially designated by the serviceman to be notified in emergency, the War Department contemplates that the recipient will adequately inform any other relatives, dependents or other parties interested. The bulletin is sent to the "emergency addressee" of Army personnel who are reported missing, missing in action, prisoner of war or interned in a neutral country and its provisions apply in all such cases.

PAY

Pay and allowances at the rate received at the time of beginning of absence continue to be credited during absence, together with any increase to which the absentee may become legally entitled during his absence.

Accrued pay and allowances may not be transmitted to an absentee, such as a prisoner of war, nor may payment thereof be made to any other person. The accrued pay constitutes a credit, part of which may be disbursed by allotments of pay, or by contributions toward family allowances for dependents of enlisted men but in no other way. Every allotment payment, or family allowance contribution, is a charge against the individual's accrued pay which is reduced accordingly. (Family allowances may be granted for dependents of enlisted men only. Allotments may be made from the pay of either officers or enlisted men. An enlisted man may have both allotments and family allowances in effect at the same time and to the same or to different payees.)

It is now provided by law that accrued pay shall not be reduced by deduction of any amounts that a person in the hands of an enemy may receive from the captor government as pay or allowances.

It is the general policy of the Secretary of War to conserve accruals of pay of absentees making only such disbursements therefrom as are deemed essential.

CONTINUANCE OF ALLOTMENTS AND FAMILY ALLOWANCES

Every endeavor is made to encourage persons in service, and particularly those going overseas, to make such voluntary allotments from their pay as they desire for support of dependents and other authorized purposes. It is assumed that enlisted men or their dependents will have applied, promptly upon or following induction, for authorized family allowances for dependents. To insure continuity it is the general practice to continue the payment of all allotments and family allowances in effect at the date of commencement of absence in any missing status. No request or other action by the payee, other than registering any change of address, is necessary. The payments are continued until the absence ends, subject to such changes or discontinuances as circumstances may warrant.

CHANGES IN ALLOTMENTS

During a person's absence in any casualty status the allotments in effect at the beginning of his absence may be changed either upon or without his request. They may be decreased or discontinued whenever such action is in the interests of the absentee, of dependents, or of the Government. Any dependent or other person should bring to the attention of the department any facts which warrant such a change.

Existing allotments in effect at beginning of absence may be increased either upon request of the allotter or by direction of the Secretary of War whenever they are insufficient in amount. Requests for such increases should be made and the necessity established by dependents or others concerned. Dependents are expected to request such increases as may actually be necessary but no more. Action upon requests is as directed by the Secretary of War or person designated to act for him.

NEW ALLOTMENTS

In the absence of an allotment at time of beginning of absence new allotments may be made upon or without the request of the absentee for any authorized purpose. The amount will be the minimum necessary for the purpose. Authorized purposes are support or well-being of dependents, paying life insurance premiums, preserving or protecting existing property or financial interests, reducing or paying interest-bearing indebtedness. On the other hand authorized purposes do not include new ventures such as investments in property or securities or acquiring new business interests or new insurance. The holding of a general power of attorney can not be deemed an authorization for any such new ventures. Requests for new allotments should be made and the necessity established by dependents or others concerned, requests being for whatever may be actually necessary but no more. Particular attention of relatives of absentees is called to making certain that commercial or governmental life insurance premiums continue to be paid by allotment or otherwise.

Chapter 58

Mom, Baby and No Father

What did that War Department letter do to my Mom, to my grandmothers? The entire family had to be in total turmoil and despair. The happiness of a brand-new baby, trying so hard to feel all the joy that this special time brings to a family. There was a looming elephant in the room. Are they all talking about it? If I know my Mom, if she was able to leave the house, she was at church with her mother. Maw would have been saying her rosary every night as she did all her life. And my other grandmother, Dad's mom was walking to Lourdes Church in the city every day, praying for the safe return of her son. This was the way they were spending their time; I just know it.

My Mom was hanging on to those repeated words in many of Dad's letters, **"If you don't hear from me there is always a good reason."** Over and over again this would have been her mantra, this is what would have given her the hope that she hung on to along with her faith. She and the rest of my Irish Catholic family had a very strong faith, and they prayed, A LOT!

Chapter 59

PRAYERS ARE ANSWERED

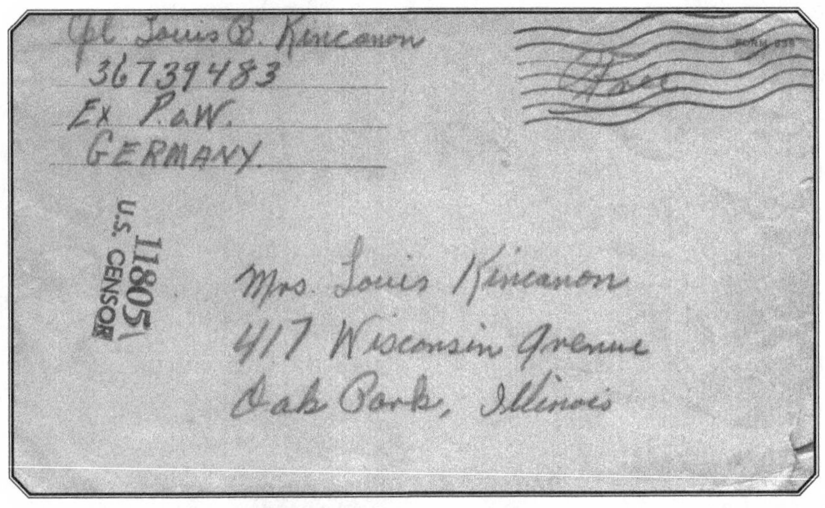

F59.1 A letter arrived! No Date on this letter and No Envelope

Finally! Word from Dad!! May 1, 1945 almost six months after my Dad's last communication.

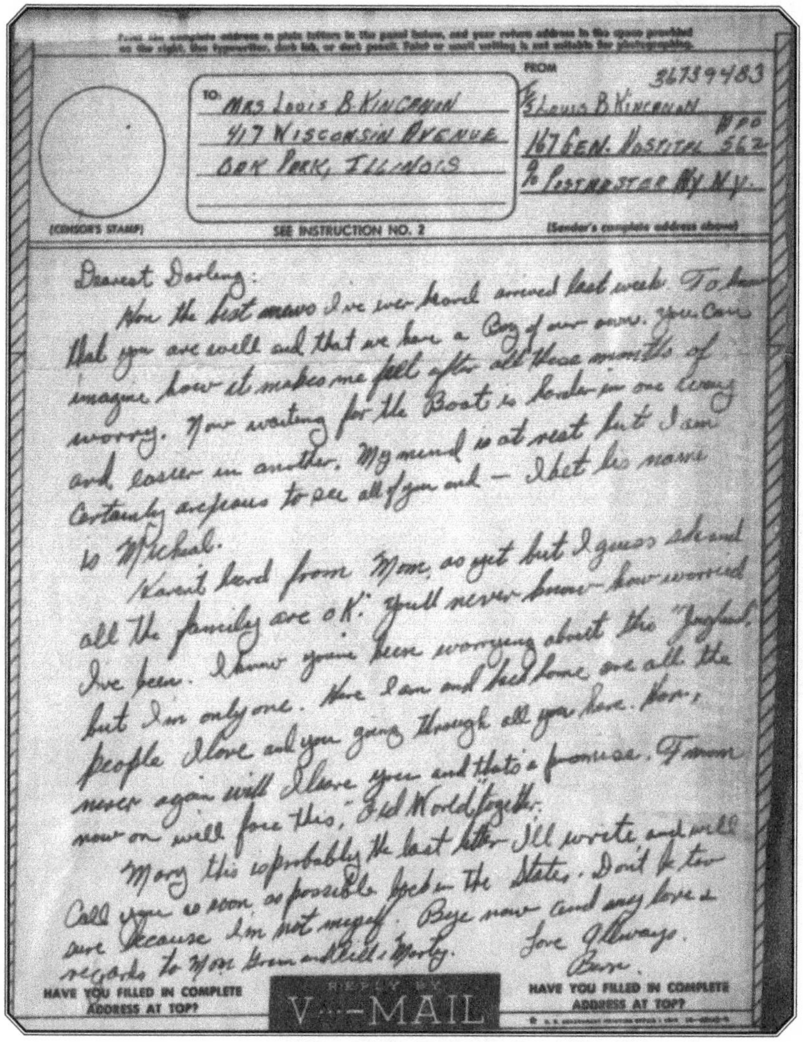

TO: MRS LOUIS B KINCANNON
417 WISCONSIN AVENUE
OAK PARK, ILLINOIS

FROM 36739483
Louis B Kincannon
167 GEN. HOSPITAL APO 562
% POSTMASTER NY NY

(CENSOR'S STAMP) SEE INSTRUCTION NO. 2 (Sender's complete address above)

Dearest Darling:
Now the best news I've ever heard arrived last week. To know
that you are well and that we have a Boy of our own. You can
imagine how it makes me feel after all these months of
worry. Now waiting for the Boat is harder in one way
and easier in another. My mind is at rest but I am
Certainly anxious to see all of you and — I bet his name
is Michael.
Haven't heard from Mom as yet but I guess she and
all the family are OK. You'll never know how worried
I've been. I know you've been worrying about the "Jungle,"
but I'm only one. Here I am and back home are all the
people I love and you going through all you have. Honey,
never again will I leave you and that's a promise. From
now on we'll face this "Old World" together.
Mary this is probably the last letter I'll write and will
Call you as soon as possible back in the States. Don't be too
sure because I'm not myself. Bye now and my love &
regards to Mom Gram and Bill & Marty.

Love Always.
Bus.

HAVE YOU FILLED IN COMPLETE ADDRESS AT TOP?

REPLY BY V—MAIL

HAVE YOU FILLED IN COMPLETE ADDRESS AT TOP?

Mail was moving slow. This was a request for a health and welfare check on Mom, coming from the Red Cross May 30, 1945. It is unknown if Mom had heard from Dad yet because of the mail. No matter the dates on the letters, my recollection is Mom did not get any word from Dad or the Army until early June 1945. But I have kept all the letters in chronological order.

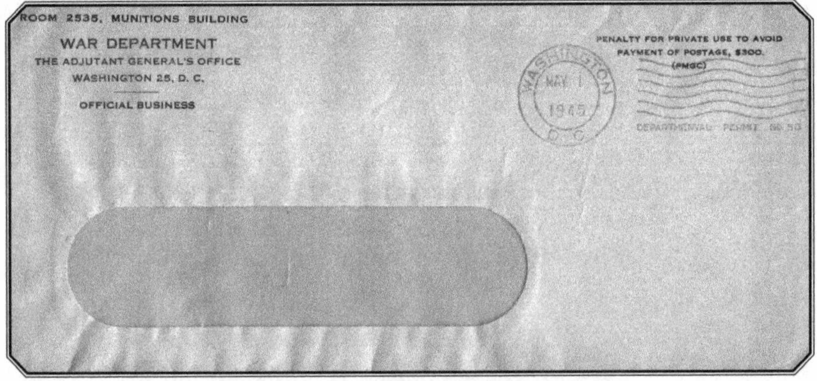

F59.2 May 9, 1945

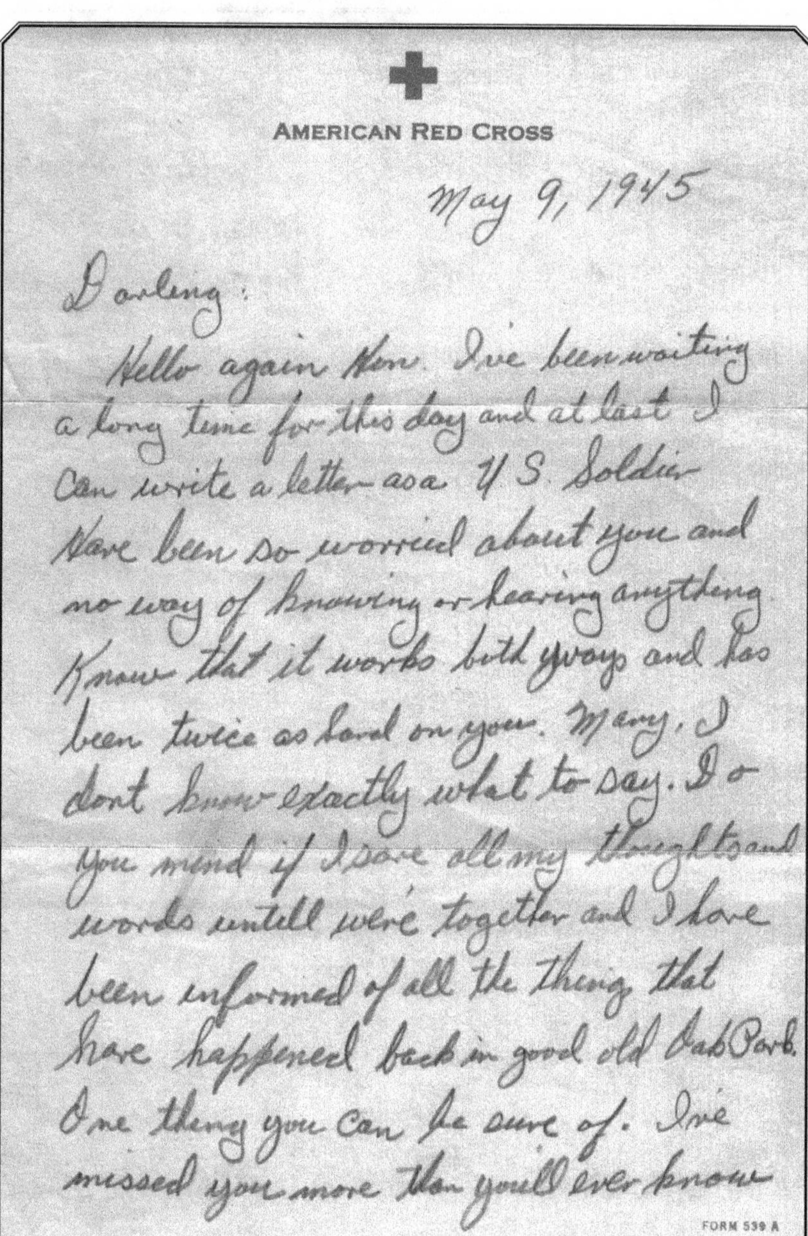

AMERICAN RED CROSS

May 9, 1945

Darling:

Hello again Hon. I've been waiting a long time for this day and at last I can write a letter as a U.S. Soldier. Have been so worried about you and no way of knowing or hearing anything. Know that it works both ways and has been twice as hard on you. Mary, I dont know exactly what to say. Do you mind if I save all my thoughts and words untill we're together and I have been informed of all the thing that have happened back in good old Oak Park. One thing you can be sure of. I've missed you more than you'll ever know

FORM 539 A

and just let me get back home again to prove how much I love you. I owe you so much happiness and hope I never cause you another anxious moment. Life plays some funny tricks sometimes and it hit the Jackpot on us but well make up for it. Things could allways be worse and whats more I can still pitch Baseball, Oh Boy. Darling, please excuse me for now and I'll be seeing all of you soon. Should be home by the 1st of June and I'll get in touch with you as soon as possible. If its a bit later dont worry because were definetely slated for the States. Bye for now and give my love to Mom, Gram, Bill and the family. Hon, I love you. Bern.

AMERICAN RED CROSS
HOSPITAL SERVICE RECORD.

Last Name Kincanon First Name Louis B

ASN 36739483 Rank T/5

Initial Contact: 5-30-45 Kincanon requested health and welfare report on wife, Mary E. Kincanon, 417 Wisconsin Ave, Oak Park Illinois. Had been RAMP and so had no news for sometime. Baby expected in April.

Date 5-30-45 Signature [illegible]
Hosp. 241st Gen. Title AFD

Subsequent Data:

RAMP (Recovered Allied Military Personnel)

F59.3 This states initial contact 5-30-45 and was requesting a wellness check again on June 5, 1945 on Mom and baby

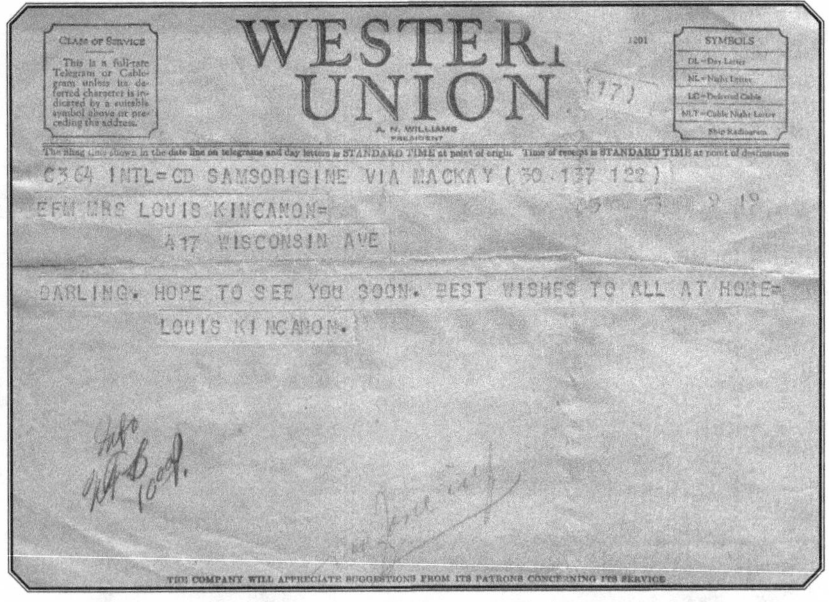

WESTERN UNION

A. N. WILLIAMS
PRESIDENT

CLASS OF SERVICE

This is a full-rate Telegram or Cablegram unless its deferred character is indicated by a suitable symbol above or preceding the address.

SYMBOLS
DL=Day Letter
NL=Night Letter
LC=Deferred Cable
NLT=Cable Night Letter
Ship Radiogram

The filing time shown in the date line on telegrams and day letters is STANDARD TIME at point of origin. Time of receipt is STANDARD TIME at point of destination

C364 INTL=CD SAMSORIGINE VIA MACKAY (30 137 122)

EFM MRS LOUIS KINCANON=

A17 WISCONSIN AVE

DARLING. HOPE TO SEE YOU SOON. BEST WISHES TO ALL AT HOME=

LOUIS KINCANON.

THE COMPANY WILL APPRECIATE SUGGESTIONS FROM ITS PATRONS CONCERNING ITS SERVICE

F59.4 Western Union Telegram Dated May 23, 1945

83 More Freed

The Office of War Information announced today the names of 83 more Chicago area soldiers freed from prison camps in Germany.

F59.5 Headline 83 More Freed

Third row top of page
Kincanon T/5 Louis B. son of Mrs. Mary Kincanon
1734 Winnemac Ave.

Official Word Dad has been returned to Military Control May 11, 1945, but the telegram was delivered June 1, 1945.

From what I remember, Mom told me that this telegram was the first notice she received that Dad was alive.

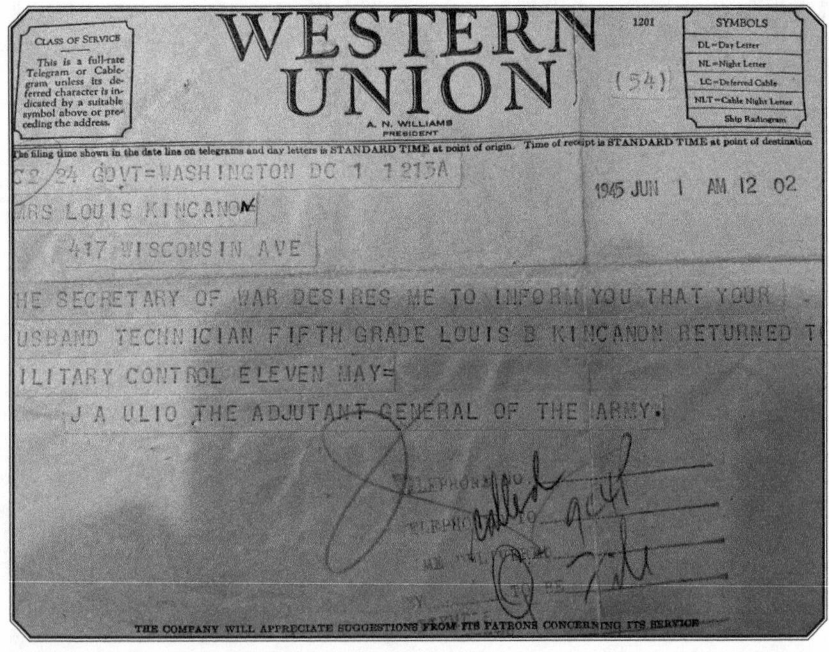
WESTERN UNION
A. N. WILLIAMS PRESIDENT
1201
(54)
CLASS OF SERVICE
This is a full-rate Telegram or Cablegram unless its deferred character is indicated by a suitable symbol above or preceding the address.
SYMBOLS
DL=Day Letter
NL=Night Letter
LC=Deferred Cable
NLT=Cable Night Letter
Ship Radiogram
The filing time shown in the date line on telegrams and day letters is STANDARD TIME at point of origin. Time of receipt is STANDARD TIME at point of destination

C2 24 GOVT=WASHINGTON DC 1 1215A
1945 JUN 1 AM 12 02
MRS LOUIS KINCANON
417 WISCONSIN AVE

THE SECRETARY OF WAR DESIRES ME TO INFORM YOU THAT YOUR HUSBAND TECHNICIAN FIFTH GRADE LOUIS B KINCANON RETURNED TO MILITARY CONTROL ELEVEN MAY=

J A ULIO THE ADJUTANT GENERAL OF THE ARMY.

called 9:41

THE COMPANY WILL APPRECIATE SUGGESTIONS FROM ITS PATRONS CONCERNING ITS SERVICE

F59.6 After months of no word and worry, a telegram finally arrived.

Mrs. Mary Kincanon
1734 Winnemac Avenue
Chicago, Illinois

AMERICAN RED CROSS

May 29, 1945.

Dear Mom & Girls:

Well, they did transfer me to a different hospital and I'm waiting to be sent to the coast where all the ex P.W.'s are waiting shipment home. Transportation is a big problem over here now but Gen. Eisenhower promised to send all Prisoners home as soon as possible. A heck of a lot of them have arrived back in the States already but just knowing I'm going home soon satisfies me. My leg has healed up fine and am in perfect health but as always I'm still worried about all of you at home. There just isn't any possible way for me to hear from you it seems. Now that I'm on the move all the time, I guess I'll have to wait until the old boat reaches New York.

FORM 539 A

Mom, you've heard stories of the weather in France during the last War. Well, they weren't exaggerated a bit. It does rain all the time in this lousy country. We had one spell of beautiful Summer weather but since then —
Last Dec 1, when we arrived in France we stayed here for 10 days in an open pasture and sure enough it rained every day. Then we went into Belgium and it was snowing there. The weather in Chicago may get miserable at times but never again do I want to leave that City.
Now this is what they plan to do with all P.W.s When we hit the States we are taken to some Camp and are paid in full for all the time we've been captured. After that comes our furlough either 30 or 60 days, I'm not sure. From there on its a mystery. Some say discharge others reassignment to a new outfit. Everybody does agree on one thing though. They are pretty sure we'll never

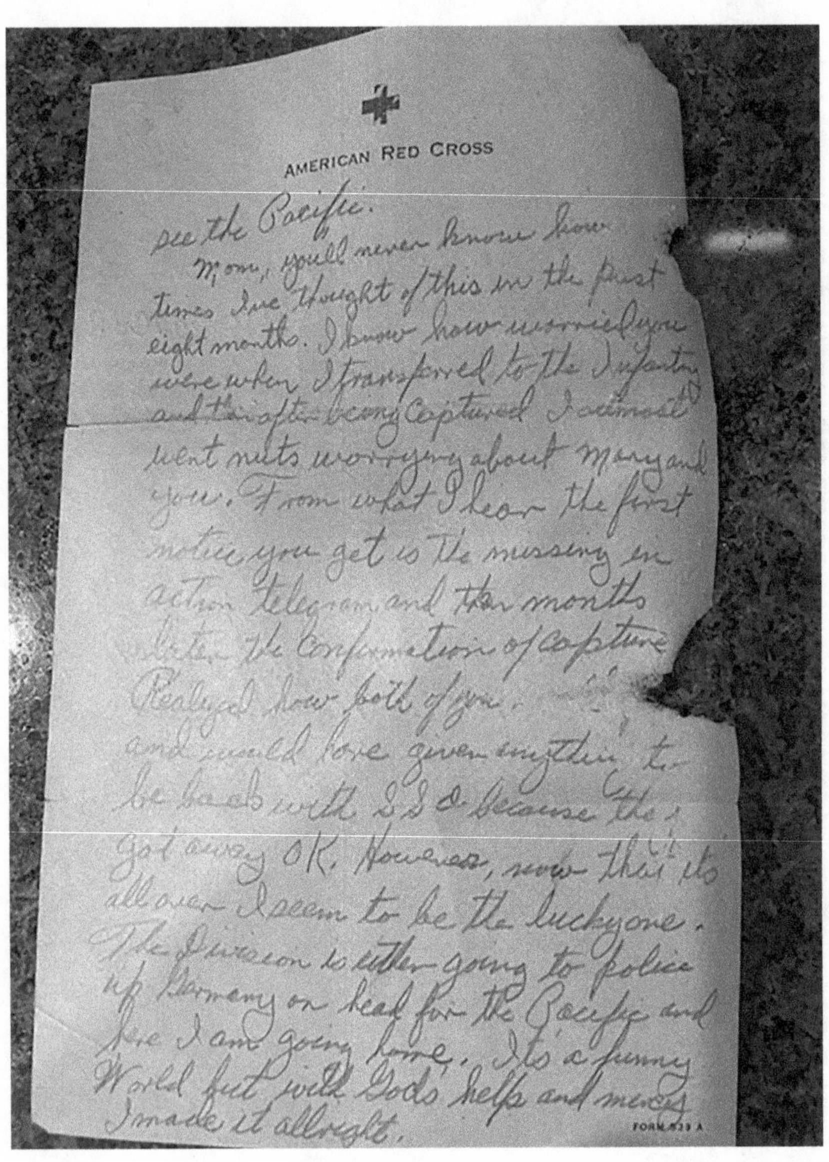

AMERICAN RED CROSS

see the Pacific.
Mom, you'll never know how
times I've thought of this in the past
eight months. I know how worried you
were when I transferred to the Infantry
and then after being captured I almost
went nuts worrying about Mary and
you. From what I hear the first
notice you get is the missing in
action telegram and then months
later the confirmation of capture.
Realized how both of you [illegible]
and would have given anythin' to
be back with S S D because they
got away OK. However, now that it's
all over I seem to be the lucky one.
The Division is either going to police
up Germany or head for the Pacific and
here I am going home. It's a funny
World but with God's help and mercy
I made it allright.

FORM 539 A

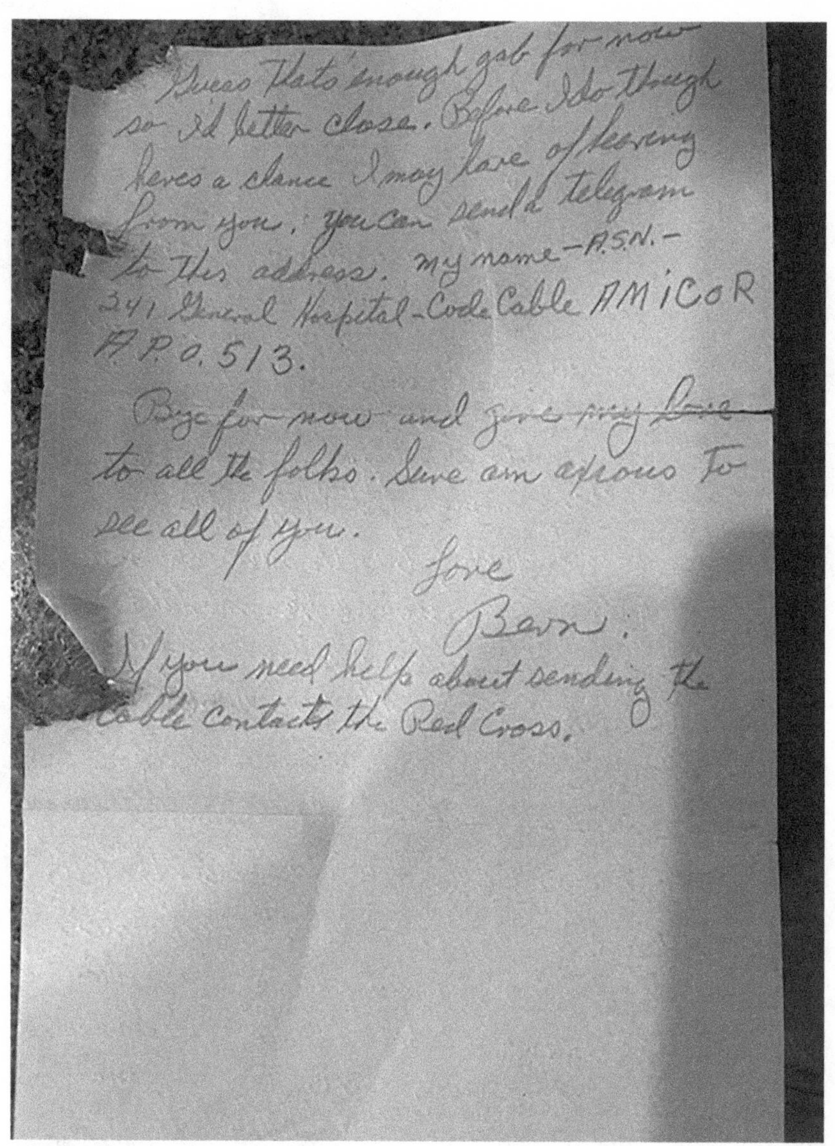
Guess that's enough gab for now
so I'd better close. Before I do though
here's a chance I may have of hearing
from you, you can send a telegram
to this address. my name - A.S.N. -
341 General Hospital - Code Cable AMICOR
A.P.O. 513.

Bye for now and give my love
to all the folks. Sure am anxious to
see all of you.

Love
Bern.

If you need help about sending the
cable contact the Red Cross.

Chapter 60

Back in the USA

June 1, 1945. It seems by the chronological order of things that there were letters written to Mom, but the June 1 telegram was her first contact according to what she had told me.

By this time their new baby boy was almost two months old. Dad had prayed that his new wife and son were in good health and according to his letter Dad said, "I am sure his name is Michael."

Previously, in **Chapter 3** I wrote about the fact that there is a story just in my brother's name?

Well, it is time for the explanation. I know this story by heart, as it was one of the only stories from that time period that was told over and over again. There was an earlier letter, dated April 15, 1943 almost two years to the day before my brother's arrival. That letter was even before Mom and Dad were married, but they were making plans for their future. The name of their child was to be Michael, Michael Bernard. It was to be so.

Mom was pregnant when Dad was missing. No word if he was alive, dead, injured, or captured. Month's go by and still no word. On April 12, 1945 a little boy is born to Mary and Bernie, but Bernie was not there. It had been so long with no word, but she remained faithful in her belief that he would return to them. But, she reversed their decision, and their little boy's name on his birth certificate is; Bernard Michael Kincanon.

It isn't until Dad comes home after his release from the prison camp after the war ended; it is June 1945. Bernard Michael was two months old and the tradition of the middle name was back, in a new generation. Bernard Michael would be called Michael. The next two children born to Mom and Dad were not given a middle name. Their second son Lawrence was born thirteen months after Michael, and then along came their first daughter, Kathleen (me), seven years later, I have no middle name. Mom and Dad were determined to squash that tradition. Twenty-two months later my sister, Lynn, was born; testing the waters, Lynn was given a middle name, Marie. Are you surprised it isn't Vera, after Dad's favorite war time singer, Vera Lynn? I guess by the time they got to my sister, they were confident they broke the curse of the middle name tradition, because William, our baby brother has a middle name, Louis. So, now you have the full story of Michael's name and how it came to be, even before he was born.

Chapter 61

Captured / POW

Now we know that Dad was captured on December 16, 1944 at the Battle of the Bulge, three days after his last letter to Mom and just prior to his capture. Thousands of men died that day, thousands were injured, others like my father were captured and relegated to the Prison Camps in Germany. There are not many stories that I can tell you about his time there, because he rarely spoke of it. I am not sure how much he shared with Mom. Now we will never know. Maybe he spared her the details of what he had to endure, maybe she had her own ideas because she knew the man that returned was somehow different from the man that left to serve.

One memory he did share with us, was how blistering, cold it was. Dad told us it was the coldest he had ever been in his entire life. Another experience he was willing to share was regarding the food, he visibly shivered when he told us. One such vivid memory for him was when they were given soup to eat and saw right away there were maggots in it. As starving as he was, he could not bring himself to eat it. Dad reminisced about one of the other men, who was able to look past the maggots and even offered my dad a ring for his soup. Dad gladly but also a bit reluctantly gave up his soup because at the time he had no idea when his next meal would come. I am not sure if he actually took the poor guys ring.

He did have a couple of funny and not so funny German words he picked up along the way. Later as I remember he found out what a couple of them actually meant and he stopped using them all together. One was **"Dummkopf"** which means a stupid person, dumbbell, or blockhead. Using a word like that was not Dad's style at all.

I do remember Mom saying the men spent many days at the Red Cross after their release because many of them were so malnourished and weak. I remember my Dad said he was full of fever blisters that were so painful, not to mention he was severely underweight.

Below are some of my Dad's POW papers and pictures of his actual prison camp.

Stalag IV B № 16246

Dem Kriegsgefangenen Nr. 313062 IV B

Name: Kincanon, Louis B

ist heute abgenommen worden:

Der Abnehmende:

Datum: 30/XII.44 Name:

Dienstgrad:

1) 1. Blatt als Quittung f. d. Kr. Gef. 2. Blatt als Fahne an den abgenommenen Gegenstand
2. Blatt m. abgenommenem Gegenstand und 3. Blatt an A. O. Kr. Gef.
2) 2. Blatt mit abgenommenem Gegenstand an Verwaltung. 3. Blatt zu den A. O. Akten.

F61.1 Classification POW Germany December 1944-May 1945

To be RETAINED PERMANENTLY by Allied PW for Identification purposes. 361
(A etre rempli par les P.G. pour identification)

Serial No.
No. Mle de recrutment 36739483

Nationality American

Last Name
Nom KINCANON

Initials
Initiale du prenom LOUIS B

Rank
Grade T/5

Regiment, Squadron, Ship or Unit 423 INF. 106 INF. DIV.

Holder's Signature
Signature de l'interesse Louis B. Kincanon

POW No.
MLE de P.G. 313062

Last PW Camp
Dernier Camp 3A

Signature of P.W.
Camp Contact Officer

Issued at ... on ... 194..

F61.2 Dad's POW Identification

Notice of right to appeal

Appeal from classification by local board must be made within 10 days after the mailing of this notice. You may file a written notice of appeal with the local board, or you may go to the office of the local board and sign appeal form on back of Selective Service Questionnaire (Form 40).

Within the same 10-day period you may file a written request for personal appearance before the local board. If this is done, the time in which you may appeal is extended to 10 days from the date of mailing of a new Notice of Classification (Form 57) after such personal appearance.

If an appeal has been taken and you are classified by the board of appeal in either Class I-A, I-A-O, or IV-E and one or more members of the board of appeal dissented from such classification, you may file appeal to the President with your local board within 10 days after the mailing of notice of such classification.

For advice, see your Government appeal agent.

The law requires you: (1) To keep in touch with your local board; (2) to notify it of any change of address; (3) to notify it of any fact which might change your classification; (4) to comply with the instructions on the notice of classification part of this form. GPO 16—31524-1

Cut along this line

NOTICE OF CLASSIFICATION App. not Req.

Louis Bernard Kincanon
(First name) (Middle name) (Last name)

Order No. 2885 has been classified in Class I-C Disc.

(Until — , 19....)
(Insert date for Class II-A and II-B only)

by ☒ Local Board.
☐ Board of Appeal (by vote of ..... to .....).
☐ President.

12-7-45, 19.... C. L. [signature]
(Date of mailing) (Member of local board)

The law requires you, subject to heavy penalty for violation, to have this notice, in addition to your Registration Certificate (Form 2), in your personal possession at all times—to exhibit it upon request to authorized officials—to surrender it, upon entering the armed forces, to your commanding officer.

DSS Form 57. (Rev. 12-10-43.)

(Registrant must sign here)

Cut along this line to detach card

F61.3 Dad's Discharge Classification

F61.4 December 7, 1945 Here is a picture of where Dad was held in Germany

F61.5 Dad's Prison Camp in Germany

Because of the internet we have such an amazing opportunity to find information that we had no idea existed. What you are about to see in the picture below is one such item, and there are more which I will share. This particular item blew my family and I away. Our entire family could not believe our eyes when we saw this. My nephew Tim, Michael's son, he is the oldest of Mom and Dad's grandchildren. He had spent some time researching WWII and Dad's history in the war. When doing so he came across a picture of a dollar bill on a Facebook post which was done by someone looking for anyone who may have served and been in the prison camp along with his grandfather, George Coleman. He was in possession of a dollar bill that was signed by many of the men in his camp. The bill was posted on-line with a question to the public if there was anyone that knew these men on the dollar bill. When my family saw this bill, we immediately recognized my father's signature. It was clear as day. I could recognize his handwriting anywhere, and so could my brother's as they all write just like him.

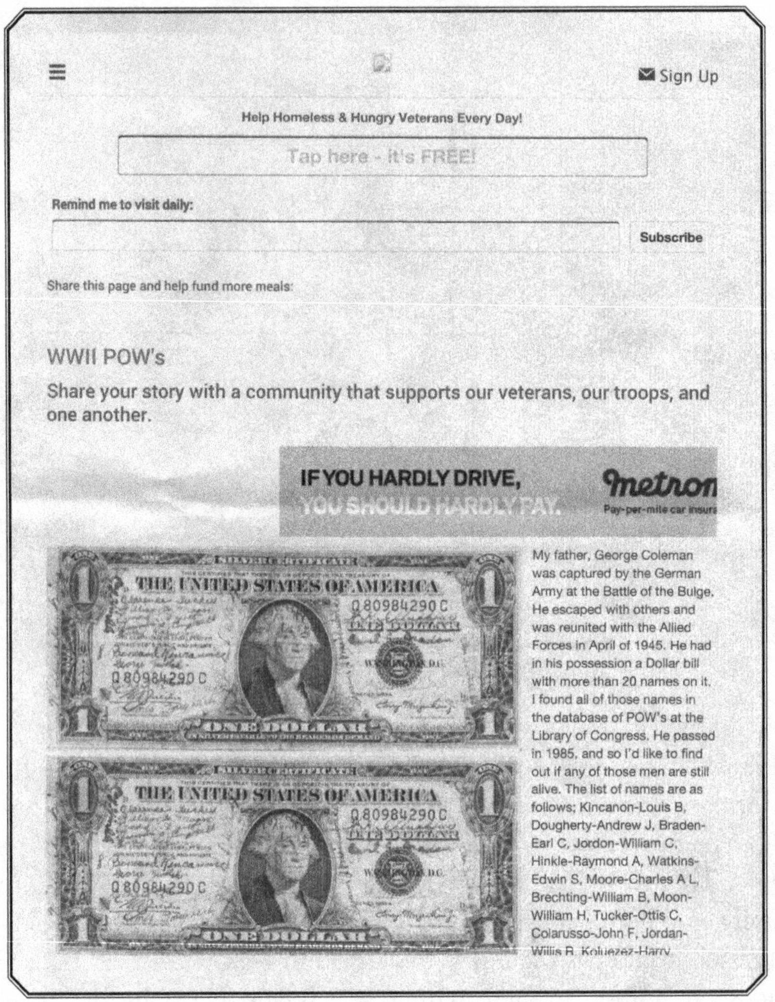

F61.6 Facebook post along with the dollar bill

Here is a close up, my Dad's name L. Bernard Kincanon is located right above the serial number **Q80984290C.**

The saddest part about this amazing find; Mom or Dad were not here to see it. I would have loved to have seen Dad's reaction!

THE UNITED STATES OF AMERICA
Q 80984290 C
Q 80984290 C
ONE DOLLAR

F61.7

1945

January 15, 1945

Monday 9:30 P.M. (The only letter penned by my Mom, ended in mid-sentence. No idea why)

My Darling:

Well honey, no mail again today. I keep remembering that you've said over and over again that if there is a delay in the mail there's always a good reason. Tonight, the Secretary of War released casualty figures since December 16th and darling I could have cried when I saw them. When I think of all you boys over there going through so much our prayers are with you always.

Well, Bernie I work one more week and then I'm finished. Lilian came back to work today so they won't need me after this week. Gosh, I am so glad I was able to work this long. This afternoon I deposited my poker winnings in the bank. I wrote you last night that I won $14.80.

Honey did I tell you that my cousin Jack from Hayward that was wounded in France is back in the States? He got back a couple days ago and he's in a hospital in New York waiting to be transferred to one near home. He is the one who was the second lieutenant in the infantry.

Mom can't wait till I'm home all day and can have supper ready for her at night. At least I'll get a lot of practice honey and when we have our own place, I'll be an expert. Darling, that is one thing I can hardly wait for. We'll be so very happy when we are together again. I love you so much Bernie and I will always. I was thinking last night how lonesome it was when you were in Kansas but what was that compared to this loneliness that we are feeling now? But I guess whenever……..

April 28, 1945

UTM/cmm

IN REPLY REFER TO

AGPC 201 Kincanon, Louis D.
(19 Feb 45) 36 739 483

WAR DEPARTMENT
THE ADJUTANT GENERAL'S OFFICE
WASHINGTON 25, D. C.

28 April 1945

Mrs. Louis Kincanon
417 Wisconsin Avenue
Oak Park, Illinois

Dear Mrs. Kincanon:

There has been forwarded to this office from overseas, your letter of inquiry concerning your husband, Corporal Louis B. Kincanon who has been missing in action in Germany since 21 December 1944.

Your distress since he was reported a casualty, and your desire to obtain further information regarding him is most understandable. A report now available in the War Department shows that on 11 December 1944 the regiment in which your husband was ammunition handler moved up to a defensive position on the battle line in the vicinity of Radscheid, Germany. On 16 December 1944 the German attack began and on 18 December 1944 all communications with the regiment was lost. Available evidence indicates that the regiment was surrounded by German units.

I wish to assure you that upon receipt of any additional information regarding your husband it will be communicated to you immediately. It is regretted that the War Department has no further details as of 18 April 1945.

My sympathy continues with you.

Sincerely yours,

J. A. ULIO
Major General
The Adjutant General

1 Inclosure

May 23,1945 (Not received until June 1945)

Western Union Telegram

DARLING: HOPE TO SEE YOU SOON. BEST WISHES TO ALL AT HOME. LOUIS KINCANON

June 1, 1945

Western Union Telegram
12:02 AM

THE SECRETARY OF WAR DESIRES ME TO INFORM YOU THAT YOUR HUSBAND TECHNICIAN 5TH GRADE LOUIS BE KINCANON RETURNED TO MILITARY CONTROL ELEVEN MAY.

SIGNED

JA ULIO THE ADJUTANT GENERAL

May 31, 1945 (Not received until June 1945)

American Red Cross

Dear Mom and Girls,

Well, they did transfer me to a different hospital, and I am waiting to be sent to the coast where all the X POW'S are waiting shipment home. Transportation is a big problem over here now, but General EISENHOWER promised to send all prisoners home as soon as possible. A heck of a lot of them have arrived back in the states already, but just know I am going home soon satisfies me. My leg has healed up fine and I am in perfect health, but as always, I am still worried about all of you at home. There just isn't any possible way for me to hear from you it seems. Now that I am on the move all the time. I guess I'll have to wait until the old boat reaches New York.

Mom, you've heard stories of the weather in France during the last war. Well, they weren't exaggerating a bit. It does rain all the time in this lousy country. We had one spell of beautiful summer weather, but since then______________. Last December 1, when we arrived in France, we stayed here for 10 days in an open pasture and sure enough it rained every day. Then we went into Belgium and it snowed every day there. The weather in Chicago may get miserable at times but never again do I want to leave that city. Now, this is what the plan to do with all the PW's. When we hit the states, we are taken to some camp and are paid in full for all the time we've been captured. After that comes our furlough either 30 or 60 days, I'm not sure. From there on it's a mystery. Some say discharge others, reassignment to a new outfit. Everybody does agree on one thing though, they are pretty sure we'll never see the Pacific.

Mom, you'll never know how many times I've thought of this in then past eight months. I know how worried you were when I transferred to the infantry, and then after being captured, I almost went nuts worrying about Mary and you. From what I heard the first notice you get is the Missing in Action telegram and then months later the confirmation of capture. I realized how both of you would be worrying, and I would have given anything to be back with SSO, (special service ops) because they got away OK. However, now that it's all over I seem to be the lucky one.

The division is either going to police up Germany or head for the pacific and here I am going home. It's a funny world, but with God's help and mercy I made it alright.

Guess that's enough gab for now, so I better close. Before I do though, here's a chance I may have of hearing from you. You can send a telegram to this address.

My name- ASN-241 General Hospital- Code Cable AMICOR A.P.O. 513

Bye for now and give my love to all the folks. Sure am anxious to see all of you.

Love, Bern

If you need help about sending the cable contact the Red Cross.

January 3,1945
(this letter was written but not received until June 1945) I am putting it in the order it was received

Darling:

I hope by now you have been notified that I am a Prisoner of Germany. Know it has been a long time since you've heard from me and I'm sure anxious to have you know I'm alright. This couldn't have happened at a worse time for you Mary and I'm worried about you constantly. Take care of yourself now and I'll pray every day that you'll be alright when the baby comes. Have been to mass every morning since arriving here and will continue to attend daily for all the folks at home. Honey we are allowed to write two letters and four cards a month, so I'll split them up between you and Mom. Be sure and tell her all the news in this letter and she'll feel better. That's all for now Mary so give my love and regards to everyone.

Bye now and love always,
Bern

Chapter 62

Family and Friends

Mom and Dad are together, raising their family in Oak Park, doing all the things families do. They had many things they loved to do together and many of them if not all of them we did as a family. Sometimes, that was as simple as being outside or sitting on the front porch. Mom and Dad never really went away for any length of time without us and they were not in a position financially to take vacations with a family of five children. I never lived down one trip that we did take by car to Florida. It was just the two boys and I at this point in time. I was an infant in the back seat, maybe in a bassinet. Car seats were not mandatory back then. It was summer and the old 1950's car did not have air conditioning. The green-house effect had me boiling in the back seat, with no one paying attention to me. The story goes, I got everyone's attention the only way I could. It was most definitely a heat stroke that caused such an explosion but what can I say, it got everyone's attention. Dad pulled over and everyone flew out of the car trying to take a breath of fresh air. Okay, did anyone think to take me with them out of that hot car? The only other family vacation I recall was by car again to Florida, of course, to see Maw. All the kids were born, but I don't think the two older boys were with us. However, I do recall, my other grandmother was along for the trip.

We did some traveling to southern Illinois to see cousins that remained on the farm and worked the farm. I always loved it there. I think I would have enjoyed the farm life as long as I could have had a horse, which was always my childhood dream. Secretly, (not really) it is still a dream.

Baseball trips were also a reason for leaving home, but not overnight. While writing this I recall one of Dad's letters where he said, once he gets home from the Army, he will never want to leave home again. Maybe that was part of the reason we stayed close to home.

Mom and Dad were both avid readers. In the summer, my Dad would be on the front porch moving his chair with the sun and Mom would be in the back of the house on the screened in porch. There was always a stack of magazines and books out on the porch to read, and Mom's half-filled glass of iced tea would be sweating on one of those magazines.

We were usually somewhere outside, the park was only a block away, and there were so many kids on the block that we always had somewhere to go and play. We lived next to a church, so it was a great place to play four-square.

Terry Jirasek was one of my best friends, and she lived right across the street from us. She and I were one day apart in age. Terry was one day older than me, which was always an issue when we were kids, but it ended up being funnier as we got older because then I could turn it around and I could tell her, she was older than me! The coolest thing is we were born in the same hospital one day apart. St. Anne's Hospital in Chicago, Illinois. This meant, we were in the very same nursery together. Her family moved on our block when we were both five years old. Our parents ended up recognizing each other from the hospital nursery. Both of the new dads were at the nursery windows looking in on their new little girls. In those days the moms were able to stay in the hospital a week or more, so there was plenty of time to get to know the other people on your floor.

When Terry moved in, we were both only five years old. We were young enough that we were not allowed to cross the street; so, we would sit on the curb and roll a big ball across the street to each other. We were very creative in the ways we would find ways to play with each other. We had a very long string and an aluminum can on each side, and we would have it strung from our bedrooms upstairs, so we could talk to each other. I really can't remember if that actually worked, but we thought it did at the time. Flashlights were also fun, I think we also tried to learn Morse Code.

One day which is seared in my memory; I was twelve years old, and my sister Lynn was ten and Bill was about three. We were down at the end of our block just north of our home. Our friend Mary Beth Stanacek lived there and we would play there every so often when her mom would allow us to be there. We were so lucky to have a really fun group of girls close in age. We all had great imaginations. Terry Jirasek, Kathy Gubbins, Marybeth, and my sister Lynn, and I were always hanging out together. We had a singing group and called ourselves ***"The Question Marks."*** We used to sing many of the Beatles songs, and one of our favorite songs was Roy Orbison's Pretty Woman. On one of those days while down at Mary Beth's house we were called home in the middle of the day.

When we were running home, we could see flashing red lights that looked so close to where we lived, and as we got closer, we could see it was an ambulance right in front of our house. As I ran up those familiar front porch stairs, I ran in the front door, and I could see my Dad lying on a couch in our small TV room. That was the first room straight on from the front door. A doctor, at least the stethoscope hanging around his neck led me to believe he was a doctor, or he was some strange guy that was standing over my Dad. Daddy looked white as a ghost and was not moving, but I remember seeing him lying there with his hands crossed over his chest like he was dead. I was so scared! The man was taking Dad's blood pressure, he had that thing around his neck and listening to his heart while trying to ask him questions. A couple men helped put him on a stretcher and outside to the ambulance that was waiting for him. I distinctly remember the little kid next door watching the whole thing and when he reached our house he ran over and asked, ***"is he dead?"*** He looked dead!

My Dad was taken away in that ambulance. I do not know where Mom was, did she go with him in the ambulance? All I know is that I ran upstairs to the safety of my closet and cried my eyes out. Alone. I literally could not stop crying and when I finally did come downstairs, I was still pretty hysterical and I remember my older brother Michael slapped me to snap me out of my hysteria. I think the little neighbor boy asking that question scared me so much and I was afraid it was true. My Dad was only forty-eight years old when he had his first heart attack. It would not be his last.

Dad took this very scary event with his health seriously and as a result changed many things about his lifestyle. He quit smoking, ate better and lost some weight. Dad made changes to make sure he stayed around for his family.

Breaking the two boys two girls tie;

Our family was even-steven, two boys and two girls. Now there was another baby on the way five years after my younger sister Lynn. It is only natural the vote was split on what the next bundle of joy should be. Lynn and I wanted a girl so bad. We were afraid another boy would just mean more sport's games that we would have to go to. My older brother Michael played baseball. He was very talented, and Dad and Mom would go see every game. The best part for my sister and I were the parks we could go play in or the trees we would find to climb. I stayed as far away from the game as I could because I found out early on that I was a magnet for foul balls! The high branches of big trees seemed to be a safe place to escape what had become inevitable. A bonk on the head. One time I was walking along minding my own business, someone yells, "heads up," and I ran, only to run right into that foul ball that hit me right on the head. My Dad had to carry me out of the park with a big knot on my forehead. I guess that was one way to get my Dad's attention. It took me awhile, after all I was only six or seven years old to understand that "heads up" meant to look up and keep your eye on the ball! *OHHHHH that makes sense.* But, to this day no one really wants to sit next to me at what are now my nephew's baseball games. Yes! I go to the games and yes, I have traveled out of state to see him play and will continue to do so. All the while, I will be paying attention to the ball. It won't surprise you to know he is a fantastic right-handed pitcher and currently pitching for the Chicago White Sox.

Dad had come very close to pitching in the Big Leagues, but the Army ruined his arm. It ruined more than that, I think! Dad as they say, lived vicariously through his sons. He wanted the best for them, and he wanted everything for his very talented first son, Michael. He wanted for him what he couldn't have. What he lost! Dad was very hard on Michael. I remember many dinners that were ruined because Michael had a bad game. He didn't throw the right pitch, walked too many guys, I don't know. I never understood it. I hated it. I hated that my older brother was getting yelled at, or ignored, either one was punishment. The fights or arguments in our family were mostly about sports, baseball. So, another boy, another possible athlete was not on the girls wish list.

Lynn and I were across the alley at the Hawley's house. I have no idea where the boys were at the time. Annrose and Bill Hawley were like my second family. They have a daughter Billie Ann that is eight months older than I am. She is an only child and we could pass for sisters. We had the same hair color; we were about the same height and we loved being together. We still do. Our friendship has lasted over sixty years. There were many sleep overs with popcorn and movies. The Hawley's used to take me on vacation with them every year up to their summer home in Valparaiso Indiana. It was a great escape being with them. Writing this right now makes me wonder how my over nights at the Hawley's and my get away vacations affected my little sister at home, without me. Boy, being young little kids, we can be so self-centered and selfish.

Mom and Dad were great friends with them too, and it was no wonder that they were the people we were entrusted to when they went to the hospital. I know Annrose was not happy when mom told her she was pregnant. They had just gotten all of us kids in school full time and the coffee clutches could begin. Annrose was really looking forward to the mornings when the kids left and the coffee and maybe a sweet role could be shared over some great conversation and laughter, because with Mom and Annrose, there was always laughter. I can hear them now in my mind. Annrose had the best laugh! But now Mom had another baby coming home and it through a monkey wrench in their best laid plans.

All of us were in the kitchen, having a snack, or lunch and their mustard yellow phone was hanging on the wall, and when it rang, we all knew we were about to know who won the tip of the scale! The Boys or The Girls? On January 9, 1960 William Louis Kincanon was born!

It was a Boy, and I think Annrose felt for Lynn and me, as much as we felt sorry for ourselves! Well, that little boy was a life saver for us all. My little brother Bill, who at the time of this writing is turning sixty years old in less than a month, is my best friend. We have been so close, hanging out for years together in hard times, and great times. I love him with all my heart! I would do anything for him, and I know he feels the same way about me. That kid, that boy, gave my parents a whole new lease on life. He too, was so talented. He could pitch, he could hit, he was an all-around excellent athlete. He was MVP at Oak Park River Forest High School in Basketball and Baseball. He was drafted as a right-handed pitcher for The Cincinnati Reds. Are you seeing a pattern here? He gave my parents so much joy, thank God he was a Boy!

Chapter 63

EMPTY NESTERS

When all the kids were out of the house, and the nest was empty, Mom and Dad had a very nice group of friends that they socialized with often. Some of them were long-time friends that were empty nesters too and others joined the group later in life. It couldn't have been better for my parents because guess what these friends loved to do? They loved to play cards! They would all get together and play pinochle for hours on end. One thing that was different with these games were the winnings or losses. I think maximum was one dollar, it never broke the bank thankfully, as everyone was on a fixed income.

There were a couple of really nice trips that these friends went on together. One trip they ventured out on was with another couple, the White's. They all rented an RV and drove out west to visit Annrose and Bill Hawley, who had moved to Arizona a few years earlier. Annrose and Bill moving was very hard on my parents. They had been great friends for years. I never pictured my Dad traveling in an RV, but I think the idea of seeing his old pal Bill made the trip worth a little discomfort. There are certainly some wonderful pictures from that trip I will share. They all looked like they were having such a wonderful time in the photos, and I know Mom talked about that trip for many years.

F63.1 My Dad, Bernie, Mr. Hawley (pops), Joanne White, Annrose Hawley, and Harry White

F63.2. Pops and Annrose

F63.3 Mom and Dad

MF63.4 Dad and Pops

F63.5 Mom and Annrose

F63.6 Pops, Mom, Dad, Annrose, Harry

F63.7 Pops, Dad, Mom, and Annrose

F63.8. Harry, Dad, Mom, and Joanne White and RV

F63.9 I Love this Picture! Annrose and Dad.

F63.10 Pops, Mom, Annrose, Dad and Harry

F63.11 Mom and Dad in Florida

F63.12 Mom and Dad visiting Lynn in Williamsburg Virginia

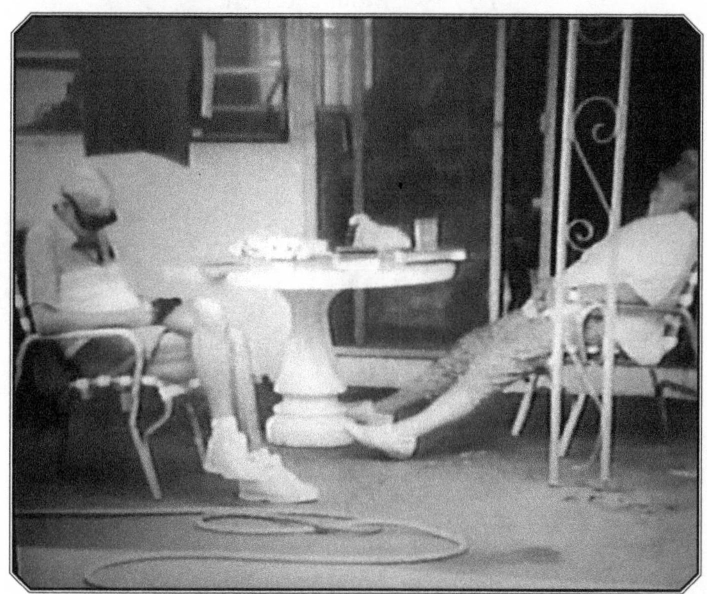

F63.13 Mom and Dad at Maw's house in Florida

F63.14 Mom and Dad
Wedding June 3, 1944

F63.15 Mom and Dad
50th Wedding Anniversary
June 1994

Chapter 64

Daddy's Decline

Mom and Dad had a full life together. I mentioned in a previous chapter about Daddy's fall down a long flight of stairs in our home in Oak Park. Soon after they moved to a ranch home and they did very well there for a time. This is the home where my Dad's decline was something we watched with an eye on denial. I spent a lot of time with my parents. I had a pretty flexible schedule, so I would help Mom whenever there was an appointment or more frequently a scare with Dad's health. There were starting to be many such occasions. During this period of time, I was in my late thirties. This is when Dad began to look at me as a daughter that he was proud of, and he thanked me often. This was also a time period when Dad also acknowledged and said to me ***"I'm sorry Kathleen, I could have done better by my daughters."*** This was a long-awaited validation that I needed from him my entire life. I accepted his apology immediately because I knew he was being sincere. I had always wanted to hear those words from him. It was a turning point for us and one that was a long time coming, but it was not a minute too soon. I certainly was painfully aware of all the changes that were happening with Dad. It seemed every week there was a new challenge, something that took him longer to do, or worse yet, something that he would never do again. It was so sad to witness.

Dad used to come to the gym with me at the Oak Brook Park District in Oak Brook, Illinois. He would drive and meet me there almost every day. On this particular day he came to my home in Downers Grove, Illinois and he followed me to the recreation center. We turned north on Jorie Street, the same street every day. I made the turn and checked my rear-view mirror for Dad. He was not there! He was just behind me. ***Where did he go?*** I spent the next three hours driving around looking for him. Literally it was three hours! There were no cell phones, so there was no way to reach him, if I did have one, he didn't, and I would not have been comfortable calling him while he was driving anyway. When I finally went home to my house Dad was in my drive way sitting in his car, all confused. I have to say I was so relieved to see him, and at the same time scared to death of what he was doing and how he got there. Dad told me he got totally turned around and so confused he just came here and sat waiting for me. I think that was the last day he drove alone. Mom took his keys away and I do not even know if he realized it. Until one day, Mom and I were out, and Dad was left home alone in their home. When Mom and I returned back home to their townhome, we turned their corner into their cul-de-sac and immediately noticed their garage door was open. Mom and I looked at each other with total fear on our faces. We immediately thought as we got closer that Daddy and the car would be gone. Thankfully, as we approached the driveway we could see the taillights of their car still parked in its spot, what we were not prepared for after that sigh of relief was to see Dad just sitting there in the driver's seat. When Mom and I approached the car, I know we startled him by knocking on the car window. I opened the door and asked Dad what he was doing sitting out there in the garage. His sad face nearly broke my heart. All he wanted to do was go to the drug store, but he could not figure out how to start the car. It was the saddest thing to witness and I could not help but cry. Mom was just stuck in her initial reaction of shock seeing the garage door open and reflecting on how awful it would have been if he had found the keys. Day after day things were deteriorating and when I say this, it was not over night! It was a long, long process. It was over a five-year period, of witnessing one thing after another. There were some falls, hospital visits, doctor visits, new medications, good days, and bad days. He was losing interest in the things he always loved and lived for his entire life. Dad never thought to turn on the TV for a baseball game, he just had lost interest.

We had my son Tim's wedding in 1998 and Dad was pretty good that day, but he was definitely ready to go home long before everyone else. We actually extended the time the reception was to end, and by then Dad was actually snoozing in his seat. We all just let him be and the party went on. By the year 2000, Joe and I moved from Homer Glen, Illinois where we lived since 1995 to Downers Grove, Illinois, which was a great move for us and a little closer in travel time to Mom and Dad's home. I will take this opportunity to mention that my husband Joe was an amazing son-in-law to my Mom and Dad. He was there for them whenever he was needed. He always went above and beyond to help them in every way. My Mom absolutely loved him, and they had a very special relationship.

When we made the move to Downers Grove in May of 2000, Dad was getting weaker and less able to be alone with every passing day. On this particular day, November 16, 2000, Mom, Dad and I went to an appointment to their attorney's office. Mom felt with everything going on with Dad, she needed to update her will. Mom and Dad inherited some money in January of that year, from Dad's Aunt Caddy. Aunt Caddie and Uncle Charlie did not have any children of their own. Caddie outlived Charlie by at least twenty years. She was a hoot, and spry as could be. She died from leukemia which was a quick diagnosis and a very quick end to a very well lived life. She died in January 2000. Because she and Charlie had no children and she loved my Dad and Mom like they were her own children, she left them the bulk of her estate. Mom wanted to make sure everything was in order, should something happen to Dad. They were not used to having any sum of money that would ever require making sure things were in order, this was all new to her. We pulled into the parking lot at the attorney's office. It was November and it was very cold outside. There were landscapers in the lot at the office building changing out the planters for the Christmas holiday. I do not know why I noticed that as soon as we pulled into the lot, but the upheaval of the old plants out of the planters at the end of their life, was a metaphor for what we were about to experience with my Dad. We had planned ahead and had a wheelchair for my Dad. I was driving, he was in the back seat and Mom was in the front with me. I got out and opened his door to help him out. He was in a green parka like coat, warm and cozy. Before Dad got out of the car, I went to the trunk to get the wheelchair out. I brought it over to his car door by the back seat. He went to stand up to get out of the car. I remember this like it was yesterday. I told Dad to turn around, so he could sit in the chair. The blank stare on his face was as if he was looking right through me. I could see he had absolutely no idea what I was asking him to do. I know when I was trying to get him to turn around, he just could not tell his brain to do this one simple motion. The minute he went to try to turn, he literally started to slide down the car and ended up sliding all the way down to the ground. I was trying to stop the centrifugal force next to me, but my Dad was over six feet tall and I could not stop what was happening. Suddenly he was on the cold, winter ground. Mom and I were trying to figure out what to do without showing Dad how stressed we were. I know I was not being very successful at that. This exact moment is when I remembered the landscapers working on the pots in front of the building. I left Mom with Dad and went over to ask for help. The gentleman I came upon was a really nice older gentleman, he did not speak English and I did not speak Spanish. I tried asking for help using simple words I knew. He followed me to our car. He saw the trunk open which by his reaction I believe it scared him a little bit. He went to back up and leave but I said, ***"POR FAVOR MI PAPA."*** I have no idea where that came from, but it came out of my mouth. He then noticed my Dad sitting on the cold ground. He ran right over to him and he helped us get him into the wheelchair. It was so exhausting, but I am not sure if it was more for us or my Dad. I gave that nice man a tip for helping me and said thank you as best I could in Spanish. We got up to our appointment and I remember sitting in the waiting room, with my Dad in the wheelchair sitting right in front of me. I had my arms wrapped tight around my Dad from behind while he was still in his big parka coat. I was hugging him and crying, saying out loud to my Mom how sorry I was for being so impatient with him in the parking lot earlier. I was so ashamed of myself, and at the same time I could not stop hugging him.

We were called in to the office, the will was already prepared. All they both needed to do was sign it. All Dad needed to do was sign his name. Oh my god, Daddy could not sign his name! I cannot explain to you what that was like, to watch your Dad with pen in hand, the man that penned all the letters in this book, he did not know where to put the pen to paper and write his own name.

Devastating! He signed the will with an "X."

PROOF OF WILL

STATE OF ILLINOIS)
) Self-Proving Affidavit
COUNTY OF DU PAGE)

We, **LOUIS B. KINCANON**, and Paula Kovarik, Carol Wolin and Arlene Wender, the Testator and the witnesses, respectively, whose names are signed to the attached or foregoing instrument, being first duly sworn, do hereby declare to the undersigned authority that the Testator signed and executed the instrument as his Last Will and that he had signed willingly (or willingly directed another to sign for him), and that he executed it as his free and voluntary act for the purposes therein expressed, and that each of the witnesses, in the presence and hearing of the Testator, and in the presence of each other, signed the Will as witness and to the best of our knowledge the Testator was at that time eighteen years of age or older, of sound mind, and under no constraint or undue influence.

LOUIS B. KINCANON

Paula Kovarik
Witness

Carol Wolin
Witness

Arlene Wender
Witness

Subscribed, sworn to, and acknowledged before me by **LOUIS B. KINCANON**, the Testator and subscribed and sworn to before me by Paula Kovarik, Carol Wolin and Arlene Wender, witnesses, this 15th day of November, 2000.

(Seal)
Notary Public for Illinois

OFFICIAL SEAL
LOUIS V PAVONE
NOTARY PUBLIC, STATE OF ILLINOIS
MY COMMISSION EXPIRES: 12/10/00

Last Will and Testament of LOUIS B. KINCANON Page 7

F64.1 A copy of that will and my dad's name is an "X."

By the time we left the attorney's office it was early afternoon. This day was a turning point for both of us. We were so thoroughly exhausted. We looked at each other and we both had the same thoughts. *What in the world do we do now?* Mom and I knew on this day November 16, 2000 things were going to change, and not for the better. We made the decision to check out her options. We went by three or four nursing homes on the way home to check them out. Mom was so worried after what we had experienced that day and the days leading up to this, that she was reaching a point where she knew she could not take care of him on her own. She was not strong enough on her own, to help Dad if he fell. She could not help him get into the bathroom, or the shower. She was staring her own limitations right in the face. How in the world did this feel? After everything they had been through together, how do you make the decision about the one you have loved for almost sixty years? I remember going home with Mom. I remember it like it was yesterday. *Was today the day?* Was this the day Dad was leaving his home for another, to be cared for by strangers? We got him home, and just getting him in the house was near impossible. It was almost like the decision was being made for us by my Father's lack of ability. That is when I brought up to Mom, how about the VA Hospital. My Dad, never in all his years post war used any of his benefits from the VA. I have no idea why. My own opinion is he wanted nothing to do with anything that had to do with the war, not even his benefits that he earned as a vet, not to mention as a POW. We both tried getting Dad in the house, which took us forever. We got him to his bed and knew right then; the decision was made. We were calling an ambulance and taking Dad to the VA Hospital in Maywood, Illinois. Mom went into the filing cabinet with all Dad's paperwork. She was looking for his discharge papers and his POW papers. I remember her rattling off Dad's I.D. number like it was their phone number. She knew it by heart. I would guess she wrote it a thousand times on the envelopes to her husband. The ambulance was called, and they put Dad ever so gently on the stretcher. Mom and I both knew when he was wheeled out of the front door of their town home, it was the last time he would cross their threshold. We both were visibly upset knowing this. Were we doing the right thing?

Was this really the right decision at this time, this very night? For any family that has had to go through this decision, I feel your pain. It is so hard, and you question that decision for the rest of your life. I am questioning it right now and it is 20 years later, almost to the day.

Mom and I followed the ambulance to Maywood Il. and called other family members on the way to the hospital, trying hard to explain the day's events that unfolded with Dad, starting at the attorney's office. Even though my sister and my brothers knew what we had been denying for the past several months was leading to this, it was still a shock. Our Dad, our Father, was going into the VA Hospital and in all likelihood, he was not coming home. It was November 16, 2000 exactly one week before Thanksgiving. When we arrived at the Hospital, we were with the ambulance and initially greeted very hospitably. They asked all the usual questions, his name and other pertinent information. But, since my Dad had never been there, he was not registered as a vet. The man said to me, ***"I am sorry, but "we cannot accept your father, he is not in our system.***" Well, you have never seen me so angry! I told that man in no uncertain terms that my Dad was a WWII prisoner of war. I also instructed him to bring us the person in charge. When the administrator came to talk with us he asked us if we had Dad's papers. Of course, Mom had all the paperwork that was needed for his admission and Dad was taken to his private room. All family members that were local were with him that night. My sister arrived a day later from her home in Colorado to be with our Dad. The VA hospital staff treated our Dad very well. He was comfortable and well cared for by everyone there. I am not sure if he really knew where he was. I do remember he was worried about the cost of Jell-O which was all he would eat for the next thirty days. Dad and Mom both had a DNR (do not resuscitate) in their will, neither of them wanted any extreme measures keeping them alive. One specific instruction for both of them was absolutely no feeding tubes. Thirty days to the day after admission, our family was there, by Dad's side for his last rights and prayers.

It was on the 56th anniversary to the day of our father's capture at the Battle of the Bulge, that our father passed away and was at peace, December 16, 2000.

Chapter 65

Life After Dad

Mom lived alone in their town home for eight more years after Dad died. She remained pretty independent and stayed very busy. She still worked for Pete's sake. Mom was eighty-two years old and still drove to work every day to Life Touch Studio in Aurora, Illinois from Darien, Illinois. Life Touch was the photography company that did school pictures for many of the grammar schools in the western suburbs. When Mom first started working there, she used to take the pictures. It was part of her job to make sure the kids' looked their best. Mom would make sure their hair was brushed and as hard as she tried, she could not always get them to smile before pressing the shutter on the camera. The job started to become hard for her. Part of her duties also included carrying all the photography equipment into each of the schools. Depending on the school this would prove very difficult for Mom. In many of the schools there were no elevators and the long staircases up and down would be too much for her with the heavy equipment she had to carry. There came a time when this part of the job was just too much for her physically. When it became apparent Mom could no longer do that part of the job she told her boss she would have to make a change. The bosses at Lifetouch did not want to lose such a loyal employee, not to mention a woman like Mom that was fun to be around. They immediately gave her a job in the office in Aurora. Mom made friends easily and had many friends there that loved her! Mom's new job in the office was handling all the orders that would come in from the families of the school children, she was in charge of counting the money and to complete the accounting reports.

One day, at work, Mom was in the office, she went to turn around and her foot got caught up in the computer wires under her boss's desk. She went flying forward and jammed her shoulder into a door frame. This accident required my poor Mom to need a shoulder replacement. Much to Mom's chagrin, she was unable to return to work after that. Mom had to spend quite a bit of time at a rehab facility in Naperville, Illinois until she was able to be on her own again. At eighty-two years old, my Mom was collecting workman's compensation. It was very hard on her. Even after months of rehab she was still unable to lift her arm up to her ear. Doing her own hair was nearly impossible.

It was a good thing she had a standing appointment every Friday at Paula Pinkerton's Salon in Downers Grove. A wash set and style, by her friend Paula was a weekly thing for her. We had known Paula since she was eighteen years old. During my job at Oak Brook Hills Hotel and Resort, Paula was a young new stylist at the Beauty Salon right next to my gift shop. Years later, Paula left the salon and opened up her own business and Mom followed her. She became one of my Mom's best friends. Mom loved her, and Paula loved my Mom. She used to bring Mom pea soup, bake cookies with her over the holidays, and treat her like her own mother. The relationship between them was one that I was so grateful for. I knew that Paula was taking great care of Mom and that she loved her. Anyone who loved my Mom and treated her like she deserved to be treated is family to me. Paula and I often have many tearful conversations about her.

At the time of this writing, Paula has recently moved to South Carolina. She is very special to me and always will be. Paula, thank you for being such a kind friend to our Mother. She loved you and your stories! She would be so happy for you that you have found happiness with your man. Mom would also be so proud of Paula's daughter, Peyton, she is an amazing girl who is turning into an amazing woman!

Every Friday, after Mom's appointment with Paula she would pull up in my driveway to spend the rest of the day with me, her great-grandson, Colin, and great-granddaughter, Kellie. The summers were so much fun, we would spend the day together in our back yard. The kids loved GiGi and she was crazy about them. We did so many fun things with the kids. We would go to The Morton Arboretum, downtown Chicago, and the children's museum in Naperville. Joe and I had a hot tub that we would keep cool like a kiddie pool for the hot summer days. It was the next best thing to having a pool in those days.

Colin and Mom used to play school together; the kids and I still laugh about those times. Mom was a terrible student and Colin would grade her accordingly. I think her grade was always a "Z" (Colin's grading scale). And on a scale from A-Z, "Z" was the worst grade ever. Colin was a terrible teacher and Mom had no problem letting him know. We used to have so much fun with this little game. It was always so nice having Mom with me on my days with the kids. There was such a strong bond that developed between the kids and their great grandmother, GiGi. Both of them have so many fond memories and we keep her alive by talking about her often. Kellie will always look at me with such a sweet eye, wondering if the tears will be coming since we are talking about my Mom. There are definitely days where that is true. I miss my Mother every day.

They will get to know much more about her and the great grandfather they never met, through this book. That is one of my greatest hopes with these writings.

I have so many wonderful memories with my Mom! We have taken many wonderful trips together. The biggest extravagance was a trip to France in 2001. It was only a little more than six months since Dad had died. There was a great opportunity to go on a trip to Paris, France. I think it was just what both of us needed at the time. We went with a tour group. The head tour guide, Patrick, was a French chef that took twenty-five to thirty-five people on these tours every year. It was an unbelievable experience. We had nine course meals at five-star restaurants every night. We were in Leon, Rheims, Paris… eating at the most historic of places. We drank Champaign where Dom Perion discovered Champaign while overlooking vineyards and rose gardens. We ate chocolate crapes from vending carts on the streets of France. We walked along the Champs-Èlysèes and, visited the Louvre. It is a trip I hold dear in my memory and I am so thankful we did it together.

My husband Joe and I took Mom on her first cruise, which she loved. We had a suite on the concierge level of the ship on Princess Cruise Line. We had a very large room with a gorgeous view from our balcony. Mom of course got the most comfortable bed! We went off the ship to see the islands, we found it was easier to have a wheelchair for these excursions. Mom loved the shows in the evening, the never-ending food choices and our company.

Mom and I were traveling buddies. We took many trips to Colorado to see my sister Lynn. Before Colorado Lynn lived in Virginia, Michigan, Florida, and Washington D.C. The one thing about Lynn living out of state, we always had many lovely places to visit. Joe was a part of many of these trips, but some many we took alone. I always regretted that Joe and Lynn did not come to France with us. Obviously, with the trips we were able to take, Mom was pretty active, but she had some limitations.

Mom would not let much keep her down. One perfect example, Mom and Dad went into Berwyn, Illinois to have breakfast at one of their favorite places years before Dad died. They were still living in Oak Park at the time. Mom got out of her car in the back-parking lot, fell and twisted her ankle in a pot hole. The way she twisted the one ankle and then fell on her other ankle, she ended up breaking both ankles at the same time. I thought this was the end of Mom being mobile. I know her mother broke her leg very early on in her life, maybe in her early 70's, and ended up so afraid she put herself in a wheelchair and never walked again. I was afraid the same thing would happen with my Mom. That was not the case. Mom was very adamant that was not going to be her future and she worked really hard at rehab to walk again, albeit slower and with more trepidation. There were times I would be walking with Mom and she would literally be talking to herself out loud to ***"keep walking"*** and ***"watch where you are walking."***

While I was reading my Dad's letters, I realized my Mom must have been a bit of a klutz. There were quite a few references in my Dad's letters to her falling. If it was the case back then at a young age in her twenties, it became even more of her signature later in life. I cannot tell you how many phone calls I would get that she had fallen.

They all started out the same, ***"Kathleen…I fell."***

I was always the first phone call my Mom made even when it made absolutely no sense to be that first call.

One such call was from her home in Darien, Dad had already passed. I want to say it was around 2005 or 2006. My phone rang, it was my Mom, saying, ***"Kathleen, my house is on fire!"*** I was stunned, but not too stunned to ask if she called the Fire Department and if she was out of the house. The answer to both questions was no. I urged her immediately to ***"hang up get out of the house and call 911."*** OMG! By the time I got to Darien from Downers Grove there were five or six firetrucks in her small cul-de-sac. The fire was started because she had hired a plumber because of a leaky outside spigot. In order to get to the spigot to fix the leak they had to cut her inside wall in her master bedroom. The plumber, while sweating the pipes with the torch, caught the insulation on fire. It went up the inside of the wall and caught her unit, the unit next door, and the unit above her on fire. Mom was out of her home for over six months. The man upstairs was very unkind to her after that, but I sure don't know why, he got an entirely brand-new updated home. It wasn't like my Mom was the one sweating the pipes. I bet when he went to sell his place, he did well because of all those brand-new updates! No one was hurt, that was the main thing.

Mom lived by Joe and me for a while but for some of the time while she was out of her home she had a large suite at Oak Brook Hills Hotel where I had worked before becoming a Realtor. My previous boss, Randy, (he was the golf pro at the resort), made sure she was comfortable while she was a guest there. We had many nice gatherings during her stay.

Mom continued her social life of playing pinochle with all the men and women at the Darien Park district. This was an activity she was committed to at least a couple days a week. That happened to be another place where I received an emergency call. Mom had fallen in their parking lot and really hit her head hard. I will put a picture here, but a warning, they are graphic. Mom wanted a hat on thinking it would help the way it looked! ***Uh, no mom, it did not help.***

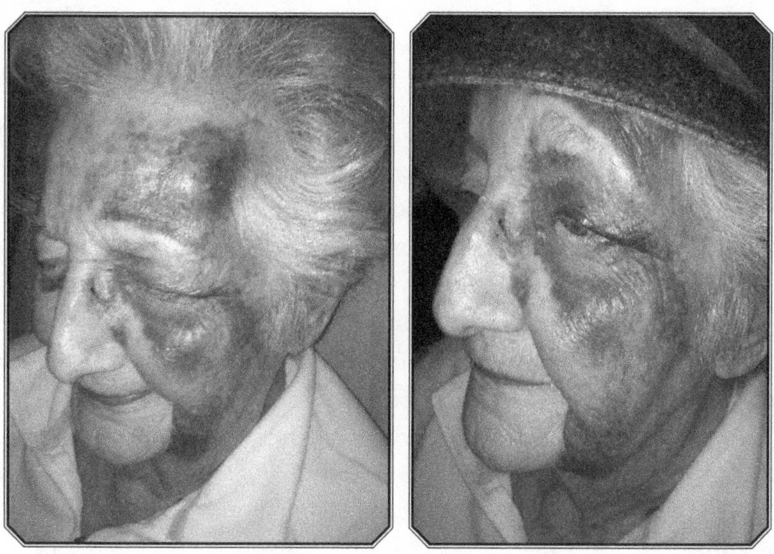

F65.1 This was a fall she had in the summer of 2012 in Darien.

Chapter 66

Mom Moves In

Joe and I started doing the shopping for Mom because she was starting to slow down. Doing the shopping and unloading it herself was becoming very hard for her. There were times when we would sit down together and order from Pea Pod which delivered the groceries to her kitchen. I remember very clearly one of our days together. Mom and I were sitting at my computer in my office going over her shopping list. Mom just came out and said to me, *"I'm getting very lonely living alone."* I often wonder how long she was feeling this way. How many times had she practiced what she was going to say to me? How many times did she run through in her mind what I would say to her? I know my Mom, and this one sentence had to be one of the most difficult ones for her to utter. It did not matter that she and I were so close and that we loved spending time together. This was a momentous decision for all of us. This was my very independent Mom, giving up a piece of her independence. This was huge on so many levels. I am sure she was not even thinking that Joe and I had on many occasions told her she would always be welcome to come and live with us. Many things are said, but are they always meant? Do you ever think they will come to pass? Well Mom, say no more, if you are telling me you are lonely, that made me so sad, but not at all surprised. I honestly did not see how she last as long as she did by herself. My recollection is from the time she told me that to the time she moved in was not more than a month or so. We had some decisions to make on the logistics.

The timing of this life changing decision was right at the same time of the downturn in the real estate market, and things were getting financially tight for us. Joe and I had a big 3000 square foot home in north Downers Grove, and with real estate being my main source of income, we were starting to feel the pinch of the big mortgage payment every month. We talked to Mom and decided to look for a ranch home to rent, then we could rent out our home and save some money. We ended up doing that for one year. We found a perfect solution in Downers Grove not too far from our home. It was a sprawling ranch with five bedrooms. Mom could have her own family/ TV room and her own bedroom. We had a few things we had to change at our own expense and with the owner's permission. It had very old loose carpeting which was a sure tripping hazard for mom and her walker. It also needed a fresh coat of paint. We were told it was ok to replace the carpet, and paint. Sure, why not, we were definitely making an improvement to their property for them at no cost. But, the best part for Mom, it was a one level home, and now she had the company of Joe and I, our Great Dane Zoe, and the grandkids on a regular basis. Colin and Kellie still talk about our spaghetti nights every Wednesday and we all really miss her meatballs! That first year went by very quickly. Our tenants in our home in Downers Grove were getting really flakey and to be honest we were really missing our home and our neighbors. One year later we decided to move back. The one problem we had was our home was on three levels and had a detached garage, which would be harder on Mom in inclement weather. The home had a first floor walk out, which would be considered the lower level, with a well-appointed finished family room with a fireplace, a wonderful brand-new bathroom with a double Jacuzzi tub and a separate walk in shower. This part of the lower level also had a separate space on the other side of an amazing staircase where I had my office set up. There was a wall of built in cabinets for storage and another for coats. It worked so well for us. There was only one problem, the walk out also meant a large staircase to get to the main level. The main level of the home consisted of a large master bedroom with a wall of huge closets with built-ins, a large living room with another fireplace and a dining room that was the same size as the living room. We installed gorgeous hardwood floors throughout this level which would be easier for Mom to get around with her walker. The full kitchen was also on this level. All five of us discussed the situation regarding the stairway to the main level and we came up with a solution. We had a chairlift installed for mom. This gave Mom the freedom she needed and the assistance to come and go as she wanted. By the picture I think you can tell she loved it!

F66.1 Mom testing out her chairlift

Our bedroom was a first-floor master, so Joe and I gave up that room and went upstairs to the third floor where there were three other bedrooms and a full bath. The only tweak we had to make was an addition of a separate zone for air conditioning, as it got very hot up there in the heat of the summer. Who knew? We really did not use the upstairs very often unless we had overnight guests. Mom actually helped us pay for the additional zone since she felt she had displaced us from our room. We accepted that help. It worked out perfectly. Mom really had the entire first floor as her own with the living room serving as her family room with a TV, fireplace, and a large picture window to see the world outside. We lived on a great block on Washington Street, just a couple blocks from town. Many commuters walked by our home every day. The farmer's market was a block away. It was the perfect home for all of us. Who knew years before, that this home I fell in love with years earlier when I sold it to clients, then ended up buying it from them when they called me to list it when they were moving to Boston, would end up being the best decision. It worked out so well for everyone.

Our home always seems to be the home where our family gathers, and now that our Mom was living with us, it was even more so. That was fine with us. We had an awesome back yard. My sister is a wonderful gardener and helped me over the years to plant lovely perennials, bushes, and small trees like the service berry bush we planted right outside our back door. We had a colorful view every season of the year. Mom and I along with our Great Dane would spend many mornings out in the yard. It was a peaceful serene part of our home that we both loved. We invited family on most weekends to BBQ and visit mom. Most Sundays, one of my brothers, Bill or Larry would make plans with Mom and have their own time with her. This was also good for Joe and me to have some alone time.

Mornings were a very lovely time with Mom. Joe and Mom would be in the kitchen, having their coffee, Mom would have her oatmeal, and they would work the New York Times crossword puzzle together. Mom was still sharp as a tack and she amazed Joe many times with how really smart she was. By the time I got up, Joe had already left for work, but he had made a copy of the Sudoku and scramble puzzles for me and Mom. These were the ones Mom and I would do together.

There were certain days Mom had her own schedule; Friday's she had her standing hair appointment with Paula, and on Monday's and Wednesday's she played pinochle. She kept busy and was never underfoot. Mom was very respectful of our space which we really appreciated.

Her closets, those famous closets, still needed attention way too often. We had our shows we loved to watch together. The Good Wife was one of our favorites. Mom loved both of the Bachelor and Bachelorette shows. I would watch them with her, but they were not my favorite. She and her friend Anita would call each other after each show and discuss all the crazy men or women from the nights show. That was funnier and more entertaining than watching the show.

I will say she was not the best at picking up after herself, her crumbs and oatmeal flakes were always on the kitchen floor, not to mention a lot of salt. Mom had her superstitions; if you spilled the salt shaker then you had to throw the salt over your left shoulder. Hence, the salt on the floor. I once told her I have swept more since she moved in than I have in my entire life. Her reply was, *"oh that's nothing."*

Chapter 67

The Final Fall

While Mom lived with us things were good, really good. Do not get me wrong, we had our days when she drove me crazy and I am sure the same could be said for me. I know Joe drove her crazy at times too. I made some pretty desperate phone calls to my brothers and sister asking for help and a little relief. These times usually came when I was really busy at work, mom had fallen or needed help with one thing or another and I did not have time. She would get pouty and quiet. These hiccups never lasted long, and I always felt terrible afterwards. My brothers Bill and Larry became more involved in helping me and life went on. I cannot count how many times I was in the emergency room with Mom or at doctor appointments with her. At one of her usual check-ups, she was not feeling well, I was always in the room with her. This particular time her doctor sent her right over to the ER at Hinsdale hospital. Mom had **COPD** and was very susceptible to pneumonia, she also got bronchitis on a regular basis. The falls, there were more than I could count. At this stage, Mom was supposed to use her walker, there was just too much risk without it. I used to call my siblings and say to them, *"Guess where I am?"* It was always a prelude to *"I am at the hospital with Mom."*

She was pretty good at using her walker, but not great. On this one particular Sunday, about a week before Thanksgiving in 2012, we were all getting excited for a visit from my older brother Michael.

He was coming in the day after Thanksgiving for a visit from Florida where he has lived since he retired in 2001, a year after Dad died.

Mom was in our kitchen putting a roast in the oven for dinner, I was downstairs working in my office. Joe was on the couch reading the Sunday paper. Mom took a couple steps away from the stove to put something back in the refrigerator without her walker. She fell and fell hard. I heard the worst sound and her scream. We flew upstairs to find her lying on the floor. She was crying and moaning in such pain. I was down on the floor with her and she was crying and saying to me *"I have ruined everything."* I know she was talking about Michael's upcoming visit. Joe called 911 and within minutes two or three men were in our kitchen standing over my Mom. She could not move, and they were trying to evaluate where her injury was. I could hardly stand there and watch as they tried to move her and get her on a stretcher. I have seen her in pain before, but I knew this was different.

Following the ambulance to the hospital, I was making those familiar calls to my family only this time I know there was more distress in my voice. It was unusual that I was actually with Mom when she fell, so this felt different for more than one reason. This entire scenario is so hard to re-live in this writing. I can see it all right now in my mind's eye and it is so hard. Just one more careful step, a step with her walker rather than deciding not, maybe a decision to go out to dinner so Mom was not upstairs cooking, which she still loved to do.

Nothing but: IF, IF, IF, IF, IF, IF, IF, IF, IF, IF, IF!

The diagnosis was a broken leg and surgery was scheduled for the next morning.

F67.1 Our kitchen where mom fell.

F67.2 My Brother Michael and granddaughter
Kellie at the Hospital Visiting Mom

F67.2 My sister Lynn and grandson Colin at the Hospital visiting Mom

The look on my sister's face tells me she knew what was ahead.

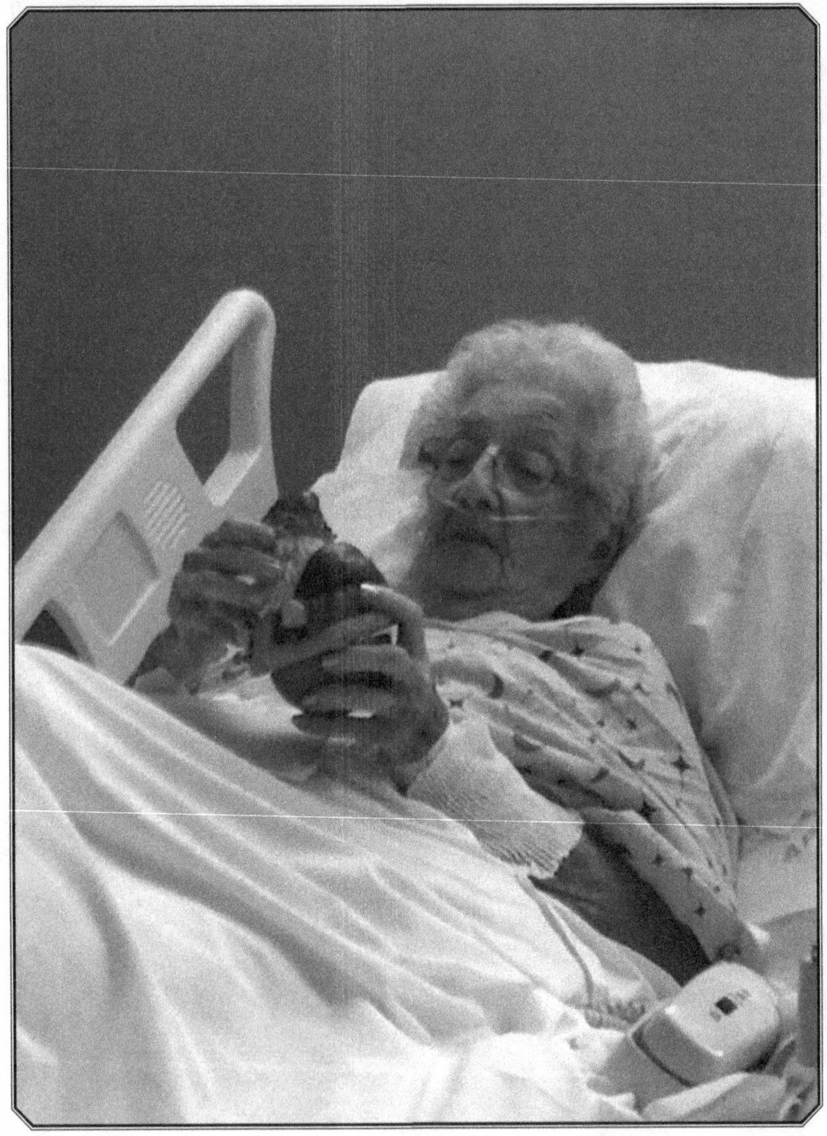

F67.4 Mom a day or two after surgery

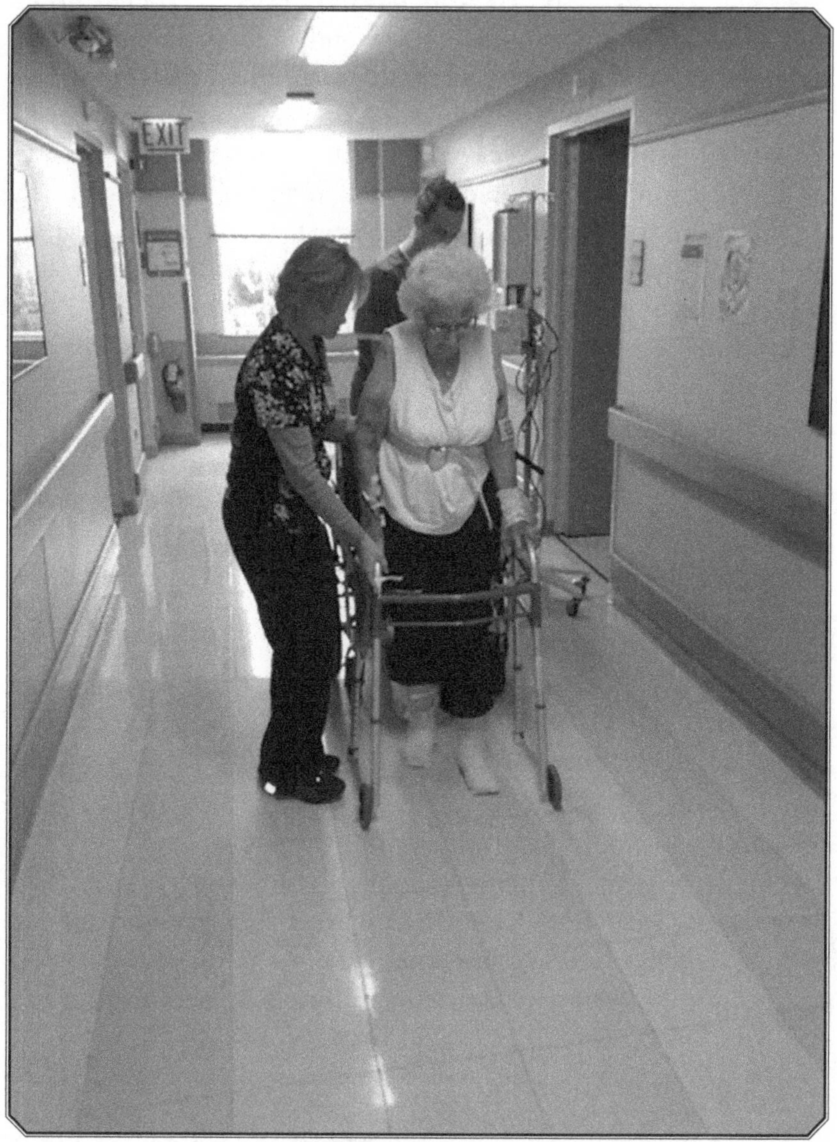

F67.5 Mom doing her daily rehab at Hinsdale Hospital

Mom came through the surgery very well, they had to put a rod in her femur, but they felt she would do well after extensive rehab. They put her on a pretty aggressive schedule, three days of rehab and one day of occupational rehab. Her wound was causing her some trouble, they kept a draining machine attached to the wound which was a bit annoying. We were hopeful, and she was looking pretty good. Her attitude was a very typical attitude for our Mom. She was so mad at herself for the stupid fall, but determined she was going to get better and be back to her normal routine.

Days into her rehab her surgeon made a decision that would mark the beginning of her end. He felt the rod had shifted a little and wanted her to reduce her rehab schedule. Due to this shift in rehabilitation schedule, she could no longer stay in the Hinsdale facility. She had to go to another place since she was not on the fast track any longer. She had a pretty good experience once before at another place which shall remain nameless or I could get sued for telling the truth. Some of the staff recognized my Mom when she checked in and they were visibly happy to see her. She was a welcomed change from some of the patients they usually got. She was nice, funny, did not complain and she was very engaging. A big difference from some of the people you would see sleeping, slumped over in their wheelchairs in the hallway. Or, the combative ones that fought the help they were being given. I was there with her every day. My brothers also visited her often. Mom was one of the lucky ones, she had advocates there for her, where some of those poor souls in there never once had a visitor. Her rehab was a little slower and she was growing frustrated with her progress. I started to see small little changes in her. She was not looking herself. Mom was diagnosed with a urinary tract infection and had a catheter put in her. She started sleeping more and she was just not Mom. One day I got there about nine in the morning and I had to wake her. I got her up and into the common room for a while. Someone there was playing the piano and we enjoyed listening to her. She was playing for her grandpa. Mom looked visibly tired, and not only tired, she was looking drawn, pale, and old. I was getting really worried about her. I brought her back to her room and she fell asleep right before they brought her lunch in to her. I tried to wake her, but she did not want to eat. Unfortunately, I had to leave for an appointment and did not get back until four o'clock. I walked in her room and she was in the same position as she was when I left at noon. Her food tray was still in her room, which told me no one had come into her room for four hours. I went over to her and she would not wake up, as I am trying to wake her I felt her bed, bedding, and her gown. She was soaking wet through and through. Her IV had leaked all over her. These were antibiotics for her UTI which obviously she was not getting. I went flying down the hall yelling to "Call 911, NOW"! The male nurse practitioner on duty came into the room and my Mom was literally slurring her words. He said to me, this is not Mary, what happened to her? I was so infuriated at this question, I yelled back at him ***"that is what I am asking you!"*** The EMT men came and took her over to Hinsdale hospital. I was filming at the time and telling them to make note of the fact she is soaked with her IV fluid. I also recorded the fact her lunch was still in the room from noon until the time of my return, which was four hours later. The emergency room doctor that took care of her was really great. I do not remember her name, but after all her labs came back, she told me my Mom would not have survived the night if I had not gotten her there. Mom was extremely dehydrated. Also, she had MRSA. a bacterial blood infection. The infection was likely from her UTI and her catheter. Another thought was that she had an infection on her eyelid that they had been treating at Hinsdale Hospital rehab. At any rate no matter where it came from, it had been left untreated. The rehab facility kept telling me they could not put her on antibiotics until they had the results and knew what they were fighting. All of a sudden Mom had a yellow sign on her door, and we had to put a gown and gloves on before we went into her room. The doctors told us the MRSA went to her heart, and they were doing everything they could. Mom noticed and complained that no one came to re-start her rehab. We found this curious, but it seemed to me they were waiting for Mom to gain her strength back. I don't know how many days Mom was in the hospital, but there came a time when they had a family meeting and told us they have done all they can do. I don't think any of us knew what that really meant at the time. Mom was still in good spirits and wide awake and seemingly back to herself. We had to make a decision where she was going. We did know she was NOT going back to the place she came from, the place that neglected her, the place that I hold responsible for her death.

I had a good friend, Eden, that was very involved with health care and health care facilities. She recommended Burgess Square in Westmont, Illinois which was a good location for all of us. So, Burgess it was. The people were wonderful there. They were kind, attentive and very caring. They included all of us in all the details of Mom's care. When the news of all this was shared with the entire family, near and far, my sister Lynn took a leave from her job, my niece Kristen and my brother Michael left Florida all to be by our Mother's side. Lynn is a nurse practitioner for a large heart group in Colorado. I cannot tell you what it meant to have her with me during this time. She never left mom's side. After what had happened at the other place, Lynn was staying in her room every night and making sure our mother was being looked after. Kristen and Michael stayed with Joe and me at our home. The fact that Kristen was here meant so much to me and to her grandmother. It was not easy, seeing her decline, which in all of our opinions could have been avoided.

Chapter 68

Losing the Fight

Within a week or so of Mom's admission to Burgess, the doctors started talking about Palliative Care. This was a term I had never heard before. Lynn had to explain it to us. I could not believe what I was hearing. Mom was not going to recover from this, the MRSA was going to take her from us.

Mom was a part of every decision. She was aware of all that was going on. The entire family was there with her every day and every night. I am not talking about just the five of us. The entire family was by her side, grandchildren, great-grandchildren, Paula, Peyton, Jim. So many that loved our Mom were there to let her know. Those days and nights my mom spent telling everyone how she felt about them, and we had the same opportunity to tell her. I would tell her every day I came in her room that I loved her, and I remember the one day she asked me if she had to keep saying it back to me?

She was getting weaker.

Mom told, not asked, her one granddaughter, Kerry with the voice of an angel to sing at her funeral mass. Kerry did sing at her mass, how she did it I do not know, but she did.

Mom asked all her grandsons and her granddaughters to be pallbearers for her, and they were.

Mom asked to see Jim, my first husband. He owned his own business; he is a funeral director and his job is to pick up the deceased for the funeral homes. Mom first told Jim that she loved him and always did, Jim told her he loved her too. Mom then asked him to "please be the one to pick her up," she continued by saying, ***"I know you don't want to, but please do it for me, just don't look!"***

Everyone witnessing this exchanged had tears in their eyes, me, I was sobbing. She did manage to get a laugh out of us too.

It was a given that my husband Joe who was also a funeral director was going to handle her arrangements.

Mom had so much grace and dignity, she was as strong in her dying as she was in her living.

The family gathered and remained with her every minute until she took her last breath on February 3, 2013. She was eighty-nine years old.

Chapter 69

Their Legacy

Losing our Mom was so traumatic. She was my best friend. I loved her deeply and I miss her every single day. We All do!

Mom and Dad have left behind a legacy that they can be proud of! Five children, eight grandchildren, and eight great- grandchildren.

Michael Bernard Kincanon & Marge Kincanon
Married January 27, 1968
Timothy Michael and Kristen Elizabeth
No Children No Children

Michael.

We have heard a lot about Michael throughout the book, the first born. He was the twinkle in Dad's eye long before conception.

Michael was from all accounts a really good little boy. His first years were spent in Chicago where Mom and Dad lived after Dad came home. One of my Mom's aunts, Aunt May, owned a two flat on Congress Street where we lived on the first floor. Michael was very talented in sports and loved playing, you guessed it, Baseball.

When I was a little girl, I thought he walked on water. He was a great older brother and very protective. Michael went to Fenwick

High School initially and then left there to go to Oak Park River Forest High School where he excelled in basketball and baseball. After high school graduation he went to Wright Jr. college, and from there went to Bradley University in Peoria, Illinois. Through the years and during his teaching career he earned his master's degree. Michael taught at Addison Trail high school in Addison, Illinois where he coached basketball and baseball and taught golf, drivers' education, and health. During his college years he was introduced by some friends to Margie Purcell. She attended Clark College in Dubuque, Iowa. One of our neighbors in Oak Park who lived down our street on Euclid Avenue was Kay Stanacek, she was Marge's roommate at college and introduced the two of them. I remember I was ten or eleven years old when they started dating and I was not too sure about this girl he was bringing around. I thought he was acting weird when I saw him sitting in his room with her picture on his knees while writing her letters. I remember thinking how pretty she was and noticing she had really pretty nails and really long eyelashes. I know I used to ask her if her eyelashes were real. She must have thought I was a real pain in the neck. I wouldn't have blamed her. Margie and I became really close and I always knew I could go to her with any issues and find support, and through the years I did, she was always there for me. Michael and Marge married on January 27, 1968. All four of Michael's family have been living in Florida since 2001. Michael retired from teaching and moved soon after. I was really sad to see him move out of state, we were very close and used to do many things together, not to mention he was a great support to have close by for Mom. I know it was really hard on our Mom when he moved away, especially since it was so soon after our Dad had passed. But Michael worked very hard his entire life and he deserved to retire with his family where he and Marge were destined to be. They have a lovely home and they are so fortunate that their kids followed their lead and moved south. I visit them often and Michael will make a trip up north once a year for a visit, as long as there is no snow on the ground. Oh, I take that back, he did come to Downers Grove as a surprise for my fiftieth birthday celebration. He arrived dressed like a model, tan skinned, khaki pants, a light-colored orange shirt, and loafer shoes without socks. He rang the front doorbell, no one came to our front door. My sister Lynn was visiting too, but I knew she was coming. Mom said, "go see who is at the door," I ran upstairs and opened the door to see my brother Michael, standing in a foot of snow, no socks, freezing. I screamed out loud "Oh My God" he said, "let me in!" I was thrilled to see him. Little did I know my amazing husband had a big fiftieth surprise party planned for the next night, but this was the real surprise!

Michael and Marge just celebrated fifty-two Years of marriage at the time of this writing. They have two amazing kids, Tim and Kristen.

Tim

Tim was Mom and Dad's first grandchild. He is a police officer in Florida where his skills are used in many high stress situations because of his background and training. Tim is my Godson, and I am very proud of what he does. I cannot even imagine what he has to deal with as a first responder. This writing is during the Covid-19 pandemic and he has had to deal with being a first responder with his Crisis Response Team. He ended up getting the virus which made him pretty sick. Thankfully he fully recovered and is back at work. Unfortunately, it is during a time of much unrest in our country due to race relations and continuing to deal with the virus and what that has done to the economy. It is a lot to deal with especially in his line of work. He is a hero in my mind. I pray for his safety every day.

Kristen,

My beautiful, red-headed, green-eyed niece is one in a million. She has a heart of gold. Kristen and I are very close, we always have been. She is like the daughter I never had. Since my son Tim is an only child and Tim K and Kristen are very close in age all being within a year of each other, Joe and I would take them with us on many summer outings; like the Wisconsin State Fair, Great America and many other weekend activities.

Kristen is a very hard worker and is great at anything she sets her mind to. She has a huge following of very committed people that will follow her wherever she is working. Her winning personality and amazing smile will draw you in and you will love her the minute you meet her. I know I could sit and listen to her laugh at one of her silly shows she loves and laugh right along with her without knowing what the heck is going on in the program. It is her laugh, and genuine warmth that I love so much about her. I sure wish she lived closer, but the one thing I know is she loves being "home" in Chicago and that means I get to see her quite often. Our home is the place she lands, so we get the pleasure of her company for weeks at a time!

Lawrence Kincanon and Camille Kincanon
Married September 23, 1972 - present

Richard Kincanon wife Elizabeth	and	Kerry Kincanon
Francesca Anita		Katie
Henry **Louis**		Mol
Alexandra **Mary**		

Lawrence, aka Larry

My second older brother, Larry, came only thirteen months after Michael. Almost Irish twins! Larry and Michael were the only two children for seven years. There are a lot of great pictures to show Michael and Larry as little boys together, with their cowboy outfits and similar haircuts. They were so close in age; I am sure Mom had her hands full. Dad would have gotten home from the Army when Michael was three months old. Larry was born ten months later; it did not take long for the second baby to be on his way. I am sure this is when Dad figured out their rhythm method of birth control was not working too well. It took seven more years for me to come along. Larry did not have a good experience at Fenwick, and because of this Mom and Dad made the choice to take both boys out of Fenwick and they both finished up at Oak Park River Forest High School, Mom's alma mater and all of ours now for that matter. Larry had a job working in town at the Oak Park Bakery, Mom loved that as we would get some nice desserts on the days he worked. Larry worked very hard at a couple jobs before joining the Navy in 1965.

These were tumultuous times during the Vietnam war. The draft was in full force, boys had to register at eighteen years old, just babies themselves. Dad told him he better enlist in the Navy or he will find himself in the middle of that crazy Vietnam war that my Dad did not at all support. Larry took Dad's advice and enlisted for a four-year commitment in the Navy on October 1, 1965. It was a great decision for him. Sadly, because of the war, he lost a few of his friends from the old neighborhood in that lousy war. Their names are engraved on the Memorial Wall in Washington D.C. Larry left for active duty February 1, 1966. He did his boot camp in Great Lakes, Illinois. I remember when he was graduating, I had just turned thirteen years old, and he was a part of the Navy drill team. My Mom and Dad, Mike, Marge, my sister Lynn, and my brother Bill and I all went to see him. It was one of the most impressive things I have ever seen. I couldn't believe that was my brother, marching in step and throwing his gun with a big blade on the end of it in such an amazing formation. I was really proud of him. He spent his Navy years seeing the world on a ship called the S.S. La Salle. Larry left behind a girlfriend, Camille. She was the girl I mentioned in a previous chapter. Her dad, Mr. T, owned the pizzeria in Oak Park. I am sure that was not easy on either one of them, but they did survive, rekindled their relationship when Larry came home, and they married on September 23, 1972. Larry worked for many years and retired from Illinois Bell, now AT&T. Camille worked for quite a while as a teacher and still substitutes for local school districts.

Kerry

Kerry is very talented and has a beautiful voice, she is the niece I wrote about in a previous chapter that sang at our Mom's funeral. Kerry graduated from University of Illinois. While there she was very involved in stage plays where she could develop her amazing talent. Kerry is busy raising her family in Elmhurst, Illinois.

Richard aka Rick

Rick was also very talented, he played in the marching band in high school and was very musically inclined. He also loved the stage when he was growing up. Rick is currently working at a very large prestigious insurance company. He is very involved in his church and his community along with his wife Libby. She is a teacher at a local grammar school. They have three children and are currently living in Downers Grove.

Kathleen Kincanon Crook and James Colin Crook
Married July 30, 1970- Divorced June 3, 1975
Born January 1, 1971
(Twin) Timothy Gordon Crook
(Twin) James Colin Crook Jr. died March 16, 1971

Timothy Gordon Crook and Julie Kaye Crook
Married October 24, 1998
Triplets Born October 6, 2003
Caitlin, Grace and Emma Died October 6, 2003 (Lived 1 hour)
Colin James Crook November 10, 2004
Kellie Ann Crook May 14, 2007

Kathleen Kincanon and Joe Nosek
Married October 15, 1988 – present
No Children

Kathleen

This is a little about me, your author in-case you haven't read enough.

I was born eight years after Michael, on March 9, 1953. I have very few memories from our home in Chicago before we moved to Oak Park when I was five years old. I know I went to St. Mel's for kindergarten, then we moved in December of 1958 and I had to change schools. I was enrolled at Ascension School in Oak Park, but I was not there long. That very month December 1, 1958 a terrible fire broke out at another Catholic school; Our Lady of Angel's School in Chicago at 909 North Avers Avenue. Ninety-two children and three nuns were killed in that fire. The reaction from many other Catholic kindergartens was to close down. Because of that decision I had to leave my second school within a week and attend another kindergarten. Lincoln School was a "Public School" only a couple blocks from our new home in Oak Park, and for the rest of my kindergarten year that is where I went each day. All that change was quite traumatic for a five-year-old little girl.

I loved our new neighborhood. It was so different from our home in the city. Our block had a lot of kids in this Irish Catholic neighborhood. We played games in the street, we went to the park in the winter and summer. We had a public pool close by that we would go to almost every day.

In an earlier chapter I wrote about working small jobs in my neighborhood, and how this led to meeting Jim, the boy I would marry. Jim and I did marry in July of 1970. We were very young; I was seventeen and he was nineteen. We were going to have a baby, not only were we having one baby, we were having twins! On January 1, 1971 Timothy Gordon and James Colin Jr. were born at St. Anne's Hospital. Tim was seven pounds six ounces and James was three pounds eight ounces. Jim and I did not, as the saying goes, "have a pot to pee in," and now we had twin boys. Thankfully Jim's mom and my parents were very supportive. Jimmy had to stay in the hospital and Timmy came home with us after about a seven day stay in the hospital. We split our time going back and forth to St. Ann's to be with Jimmy with the help of both sets of grandparents; Jim's sister,

Laurie; and Auntie Dot. We soon had some concerns about Jimmy, he was gaining weight which was a good thing, but he was born with jaundice, which is common in newborns. It is a higher than normal level of Bilirubin in the bloodstream. Many times, this can be treated with light therapy, but Jimmy's jaundice was not going away even with the treatments. The doctors at the hospital determined they had to do an exploratory operation to see why he was not getting better. When his operation was over, we received terrible, devastating news. Jimmy had a defective liver. He was born without a bile duct. We were told he would not survive with this condition. Mom and I were by his bedside every day, Jim too, but someone had to be with Timmy at home, so he would come and go. Because of the incubator, iv's and tubes running through this poor little baby's body, we were unable to hold him. There was only one occasion when Jimmy was actually having a good day, the nurse came in and unhooked him from all his tubes and let me hold him. It was the one and only time my little boy felt the love and warmth of his mommy. It was a day when the nurses felt Jimmy was making a turn for the better and maybe God was working a miracle on our little boy. We know now that one day was a gift, it was the only day I held my son. Things soon took a turn for the worst. We would watch his little belly go up and down and just wait for it to suddenly stop. It was excruciating. My Mom was a huge support for me, she was always there with me and Jimmy every single day. I always felt so guilty because I honestly did not know where I should be. I had a baby at home too. Thankfully Jim's mom, Vi, was home with Timmy. Six weeks into this vigil, Timmy entered the hospital with pyloric stenosis which is caused by a closed valve leading down into the stomach. This would cause Timmy to projectile vomit every single time I would feed him. The doctors first thought it was an allergy to the formula. I could not breast feed because I was away so much at the hospital. We tried all different formulas, goat milk, nothing worked. And at six weeks old he weighed less than when he was born. I was not waiting for the doctors to tell me to take him to the hospital any longer. My mom and I picked up my sister Lynn from school and went straight to the hospital where he was admitted. Later that day we found out the reason he was not keeping any of his formula down and were told he had to have a surgical procedure. We were told that this was pretty common in first born boys, why I have no idea. All we knew was we had both babies in the hospital at the same time, both under six weeks old.

Jimmy lost his fight for life on March 16, 1971 at two and a half months old. Timmy came through his operation and was a very healthy little guy. This was very difficult and stressful on a new marriage, not to mention a very young couple. We were without insurance, which sure added extra stress to our lives. No matter how much we loved each other, our marriage did not survive. I know we both grieved so differently, and I was too young to know that it is sometimes that way, especially with the loss of a child. Jim and I remain very close friends to this day, and we always will be, which I am so thankful for. He will always be an important part of our family.

I have had a few careers in my life, I too am a hard-working Kincanon woman. I did learn a great lesson from my Dad. I did not stay at jobs that made me miserable. I went into Real Estate in 1998 on the advice of our Realtor at the time. After twelve years of experience, in 2010 I opened my own Real Estate Company. 4C Realty, which has been very successful, and the best decision I could have made for my career. I have met some wonderful friends in my career as a Realtor and I have been so blessed to have my dearest friend Debi Simone as one of my agents. Debi is an amazing friend and I treasure her friendship more than I can say.

My company is named after the 4C's (four Crook children that have passed). They are my angels and they watch over me every day.

I met a great guy in 1987, Joe Nosek. Joe is twelve years younger than I am. I was thirty-five, divorced thirteen years, and thinking I would never marry again. I met this blue eyed, twenty-three-year-old guy while out to dinner with a friend of mine. We married eleven months later on October 15, 1988. We will be married thirty-two years at the time of this writing.

Joe gave me the support I needed to follow my dreams when I changed careers and later made the leap to business owner. Joe worked in his five generation very successful family funeral business for about twelve years. Because of family issues within the business he left his families business which was the best decision for him. Not long after Joe left, the ones left behind, ran the business into the ground. The business and all their property, that survived over 100 years went into foreclosure. Joe's grandpa always said that Joe worked that business like it was his vocation, and for the rest of them it was a paycheck. Truer words were never spoken. Joe has a way with family's during the saddest times in their life. He takes care of them with such care and empathy. He still holds his funeral director's license and friends will call on him when the need arises. After he left the family business, he went back to school, got another degree and is very successful in his banking career. He works harder and cares more about his job responsibilities than anyone I know. Joe and I did not have any children of our own, we tried, but it was not meant to be. Joe was not really up for having any children, but he tried for me. After my son died, I was certain that I did not want to risk having another child, but maturity and grieving gave me another outlook and some hope. I was also willing to adopt, but Joe was very happy with our life together. He is a wonderful grandpa to our two grandchildren. I know he would have been a great dad.

Timothy Gordon Crook

This brings me to my amazing son Tim. He is my hero. I am so blessed with one of the best sons on this planet. He is kind, generous, loving, and he wears his heart on his sleeve like his momma. One of the best things in my world is my close relationship with my son.

Tim and I went through a lot together. He was only four years old when his dad and I divorced. Jim and I tried very hard to make sure we did everything in our power to stay connected and show Tim that we are still a family even if we live apart, and forty-five years later, we are still very close. I hope my son realizes how much we both adore him. I know he has had his questions for me through the years. One of the ones that stick with me the most is when he asked me, "if Jimmy did not die, do you think you and dad would have stayed married?" Life is hard, and hindsight is 20/20, but no matter how that question in answered it would not be the right one. All of our lives are full and happy now, so I believe we are all where we are meant to be, and we are all still a very close family. Jim and I know we created someone very special and we are so blessed we had that time together. How could one ever say otherwise with what has come after us?

Tim is also a funeral director and he has taken over his dad's business helping other funeral homes with the deceased and getting them to the funeral home. I don't know another way to put it that sounds respectful. Tim also has his master's degree in computer science. His wife Julie has her degree in finance and does underwriting for a local bank. Tim is a wonderful husband to the best daughter-in-law you could ask for, I know people say that but, I really mean it. Julie and I have a great relationship. Her company is one that I enjoy every time we are together. I make a point of going out to lunch with her as often as I can and when both of our busy schedules allow. I am so proud of her, and the mother she is to her kids. She is so loving and has a great sense of humor. She and Tim are very involved with their children and all their activities.

Tim and Julie went through their own terrible losses. As a parent, you always want to protect your kids from pain. In my life the pain of losing Jimmy ranks in the top two of the pain that stays with me every day of my life. My amazing son and daughter-in-law had to endure the loss of three little girls. Caitlin, Grace, and Emma. They were triplet little girls, born too early. They each weighed 1 pound and lived on this earth for 1 hour. Our entire family went through so much grief for the loss of these three angels. I know it put me on the couch for many months. I did not think things would ever be the same for any of us. I could not believe that my son had to endure what I endured many years before. Only they had three little girls that he and Julie would have to grieve. They tried for so long to have a child. Thankfully there was a program at Good Samaritan Hospital in Downers Grove, Illinois for families who had lost children. It was called SHARE. Julie, Tim, Cathy (Julie's mom) and I attended these group sessions together. We listened as other couples shared their stories of their own loss. We found comfort there. There was actually a feeling of hope in that room. Hope that a couple can move on and try again to have more children. This entire process had such a profound effect on me. There was a feeling of real sadness because I never thought of that as a possibility for me. It also was finally a time for me to heal. Through my son Tim and his wife Julie's loss, after thirty-two years, I could finally, openly grieve the loss of my son. Tim and Julie are two of the bravest people I know. They were braver than me, that is for sure. Thankfully they were able to go after their dream of having children and we all were blessed with two of the best.

Colin James, 16 (named after Tim's twin brother James Colin).

Colin has a love for computers, politics, gaming, dancing, scouts, band, chorus and the stage. He has built his own computer from scratch and says it is better than any he could purchase. I noticed very early on that he had a love of music and his body was always in motion when there was music playing. I was fortunate enough to have my great friend, Ann who owned a dance studio; Celebrity Dance in Downers Grove, Illinois, so I asked him if he wanted to take lessons, and there was absolutely no hesitation from him. I was so happy to be able to bring him to his lessons, pay for them and his outfits when he performed. It was a kick to see how much he got into his roles and absolutely loved what he was doing. Because of his experience in dance and his outgoing personality, he was chosen as a freshman for a key role in their first musical of the year, ***The Little Mermaid***. Colin had the solo singing and dancing role as Chef Louie. He was spectacular. I am so proud of him! His dancing experience is paying off now that is for sure, and it will for the rest of his life, I have no doubt about it.

As of this writing Colin is going into his Sophomore year in high school at Glenbard South in Wheaton, Illinois. He will succeed in whatever he chooses to do.

Colin's is a very picky eater, but he does have his favorites. His love for tableside guacamole has made me a Platinum Member at one of his favorite restaurants, Uncle Julio's in Naperville. Our favorite server, Sergio, turned friend and family member, can recite our entire family's order without asking. Sergio says they have a special-order key just for Colin on the register because he is so picky. I think he gets that from me.

One of the things I love about this kid, he has many interests. He is very involved in Scouts and he is working toward his Eagle Scout. He has a love of politics and really stays very informed about what is going on in Washington D.C. I love that he is progressive in his thinking and is passionate about what is going on in the world.

We are in the year of a presidential election and the stakes cannot be higher. At the time of this writing April 15, 2020 (doing edits) the United States of America and many, many, other countries are in a "stay at home order." We are plagued right now by the Coronavirus, commonly called COVID-19. We have been told to stay in our homes since March 21, 2020, it is now April 15, 2020, and there is no end in sight. We are in a pandemic. Right now, there have been over 19,000 deaths in the United States alone. Italy's death toll is over 19,000 and worldwide the numbers are staggering, 104,000 deaths and counting. The economy has ground to a halt. Businesses are closed, Restaurants can only do carry out or delivery in some cases. People that can work from home are, and others our completely out work. Our unemployment rate has skyrocketed in record time. 3.3 million Americans have filed for unemployment and that is on the rise. Our first responders are fighting every single day to get the personal protective equipment (PPE) they need to stay safe. Masks, gowns, gloves. My sister, my son, and my nephew all are on the front lines. They are working every day to help people and they are doing it without the proper protection. The hospitals are fighting and bidding against the federal government for ventilators that are needed to keep those in need alive. What is wrong in the greatest country in the world when our people cannot have the equipment they need?

People are dying and the current Administration is doing nothing but playing a blame game. Thank God for our governors, at least in some of the states. Many that serve this president are putting their own states and their people at risk. They are failing. By the time this book is ready to hit the market we will know more about the toll that this has taken on human lives. The election will be over, and God willing the better angels will come out on top.

Kellie Ann 13

Kellie is an amazing girl; she is as sweet as they come. I am always amazed by her ability to observe everything around her. She takes notice of any changes before anyone else.

She is always full of compliments, and she never misses an opportunity to say thank you. She is a mush, and I love her hugs. I love her quick wit; she is so funny and can really land the zingers on all of us. She is absolutely one of my most favorite people to spend time with bar none. One of the things I love to do with Kellie, besides just sit around and have great heart to hearts, is play cards, or any game really. She picks up on games so easily and can whip my butt that's for sure, but she and I both have a love of the water, so we spend a lot of time in the summer relaxing in our pool. (Thank you Mom)

She reminds me of me, when it comes to her love of playing sports. What a huge advantage she has now. The opportunities for girls are amazing, where, in my day, we had no chance of getting noticed as a great athlete. Although my Dad used to always tell me "You should have been a boy Kathleen." So, I guess he noticed.

That will be the name of my next book!
I should have been a boy!

Kellie's love of basketball, volleyball and soccer keeps her very busy on traveling teams all year long. They fortunately live about three miles from Joe and I, which allows us to see the kids on a very regular basis and help out when needed.

Kellie has an amazing heart and a love of animals. We have had three Great Danes that she has grown up with. Two that she really remembers well, Zoe was her pal. Poor Zoe was a very special needs dog, she had separation anxiety like no other. She could not be left alone for one minute without taking out a doorknob or a door frame. So, Zoe and Kellie spent a lot of time together. It was very hard on her when Zoe died at only eight years old. Not even two months later we rescued another Great Dane into our family. KC named of course after Kellie and Colin; however, Kellie will tell you he was named strictly after her; **K**ellie **C**rook. Kellie and my Mom were with us when we took the trip to Ohio to go meet KC. Immediately he was all over her, kissing her. I remember she told me she thought "he kissed too much," but she learned to love that later! He adored her. He actually listened to her better than he listened to me. KC would have been nine on May 11, 2020. It always worried me how my little girl would be when we had to make the tough decision to give him peace. He was struggling the last year or so with joint problems, we tried everything to help him; Acupuncture, laser, supplements, CBD oil, swimming lessons, you name it. KC actually loved the vet that gave him his acupuncture, he would be very comfortable and relaxed while Dr. Z. gave him his treatments, he would actually take a treat from her, which meant he was happy and comfortable there with her. I think he knew he always felt better after leaving there. Dr. Barb who gave KC water therapy was wonderful and it helped him remain strong for quite a long time. Without that strength from swimming we would have lost KC long before we did. I am so grateful to all the vets and techs for their compassion and care for our boy. It all worked for a while, but as he aged, he became weaker and you could visibly see he was struggling. The decision to relieve him of his pain and discomfort came way too soon. On April 4, 2020 during the 2020 Covid-19 virus. It could not have been a worst time. Kellie, Colin, Tim and Julie were saying their good-byes to KC when Kellie asked if she could come with us to the vet. We had a short conversation about how difficult it will be for her, and her response, with tears in her eyes said, "grandma, I was there with him from the beginning when we got him, I want to be with him at the end." And, she was. Kellie got his very first kisses and she got his last kisses. She was unbelievably brave, and I know KC loved the fact that she was there with him until he took his last breath. I know that Kellie has such love, compassion and empathy in her heart and soul that her calling should be geared toward the animal world.

I have been so blessed to be a very hands on grandma. Since the kids were born, I was the Monday and Friday sitter. Later as they got a little older, I also took on every other Wednesday. These days were the most important days of the week for me. Right now, at the time of this writing Colin is sixteen and Kellie is thirteen. Sure, they could go home on the bus from school, but I still want my time with them even if it is for just an hour because they have sports, scouts or homework. Kellie tells me she looks for my car every day, "just in case." I love that!

The three of us have taken many wonderful trips together and we will continue to make the memories that will last us a lifetime.

Lynn Kincanon

No children but the best Aunt on the planet

Lynn

There is so much to say about my little sister. Lynn was born twenty-two months after me. Thank God I had her when we were little since the boys were really the focus of most of the attention in our family while we were young. Lynn was a great girl, she has the same smile in every picture as a little girl, and that is who she is, she is a smile. Never will you know a more generous lovely woman. This book at times, and even some of my writing exercises have been eye-opening and painful for me as the older sister. I had some light bulb moments and have called Lynn a couple times after writing and cried my eyes out. We are great, great, sister friends.

We made a pact a long time ago, that we do not let more than four or five months go by without one of us visiting the other. I have been taking summer trips to see Lynn with my two grandchildren for the last ten years. Now that they are older, we can find some amazing things to do with them. Last summer it was zip lining and white-water rafting. Fun times and great memories.

I was not the best older sister when we were little kids. I don't know, maybe it is normal sibling behavior not wanting your little sister to tag along with you. But as an adult looking back on it, I feel like a bully. I was bullied in grammar school and I think the bigger sin here is, I was a bully at home sometimes. Poor Lynn, I know she forgives me, I have to work on forgiving myself. I love her so much. I love her more!

Lynn is so darn talented. She amazes me all the time. She writes poetry like it is taking a breath for her. It flows from her heart and soul. One of her poems is included in this book on ***page 555.*** She is passionate about her causes which are many. The planet, the people, the governed, her friends, her family, and all animals on the planet. She is a true friend and if you have her in your life you are blessed beyond words. Lynn can also take whatever you have in your refrigerator and throw together a brilliant meal. I have zero talent for that or even seeing what is in my refrigerator.

Another major example of a very hard worker in our family is my sister. Lynn worked very hard to put herself through college. No one helped her, she worked. Here decision to become a nurse came in the 1980's. She went back to school, of course she was top in her class, she was always so smart! Lynn reconnected with an old love from college, they married and were married for over ten years, they did not have children. I think the fact that Lynn worked so hard and did not feel like her husband was contributing made the marriage end among other difficulties they could not overcome. She lived in many different states over the years, Florida, Michigan, Virginia, Minnesota, and Colorado which is now her home and has been for nearly twenty years at the time of this writing. Lynn went on to further her education and got her master's degree in nursing. She is a nurse practitioner for a large heart group in Colorado. Lynn is so amazing at what she does, but I know it is getting hard on her to keep up the pace that job requires, not only physically but mentally. And right now, she is working along with others during this pandemic. I worry about her every day. She plans on retiring in January 2021.

William Louis Kincanon and Toni Kincanon
Married December 31, 1989

Emily **Louise** Kincanon married Noah Hayman 2018
Their First Born Son Scout was born July 2020
Jack Alexander Kincanon
William Anthony Kincanon

William, aka Bill

Bill

My little brother! He was born seven years after me, and fifteen years after Michael. The span between oldest and youngest in our family is almost like three separate families. Michael and Larry were in high school when Bill was born. I know Michael has said often he does not remember much about Bill as a little boy because he was gone all the time playing sports after school and on the weekends. This is a soul-searching book these last few chapters. Reliving one's childhood can be daunting and cathartic.

When he was school age Lynn and I used to have to walk with Bill to school. We did have a long hike to get over the Eisenhower expressway to our Catholic school, Ascension. I would have been in seventh grade, Lynn fifth. We would run ahead of Billy like we were leaving him, and he would cry, then we would run back and hug him and do it again. That was so mean and know he still remembers it. He remembers every little thing we did I think.

As Bill grew up, so did I, finally! Bill and I became really great friends as he got into high school and I was in my early twenties, raising my son, Tim. Bill and Tim are only eleven years apart and Tim loves his Uncle Bill. Because I had a place of my own Bill used to come over and hang out with me. We are best friends and I treasure him.

Bill was a great athlete at **OPRF** High School. He was MVP in both basketball and baseball. Many of us used to go to his Friday night basketball games and they were the highlight of the week. As you will guess by the genes he inherited from our Dad, Bill was also a great right-handed pitcher. I loved to go watch him play. He was also a great hitter, but the dumb rules about pitchers not hitting, kept that from shining like it could have.

Bill went to college and was soon drafted by The Cincinnati Reds. It was so hard to see my brother leave home, but this was his dream and he was about to realize something he had worked very hard to accomplish come true. I took a trip to South Carolina to go see him pitch. I was so proud of him. There is a lot of competition to get to the Major Leagues. Unfortunately, for whatever reason Bill was released. This was heartbreaking for him and for our family. Dad was living vicariously through him as his own dream was never realized. It took Bill many years to get over such a major disappointment. We spent a lot of time together during this period. We hung out, watched movies, ate popcorn, but never talked about the elephant in the room. Time just passed.

Then, Bill met Toni through some mutual friends from **Oak Park River Forest** High School. It was in 1985 or 1986. They got married on New Year's Eve December of 1989. Toni was a great daughter-in-law to our Mom. She made such a great effort to be there for Mom and I know she called her every day. Mom was always so appreciative of her love and affection. It was a wonderful relationship and I know Toni misses my Mom very much, she speaks of her often.

Bill and Toni spent many years downtown working for the Chicago Board of Trade. The entire industry after over thirty years down there, blew up. The jobs dried up and both Bill and Toni lost their jobs. It was pretty devastating.

Throughout the years downtown, they were also raising a family. Their first is Emily.

Emily

Emily is my brilliant god-daughter, she was born in November 1989. Emily has a great mind and I love her outlook on the world. She has a strong sense of right and wrong and fairness. She went to Dominican College in River Forest, graduated top of her class and is currently working on her master's degree. Emily and Noah recently welcomed their first born in July. It's a boy and his name is Scout.!

The next addition to the family

Jack Aka J

What a sweetheart. He is polite and considerate; I think he is one of those kids that feels deeply for whatever he believes in. One of most favorite things about J is he is always willing to help; he has such a generosity and caring about him. They always said when Jack was young, he should be the mayor of the town. He can talk to anyone. Jack works very hard at a logistics company in Bensenville and at the time of this writing is dating a really sweet girl Emilie. Maybe by the time I am ready to publish, I will have more news!

Last but not least,

William aka Will

Will is the youngest of Bill and Toni's family and has the sweetest way about him. Will has a love of animals that is so apparent, and it is so enduring. He too, has such a great outlook on the world. He is all about fairness for everyone and has such a generous spirit. I think this is a trait all three of their children share.

Will has followed in the great baseball legacy like his father and grandfather. He was also MVP in both basketball and baseball at **Riverside Brookfield High School.** He graduated high school, went to college on a sports scholarship. He excels in baseball as a right-handed pitcher, throwing over ninety-five mph and has a few pitches that leave the batters scratching their heads. Will was drafted in 2017 by the Chicago White Sox in the eleventh round.

Will was having a great year and it all came to a sudden end with this pandemic. He and all his team were sent home. All sports were cancelled. March Madness Nope, Baseball Season, Nope! St Patrick Day Parade, Nope! No more crowds, no more parties, no more family gatherings. If you wanted sports, you had to watch reruns, if you wanted to see your family, you did so by ZOOM or Skype.

It is a whole new world. I feel like I'm in the Twilight Zone.

It is April 15, 2020

Chapter 70

Is This the End?
I think Not

There is a lot more to come for the Kincanon Family.

Thank you for taking the time to read my book. I hope you came away with some appreciation of what families face when their loved one is called to serve. I also hope you read these letters with the spirit in which they were intended. To show you the way love can grow when two people give of themselves and sacrifice for each other.

The journey I have been on, reading these letters, writing their story, learning more about my parents, has been so rewarding and eye opening. As I sat at my desk typing away on my laptop, I have laughed, and I have had many good cries as I learned about the past and how it has shaped the present. The past that I really knew nothing about until my Dad's letters brought it all to light. It left me appreciating every little thing my parents worked their entire lives to give us. A look back, brought to you by their daughter who wishes she knew even more. I cannot think of a better legacy to leave to the generations in my family that follow me.

If they are the only ones to read this book, I have accomplished what I started out to do. To tell a compelling story of the two people who gave us All life.

Thank God, Dad came home!

F70.1 1961 Lynn, Michael, Kathleen, Lawrence, William

F70.2 Michael and Lawrence
Lynn, William, Kathleen 1963

F70.3 Rick and Libby's Wedding July 2011
Michael Jack Kathy Bill Will Tim
Kerry Lynn Mom Joe Toni Julie Larry
Rick and Libby

F70.4 Some of our Family at our house in Glen Ellyn 2016
Back row: Larry Camille Tim Michael Will Bill
Kerry Julie Kathy Joe Colin Toni Lynn
Kellie KC

My husband Joe and I currently live in Glen Elly, Illinois. After Mom passed away I could not stay in our Downers Grove home. Everywhere I went my memories of Mom haunted me. I knew staying in the home where we lived with Mom was going to make it impossible to get past such a deep loss. Each room was our room, the yard was our yard.

Mom passed in February 2013 and we were in our new home by the end of May 2013.

Guess what, Mom followed me here anyway!

F70.5 Mom and KC in our back yard in Downers Grove 2012

F70.6 Mom in our Kitchen in Downers Grove

F70.7 "Gigi" and Kellie at the nursing home right before she got sick there.

F70.8 Colin and Gigi
Oh, the Love!

Word Definitions

Chapter 22 Page 171 *Brogue*: An Irish Accent when speaking English

Chapter 23 Page 176 *Gasùr*: Gaelic for small boy child

Chapter 34 Page 271 *Bivouac*: A military encampment made with tents

Chapter 17 Page 126 *Furlough*: A leave of absence especially that is granted to a member of the armed services

Chapter 50 Page 432 *V-Mail:* Short for "Victory Mail" was a particular postal system put into place during WWII and used between June 1942 through November 1945. The letters were photographed in microfilm. This system drastically reduced the amount of space needed to transport mail, freeing up room for other valuable supplies.

Chapter 59 Illustration F59.3 The Government form Wellness Check references the acronym RAMP: Recovered Allied Military Personnel

Illustration Appendix

F14.1 Letter Fort Jackson dated April 15,1943
F16.1 Letter Fort Jackson dated June 6, 1943
F17.1 Dad's Furlough picture May 1943
F17.2 Dad and Mom during Dad's Furlough May 1943
F17.3 Letter Fort Jackson dated June 10,1943
F17.4 Letter Fort Jackson dated June 13, 1943
F17.5 Dad 1942
F17.6 Mom 1942
F17.7 Mom 1943
F17.8 Dad 1943
F17.9 Letter Fort Jackson dated June 24, 1943
F18.1 Letter Fort Jackson dated June 29, 1943
F19.1 Letter Fort Jackson dated July 21, and 25th 1943
F20.1 Letter Fort Jackson dated July 31, 1943
F21.1 Vera Lynn then and now
F24.1 Letter Fort Jackson South Carolina dated August 1, 1943
F25.1 Letter Fort Jackson South Carolina dated August 15, 1943
F25.2 Letter Fort Jackson South Carolina dated August 20,1943
F26.1 Letter Fort Jackson South Carolina dated August 25, 1943
F27.1 Letter Fort Jackson South Carolina dated August 29, 1943
F28.1 Letter Fort Jackson South Carolina dated September 17, 1943
F28.2 Letter Fort Jackson South Carolina dated September 21, 1943
F28.3 Letter Fort Jackson South Carolina Station Hospital dated September 29, 1943
F28.4 Letter Fort Jackson South Carolina Station Hospital dated October 1, 1943
F28.5 Letter Fort Jackson South Carolina Red Cross Hospital dated October 2, 1943
F29.1 Letter Fort Jackson South Carolina Red Cross dated October 7, 1943
F30.1 Letter Fort Jackson South Carolina dated October 9, 1943
F31.1 Picture Maw Herrmann (Mom's mother) and unknown woman
F31.2 Picture Maw Herrmann Bea, Edith (dad's sisters) and Dad
F32.1 Letter Fort Jackson South Carolina Station Hospital dated October 12, 1943

F32.2 Letter Fort Jackson South Carolina Station Hospital dated October 18, 1943
F33.1 Letter Fort Jackson South Carolina Station Hospital dated October 26, 1943
F33.2 Letter Fort Jackson South Carolina dated October 31, 1943
F34.1 Letter Fort Jackson South Carolina Special Services dated November 4, 1943
F34.2 Letter Fort Jackson South Carolina Special Services dated November 8, 1943
F35.1 Letter Fort Jackson South Carolina Special Services dated November 13, 1943
F35.2 Letter Fort Jackson South Carolina Special Services dated November 25, 1943
F36.1 Letter Fort Jackson South Carolina Special Services dated December 17, 1943
F37.1 Letter Fort Jackson South Carolina Special Services dated December 22, 1943
F37.2 Letter Fort Jackson South Carolina Special Services dated December 25, 1943
F37.3 Photo Family Last Thanksgiving in our Oak Park Home November 1994
F37.4 Photo Family Christmas December 2018
F37.5 Photo Folded Christmas Napkin
F37.6 Photo of Beautiful place setting
F37.7 Letter Fort Jackson South Carolina Special Services dated December 29, 1943
F38.1 Letter Fort Jackson South Carolina Special Services dated January 1, 1944
F38.2 Letter Fort Jackson South Carolina Special Services dated January 2, 1944
F39.1 Letter Fort Jackson South Carolina Special Services dated January 9, 1944
F39.2 Letter Fort Jackson South Carolina Special Services dated January 12, 1944
F39.3 Letter Fort Jackson South Carolina Special Services dated January 16, 1944

F39.4 Letter Nashville Tennessee Special Services dated January 19, 1944
F40.1 Letter Nashville Tennessee Special Services dated January 26, 1944
F41.1 Letter Nashville Tennessee Special Services dated January 28,1944
F41.2 Letter Nashville Tennessee Special Services dated February 3, 1944
F41.3 Letter Nashville Tennessee Special Services dated February 5, 1944
F41.4 Letter Nashville Tennessee Special Services dated February 12, 1944
F41.5 Letter Nashville Tennessee Special Services dated February 16. 1944
F41.6 Letter Nashville Tennessee Special Services dated February 23, 1944
F42.1 Letter Nashville Tennessee Special Services dated February 26,1944
F42.2 Letter Nashville Tennessee Special Services dated February 29, 1944
F42.3 Letter Nashville Tennessee Special Services dated March 8,1944
F42.4 Letter Nashville Tennessee Special Services dated March 13, 1944
F43.1 Letter Nashville Tennessee Special Services dated March 20, 1944
F44.1 Letter Nashville Tennessee Special Services dated March 28, 1944
F44.2 Letter Nashville Tennessee Special Services dated March 31, 1944
F44.3 Letter Nashville Tennessee Special Services dated April 1, 1944
F45.1 Photo of KC our Great Dane
F45.2 Photo of KC
F45.3 Photo of Joe Kathy and KC
F45.4 Photo of Majestic KC (he was our beloved dog from 2011-2020)

F45.5 Photo of Kellie Crook Our granddaughter KC and Colin Crook our Grandson
F45.6 Photo of KC (this chapter could have been called KC)
F45.7 Letter Camp Atterbury, Indiana dated May 13, 1944
F45.8 Letter Camp Atterbury, Indiana dated May 17, 1944
F46.1 Marriage Status change from War Department
F46.2 Photo Saint Edmunds Church Oak Park, Illinois June 3, 1944
F46.3 Photo Mom and Dad Wedding Picture June 3, 1944
F46.4 Photo Outside of Saint Edmunds Church June 3, 1944
F46.5 Photo Mom's best friend Jean at their wedding
F46.6 Photo Happy Mom on her wedding day June 3, 1944
F46.7 Photo My grandmother Helen Ruhnke Herrmann (Maw)
F46.8 Photo Both of my grandmothers Helen, Magdalene, Dad's sisters, Edith and Bea
F46.9 Photo Uncle Bill (Mom's Brother) and my grandmother Helen
F46.10 Photo Friends and Family outside at wedding
F46.11 Photo Marriage License
F46.12 Photo of my grandmother's home in West Palm Beach Florida
F47.1 Letter Wichita Kansas Baseball Club dated August 15, 1944
F47.2 Letter from War Department to Mom dated August 4, 1944
F47.3 Letter Wichita Kansas Baseball Club dated August 18, 1944
F47.4 Letter Wichita Kansas Baseball Club dated August 22, 1944
F48.1 Letter Wichita Kansas Baseball Club dated August 24, 1944
F49.1 Photo Dad on Furlough dated September 1944
F49.2 Photo Dad and Mom during Furlough dated September 1944
F49.3 Photo Mom and Dog dated October 1944 states Dad "overseas"
F49.4 Letter "Somewhere in Eastern USA dated October 26, 1944
F49.5 Letter "Somewhere Overseas" dated November 2, 1944
F49.6 Letter "On the High Seas" dated November 3, 1944
F49.7 Letter "Somewhere Overseas" dated November 4, 1944
F50.1 Letter dated November 5, 1944
F50.2 Letter "Somewhere Overseas" dated November 6, 1944
F50.3 Letter "Somewhere Overseas" envelope dated November 9,1944
F51.1 Letter "Somewhere Overseas" dated November 11, 1944
F51.2 Letter "Somewhere Overseas" dated November 15, 1944

F52.1 Letter "Somewhere in England" dated November 18, 1944
F53.1 Letter "Somewhere in England" dated November 23, 1944
F53.2 Letter "Somewhere in England" dated November 25, 1944
F54.1 Letter V-Mail dated November 27, 1944
F54.2 Letter V-Mail dated December 13, 1944 (Dad's Last Letter before the Battle of the Bulge)
F54.3 History of the Battle of the Bulge
F56.1 Letter MY DARLING dated January 15, 1945 (Mom's one and only letter to Dad)
F56.2 My Sister Lynn's Poem
F57.1 Letter from The War Department Washington D.C. dated April 28, 1945
F59.1 Letter "Germany" no date or postmark 1945
F59.2 Letter "Washington D.C. dated May 9, 1945
F59.3 Government Form "Wellness Check" dated May 30, 1945
F59.4 Western Union Telegram from Dad dated May 23, 1945
F59.5 Newspaper Article "83 More Freed" no date
F59.6 Western Union Telegram dated June 1, 1945
F61.1 POW CLASSIFICATION Germany
F61.2 POW IDENTIFICATION
F61.3 POW DISCHARGE CLASSIFICATION
F61.4 Photo The prison camp where my Dad was held December 16, 1943 until the end of the war
F61.5 Photo Dad's POW Camp
F61.6 Photo Dollar Bill from prison cam with men's signatures including Dads
F61.7 Photo Enlarged photo of the Dollar Bill
F63.1 Photo Mom Dad and Friends
F63.2 Photo (Pops) Bill and Annrose Hawley
F63.3 Photo Mom and Dad on vacation with friends
F63.4 Photo Dad and Pops
F63.5 Photo Mom and Annrose
F63.6 Photo Pops, Mom, Dad, Harry, and Annrose
F63.7 Photo Pops Dad, Mom, and Annrose
F63.8 Photo Harry, Dad, Mom, and Joanne
F63.9 Photo Annrose and Dad

F63.10 Photo Pops, Mom, Annrose, Dad and Harry
F63.11 Photo Mom and Dad in Florida
F63.12 Photo Mom and Dad in Virginia
F63.13 Photo Mom and Dad at Maw's home in West Palm Beach, Florida
F63.14 Photo Mom and Dad Wedding June 3, 1944
F63.15 Photo Mom and Dad's 50th Wedding Anniversary
F64.1 Photo Mom and Dad's Last page of their will. Signed with an X
F65.1 Photo Mom's bruised face from a fall
F66.1 Photo Mom on her chairlift in our home in Downers Grove, Illinois
F67.1 Photo Mom's fall in our kitchen with the paramedics
F67.2 Photo Michael and Kellie visiting Mom at the hospital
F67.3 Photo Lynn and Colin visiting Mom at the hospital
F67.4 Photo Mom in the hospital after surgery
F67.5 Photo Mom during rehab at Hinsdale Hospital
F70.1 Photo The 5 of us 1961
F70.2 Photo The 5 of us 1963
F70.3 Photo Rick and Libby's wedding July 2012
F70.4 Photo Family Gathering our home in Glen Ellyn, Illinois 2016
F70.5 Photo Mom and KC Our yard in Downers Grove, Illinois 2012
F70.6 Photo Mom in our Kitchen Downers Grove, Illinois 2012
F70.7 Photo Mom (Gigi) and Kellie at the nursing home
F70.8 Photo Mom (Gigi) and Colin in our yard Downers Grove, Illinois

CPSIA information can be obtained
at www.ICGtesting.com
Printed in the USA
LVHW041924170422
716246LV00002B/4